Film jour... with several
books on popular culture including the ...ing *Hellraisers*,
Very Naughty Boys, ...ory of the George Harrison/Monty...

Also by Robert Sellers

*Hellraisers: The Life and Inebriated Times of Burton,
Harris, O'Toole and Reed*

*Hollywood Hellraisers: The Wild Life and Fast Times of
Brando, Dennis Hopper, Warren Beatty and Jack Nicholson*

*An A–Z of Hellraisers: A Comprehensive Compendium of
Outrageous Insobriety*

*Don't Let the Bastards Grind You Down: How One Generation of
British Actors Changed the World*

*Very Naughty Boys: The Inside Story of
HandMade Films*

*The True Adventures of the World's Greatest Stuntman
(with Vic Armstrong)*

*James Robertson Justice: What's the Bleeding Time?
A Biography (with James Hogg and Howard Watson)*

*Little Ern!: The Authorised Biography of Ernie Wise
(with James Hogg)*

What Fresh Lunacy is This?

The Authorized Biography of
Oliver Reed

Robert Sellers

Constable • London

Copyright © Robert Sellers 2013

3 5 7 9 10 8 6 4 2

The moral right of the author has been asserted.

Every effort has been made to obtain the necessary permissions with references to copyright material, both illustrative and quoted. We apologize for any omissions in this respect and will be pleased to make appropriate acknowledgements in any future edition.

A CIP catalogue record for this book
is available from the British Library.

ISBN 978-1-4721-1263-7 (B-format paperback)
ISBN 978-1-4721-0114-3 (ebook)

Printed and bound in Great Britain by
CPI Group (UK) Ltd., Croydon, CR0 4YY

Constable
is an imprint of
Constable & Robinson Ltd
100 Victoria Embankment
London EC4Y 0DY

An Hachette UK Company
www.hachette.co.uk

www.littlebrown.co.uk

'I do not live in the world of sobriety.'
Oliver Reed

Acknowledgements

I received invaluable cooperation from the family of Oliver Reed. My sincere thanks go to his brothers David and Simon, his children Mark and Sarah, and his widow Josephine. I felt privileged talking to them.

I would also like to thank the many friends and work colleagues who agreed to share their memories of Oliver, memories that were often funny, sad, traumatic, and bemusing, often all at the same time:

Carole André, Michael Apted, Vic Armstrong, David Ball, Steven Berkoff, Karen Black, Stan Boardman, Leslie Bricusse, Eleanor Bron, Barbara Carrera, Geraldine Chaplin, Stephan Chase, Michael Christensen, Bernie and Joyce Coleman, Don Coutts, Michael Craig, Wendy Craig, Jacquie Daryl, Pierre David, Brian Deacon, Quinn Donoghue, Greg Dyke, Mark Eden, Samantha Eggar, Julia Foster, Stuart Freeman, Paul and Nora Friday, Mick Fryer, Ray Galton, Terry Gilliam, Menahem Golan, Johnny Goodman, Stuart Gordon, Sheba Gray, Piers Haggard, Georgina Hale, Noel Harrison, Paul Heiney, Fraser Heston, Mike Higgins, John Hough, Glenda Jackson, Charles James, Peter James, Charles Jarrott, Kerrie Keane, Paul Koslo, Sir Christopher Lee, Mark Lester, Carol Lynley, Nico Mastorakis, Peter Medak, Murray Melvin, Eben Merrill, Jane

Merrow, Mick Monks, Oswald Morris (1999 interview), Brian Murphy, Steve Neill, Barry Norman, Pat O'Brien, Gerry O'Hara, Ian Ogilvy, Anthony Perry, Johnny Placett, Warren Raines, Reginald Rea, Muriel Reed, Selwyn Roberts, Dick Robinson, Maria Rohm, Yvonne Romain, Ken Russell, Jimmy Sangster, Janette Scott, Alan Simpson, Elke Sommer, Louise Sorel, Pierre Spengler, Graham Stuart, Brian Thompson, Barry Turner, Jonathan Vanger, Patrick Warburton, Douglas Wick, Jack Wild (1999 interview), Billy Williams, Ali Wilson, Michael Winner, Katherine Woodville, Sir John Woolf (1999 interview), Michael York, Richard Zanuck.

Pilgrimage

On 2 May, the anniversary of Oliver Reed's death, the small village cemetery of Churchtown in County Cork, Ireland, is host to a very special pilgrimage. Family and friends congregate beside a small grave, sit on the grass and chat, laugh, drink, and share stories about an extraordinary individual, not forgetting to regularly douse his grave with a gin and tonic; just so the old man doesn't feel left out.

As the years pass – remarkably it's almost fifteen since Reed's death – the number of family members who visit the grave lessens, understandably so, but a few still make the special effort to come over for the anniversary. His son Mark is especially keen to uphold the tradition, so that his dad shouldn't be alone on that day of all days.

Conveniently situated opposite a pub, the spot is visited by fans and tourists too, who pop in to buy a pint of beer to throw over him. 'I'm surprised that anything grows on that grave, the amount of alcohol it's seen,' observes Ollie's daughter Sarah. Gifts are also left at the graveside, some weird and wonderful things, like a toy bulldog in honour of Bullseye, Bill Sikes's loyal companion in *Oliver!* And money, so much in fact that one year his widow Josephine collected it all and gave it to a local charity.

But if you look closely at the inscription on the headstone

you'll notice a flaw. Oliver liked to think that as a film performer he made the air move, an essential quality in cinema, he always thought. Indeed, Orson Welles once said of him, 'Oliver was one of those rare fellows who have the ability to make the air move around them.' There was electricity about him, because you didn't know what he was going to do next. And not just on the screen but in real life too. He was so strong a personality that you could not deny him, you could not ignore him. When he walked into a room every head turned and he took control, without even trying. 'He did have this amazing energy around him, which was quite remarkable,' says Mark. 'And you can't teach someone that, they just have it.'

So the family decided they wanted 'He made the air move' engraved on his headstone. The night before it was erected, they all went down to have a look, and there it was, this brand-new gravestone in big thick slate:

Robert Oliver Reed

1938–1999

'He made the earth move.'

It was an awkward moment as they tried to explain to the stone-mason that wasn't quite what they meant. So it was changed. And if you rub your hand over the stone you can still feel the gentle hollow where the stonemason had to sand down the slate to etch in the word 'air' rather than 'earth'.

Oliver Reed died as he lived – in his own unique way. And the fact that he died in a pub has only added to the legend. While a lot of actors have a romantic notion of conking out on stage like Molière, Oliver died drinking. 'We always said, if he could have picked that for himself he would have been delighted,' says Josephine.

Of course, his death was a total nonsense. It should never have happened. He'd just done *Gladiator* and shown that he was still a fine actor and was all set for one of cinema's greatest comebacks, and then he resorted to drinking copious amounts of rum and arm-wrestling with eighteen-year-old sailors. It was a terrible waste. 'I remember the shock of his death but realizing that it was perhaps inevitable that it would happen that way,' recalls Michael York. 'Because even as Athos in *The Three Musketeers* he had a line that read, "Life is so much more rosy when seen through the bottom of a glass of ale."'

Indeed, Oliver's principal relaxation in life was going to the pub. He always said that you met a better class of person there. It was his drama class, his school, his psychiatrist, his doctor, his everything. Once asked to summarize his career, Ollie replied, with scarcely a hint of exaggeration, 'Shafting the girlies and downing the sherbie.'

A Village Boy

Back in the early sixties Ollie initiated the now infamous Wimbledon run, a glorified pub crawl that incorporated eight hostelries dotted around the village: the Rose and Crown, the Dog and Fox (where he downed his first ever pint), the Castle (now the Fire Stables), the King of Denmark (long ago demolished), the Swan, the Brewery Tap (now gone), the Hand in Hand, and the Crooked Billet, where Mark shared a pint for the last time with his dad just a few months before he died.

The rules were simple: circumnavigate the course as quickly as possible, downing a pint in each pub, and arrive back at where you started from. 'It was like a race,' recalls friend Mick Monks. 'The last one back got the next round in. It was also an endurance test because by the time you got to the fourth pub you'd have lost three people. And there was no throwing up: that meant disqualification. I think the record for whizzing round was something like an hour and ten minutes. Ollie sometimes went round twice, but he didn't always win.'

The Wimbledon run remains a tradition carried on to this day by fans and wannabe hell-raisers. Mark has seen them first-hand. 'It is remarkable how a dozen or more years on from his death there are youngsters who come into the pubs wearing T-shirts with "Ollie Reed died in action" on them. And then they go off to Malta, to Valletta, to drink in the pub where he died.

It's all a bit weird, to be honest.' At the same time it does prove the continuing significance of Oliver Reed as a cultural figure in our nation's psyche, although the ultimate tragedy is that here is a man more famous today for getting drunk on television or playing the public fool than as the distinguished actor he unquestionably was. 'That's the thing,' says Mark. 'You've got this new generation who probably don't know everything that he stood for or what he was about in terms of acting, but they still feel the need to adopt his antics, having fun and drinking, because it's a good boysie thing to go and do.'

A lot of these people miss the point entirely, that for Ollie it wasn't always about the booze. Often the drinking was just the social grease that brought people together and lowered the inhibitions. 'He loved the fact that he had the constitution of an ox,' says his daughter Sarah. 'And that he could drink people under the table and then just see the effect. It was a terrific wind-up, that was all part of it, it was all part of the crack.' It was fun and games and if it wasn't fun he wouldn't do it. 'Like the Wimbledon run,' says Mark. 'Yes, he would get arseholed, but it was much more about the fun and the challenge and the endurance of being able to do it. It wasn't really about the drinking. For him it was the journey, not the destination. So being out of his tree was not what it was about.'

The Swan was among Oliver's favourite pubs in Wimbledon village: it was where he played darts and met up with his mates for drinks and laughter. His brother Simon remembers popping in one evening – this must have been in the mid-sixties – on the way to the cinema with a date. 'We went inside and Ollie was there with about six guys. He saw me and said, "Sit down, Sausage." He always used to call me Sausage. "Can I get you a drink?" I could see they'd been at it all day.' Everyone was playing a card game called Jacks. Now, Ollie was a sucker for pub games, the more ludicrous the better. There was, for instance, the Slippery Pole Contest, held every year during the seventies at the Royal Oak in Rusper, West Sussex. It featured a piece of old gas pipe supported by a trestle at either end over a load of manure-covered straw. The idea was to edge along the pipe, which was covered in washing-up liquid, and with a heavy cushion try to knock your opponent off. Ollie realized that if he wore an extra pair of jeans the absorbability would be better and so allow him a greater grip on the pipe. Alas, one year the organizers used a very strong detergent. Mark remembers the consequences for Ollie. 'After the competition he carried on drinking through the night with the same jeans on and the next day he thought, that's a bit uncomfortable, and basically the corrosive qualities in this soap had taken all the skin off his goolies. At the time he was making *The Class of Miss MacMichael* (1978) with Glenda Jackson, so when he wasn't required for a scene he was walking round in a kilt with camomile lotion all over his knackers.'

More bizarre was a contest to see which two men could keep the longest French kiss going, the prize being a case of Scotch. Ollie's opponent one night made the mistake of divulging to Ollie's pal Michael Christensen his intention of filling his mouth with Colman's mustard. Michael recalls, 'I told Ollie what this bloke was up to, so just before the bout he emptied an ashtray into his own mouth and as they came together mustard and fags squirted everywhere. It lasted about three seconds. It was called a draw.'

Jacks was a particular favourite among the pub games Ollie liked to play. The rules were that you dealt out cards and the first person to draw a Jack had to order a drink, putting into the same glass shots of hard liquor for however many players there were. The second person to draw a Jack sipped the drink, the third Jack downed it in one, and the fourth Jack paid for it. 'And I don't know if it was by luck or design,' says Simon, 'but I had two of these within about twenty minutes of arriving: that's fourteen spirits, full on. It soon began to take effect.' He stumbled over to Ollie to explain that he had to go because his date was waiting. 'Tell you what, Sausage,' said Ollie, 'the best thing you can do is to come outside and get some fresh air.' The two men went for a stroll on Wimbledon Common and carried on walking towards a large pond. 'Keep going,' cried Ollie as Simon walked straight into the murky water. 'He wanted to see me shit-faced, and now he'd got me wrecked as well because I came out the other side of this pond with bits of twig, mud, and crap all over me, and this girl took one look and said, "That's it!" and stormed off. Actually, however good it may have turned out with her, it wasn't as funny as that incident. I laughed all night.'

Most of the pubs Ollie drank in were situated around the village, and he rarely ventured into London's West End or even down to the pubs in Wimbledon town a short distance away. He felt safe in the village, where everyone knew him and looked out for him, especially when he started to become famous. That was the reason why he loved the place so much, spending the first thirty years of his life there. It was an anchor in an often turbulent existence, and why the great majority of the friends that really lasted all through his life were Wimbledon people.

Ollie was very much a local character in Wimbledon, as was his father. Most people knew Peter Reed. He was unmistakable as he took his afternoon constitutional around the village: distinguished-looking, very upright, and tall, he never left the house without a smart suit on. 'He was a very refined gentleman,' is how Joyce Coleman, then the landlady of the Dog and Fox, remembers him. 'And he was always immaculate, always. He'd walk through the village like he was the local squire.'

A newspaper racing correspondent, Peter Reed had married Marcia Beryl Andrews, the daughter of a London businessman, and they lived modestly in a small cottage in the village of Fetcham in Surrey, a short drive away from Epsom racecourse. Here Marcia had given birth to their first child on

7 February 1936, a boy they christened David Anthony Reed. It was an event that may well have prompted them to move to Wimbledon, so as to be closer to their respective families.

They rented a spacious detached property at 9 Durrington Park Road, near Raynes Park railway station, which sent weary commuters up to Waterloo and the vast metropolis of London. The house was also close to Wimbledon Common and a good, spirited walk from the All England Lawn Tennis Club. In short, this was a suburb about as middle class as they come. And it was into these genteel surroundings that Oliver Reed ('Robert Oliver' on his birth certificate) was born on 13 February 1938.

His earliest years Oliver would recall as disconnected images: 'A burning fire in a grate. A potty overturned on a linoleum floor. The taste of cold urine. A world of legs – table legs, chair legs, sideboard legs, human legs.' David, a full two years older, is able to remember things a little more clearly, although again these are 'just little flashes of memories'. He describes, from a distance of over seventy years, a household that might have looked to the casual observer to be residing in an Edwardian time warp. There was a man downstairs who was the family's dogsbody, gardener, car washer and so on, and upstairs a nanny who looked after both children, to all intents and purposes so that Marcia didn't have to. At six o'clock every evening David and Oliver would be brought downstairs and presented; 'and that was the only time we were seen by our parents,' recalls David.

Moving from Durrington Park, the Reeds rented a house in North View, right on the edge of Wimbledon Common. 'My first memory of us living as a family was at North View,' says David. 'I remember being given a grown-up gas mask and Oliver was given a Mickey Mouse one which had a little nose on the front. The other thing I remember is the house had French windows out on to a garden, and Ollie went out one day and kicked over all these flowerpots and my father went up and gave him a two-shilling bit, saying, "You're the only person who'd go out and knock over six flowerpots in a row."'

On the outbreak of war with Germany Peter made a monumental decision that not only had a bearing on his own circumstances but deeply affected Oliver throughout adulthood and right up until the very last moments of his life. The thought of ordinary decent men killing each other, no matter what country they were from, was barbaric, Peter announced, and so he'd registered to become a conscientious objector. It was a laudable point of view, but a tough argument to win in the face of the threat from Hitler and Nazism. Marcia didn't sympathize in the slightest with the principles behind her husband's stance: all she saw was a coward and a man for whom all her love had evaporated. Their marriage was effectively over and for months the household crackled with tension.

Ollie and David were blissfully ignorant of what was happening, though keenly aware that outside their home things had definitely changed. With shocking impertinence the war had encroached upon the tranquil urbanity of Wimbledon. Trenches had been dug on the Common, accompanied by anti-aircraft, or ack-ack, gun placements, and sergeants were throwing thunderflashes at soldiers to get them used to explosions. Occasionally the two brothers would forage for pieces of shrapnel or the strange tin foil, black on one side, silver on the other, that the Germans dropped to create a cloud on Britain's radar screens. 'I also recall there was a prisoner-of-war camp at the front of King's College [School] on the Common,' says David. 'And we could go and talk to the prisoners almost daily through the wire.'

While it didn't get the worst of it by any means, Wimbledon didn't entirely escape the tyranny of the bombing raids on civilian London. As he was only two it's doubtful Oliver could later remember the afternoon of 16 August 1940, when a huge tonnage of bombs fell on the area, causing loss of life and damage to property. Or had he gone from the family home by then, snatched away by Marcia and vanishing like a pantomime genie in a puff of smoke? Peter had not the first idea where Marcia had taken him; he was left behind with David to rummage through the wreckage of his marriage and work out alone what had gone wrong. Clearly the couple had been a mismatch almost from the off. 'My father wasn't a difficult person,' says David. 'He was a very easy-going person, too easy-going perhaps. Juliet, his sister, always used to say that he had no ambition.' Maybe life in Wimbledon with Peter was just too plain dull for Marcia, who craved excitement and whirlwind affairs. 'And she had a series of them,' admits David. 'My mother was quite theatrical and a bit larger than life, so my father was probably too stable for her.'

Marcia had taken Ollie with her to Bledlow, a quaint village nestled in the Chiltern Hills of Buckinghamshire. Home was a picture-postcard thatched cottage, the sort of emblem of England that people were laying down their lives to preserve. It belonged to a senior RAF officer at a nearby airbase, Marcia's lover, and came complete with the matronly Morgy, cook and sometimes nanny, who read Winnie the Pooh stories to the young Oliver during air raids as they crouched inside a Morrison shelter in the kitchen. A. A. Milne's magical creation was a firm favourite of Oliver's childhood, as was Rupert the Bear, whose adventures in and around the village of Nutwood enchanted him and fed his imagination.

Worried the cottage could take a direct hit, Marcia's lover built an Anderson shelter, made of corrugated iron, out in the garden and insisted it be used during air raids. Then early one morning Oliver was startled by a brain-piercing metallic scream. A flaming Messerschmitt had skimmed the roof and set the thatch alight, before crashing into a neighbouring field. Oliver was to recall his mother's beau gallantly legging it up a ladder and everyone passing him buckets of water to douse the flames. Once that show was over, Oliver's curiosity hastened him to where the wreckage lay. It was an enemy aircraft all right, with a swastika on its side. Already kids were scrambling around it, taking souvenirs. Walking to the front, where the nose lay concertinaed in a grassy bank, Oliver peered through the broken windscreen and saw the pilot slumped over the controls, his face smeared with blood. 'I was horrified. It was the first time I had seen a dead man and I started to cry.'

This was an altogether rare encounter with the realities of war. For the most part young Oliver enjoyed an idyllic life at Bledlow, his days spent happily playing in woods and fields, buying sweets in the post office, and drinking lemonade outside the village pub. The Red Lion was the heart and soul of the community, 'always full of reassuring noise and uniforms and the fug of sour beer and tobacco,' remembered Oliver, whose lifetime love affair with booze and public houses of every description may very well have its roots in the nostalgic glow of these early visits. There was also a heritage of drinking in the Reed family. 'My mother drank, not to excess, but she did drink,' says David. 'And as a treat at Sunday lunch when Ollie and I were very young we would be allowed a glass of beer, not a pint, just a small glass.'

Drink was also a feature of soirées Marcia indulged in at the cottage, attended by her lover's friends from Bomber Command. From his bedroom Oliver could hear the sound of clinking glasses and laughter, or he'd wander to the top of the stairs to observe things a little better. On special occasions Marcia allowed him to stay up late and serve drinks and sandwiches from a tray to the men, many of whom had seen action, some in the Battle of Britain. 'They were young and full of extravagance, indulgence, elegance and arrogance,' remembered Oliver, and they had names like Pip, wore handlebar moustaches and smoked pipes, a stereotypical image later so beloved of British war films. Oliver felt exhilarated by their rowdy bonhomie.

Already exposed to alcohol and a drinking culture, he was still at an impressionable age when sex entered his life. Barely five, he had just pulled down the knickers of an obliging local lass in a game of doctors and nurses when her mother walked into the room. That little girl, whose mother part-owned the Red Lion, grew up to be Samantha Eggar, who went on to enjoy a successful acting career in films including *The Collector* and *Doctor Dolittle*. In his autobiography, published in 1979, Oliver claimed that Samantha was 'my first love'. Today Samantha fondly remembers Oliver as her earliest playmate. 'Then years later Oliver and I worked together in two films and he was worth every cent of his notorious but endearing self.'

It was around this time that Peter made contact again. Tracking Marcia down was hardly a job for Sherlock Holmes: he'd simply made enquiries at the Ministry of Food and located her through the family's ration book. Was he still in love with her? Perhaps so, but Peter was no fool and knew she was never coming back, instead he was rather hoping to farm out David to her care. Still refusing to fight, Peter had been working for the Civil Defence driving an ambulance during the Blitz of 1940. 'This all happened while I was away at school,' recalls David. 'I remember he used to drive down in the ambulance to see me sometimes. But when my school was bombed it was decided it was too dangerous for me to stay and so they carted me down to Bledlow.'

It was rather a shock for Oliver when his elder brother turned up at the cottage, since in the few years that had passed he'd forgotten all about him. At first Oliver didn't react well to the intruder: running upstairs, he picked up his dog, a little mongrel called Fizzy, and hurled him over the banisters. It was an odd statement. 'I think I wanted to impress him,' recalled Oliver. Summoned downstairs, the two boys faced each other. David put out his hand. 'Hello, Ollie.' Adult faces looked sternly at Oliver. 'You remember David?' they asked. No, he didn't, and there seemed to be no family resemblance at all. In fact, the two brothers couldn't have been more different in both temperament and looks, and they were chalk and cheese their entire lives.

Anyway, Ollie took his mum's word for it that they were brothers and for him it was quite a novelty, because most kids got smelly babies for brothers whereas this one was already fairly grown up. Quickly they forged a close bond. In other words, Ollie smashed things, David mended them. 'My conscious memory of really developing as brothers is from Bledlow on,' says David. 'We started going off to school together and became very close in quite a short space of time. I remember one of our first incidents: I was throwing cold water over him in the bathroom and he was jumping and slipped and broke his nose.'

The two brothers romped all over Bledlow, chased cows, waved at land girls in their green pullovers, went scrumping, and dug for victory on allotments. 'It was an idyllic country existence,' says David. For him these are memories that are not dimmed by the passing of time but bright and clear and vivid, cherishable too, of an age of innocence and a young brother he loved. 'I remember we used to go up to the village shop and they had a tame jackdaw that would sit on the handlebars of our cycles. I remember great excitement at the haymaking with these large threshing machines. And even though the war was on and everything was rationed, farmers could still breed chickens and pigs, so we were never short of eggs and things like that. It was an idyllic childhood, it really was, and a vanished era. And the funny thing is that both Ollie and I ended up living in the country because instinctively we preferred country life to metropolitan life.'

With the airfield nearby and bombers going off and returning, Ollie and David were conscious of the war but remained largely unaffected by it, having created their own private little world.

'Because of all the disruption caused by our parents, Ollie and I relied on each other and led our own sort of lives.'

David tells a charming story that seems to sum this up better than anything else. There was a comic strip character both of them loved to read about who had the ability to fly with the aid of two feathers on his ankles. 'Well, Ollie and I got talking about this and so we put feathers on our ankles and tried to fly, but we couldn't. "I know what we'll do," I said. "We'll make a parachute."' Somewhere they managed to get their hands on a large tent panel with brass rings around the edge. Then they poked string through each of the rings and tied it on to their belts. 'We decided to give our parachute a trial run and so it was decided, I being the wisest one, that Ollie climb a tree and jump out of it. It was at the point, when Ollie was at the top of this tree about to fling himself off, that our mother came out and saw what was going on and threw a wobbly. "Come down immediately!" We spent hours and hours together.'

Some of that time was spent watching the airmen undergo survival training. This largely entailed throwing themselves off a bridge into the River Thames under the instruction of a squadron leader who, Oliver remembered, 'had a face like a badger's bum'. Overawed by the spectacle, little Ollie thought he'd have a go and jumped off the highest parapet, only suddenly realizing he couldn't swim. After swallowing a mouthful of water he was dragged out by one of the airmen and tipped upside down. This airman went by the strange nickname of Lovely Gravy and he and Oliver saw a lot of each other over the next few months. He taught the youngster how to swim and catch sticklebacks, and regaled him with tales of night-time bombing raids on the factories along the Rhine.

Made to feel special by Lovely Gravy, Oliver only later came to the conclusion that the airman was probably trying to ingratiate himself into the affections of Marcia, who by 1943 had acquired a bit of a reputation in the area. Like so many women in wartime, she was dazzled by arriving Yanks, in this case staff officers with the Eighth Air Force, which had established its headquarters at the nearby Abbey School for girls in High Wycombe. Luckily for regional population forecasts, the school had been evacuated of its pupils. Marcia's popular soirées now took on a distinctly American flavour, with more than one officer paying solo visits. Marcia loved the attention this gave her, and she was often at her best playing the hostess, effortlessly turning on the charm and sophisticated elegance. Oliver, though, was to remember his mother a little differently, as a woman from whom 'there had never been any hugs and kisses'.

After he spitefully hit a local boy round the head with a hoe as they were planting seedlings, Oliver ran home and, fearing reprisals, collected his few belongings from his bedroom and announced he was leaving home. 'I'm not stopping you,' said Marcia, in the middle of her tea, and turned her back on him. The little lad was shell-shocked. 'I couldn't believe it. My first great decision ignored.' He stomped out and sat for a while on top of the Anderson shelter mulling over life in general and whether or not it was worth carrying on if his own mother was going to snub him. It started to get dark and strange rumblings were coming from his tummy. Time to take drastic action. He climbed a tree and threatened to jump, minus even his makeshift parachute. This brought everyone outside and with it pleadings for him to come down safely. It was his first captive audience and Oliver revelled in the attention.

Would he really have jumped, 'or was I asking my mother to tell everyone she loved me best of all?' All Oliver remembered was that when he finally came down he chose to run and throw his arms around Morgy rather than Marcia.

After all her fraternizing with the Americans, Marcia's relationship with her RAF beau was on shaky ground. On hearing he was to be stationed at an airbase in Yorkshire she refused to countenance a move up north. Not only that: she rejected his offer of marriage and pledge to adopt her two sons, and returned to Wimbledon. Not to Peter, though, but darling Daddy, who welcomed her back with open arms.

Oliver found 74 Marryat Road a very different household from the one he'd just come from, and his grandfather a very different kind of male influence in his life than the largely anonymous RAF lover. You couldn't help but notice Lancelot Andrews, especially after he'd had a few drinks, when, Ollie recalled, he would parade around the front room and the garden waving a Union Jack and singing 'Rule Britannia'. He reserved a particular hatred for the Germans, a hang-up from a rather bad time in the First World War, when he'd had the misfortune to be gassed in the trenches. David lived there too and remembers that at bedtime Lancelot would act like a horse and each boy would take it in turn to sit on him as he carried them upstairs to the bedroom on his back.

Lancelot had done pretty well for himself by climbing the executive ladder at the fruit importers Fyffes, and lived a comfortable life. And there was Granny Olivia, Marcia's mother, the daughter of a Sussex farmer, whom the boys cherished deeply. Of his father Oliver saw very little: he was persona non grata with Lancelot, who, because his son was suffering as a Japanese POW, didn't take kindly to 'bloody conchies'. This antipathy wasn't hidden from the impressionable Oliver, who was now of an age to believe that his mother must have held his father in similar contempt.

A Fractured Education

Oliver's education was to follow a convoluted path, beginning at Wimbledon Common Preparatory School, known fondly as 'Squirrels' and founded in 1919 as a place of learning for the sons of local gentry. 'Industry with Cheerfulness' was the school's motto and its class sizes were small, but even with the advantage of close tutoring Oliver did not shine in lessons. His only interest, it appeared, was in nature. Walking home after school he always made a point of visiting the home of the headmistress to help feed the multitude of stray cats she'd managed to rescue from local bomb sites.

Years later Ollie enrolled his son Mark at Squirrels and always made an effort to attend sports day, wearing his old school cap and scarf, and never shying from performing in the parents' race. 'He was very quick,' recalls Barry Turner, the school's former assistant head. 'But what I remember most about those occasions is that he was always very reverential to my mother, who'd been the school's principal. He took great pains to be seen to be very polite, bowing and scraping in her presence. Oliver was a most memorable character.'

By the summer of 1944 Hitler had begun upping the ante by launching hundreds of V-1 flying bombs, or Doodlebugs as the press dubbed them. Such indiscriminate bombing, barbaric in the extreme, terrified Londoners. In late July Lancelot was leaving his bank in the centre of Wimbledon when a Doodlebug struck and the force of the explosion hurled him fifty yards, killing him instantly. Within a few weeks David and Oliver were sent to Hoe Place Preparatory School in Woking, some twenty miles away. David isn't entirely convinced that the bombing was the sole reason for their departure. 'We were a bit of a problem, I think, for both of our parents. That's the reason why we both went off to boarding school at what was a very young age.'

The day of their leaving had begun so brightly. Peter arrived at the house and for a fleeting moment he and Marcia were reunited. Oliver recalled it as one of the very few occasions when he saw both of his parents in the same room together. As the boys were driven down to the school it became patently clear to Oliver that their mother and father hadn't been entirely frank with them. The fact that he'd been told to pack some clothes into a suitcase should have been a clue, but the full extent of the horror to come only emerged after he and David had been deposited on the school's gravel driveway and introduced to a lot of serious people in flowing gowns. When his parents got back into their car and sped off, Oliver howled like a wounded animal. 'My screams shattered even the most tearful boys into amazed silence.' It took several days for the tears to subside, and even though David was there with him, this crushing feeling of loneliness and of being deserted would not go away. 'I cried in the lavatory and the rhododendron bushes.' At night Oliver sank his face deep into his pillow to muffle the sobbing. He missed his old life and wanted it back, but even that was already gone when news arrived that Lovely Gravy had been shot down and was dead.

Marcia visited on occasion and David and Oliver would cherish those days. She brought with her sweets and regaled them with stories of her new life as an actress, touring the country in repertory theatre, a career the two boys followed avidly from afar. 'We'd have a map of England with little pins on it showing us where she was playing,' remembers David. Peter also visited, sometimes with another woman, who smiled at the children a little too earnestly. Her name was Kathleen Mary Cannon, although she preferred people she liked to call her Kay. She was a widower who worked at the fashion chain Wallis, and Peter had fallen desperately in love with her. His father was always slightly self-reserved, David remembers, and his way of revealing that Kay was someone special in his life was a suggestion that he could get the boys some socks knitted in school colours. 'That was the first indication Oliver and I ever had that there was someone else on the scene as far as he was concerned.'

Oliver's memories of Hoe Place are typical of those who had to endure life at boarding school: smelly, soulless dormitories and a ridiculous school uniform, in this case a pink hat. There was also the obligatory monstrous matron, who tended to Oliver when he caught a particularly virulent strain of measles that left one of his eyes permanently damaged with a squint that he did his best to hide. The headmaster, whose breath invariably smelt of malt whisky, was a Mr Sinker, so he inevitably went by the nickname 'Stinker'. If it were possible, Mr Sinker was even more rabidly patriotic than dear old Lancelot, and the classrooms were festooned with military posters and maps showing in bright red the all-conquering exploits of the British Empire.

As at Squirrels, lessons were a distraction for Oliver. He judged the teachers to be decrepit relics of a bygone age. Often his impatience with them resulted in a smack across the head with a ruler, or he'd be lifted from his desk by one ear and deposited in the corridor. Such antics, realized Ollie, drew the attention and enjoyment of his mates and he began wearing the persona of class clown with pride. 'No memory of learning clutters my memory of Hoe Place.'

They were out after a few months anyway, because Peter could no longer meet the fees, as he was finding work hard to come by, and for a time the boys found themselves allocated to various relatives. David still remembers sitting next to his grandmother's radio with Ollie listening to the latest instalment of *Dick Barton*. Sundry aunts and uncles also treated them to Saturday-morning picture shows where they followed the adventures of heroic figures like the Lone Ranger. 'We lived in very simplistic times,' says David. 'It was the days of radio, there was no television. And because it was largely radio your imagination was left to put faces on the voices, you could imagine them as you wished: much better than it is for modern kids, where everything is there in front of them and no imagination is required at all.'

In yet another new school concerns began to be raised that Oliver's education was suffering perhaps more than David's. While his brother already knew his alphabet and could spell complicated words like 'cul-de-sac', Ollie stuttered with even the simplest words, much to everyone's exasperation. 'He's impossible. What can we do with the boy?' It was decided to place him back into the care of his father, who had now settled into married bliss with Kay in an apartment in Merton Mansions in Bushey Road, Raynes Park, near Wimbledon.

Suddenly acquiring two sons would be daunting for any new wife, but Kay pretty much took it in her stride. When the boys turned up, Oliver put out his hand and said, 'Hello. Are you my new mummy?' With the flat now too small for them all to live in, Peter and Kay rented a farmhouse near the village of Langton Green on the outskirts of Tunbridge Wells in Kent. The day of the move arrived with everyone clambering into Peter's Austin Seven. For Ollie, the highlight of the journey was making cocoa bombs out of tissue paper which he and David threw at poor cyclists coming the other way. On arriving at the house the family had to knock at a nearby farm to borrow some shears

17

to battle their way through a mass of brambles and stinging nettles to the front door. The house, unlived in for years, was similarly neglected: the front door creaked like the soundtrack of a horror film and the floorboards buckled underfoot. For the children, though, it was an enchanted place and the next morning they set about exploring, especially the cellar, where Peter told them smugglers used to hide their booty from the king's men.

Because Peter had found a job with a firm of London bookmakers, he and Kay decided to live at Merton Mansions for the week and drive the forty-odd miles each Friday night to stay the weekend with Oliver and David. It was a strange arrangement: they would go on car trips together as a family, but most of the time Peter spent up in an attic room pounding away at his typewriter, trying to resurrect his career as a freelance racing journalist. Then, come Sunday evening, he and Kay would pack up and return to London, leaving Ollie and David with very little discipline or supervision. 'Over time we had two or three au pair girls looking after us,' recalls David. 'But largely we were left alone. We went out scrumping, we camped, we lived an outdoor existence and developed this ability to just lead our own lives. We had total freedom because no one was really there looking after us, so again we really bonded as brothers.'

One of these au pairs was French and went by the name of Monique. One morning the boys were playing up in the attic when Ollie put his foot through the ceiling of the bathroom beneath them and there was poor Monique taking a bath at the time. 'God knows what we were really doing up there,' says David. 'Certainly not with the intent of spying on Monique. But Ollie's foot did make a very big hole and no doubt he had a splendid view of Monique below in the bath.'

Nineteen forty-seven began with a hellish freeze that broke records and almost brought Britain to a standstill. For Oliver the snow was a mixed blessing: there was no school and he could ride his sledge in the steep cow field at the back of the house, but usually there would be no water for his bath because the pipes were frozen solid. Peter came up with the inspired notion of taking a blowtorch to them, but instead he set the surrounding dry timber ablaze and the two boys put the fire out by lobbing snowballs at it.

The weather remained bitingly cold until well into March. It was a winter Oliver would never forget. Back at school, he failed to impress yet again. 'I sank to the bottom of the class in a bubblehead of daydreams.' For a term he and David attended Langton Green Primary while they waited for a place at another boarding school. According to David, this was the only time the Reed boys ever attended a state school. 'It was also the first time we ever went to a mixed school, and there were girls there!'

What was holding Ollie back at school was his reading and writing; even as an adult he was hopeless at spelling. His inability to get letters or numbers in the right order on the page or even the right way round condemned him to lessons with children a year below him. At first his dunce status was laid at the door of his squint and a specialist in London was consulted, but things did not improve. Eventually he went into hospital for an operation, sharing a ward with grown men, many of them ex-army, really rough types who were forever trying to put their hands up the skirts of the young nurses.

Oliver had noticed that some of the men's heads were wrapped in bandages and their eyes covered with gauze pads. One day he plucked up enough courage to ask what all this might mean for him. 'Well, lad,' one said. 'They'll hook back your eyelids, pull out your eyeballs, cut 'em up a bit and shove 'em back in again.' It sounded barbaric but that's almost exactly what they did. When Peter and Kay arrived at the hospital and saw poor little Oliver sitting up in bed resembling a panda with a bashed-up nose crusty with dried blood, they both burst into tears. 'As it was described to me,' says David, 'the doctors took the eyeball out and tightened one of the muscles to straighten the eye up. Oliver had a definite cast one side, so he looked straight with one eye and the other always looked askew. And he always had a slight weakness there, and that's why, if you see him in movies, he very often looks vaguely sideways to cover that. He wasn't very good at ball games either, in adult life, like tennis or badminton. He'd put the racket right in front of his face and you had to serve it straight at him otherwise you were a rotter.'

Even after the operation, worries persisted about Oliver's poor grasp of learning, while his teachers' indifference towards him caused him to have angry outbursts. His school reports reveal a boy who either doesn't seem to be trying or simply can't cope. 'His extremely poor standard of work has been a great disappointment,' reads one. On the subject of mathematics a teacher wrote: 'He's very confused and makes little or no effort to conquer the elementary.' And, revealingly, this: 'In class quiet, but dreamy. Out of class quick flashes of temper when things go wrong.' This wasn't the only report to make issue of Ollie's quick temper.

Amid the negative verdicts there were chinks of light. Nearly every child has one or two subjects at which they show at least a little promise, and for Oliver these were geography and drawing. One school report reads: 'Drawing very good, original ideas.' Perhaps Oliver felt drawing was one of the few subjects in which he could allow his vivid imagination full rein. 'He was a great cartoonist,' confirms his widow Josephine. 'He had this great flair for scribbling cartoon characters, he'd often draw them in his scripts.'

There is also an interesting handwritten letter to Peter from a no doubt exasperated headmaster that more than adequately sums up his younger son's academic progress: 'Frankly, I do not think he will profit by remaining . . . I cannot move him down as he is already six months over the average age of his present class.' David puts it more bluntly. 'He was asked to leave. That letter was a very polite way of saying, "Take your child away."'

Ollie was thirty-eight years old and taking a piss in a pub toilet when he saw a piece of graffiti scrawled on the wall in front of him: 'Dyslexia rules – KO.' Dyslexia was a word that wasn't used when he was growing up. Nobody apart from medical people knew anything about it, and if you had dyslexia you were simply considered a bit thick. In the intervening years it had become more widely understood, but it was too late for Oliver. At least he'd found the reason why he'd done so poorly at school, why teachers in the end simply gave up on him, but the damage had already been done. For the whole of his life he was deeply self-conscious about his lack of education. 'He was nobody's fool,' says David. 'But he always felt intellectually he wasn't the equal of others, so rather than expose himself to the threat of being discovered he would shout loudly or act loudly.'

To overcome his dyslexia when he became an actor, Oliver would study his scripts carefully and methodically, spending hours memorizing his lines. If he had trouble with a certain word or sentence he'd simply write it down and go over it again and again until it stuck. Oliver was fortunate in that he had a very good memory and over time he learned to live with his dyslexia, and to a great extent overcame it.

And what of Marcia during his education, for her absence is thunderous? It seems that David and Ollie were an impediment to her overriding desire to gallivant around and have fun. David's wife Muriel doesn't mince her words when she calls Marcia 'a very self-centred, selfish woman; all she could think about was herself. But she was very beautiful. And she loved men and had an enormous amount of affairs, and the boys got in her way. She adored Ollie, but in actual fact she never really cared for her children. She hardly ever made an effort to go and see them at boarding school. She didn't have any motherly instincts at all.'

Because Marcia was such a gaping hole in the boys' lives there was always an attraction in going to see her, even if they had to tell fibs about it to Kay. 'You didn't mention Marcia's name around Kay,' reveals David. 'So our visits always had to be done rather surreptitiously.' Marcia had recently moved in with another man, Bill Sulis, and they lived near Worthing. David remembers one occasion when he and Ollie cycled there from Tunbridge Wells just to see their mother, a round trip of nearly ninety miles. 'Can you imagine, cycling to Worthing, for two boys, a bloody long way? And Ollie's bike got a puncture and we didn't have the means of repairing it, so we stuffed the tyre with grass. We made it in the end, though.'

Kay's unwillingness to even hear Marcia's name mentioned was perhaps born of anger at the way she'd treated Peter, but also the fact that she was now expecting his child and felt proprietorial about starting her own family with him. On 5 August 1947 the baby duly arrived and was christened Peter Simon Reed. A proud Peter drove his wife and newborn son from the hospital to their home, where Ollie was waiting at the bottom of the lane and given the task of carrying indoors his new brother, who was asleep in a small wicker basket.

By the time Oliver had reached the age of about ten he was already built like the proverbial brick shithouse, a fearsome sight only slightly offset by the fact he still wore, at his father's insistence, short trousers. 'I looked like Charles Bronson dressed up as a Boy Scout.' Anger at his teachers had also given way to outright rebelliousness, which, while it made him a hero to the other boys, also resulted in harsh punishment and sometimes expulsion. However, Simon, as the youngest boy was always known, believes Oliver's discipline problem at school ran much deeper. 'It was plain insecurity. The anti-establishment thing came later on, that's for sure, but at that stage he was just a troubled boy who was going through a troubled time because of the problems with my dad and his ex-wife, and Ollie took the side of the ex-wife. And there was also something in his nature that was provocative, seeking out confrontation; all that stuff was going on.'

Back in Wimbledon, Peter hoped to enrol Oliver at the prestigious King's College School and so placed him at a preparatory school in the hope that it might improve him academically. In September 1949 Oliver started at Rokeby School in nearby Kingston upon Thames. Alas, the results were much as before and within six months Peter was informed by the headmaster that basically Oliver hadn't a cat in hell's chance of making it into King's. 'Not up to standard,' he reported in unequivocal terms. 'Leaves at my suggestion.'

Peter had no option left now but to send Oliver to a private establishment that specialized in taking boys who had failed to gain the qualifications needed to get into a top-rank public school. Ewell Castle, which Oliver referred to as 'a school for dunces', stood in fifteen acres of private land on the edge of the Surrey countryside, just outside London. Built on part of the site of the ruins of Henry VIII's Nonsuch Palace, the school looked like a boys-only version of St Trinian's. It was a grand place indeed and Oliver was to enjoy his time there. 'The secret society of schoolboy ritual appealed to me.'

Ollie came face to face with this on his very first night there, in the form of an initiation test that he recognized as a 'primitive ordeal – a test of character'. Stripped and blindfolded, he was made to crawl along the corridor and kiss the 'Blarney Stone'. As he imitated loud snogging noises his head was thrust forward and his nose touched bare flesh, followed by a jet blast of foul air into his mouth. The blindfold was removed and there was the 'Blarney Stone'. 'It was the bare arse of the fattest boy in the school. He was amazing. He could fart at will.'

Oliver's stay at Ewell Castle was the longest of any school

and also the most rewarding. Initially he and David were boarders, until they moved in with their father and Kay and became day boys, travelling to the school by bus. For two years Oliver made a point of sharing his double desk with a pupil called Charles James, who all these years later is still mystified as to why it was he that Oliver took a special shine to, since Ollie was by nature a secretive and solitary boy. 'Oliver didn't have many friends at the school. A lot of the boys went round in groups but he didn't, he really was a loner. I was one of the few people who were close to him.' During winter they used to hang out in the corridor together between lessons, huddled round a radiator to extract some warmth from it. In summer they'd wander around the school grounds or go down to the village. On Wednesday afternoons, which were free time since pupils were obliged to come in on Saturday, they might see a film at the local fleapit.

One benefit of being Ollie's friend was that nobody picked on you. 'If I was having problems with anybody Ollie would jump into the fray in a threatening manner,' recalls James. 'Or if there was trouble brewing he'd give you a penetrating stare.' At Ewell Castle Oliver learned an important lesson: life was cruel and the strongest succeeded while the weak got abused and ignored. And so he chose to become a bully; the little boy who cried in the rhododendron bush at Hoe Place had been buried for ever. 'I was bully boy Reed. Jack the Lad. I had swagger.' Very quickly Ollie forged a reputation at school as someone to whom you showed the utmost respect. 'You didn't argue with Ollie,' says James. 'He was a powerful chap, everybody was sort of in awe of him. He really was a strange mixture in many ways, he was a cultured boy, very well mannered, as was his brother, but could be very tough: you didn't cross him.'

Oliver's own comeuppance arrived one day in the shape of a hard-nosed little Scottish boy who, when Ollie made a disrespectful remark, punched him in the head and sent him reeling. 'From then on Ollie kept well away from this kid,' says James. 'But everybody else was in awe of Oliver.'

Academically things were still tough. It didn't help that Ollie never bothered to do his homework and every morning grabbed James's exercise book to quickly copy out his work before class. At home Peter was reaching infuriating heights of exasperation. One of Simon's earliest memories is of the time his father tried to teach Ollie how to spell the word 'hippopotamus', indeed vowing that he would be barred from leaving the house until he got it right. Of course, 'hippopotamus' was like a foreign land to Oliver: he hadn't the first clue where to start. Simon watched all this unfold and, being then what he now describes as 'a bit of a smart-arse', retired to his bedroom to have a go at it himself. Having mastered the word he walked triumphantly back into the room and spelt it out perfectly, no doubt to the embarrassment of Ollie. 'God knows why he didn't hate me because of that,' Simon says. 'It was a pretty disgusting thing to have done.'

Using his physical attributes, Oliver instead began to excel as an athlete. He made the school boxing team but it was on the running track that his strength truly lay, particularly over long distances. He'd pad round the school field on his own, lap after lap, hour after hour, in training. He was incredibly determined and if there was a challenge he would meet it and win. Ewell Castle had a good cross-country team and Ollie was soon its star, taking part in schoolboy championships. 'That was his major claim at school,' says James. 'Athletics.'

The games master, and also Ollie's housemaster, was Geoff Coles, a Ewell old boy who'd returned to the school after the war from the Fleet Air Arm. As perhaps the first teacher to recognize Ollie's difficulties, he would play a crucial role in his early development. With Coles's help and encouragement Ollie developed an aptitude for reading and learning poetry and it wasn't long before he began to do better at English literature.

'He was very keen on things like Shakespeare,' remembers James. 'We did *Twelfth Night* at school, and he was always very good at reciting, he put everything into it. The majority of schoolboys at that age aren't particularly interested in learning Shakespeare but Ollie was. He really threw himself into it.'

Yet if this was the first flowering of Oliver's acting ambitions, he gave no indication of it. James for one does not recall at any time his friend mentioning a possible career as an actor even though he exhibited some of the skills. 'He was a very good mimic. He'd stand up in front of the class before a master came in giving impressions of people like Robert Mitchum and James Stewart and the films that he'd seen them in. He had them off to a tee and used to have the whole class in stitches.'

Oliver was never to forget the kindness shown to him by Geoff Coles and remained in touch with him for the rest of his life. Coles was a keen motorcyclist and Ollie later bought him a top-of-the-range bike on which he travelled all over Europe, never failing to send his former pupil postcards from all the places he visited.

Coles wasn't the only master to take an interest in the young Oliver. Mr Douglas taught him English literature and had been connected in some capacity with the theatre; he was always quoting plays and actors' names. 'He favoured and dwelt on Ollie very much,' says James. 'He was always very impressed in anything Ollie did at the school. It was a strange relationship.'

James can't be sure that Mr Douglas wasn't homosexual but Ewell Castle was not alone among schools of this kind in having its fair share of scandals and masters being forced to leave. The problem was, you never saw a female there, apart from the matron, who didn't really count, because all the teachers and other staff were men. So, in spite of the copies of *Health and Efficiency* magazine that circulated about the place until the pages disintegrated, Oliver and his fellow pupils 'were no wiser about the facts of life than Irish virgins entering a Victorian nunnery'. Certainly Peter didn't want Oliver's education sidetracked by urgings going on below the belt, and, like most parents of that generation, believed the thorny subject of the birds and the bees was to be avoided at all costs; ignorance was seen as the best form of contraceptive. When Peter spotted his son out of school one afternoon chatting up some girls, he phoned the headmaster. Another time Ollie was discovered canoodling with a girl on a local bus and severely reprimanded by the headmaster.

Discipline at Ewell Castle was borderline Colditz. Boys would be beaten for getting poor marks. Certainly bad behaviour was swiftly dealt with and Oliver often fell foul of the headmaster and his dreaded bamboo cane. 'Whenever he got six of the best he wouldn't flinch,' says James. 'That didn't seem to bother him at all.' Just as well, since the outrageous prankster and rascal-to-be was beginning to take shape. 'He'd do one or two outrageous things from time to time,' James recalls. 'On one occasion he took bets off us all that he would not jump into the school's open-air swimming pool with all his clothes on. We all agreed and he went round collecting the money and then jumped straight into the water. Needless to say, the master came along and all hell broke loose and he was soundly beaten.' The school also had a strict uniform code, but the teddy boys were all the rage and so Ollie would turn up wearing drainpipe trousers and sporting a DA, or duck's arse, a hairstyle popularized by Tony Curtis. Both totally against school rules, 'but Ollie seemed to get away with it,' says James.

This defiance carried over into the classroom. Ewell had a science laboratory and the headmaster used to take Ollie's class for both physics and science. 'I used to sit in the raised seating at the back with Ollie,' James remembers. 'And he always used to bring with him a copy of the *Reveille*, which was a pin-up newspaper with scantily dressed women, and he never listened to what the science master would say, he'd just sit there reading the *Reveille* under the desk. And he seemed to get away with that too.'

The only thing Oliver seemed to take seriously was athletics. After Ollie came third in the All England Cross Country Championships, Geoff Coles made him captain of athletics in his final year. It was a prestigious appointment in which Ollie took extreme pride. 'Boys don't admire the intellectual at school,' he once said. 'When a kid reaches puberty it's physical prowess that's looked up to – not brains.' True enough, while Ollie still required fingers to add up, he had few equals on the athletics field and relished each sports day. Indeed, so confident of his abilities was he that in his final year he entered himself for every single event. Such bravado was not welcomed by his father. Peter never understood his son's obsession with proving himself physically, or 'what it meant for a non-starter in academics to breast the tape as Victor Ludorum in athletics', as Ollie described it: all he saw was aggression and rabid ambition, and it turned his stomach. To Peter it was plain showing off, and he refused to attend the event. 'He wouldn't go to see it because he didn't want to applaud this kind of fanaticism,' says Simon.

One can only imagine the emotional distress Ollie must have felt over his father's decision. But this sort of attitude was very typical of Peter and it was the same story when, a few years later, Simon began to achieve a similar status in school sport. 'I was captain of a very successful cricket team and I was a very aggressive player, I celebrated far too much. There was a bit of Ollie in me there, I think. Pete would always arrive for the start of a match and watch me bowl – I was a fairly decent bowler – but on those occasions when I knew it was going to be my day and I was going to take wicket after wicket after wicket, on those days I would see my dad's old car chuntering out of the school gate because he didn't want to see it, particularly if this aggression was coming out, he didn't want to see me behave like that.'

That sports day was a pivotal moment in Oliver's early life. He won every single event and at the prize-giving the teacher's announcement of 'Won by Oliver Reed' was greeted by cheers from his classmates. It was a feeling and an achievement Oliver never forgot. 'The fathers of boys who could spell came up and shook my hand.'

Travelling home afterwards, a rucksack flung over his shoulder with all the cups he'd won clanking and clinking noisily, Oliver was stopped on Wimbledon High Street by two policemen. Not for a minute did they believe this kid's cockamamie story about winning them all, especially when, on closer examination, it was evident they were made of real silver. 'The police thought he must have nicked them,' says Simon. 'So my dad had to go to Wimbledon police station, which just compounded the situation, because here he was trying to put a dampener on Oliver. Pete was forever saying to Ollie, calm down, it's not important, it doesn't matter, and now he had to go to the police station to get him out. That was the problem really: Ollie was fervently ambitious, just absolutely fanatically ambitious, and very tough, and Peter was not tough.'

Nor was he much pleased when Oliver showed off his trophy haul after they got back home. Ollie was expecting some kind of praise, but his father gave him none, instead saying that he'd only won the prizes because of his size and strength compared with the other boys, and adding, 'What are you trying to prove, boy?' Peter believed that mind always won out over brawn in the real world and used the example of a gorilla captured by a far weaker but more intelligent human able to spring a trap using a banana. 'So if you want to be an ape, Oliver, by all means continue running round the field. But it will get you nowhere in later life. So don't bring your cups back here to impress me.'

For a sixteen-year-old who had at last found something he excelled in at school, to have those achievements thrown back in his face by his own father must have been deeply painful. Fleeing out of the house, Oliver ran to Peter's mother, Granny May, who called in the maid and the gardener, and told them, 'Look what my clever grandson has won.' For Oliver it was consolation of a kind, but it did nothing to hide the stark reality of his father's wounding indifference.

Father and Son

Oliver left Ewell Castle an O-level dropout, possessing a mathematical mind, in his words, 'as astute as a calculator without a battery'. Peter was more succinct, suggesting his son was fit only to be a burglar or an actor. He really was at a loss as to what to do with him now he was no longer in the clutches of the education system, as David remembers: 'My father and I used to say, well, what's Ollie going to do with his life, because he was always getting into trouble.'

Glad to be rid of school at last, Ollie nevertheless didn't find life any easier in the cramped confines of the Merton Mansions flat, where he felt unloved, unwanted and a burden. Living 24/7 under the same roof as his father led to horrendous, quite often explosive, tension. 'There were constant rows going on,' is how Simon remembers it. 'Even in those early days Oliver was a feisty character. It was always a difficult relationship between them because my dad was a very mild and peaceful man, but he was provocative, very bright, his language could be rich and strong, so he would tell Oliver what he thought needed to be said. Oliver didn't always appreciate this, so they were either falling out or falling in love with each other.'

The fact that Peter had always been a little bit uncomfortable with Oliver being Marcia's favourite also added to the friction. Where David was fair-skinned and blonde and took after his father in both looks and personality, Ollie, with his free spirit and dark, almost exotic, features, came very much from Marcia's side of the family, who were supposedly of Moorish descent. It must have been the reason why, in moments of anger, Peter would spitefully call Oliver 'gypsy boy', not merely because of his olive complexion but because, as Ollie later said, 'I wouldn't conform to his Victorian ideas.'

But there was something else too, something dark and deeply ingrained, inside Oliver. He'd never been comfortable with his father for being a conscientious objector, nor able to forgive him for it. 'To Ollie that was cowardice,' says David. Ollie's stance on this not only polluted whatever relationship he might have chosen to have with his father while Peter was still alive but remained with him for the rest of his own life. 'Oliver didn't think my dad was a real man, that he wasn't the father he wanted him to be,' admits Simon. 'Deep down he loved him, but he didn't like what he stood for, this pacifist nature and being a conscientious objector. He hated that and could never come to terms with it. I think initially he was ashamed and then found it tough to deal with. As he got older he may have understood it more but it was underpinning a lot of his behaviour.'

Throughout his adult life Oliver compensated, consciously or otherwise, for the shameful stain he felt his father's 'cowardice' had left on the family honour, by indulging in displays of rabid patriotism. In interviews he often referred to himself as 'Mr England', flew the Union Jack in front of his house, forced people in pubs to stand up and join him in drunken choruses of 'God Save the Queen', and had a vehement opposition to foreigners, particularly the French and the Germans. All very funny, and some of it no doubt exaggerated for public consumption, but this patriotism, when fuelled by alcohol, had the propensity to get dangerously out of control. Shooting a film in Austria, Ollie was dismayed to find a pub decorated with every major national flag in the world save for Britain's.

Grabbing hold of the startled manager, he threatened, 'I'm coming back tomorrow night. If you haven't got a Union Jack by then I'm going to trash this place.' The following evening no Union Jack fluttered over the bar and within seconds Ollie was hurling chairs through the window.

Ollie's life was also punctuated by ridiculous tests of strength, almost always when he was drinking. One in particular had him grabbing the back of a chair and performing a perfect planche, a phenomenal physical feat in which the body is held parallel to the ground by the arms, but for what purpose? His son Mark never saw the point. 'Don't do that, Dad,' he'd protest, because invariably Ollie would go purple in the face when attempting it. 'Just don't do it. One day a little capillary up there will just pop and it will be lights out, so why are you doing it? To impress who? There's no need to do that sort of stuff.' There was, though, and that was the whole point: it was to prove some kind of warped notion of masculinity. It was the same reason why Ollie could never back down from a fight if someone wanted to take him on. It was almost as if he had constantly to prove he was a man. 'And he would have been aware of that himself,' believes Josephine. 'He would do these silly feats of strength at times that were definitely pushing it. And he knew he was pushing it and why he was pushing it.' Think of what he was doing just hours before he collapsed and died in that pub in Malta, challenging sailors half his age to arm-wrestling bouts. What Mark always feared would happen eventually did: Ollie's body gave up on him.

Charles James saw early signs of this in Oliver at Ewell Castle, when practically every day he engaged in arm-wrestling competitions with other boys. 'It seemed to be his favourite occupation at school, he was very keen on that. The other thing he did was to lie on the classroom floor and with one arm lift up a chair by just one of its legs. He did crazy things like that. He was a bit of an exhibitionist.'

33

The teenage Ollie was all about aggression, a show of masculinity that Simon believes also came from 'a deep insecurity'. That aggression manifested itself in sudden fits of temper. 'If you think of the most difficult teenager, you have just a fraction of what it was like for my parents trying to live with Oliver.' Often Peter threw him out of the house and there'd be peace and quiet for a week, only for Ollie to return and then another row would start up and out he went again, often for days at a time. It was a vicious circle.

There must also have been some resentment towards his father for his part in the marriage break-up, as well as towards his stepmother Kay, whom Jacquie Daryl, Ollie's partner for the entire seventies, says Oliver 'hated'. That is a very strong word, 'but he did hate Kay. I don't know why, he just didn't like her at all, which was so sad.' It was an extremely difficult period for everyone. It wasn't Kay's fault that she'd replaced Marcia or that he'd been packed off to live with various relatives. 'I just think it was difficult for Ollie to love my mum,' Simon accepts. 'It's true, Oliver and Kay didn't really have a very close relationship, but I don't remember rows between them, in fact she would be more or less the peacemaker between Pete and Ollie, trying to keep the peace as best she could.'

Every time Oliver was kicked out he'd make his way over to Marcia's mother, Granny Olivia, or 'Granny Dardin' as she liked to be called, who ever since his youngest days had been a stalwart in his life. She was much more reliable than Peter's mother, Granny May, who, as David says, 'was a wonderful relative that Ollie and I were very close to, but she was always sort of somewhat up there, not down on the ground. Whereas Granny Dardin was very hands on and in times of trouble was there for us, an absolute constant. Ollie and I knew that 74 Marryat Road, where she lived, was a secure place while all this trouble and upheaval was going on in our lives.'

In the early seventies, when Oliver used his superstar wages to buy Broome Hall, a magnificent country mansion, Granny Dardin was a frequent visitor. David used to collect her on a Friday in Wimbledon and drive her down there to stay the weekend. 'And Ollie did his best to get her drunk, and there she was, approaching ninety, getting a bit wobbly. She was a very important person in both of our lives.'

Back at Merton Mansions the rows between Peter and Ollie raged on. And there was always going to be that one argument that went too far. Peter had insisted on a curfew of nine o'clock, but when Oliver came in one night at some ungodly hour tempers were lost and some of Ollie's verbal blasts were directed at a tearful Kay. Furious, Peter ordered him to his room to write out several times: 'I must not be rude to my mother. I have been insolent and I must not do it again', as if he were still in kindergarten. Bollocks to that, said Oliver, and jumping on his bike made a fast getaway. He was approaching the Common when Peter caught up with him in his car and screamed out of the window, 'Come back, gypsy boy. You'll end up like your mother.' Oliver sprinted for the sanctuary of the woods and his father lost him. They would not see each other for the next five years.

Oliver now went to live on a permanent basis with Granny Dardin and gained a modicum of independence by withdrawing money from a Post Office savings account he'd had since early boyhood. His grandmother allowed him the freedom of the house and gave him his own key so that he could come and go like a lodger. With a tube and train station nearby, the eager seventeen-year-old began exploring central London with a keen eye. Almost instinctively he was drawn to the bright lights of Soho, with its buskers, pimps and teddy boys, and it didn't take him long to wind up in one of the many strip joints that dotted the area. What happened there on one visit passed by almost in a blur. Violence kicked off between rival football fans and without thinking Ollie grabbed two and hurled them hard against a wall. As a third contemplated levelling a right hook against the Reed nose a pair of burly bouncers walked over and the hooligan fled. When the manager was told what had happened, Ollie was offered a job on the spot.

The club was in St Anne's Court, just off Dean Street, in the heart of Soho, and at first Ollie couldn't believe his luck. Here he was being paid five bob (25p) to stand around watching women take their clothes off, and occasionally escorting a dirty old man in a mac off the premises. But the novelty quickly wore off as he got to know the girls: sad, pathetic waifs who travelled all over London to perform in grubby clubs, 'showing more inside thigh as they got in and out of taxis than they did on stage'. One girl, Liz, had an act that climaxed with her astride a chair sporting a G-string that, Ollie recalled, 'was about as alluring as a Pontypool prop forward's jockstrap'.

Ollie was soon put to work in a more upmarket nightclub, but quickly discovered it was a knocking shop. After working there for a month he was taking a leak one night when he heard a commotion outside and shouts of 'Police!' He clambered through the toilet window, ran all the way to Waterloo Station and caught a train home. It took him a couple of weeks to muster the courage to return, only to find the place boarded up and the management done for living on immoral earnings. There was a twinge of sadness about it: crooks all of them, yes, but such interesting people. Ollie found the nearest pub and drank a toast to them, ending up pissed and nursing a horrendous hangover. He was supposed to be at his new job, putting flower and vegetable seeds into packets for £2 a week at a garden centre in Raynes Park. It was mind-numbingly dull. He decided to go to bed instead and never went back.

Son of a Bastard

Word reached Oliver that Granny May wasn't long for this earth. Since running away from home and going to live with Granny Dardin, he had cut himself off somewhat from Granny May, which caused him some concern. In more ways than one Granny May was an extraordinary woman. David remembers her as being 'very correct, very proud, but she wasn't aloof. I remember she would sit there very regal, very old-fashioned. She was also very tall and she wore extraordinary hats, always with a veil, a very theatrical veil. I think she had been on the stage. She was known as a character in Wimbledon because she'd walk imperiously around the village.'

At this time in her mid-eighties, Granny May lived at 12 Lingfield Road in a house bought for her by Oliver's uncle, the film director Carol Reed. For some months now she had spent her days a near-invalid, propped up in bed either reading or delighting in the photographs of her children and grandchildren that adorned the walls. It was into this room that Oliver crept one afternoon to sit next to her. Hours passed and when he got up to leave he kissed her gently and lovingly on the cheek. Granny May smiled and whispered, 'I'm quite tall, Oliver. I only hope they make the coffin long enough.'

The very next day Oliver heard that she had died during the

night. He ran over to the house and tried to climb through the downstairs window to see if the coffin was indeed long enough, but was shooed away by the servants. Walking into the garden, he was suddenly overwhelmed by emotion and burst into tears. 'She was the only one who understood me, listened to me, encouraged me, kissed me,' Oliver later wrote.

Oliver did not attend the funeral, fearful of meeting his father there most likely, but instead cherished his final moments with Granny May, when she'd taken his hand and placed in it Rudyard Kipling's poem 'If'. Ollie treasured that piece of paper, which had been given to his grandmother by his grandfather and was the only link he had to a quite remarkable man. From earlier conversations with his father Ollie knew all about Granny May's past, which was, he thought, a terrific story and one he later regretted never having made into a film. Her love affair with the great Victorian actor-manager Sir Herbert Beerbohm Tree and the illegitimate children she bore him, including Sir Carol Reed and Oliver's father Peter, was a secret that some sections of the Reed family had tried their best to erase, out of pure shame. Back in those days illegitimate children were simply not tolerated by society and were regarded as a blot on a family's good name. 'Our family was very Victorian,' says David. 'Neither Carol nor any of the elder members of the family *ever* talked about it. I mean, Carol wouldn't have it mentioned that Beerbohm was his father and I remember it was a very strict rule that we never referred to it, it was to be kept very much under the carpet. Although our father always mentioned Tree, so we knew about it, many of the others were old-fashioned enough that it was not the done thing – because they were all bastards. I proudly declare I'm a son of a bastard.' And what a line to be descended from.

Oliver called Herbert Beerbohm Tree 'the most flamboyant, daring and versatile actor-manager in the record of the

British stage'. Certainly there was grandeur about the man, who had, according to his biographer Madeleine Bingham, 'a vagabond nature'. His social circle included the likes of Whistler and Oscar Wilde, he performed all the great Shakespearean roles to critical acclaim and popular success, acted opposite Lily Langtry, traded insults with George Bernard Shaw, founded the Royal Academy of Dramatic Art, and built Her Majesty's Theatre in the Haymarket, still one of the most beautiful in Britain. For services to the theatre he was knighted in 1909.

Researching the life of Tree, one is struck by how many similarities there are in both his personality and lifestyle to Oliver's; so many in fact that one is left wondering how much of him in his grandson was genetic and how much was manufactured. 'Ollie was very affected by Tree,' says Simon. 'He almost skipped my father's generation to be like Herbert in every way.' Oliver's daughter Sarah recalls that her father 'worshipped the history of Herbert'. He'd even engage in conversations with him. Whenever Oliver was stuck about how to play a certain character he'd lie in the bath for hours, a flannel over his face, and ask the spirit of Tree for advice. Then it would click. 'I've got it. I've got the character,' he'd say, rushing downstairs to announce, 'Herbert came.' We should take this with a very large dose of salt, of course. David likens it to some kind of 'romanticism', adding, 'I don't know if there's any more to it than that.'

Yet the similarities between the two men are intriguing. For starters, they shared a poor education. Tree never came to terms with even rudimentary mathematics and in adult life liked to give the impression that he hardly went near books. 'I never read. I'm afraid of cramping my style.' It was a blatant lie, just like Oliver's often made claim, including in his autobiography, that the only book he ever read from cover to cover was Kenneth Grahame's *The Wind in the Willows*.

Tall, slim, with carrot-coloured hair and, thanks to his Eastern European background, blessed with exotic, dark features, Tree tended to be cast as the villain early in his career; as was Oliver in Hammer films. By the late 1880s Tree was a popular figure in the West End and a great lover of life. Actress Julia Nielson remarked that he behaved 'like a schoolboy' in his private hours but at the theatre was always dedicated to the job at hand. Very much like Oliver, the ultimate professional on set, but at night invariably a hell-raising maniac.

Both men were great womanizers, indulging in casual affairs with their leading ladies in spite of being married. Tree's wife was Maud Holt, eleven years his junior, an actress whom, after several lead roles in his company, he began to use less and less, preferring her to be, in his words, 'a domestic angel', looking after the children and entertaining his guests. A traditionalist point of view that certainly found resonance with Oliver.

That Tree had taken a mistress, Beatrice May Pinney, Oliver's Granny May, was scarcely a secret within the theatrical fraternity. Incredibly their affair, or shall we call it a romance, lasted some twenty years and produced six illegitimate children. There was Claude (born 1891) and Robin (born 1903), or Uncle Robin to Ollie, one of his favourite relatives as a boy. Peter used to say that Ollie and Robin were very alike in that Robin 'attacks to defend his shyness'. Some of the tales Ollie was told about Robin's wild youth instantly placed him on a pedestal, for instance the time he visited New York and stopped the traffic on Broadway by standing on his head in the street. He also walked across the frozen Hudson River, broke through the ice with an axe, and dived into the freezing water for a mad wager. Then there was Guy (born 1905), who became an artist and restored old paintings, Carol Reed (born 1906), and Juliet (born 1910), the couple's only daughter. And finally there was Peter, the last to arrive, in 1911.

Somewhere in the middle of all this Beatrice decided to

change her name by deed poll from Pinney to Reed, announcing, 'I am but a broken Reed at the foot of the mighty Tree.'

While Tree was busy manufacturing what was in essence a second family which ended up twice the size of his legitimate one, his career in the theatre was attaining new heights. In many ways he was ahead of his time. He produced a Shakespeare festival, putting on six of the Bard's plays in a week and performing in all of them. His was the first London theatre to stage Ibsen's *An Enemy of the People* and Oscar Wilde's *A Woman of No Importance*. His impeccable taste was occasionally suspect, though. A friend arrived at Tree's home one afternoon to read his latest play. During the second act Tree stood up, waving his hands. 'You must be mad,' he said. 'It will never be popular.' The friend was J. M. Barrie. The play was *Peter Pan*.

In 1904 Tree staged a successful production of *Oliver Twist*, playing Fagin. It was still packing them in two years later when Beatrice gave birth to Carol, who would go on to direct arguably the best version of Dickens's classic tale. But for many, Tree's finest triumph was the staging of *Pygmalion* in 1914, which gave George Bernard Shaw his first great commercial success. The two men did not get on and relations were strained during rehearsals. Shaw, who was directing Tree as Professor Higgins, learned to live with the actor's eccentricities and said, 'If he had not been so amusing, so ingenious and so entirely well intentioned, he would have driven me crazy.' Such sentiments were to be repeated many times about his notorious grandson.

Following a trip to Hollywood to make a silent film version of *Macbeth* – with himself in the title role, John Emerson directing and D. W. Griffith as producer – Tree returned to England and suffered a fall in a friend's house. After recuperating from surgery he died of pulmonary blood clots in 1917. Peter Reed was then just six years old and for the remainder of his life had only a few memories and impressions of his father. One of his favourites, which Ollie remembered being told, was that at the breakfast table he would sometimes rub marmalade into his sons' hair and roar with laughter, 'Now we are *all* redheads.'

It's hard to doubt that Oliver grew up feeling special as a child, coming as he did from a family that had Tree and Carol Reed among its ranks. Add to that pair Max Beerbohm, Tree's younger half-brother, a world-renowned caricaturist, writer and wit. 'Ollie and I were brought up with Max broadcasting on the radio at Christmas from Italy, where he lived,' recalls David. 'The BBC used to go down there and virtually ask him to talk about anything because he was credited with the greatest command of the English language.' David also read Max's one and only novel, *Zuleika Dobson*, a tale about life at Oxford University in Edwardian times. Oliver must have read it too, since he later bought the film rights, but was never to see it materialize on screen. 'So, growing up, Ollie and I were aware we had this wonderful heritage.' A heritage that may very well have influenced Oliver's decision to become an actor.

There's someone else too, another possible ancestor who was to have a profound influence on a young and impressionable Oliver: Peter the Great, Tsar of Russia from 1672 to 1725 and one of the bloodiest monarchs in history. Again the connection was courtesy of Granny May, whose mother Henrietta Rowlatt was the daughter of Canon Rowlatt of Exeter, whose family was said to have been founded by a bastard child of the Tsar. The story goes that Peter the Great came to England in 1698 to study shipbuilding with the intention of starting his own navy, fell in love with a local girl, took her back to St Petersburg, and had two children who ultimately returned to England.

Discovering and hearing stories about this grand forebear added a certain exoticism to Ollie's childhood daydreams and fuelled his imagination. 'I was a lost prince,' he said, and he would fantasize about riding with Boadicea against the invading Roman hordes or donning the armour of the Black

Knight. 'It was half play, half dream. The romantic musing of a dunce.' He even half-expected to be whisked off at any moment to rule some desert kingdom or far-flung dark European realm, as he couldn't help but feel 'a certain contempt for the common lot I played with and rubbed shoulders with at ink-stained desks'. It never happened, but in his chosen profession of acting wasn't Oliver still 'living out my fantasies'?

While insufficient evidence exists to support any claim of alignment to this royal bloodline, the point is that Oliver grew up believing it to be true. It wasn't until the late seventies that he finally set about researching into the matter himself, at great expense. One of his cousins, John Brooke-Little, was a world-renowned writer on heraldic subjects at the College of Arms in London. After much foraging in the past, Brooke-Little produced a fairly comprehensive family tree that went back centuries. Ollie also carried out his own research and, as he read more about Peter the Great, 'I felt a frightening relaxation about the odd touches of paranoia and the strange impulses that had marked my personality and driven me to buck the system with outrageous horseplay.' Was Ollie seeking to use the shadow of his illustrious ancestor as an excuse for some of his hell-raising behaviour, and asserting that this kind of infamy was in the genes?

As Tree's personality had chimed with Oliver, so Peter's exploits in England struck a chord, for instance how he'd invite noblemen to feast with him at his home and post guards at the door to prevent anyone from leaving before they had drunk a minimum of four bottles of wine. At the end of his stay his rented house in London was deemed a wreck, the kitchen floor was in rubble, three hundred panes of glass had been broken, and in tests of strength the brass locks on every door had been smashed.

While Ollie confessed that he saw much of himself in Peter, 'I don't like all I see.' In his autobiography he reproduced this remarkably apt paragraph describing the young Tsar, written by the historian Stephen Graham: 'The young Peter, drunk, pop-eyed, making dreadful faces, roaring, slashing about at random with his sword, was a fearsome host. His eyes were roaming, flashing, audacious, full of inventiveness and wild humour, or else full of adventurous cruelty, vengeful, implacable. His giant frame brooded over his guests at the table like a vulture among lesser birds. But he did not brood over his wine. No one knew what would be his next action. All learned to be apprehensive.'

Naturally there were many who doubted the veracity of Ollie's claims, not least members of his own family. 'I'm not sure if all that Peter the Great stuff isn't bullshit,' says Simon. 'I've always been terribly unconvinced, but Ollie was, he wore it like a medal. Maybe it's true.'

For his role as Father Grandier in Ken Russell's *The Devils*, Oliver was required to have all his hair and eyebrows shaved off. The film's stills photographer took a shot of the final result and Ollie bears a quite uncanny resemblance to a death mask that Peter the Great had made in 1719. 'I have to say the similarity is remarkable,' says David. 'It's quite remarkable.'

Lance Corporal Reed 23324533 – Sir!

Trading on his strength and sporting prowess, Oliver decided to become a professional boxer. 'I fancied myself as a light-heavyweight.' It was a short-lived ambition, lasting a total of two fights. His first took place in a boxing booth at a fair in Mitcham, and he won it, quite easily. 'I thought I was on to a good thing.' His second bout resulted in a very different outcome: he took an awful beating from a man who turned out to be a former professional. 'So I quit. I decided I didn't like being hit.'

Instead he found employment as an orderly at St Helier Hospital in Carshalton. At the strip joint he'd learned about women and sex, here he learned about life and death. His duties mainly involved collecting the recently departed and taking them to the mortuary. Sometimes he'd wander around the wards and play with the ill children, just to keep their spirits up, only to be told a few days later that one of them had died. It was tough to accept, staring death right in the face, 'but always the gloom was lifted by the radiance of the nurses'. They in turn warmed to his practical jokes. One night Ollie was wrapped in a sheet and wheeled on a trolley into the office where the duty nurse checked all corpses for personal items. As she lifted the sheet Oliver grabbed her hand and sat bolt upright. 'She nearly jumped out of her knickers.' Another time he hid himself in a coffin and was wheeled into a lift containing a group of medical students. Unfortunately the matron was there too and overheard his horror-film intonations of 'Let me out. I'm alive!' In the administrator's office Ollie received a severe dressing down and was warned that if he stepped out of line again he'd be fired. Pausing outside the office, he heard the matron and the governors burst out laughing.

Oliver turned eighteen in 1956 and swiftly received his call-up papers. National Service beckoned. His brother David had already undergone his stint and stayed on after the mandatory eighteen months to become an officer in the Military Police. It was a choice that surprised many because the Reed family was not particularly renowned for its military endeavours. We already know about Peter's objections, and even Carol Reed, who was made a captain during the Second World War, didn't take things seriously, absent-mindedly raising his hat whenever someone saluted him. Peter described Carol as 'blissfully unmilitary, and [behaving] as though the war was a superb invention of Evelyn Waugh's'.

At least Oliver was keen; unlike those who swallowed perfume in an effort to fail the army medical. His first choice was to join the Royal Military Police, the Red Caps, but because of his stint as a hospital porter he was placed with the Royal Army Medical Corps (RAMC) and sent to Queen Elizabeth Barracks in Church Crookham, Hampshire, to learn to be a soldier. In other words, 'How to peel spuds, polish mess tins, paint stones, march in step and sing dirty songs.'

The barracks at Church Crookham were smartly laid out with the usual parade ground and officers' mess. The Training Companies were all housed in wooden barracks arranged in a spider formation, in other words six squad huts for about twenty men and each connected to two toilet and shower blocks. Every fortnight an intake of trainees joined and after ten or so weeks a company was basic-trained and moved on. Ollie was in D2 squad and arrived at the barracks in July 1956, settling quickly into army life as he found the experience not far removed from that of boarding school. He also loved the companionship of his fellow soldiers and, according to Reginald Rea, another cadet, who got to know Ollie well during his basic training, had no problem with discipline. 'He had no sympathy at all with any whingers or moaners.' Nor did he get into conflict with the staff, 'who were all razor-sharp creases and polish, with little sticks to prod towards us while shouting and bawling. The RSM was a very large, impressive bloke; not to be crossed.'

Considering that Ollie was to become a millionaire, it's fun to reflect on the pay he got in training, according to Rea a measly twenty-eight bob (£1.40) a week maximum, but with deductions for haircuts and barrack damages it could be as low as £1. With trainees getting up at around 5.30 a.m. and cleaning kit in the evenings, this amounted to a wage of one or two pence per hour. Because of the abysmal pay, and as most trainees smoked, there wasn't much cash left over to get seriously drunk. 'The NAAFI sold soft drinks and canned beer at around 5p a pint and fags at around 4p for twenty,' remembers Rea. 'As far as I knew, local pubs were not out of bounds, but I don't know of many trainees leaving camp during these first weeks, with all the cleaning, inspections, and guard duties. Also we had to send all civvy clothes home and trainees wore coloured shoulder flashes denoting "just started". So the pubs were left to the instructors. I only recall Ollie having soft drinks but he was a pretty heavy smoker and he did cadge fags; maybe he didn't get any money from home.' Everyone knew of Oliver's theatrical background, though, and his connection to Sir Carol Reed, and, says Rea, 'since most of the trainees were working class this put his standing up considerably.'

Barracks entertainment was not seen as a high priority but Rea does recall the odd show being put on and, most significantly, Ollie's participation in them. 'He performed comedy monologues incorporating a bit of leg-pulling of the trainers and officers using various pronounced funny accents. He also did some general comedy observations of the camp. It was a good display of his acting skills.' As was his general larking about. Because of the proximity of their surnames Oliver and Rea always stood next to each other in the pay queue and Ollie never failed to act the clown with his over-the-top marching and saluting, which once almost had the pay table over when he slipped and skidded in his hobnailed boots.

There was also the odd dance, but no woman from the local populace dared go near the drill hall, so army nurses volunteered. At one such dance Ollie flirted with a seemingly obliging lass, unaware she was the sergeant major's bit on the side. From that day forward he set out to make Ollie's life a bloody misery, marching him up and down ad nauseam and handing out every shitty job going. Far from downtrodden, Ollie surprised himself by how much he revelled in it all, the atmosphere of bullying that pervades the army, the orders that are never spoken but barked at your lughole, the personal insults, the physical toil. He couldn't get enough of it all, he was in his element.

After basic training Oliver was singled out as potential officer material for no other reason than that he had a posh voice. Exactly the same thing had happened to David. 'Like me, Oliver spoke quite well and sounded educated, we had the veneer of good breeding, which our father had invested in, so they put him up for a commission.' Off Ollie had gone for a week of tests, and was doing well: the assault course was a piece of cake and he seemed naturally to fit in among the other well-mannered 'fine fellows' and 'good chaps'. Then disaster: each candidate was required to write an essay on 'The Role of the Modern Army'. Oliver had no problem formulating a thesis but, committed to paper, it looked like the work of a twelve-year-old. The examiners were left scratching their heads and sent him to see the command psychiatrist, 'simply,' reveals David, 'because they couldn't understand how this young man who to all intents and purposes appeared to be very well educated and different from everyone else didn't come up to the standard required and wasn't able to become a young officer.'

Hurled unceremoniously back into the private ranks, Ollie decided to put himself up for the position of squad instructor. Besides a pay increase to £2 a week and a private room, Ollie was simply born for the position. 'I could sound as terrifying and inhuman as any Sergeant Major.' After completing a training course he was made a lance corporal and given his own squad of men to bully and scream at. 'I became as big a bastard as anybody who had the job of making life miserable for a body of men.' It's little wonder that Oliver became so accomplished at playing soldiers on screen, especially in the little-seen *The Triple Echo*, where his army sergeant is so frighteningly realistic that those who suffered National Service must have broken out in a cold sweat watching it.

Ollie did his job at the barracks so well that not only was he made up to a full corporal but his unit won everything in sight, and yet his men came to despise him utterly. Taking this to heart, Ollie hoped to make amends by arranging to buy them all a drink one night to celebrate their achievements; not one of them showed up. 'They refused to forgive me for doing my job properly.' Fuck them, he thought, and drank in the NAAFI on his own. There was another side to Ollie, though. He had noticed that one of the new recruits struggled with drill and had been in trouble a few times for getting it wrong. Ollie made it his personal crusade to teach the kid to get it right, all in his own spare time. The young soldier never forgot him for it.

After spending several months as an instructor at Church Crookham, Oliver was posted to the 18th Field Ambulance in Hong Kong. The long voyage on the troopship HMS *Oxfordshire* was made more arduous by the blockade of the

Suez Canal, which necessitated a slight detour round the Cape of Good Hope. One of Oliver's duties in the ambulance unit was inspecting the private parts of his colleagues for nasty sexual diseases, rife in the area, and what he found under the microscope made him never want to visit any of the local brothels. During a particularly virulent epidemic of crabs, Ollie was asked to unmask the culprit. 'I found out who it was and I said, "Listen, you little cunt, get down to the medical centre right now, shave off the hair on your bollocks and pour diesel fuel all over your nuts." And he did, the stupid bugger.'

Ollie had arrived in the Hong Kong Territories just four years after the end of the Korean War and tension was still high, with British bases strategically placed to resist any encroachment by Communist Chinese forces. Although just how Ollie and a few other stringbean recruits were supposed to hold back hundreds of tanks and thousands of troops hadn't exactly been explained to them by Whitehall. Even so, the façade of colonial strength was reassuring. The 18th Field Ambulance, based in Taipo village, was a few miles from the Chinese border and occupied several cramped Nissen huts and unappealing camouflage tents. Everyone in the unit received anti-malarials each morning. Dick Robinson was there at the same time as Ollie and still vividly recalls him. 'Oliver would have been classified as a nursing orderly, and as such we shared some time in the training of the junior nursing orderlies in basic medical first-aid techniques and field training, since the Field Ambulance was in fact an active service unit. I remember him as being an extremely smart, well-presented, well-spoken and articulate young man. I was never aware of any disciplinary matters or other problems relating to him, and always understood that he was a good and reliable NCO, which was certainly my understanding of him. To have made corporal as a National Serviceman must have revealed some positive attributes as revealed by evidence of his good presentation, behaviour and reliability.'

Ollie's mate Reg Rea was posted there briefly, before moving to a hospital in Kowloon, and remembers, 'Ollie was the depot Red Cap or security bouncer.' He can also still vividly recall the sounds, smells and sights of those incredible days and the appalling conditions many had to live and work in. 'Hong Kong was generally very nice and not too hot, but we had occasional typhoons, including a serious one called Typhoon Gloria which blew a destroyer aground and caused all sorts of damage at the hospital. There were cockroaches and ants but the city areas were OK. There was overcrowding and squalor in the poorer areas and up in the New Territories poor sanitation and water supply (sometimes available only for a few hours) and sewage spread on paddy fields.'

Rea didn't see Ollie again until a chance encounter outside a pub in Wimbledon in 1963. 'He hadn't as yet achieved fame but he was clearly more pub-based and had lots of acquaintances and was treating customers to drinks. I did find that strange because in basic training he didn't drink at all.' A couple of years later, when Ollie had established himself as a film star, Rea wrote to him and got a genuinely warm and cheerful letter back. 'I remember you well,' replied Ollie. 'In fact I often think about the lads in the army. It's just sweet to hear from you.' Responding to a query from Rea about whether he would ever consider rejoining the army, Ollie wrote: 'No I wouldn't choose to go back in. But I miss the laughs, don't you?'

Ollie breathed a sigh of relief when, after just a short stay in Taipo, the 18th Field Ambulance moved to an RAF base in Sek Kong which offered vastly superior facilities. But it was still in the middle of bloody nowhere and could only be reached by a single, winding road. There wasn't much to do in the place either, certainly women were in short supply, and Ollie referred to himself as your typical Virgin Soldier. 'To pull at a girl's knicker elastic was the peak of my excitement.' To alleviate his sexual frustrations he played sports, winning several army trophies for running. 'There was quite an active athletic competition between rival medical units,' recalls Dick Robinson. 'And perhaps since any skills we might have possessed were in the area of distance running, Ollie and myself came together in training for the cross-country race. I well remember one such instance when we were running uphill along the side of a small stream, then downhill on the opposite side, we disturbed a hornets' nest, and the training session turned into a sprint session. Fortunately we outran the hornets!' Ollie also learned to play rugby, which remained a lifelong passion, and did some more boxing. 'If you were on the boxing team, you didn't have to go and work in the cookhouse peeling potatoes. It was an easy life if you were an athlete.'

As for seeing any action, the closest Ollie came to danger was in Hong Kong when he and a bunch of mates hired a boat in Victoria Harbour, and by a combination of bad luck and idiocy managed to row themselves out into open sea. Choppy waters made it impossible to row back, so there they were floating ever closer into Communist territory. Rescue looked likely when a junk pulled alongside, but when they were recognized as British the sailors threw them back like cast-off tuna, with, 'Fuck off, pommie!' By this time it was night and pitch-dark. Luckily a breeze picked up and they were slowly pushed back in the direction of the harbour, arriving at dawn exhausted but relieved. Ollie also bragged to a reporter in 1972 that he once dived into the harbour and swam to Hong Kong Island, 'forwards and backwards'.

Regimental orders kept excessive drinking to a minimum, though Oliver and his comrades always managed an almighty booze-up at least once a month. On one highly memorable occasion they got slaughtered absolutely free of charge when the platoon was given a guided tour round a local brewery. They were led into a large, white-tiled room where a solitary pipe sticking out of the wall was turned on and out gushed beer. A sergeant pointed to a row of mugs hanging on hooks on the wall, saying, 'You've got exactly one hour.' There was a stampede. When time was up the soldiers could barely stagger to the waiting truck, which took the bumpiest road in all of China to return them to camp. 'The amount of vomit that was deposited in the back had to be smelled to be believed,' Ollie recalled. He'd also come to realize why the choice of vehicle was a tipper lorry. Back at barracks the commandant ordered the rear end to be tipped up and out slid the vomit and the soldiers in one big, revolting pile.

Extra For Hire

Oliver's National Service had drawn to an end and although he didn't think he made a particularly successful soldier he nevertheless took pride in the fact that he'd served with the RAMC. 'He loved the Royal Army Medical Corp,' says Mark. 'He used to talk about how they were the most decorated regiment in the British army.' For the rest of his life Ollie was in love with all things military. His widow Josephine says he was constantly quoting his old army number and during the Falklands war tried his best to volunteer. 'I think he phoned up and they were very kind and polite and said that perhaps he was a little old. But he was very supportive of all the armed forces.'

In 1977, when the fire service went on strike and the army's 'Green Goddess' fire engines took over, Mark was awoken at one o'clock in the morning by a grinning Ollie. 'Come on, we're going to have a drink with the bucko boys.' Mark, who was about sixteen at the time, remembers helping his father fill the car boot with Thermos flasks of booze and bottles of whisky and driving to his local fire station in Dorking. Pulling up at the gate, they were informed by the pickets that the soldiers were at a barracks in Redhill. Ollie didn't know how to get to Redhill, so drove to the nearest police station, where a helpful desk sergeant told him, 'Right, Mr Reed, you go this way, over that roundabout.' After a five-mile trek they were in Redhill but still clueless as to the whereabouts of the barracks, when Ollie spotted a police car and flashed his lights. It stopped and a copper got out. 'Oh yes, Mr Reed, we heard you were coming. I can take you as far as the barracks gate.' Off they went again, with a police escort, and finally arrived around two o'clock in the morning. 'We rang the bell,' says Mark, 'and these officers came down and helped us take in all these boxes of booze. We had a quick drink with the soldiers and then drove home again. You couldn't do something like that now. Times have changed.'

On another occasion Ollie was holidaying in Barbados when HMS *Fearless* came into port. The officers were using Ollie's hotel bar as their mess and when they arrived in their nicely pressed shore-going kit, of course his eyes lit up. 'Ah, gentlemen, would you care for a drink?' It became an amazing piss-up that turned into a game of Follow My Leader, with the navy guys trotting behind Ollie as he marched twice round the outdoor swimming pool, then on to the diving board and into the water. The next morning Ollie was sitting by the pool nursing a not inconsiderable hangover when he heard the low pulsating noise of rotor blades. A helicopter was hovering over the resort and lowering down a naval commander clutching a bottle of rum and a teddy bear as a thank you to Ollie from his fellow officers.

Back from Hong Kong and living with Granny Dardin, Ollie soon turned his thoughts to what he wanted to achieve in life. He'd no intention of returning to his old job at the hospital, but with no qualifications or training of any kind he was limited as to what he could do. The only thing he had going for him was £100 in savings and a new personal wardrobe. 'Out in Hong Kong you could get suits made very cheaply,' says David. 'So whilst he was there he got quite a big wardrobe and he came back with a trilby hat, a camel-hair coat and various good-looking suits.' Perhaps, thought Ollie, his newly acquired dapper style might entice a rich woman to marry him and keep him until his dotage. More realistically, he decided to try his hand at male modelling and joined a photographic agency. 'Oliver was extraordinarily good-looking when he was young,' says David. 'There was a mystery and a roughness and a sort of animal element to him. It was an animal attraction, his eyes were phenomenal, and gradually the film business realized it.'

Ollie had also acquired a girlfriend and this prompted a move out of Granny Dardin's into a room in Redcliffe Square, close to Brompton Cemetery. When that relationship didn't work out he was soon determined to find more obliging women and his partner in crime was an Irishman who lived upstairs. Jack Burke owned a Jaguar car won in a poker game and nicknamed 'the passion wagon', and he and Ollie tore up and down the streets of west London in an effort to impress the girls. In truth, Ollie found female company largely easy to come by. At a house party populated by young teachers he scored with a Miss Hook, who insisted she was a virgin despite a repertoire of seasoned bedroom techniques. When, post coitus, Oliver threw doubt on her claim, Miss Hook lived up to her name by walloping him round the head.

Money ran out to buy petrol for the Jaguar, and Ollie and Jack were forced to find themselves a job. Burke was a member of the film extras' union and held fanciful notions of maybe becoming an actor. To Ollie, it didn't seem like such a bad ambition: after all, he'd enjoyed Shakespeare at Ewell Castle and had all that theatrical heritage, although at school it was David who did all the optional drama classes, not Ollie. 'However, I do remember before National Service he joined an amateur dramatic group in Wimbledon. That was the first indication of going down that road.'

Like thousands of would-be actors Oliver wrote to theatrical repertory companies asking for work; he was turned down flat for lack of experience. 'That being the case, I decided to invent a career.' Overnight his CV took on the appearance of a seasoned pro's, with appearances in everything from *Othello* to the most avant-garde plays in places like Wagamoomoo in Australia. 'What I did not realize was that the people to whom I addressed my shining history knew full well that the theatres where I'd given my breathtaking performances did not exist.' Drawing another blank, Ollie decided to turn for advice to Uncle Carol, for whom he had enormous fondness and respect, even if trips to see him had been all too rare. 'You see,' says David, 'my father and Carol fell out big time and didn't talk for many a year. Carol started his career in the theatre and Peter saw him holding a spear on stage and made the remark, "What the bloody hell are you doing holding a spear!" And, rather like Ollie taking objection to things Peter told him, Carol was the same and reacted quite badly. Of course, Carol went on to a successful career but it took many, many years to get over that feud.'

By that stage Carol Reed had a string of highly respected films to his name as a director, including *The Way Ahead* (1944), a superb war drama and fitting tribute to the bravery of the ordinary soldier, *Odd Man Out* (1947), which featured James Mason as an IRA member on the run, and his masterpiece *The Third Man* (1949), often cited as the best British film ever made. He was also by then a 'sir', having the honour of being only the second British film director, after Alexander Korda, to be knighted.

Ollie had seen Sir Carol shortly before going off on National Service, visiting the set of his glossy circus romp *Trapeze* and having his photograph taken inside the circus ring with Burt Lancaster and Gina Lollobrigida. But as he walked down the King's Road in Chelsea towards Carol's opulent house at number 213, today a Grade II listed building, he was overcome by nerves. 'Not of the man, who was full of sweetness and charm, but of the powerful film director who just happened to be my father's brother.' Maybe Ollie was fearful that his visit would be misinterpreted. 'He didn't want to be seen taking advantage of the relationship,' says David. It was advice and guidance he wanted, no more.

Invited into the drawing room, Ollie sat down awkwardly and as he explained his wish to become an actor Sir Carol listened politely and intently. The stage, Ollie said, did not really hold any interest for him, he wanted to work in films. That may be so, said Uncle Carol, but he still needed some kind of formal training. RADA was suggested. Ollie shook his head: he believed all drama teachers either couldn't hack it in the real world or just weren't good enough to act. 'I also think he just wanted to get going and start earning,' says Simon. 'It was a case of, let's get some money. That's it really. I want money, I want it quickly. He saw acting as a pay cheque. Also RADA was a bit establishment.'

The next best thing, suggested Carol, was to meet the right people. 'Put yourself about a bit at the Ritz grill.' Oliver hadn't the faintest clue where the Ritz grill was, let alone the money to pay for lunch there; he currently existed on a diet of spaghetti and tomato soup and hadn't even got a shilling to put in the gas meter. He began to get the feeling that dear uncle Carol 'was drifting about in an Edwardian summer'. His next suggestion got Oliver thinking that he might very well have cracked: 'Seek out the people that can help you, Oliver, pitch a tent outside their front doors and every morning when they leave to go to the studio, step out of your tent and say, "Excuse me, I'm Oliver Reed, I would like you to give me a job."'

Carol did offer one piece of advice that Oliver would always be grateful for. If he wasn't going to bother with drama school, then he should spend as much of his spare time at the cinema, watching and observing. Henceforth Oliver's local Odeon became his university 'and my only training school'. The pub, too, was another great source of learning that served him well or his entire career. All human life was on display, the flotsam and jetsam of society, the working class, and the aristocracy mingling in the saloon and public bars, like a human zoo. 'Oliver told me once that this was the way he learned how to do a part,' reveals Bernie Coleman, owner of the Dog and Fox pub in Wimbledon. 'He loved observing people. If he came in early he'd sit by himself with a pint and just watch and listen to people.'

Ollie was remarkably perceptive and his knack for observing human nature never deserted him throughout his whole life. 'He picked up on things around him that you just wouldn't notice,' says Mark. 'They'd pass you by. But not him. Just little details that he would see and no one else. He prided himself in it.' As Ollie once said: 'Everyday life is my favourite theatre. People are my favourite actors.'

With Jack Burke's help Oliver managed to get into the film extras' union and his first job was in *Hello London*, a musical-cum-travelogue so obscure that it has virtually disappeared. Its star was Sonja Henie, three times Olympic figure-skating champion, but when she arrived in London in early 1958, after years of touring ice revues across the United States, she was very much a faded personality and Oliver couldn't help but feel disappointed. 'Her legs were muscle-bound and unattractive and didn't give me the urge to give her one.'

Ollie had been hired by the film's director Sidney Smith because of his 'hungry face', and is one of a haggle of journalists greeting Sonja as she steps down from her flight smiling inanely as if rigor mortis had set in midway across the Atlantic. Unimpressed with the costume the film production company had offered, Oliver phoned his dad and asked if he'd lend him his reporter's mac. It was the first time in something like three years that he'd contacted his father. It would be another two years before they progressed from speaking on the phone to actually sharing the same oxygen in a room.

The rest of 1958 was taken up with sporadic bits of extra work. Ollie featured in crowd scenes in Norman Wisdom's *The Square Peg*, an agreeable slice of army antics. It's the one where Norman finds he's a dead ringer for a Nazi general and swaps roles, flirts with a pre-*Avengers* Honor Blackman, causes chaos on a parade ground, says 'Mr Grimsdale' a lot, and pours champagne down Hattie Jacques's cleavage. *Life is a Circus*, directed by Val Guest, featured the Crazy Gang, the pie-and-mash equivalent of the Marx Brothers, whose mix of nerve-shredding cockney songs and insipid zaniness today looks about as funny as a dead parent. This was their last film and saw them trying to save a circus from closing down. Ollie is barely visible in the background as a punter in a few of the crowd scenes. Then there was a couple of days' work sunning himself as a passenger on a cruise ship on Pinewood Studios' back lot in *The Captain's Table*, a sort of sub-*Carry On* comedy. These jobs never paid very much, so Ollie was generally destitute, bedding down with friends or casual lovers.

Waking up one morning, he was perturbed to discover nasty red blotches across his chest, followed by blinding headaches and a 100-plus temperature. Thinking it to be nothing more than the onset of influenza, he still called in at his local GP and was alarmed when the doctor reached for the phone to order an ambulance. At the hospital it was confirmed that Oliver had bacterial meningitis, a life-threatening ailment known to strike with incredible speed, so without delay Oliver was pumped full of antibiotics and ordered to rest.

With nowhere to go, Oliver convalesced with his mother, now remarried and living in Cheshire. Oliver had yet to meet his stepfather, Bill Sulis, but had heard stories of his wild antics in the RAF, from which he was dismissed for damaging a plane while flying upside down. Such devilry immediately endeared him to Oliver and at first the appreciation appeared to be mutual. Thanks to a family fortune derived from the manufacture of rope, Bill and Marcia lived in relative splendour in a mansion set in its own grounds. Bill was determined to show off Marcia's son to the country set at various parties and hunt balls, but Ollie's prized collection of Hong Kong suits was now history save for one, and that had seen better days. 'I now regretted scrubbing it with Daz on the side of the bath to remove all the beer stains and the dried puke.' Aghast at the thought of his stepson meeting local dignitaries in anything other than flash attire, Bill loaned him a few of his dinner jackets. These, alas, did not last long: one went west after Oliver chased a farmer's daughter across a ploughed field, while another shrank to infant size when Ollie crawled home drunk one night in a rain storm. 'When my stepfather had run out of suits I went back to London.'

Marcia had arranged for her son to stay at a mews flat near Notting Hill Gate tube station that belonged to an aunt who lived in Egypt. With a secure roof over his head, Ollie began to look for work again, but this time he faced competition from a most unlikely source: his own brother. Out of the army, David had also set his sights on a career as an actor and together they made the daily rounds of casting offices and advertising agencies. It was a depressing time: Oliver had spent what was left of his army savings on a photographic portfolio but nobody was interested in hiring him. 'You're too Continental-looking,' many complained. Years later and an international star, Ollie loved going up to those same agents and producers whenever their paths crossed and saying, 'Hey, remember me? I'm Oliver Reed. You used to tell me to piss off!'

David saw a lot of his brother during this period. Their operations base was a coffee bar in Earls Court run by a man called Tiny, who of course was an enormous fellow. 'We used to meet down in the cellar and for us everything gravitated from there. We'd meet on a Friday evening and Ollie and I would buy a bottle of Merrydown cider and two straws and drink that until it gave us a buzz, and then we'd say, right, where's tonight's party?'

The Ollie that David encountered after National Service was very different from the one he last saw at Ewell Castle, if only in appearance. 'He went into an odd period of dressing very, very strangely, of going around in an open-top shirt tied in a knot above his bare waist, with a big chain around his neck with a skull on it. I suppose it was part of that period where youth were beginning to express themselves as a revolt against the stodginess of the adult world. It was the days of rock and roll, mods and rockers, and beatniks. It was the start of creating one's own culture, youth culture. The social barriers were starting to be broken down, girls and boys were getting their emancipation from the protection or governance of their parents and so earning enough to have their bedsits. We were self-supporting. It was a very important period, but it's only when you look back on it all; you didn't realize it at the time.'

Craftily David was able to make practical use of his brother's rather menacing look. At the time David hung out around Wimbledon with a chap called Mike. 'We were both rather po-faced, we'd been young subalterns in the army, so we used to go to clubs in London and pretend Ollie was our bodyguard. So there would be Mike and I dressed terribly correctly and we used to make a thing of sending Ollie across to a girl to say, my boss wants to dance with you.' A few months later when David met his future wife Muriel (Mickie to her friends) he arranged a get-together with his brother at a coffee bar. In Ollie walked, in tight-fitting jeans, the open-neck shirt, and that skull on a chain. 'I was shocked out of my brain by him,' admits Muriel.

All that time leafing through the actors' newspaper *The Stage* looking for work finally paid off when Ollie noticed a story about producers casting for a new seven-part BBC historical drama serial called *The Golden Spur*. Arriving late, he found himself at the back of a very long queue of other hopefuls.

Handed a scrap of paper with some dialogue on it, he used the time to learn it by heart, something that no one else appeared to be bothering to do. When it was his turn he rattled the speech off effortlessly, a display of professionalism that perhaps swayed the panel to give him the small role of Richard of Gloucester. It was a remarkable feat, given that Oliver had no real acting experience.

When his sole episode aired in the summer of 1959 Oliver's brooding image attracted the attention of an agent, Pat Larthe. 'You were brilliant, darling,' she said down the phone. Moderately well known in the business for supplying top models for television and magazine assignments, Pat only handled a limited number of actors, including the young Michael Caine, who joined her books at roughly the same time as Oliver. Thrilled to have an agent at last, Ollie saw this as proof that he was heading in the right direction and his days of poverty were over. The only downside to the arrangement was the 10 per cent of his earnings that Pat would claim for the next ten years. 'And she held me to that,' Ollie later complained. 'Even after I left her and went to another agent.'

Pat went to work immediately on Oliver, sending him to Pinewood for a day's work as an extra on *The League of Gentlemen*. Now considered a minor British classic, it stars Jack Hawkins as a former army officer, bitter at his early retirement, who recruits a group of disgraced colleagues to perform a bank robbery with military precision. They hire a room at a theatre club for one of their clandestine meetings and a couple of obviously gay chorus boys barge in. When one of the young actors couldn't quite manage to access his feminine side and needed to be hurriedly replaced, Ollie sensed his chance. 'I can do that!' Director Basil Dearden quickly gave him the once-over and told him to give it a go. 'And that was Oliver's very first speaking role in a film,' says David. And Ollie made the best of this opportunity, managing the almost impossible feat of out-camping Kenneth Williams with his mincing entrance, hands on hips, and a voice resembling Edith Evans overdosing on helium.

Next was *The Angry Silence*, a highly praised film featuring one of Richard Attenborough's finest performances as a factory worker who refuses to support an unjustified wildcat strike, and is ostracized and victimized by his colleagues. Ollie can be seen in several scenes set in the factory, mingling with a group of other young thuggish workers. His glowering looks are unmistakable and he handles his few lines of dialogue with a sort of naive brutishness.

Playing Attenborough's character's best friend in the film was Michael Craig, on whose original storyline the picture was based. Craig, something of a screen heart-throb in the early sixties, vividly remembers Ollie being on the film since during shooting he stayed with Craig and his first wife in their house in London and behaved impeccably. 'He was very young at the time and just out of the army, where he'd been an officer and a gent, which he still was. Oliver was very polite and good to work with. I suppose I thought he might do well as a screen actor, he was good-looking, very macho, and with presence. We ran into each other over the following years and he was always friendly until after he had the fight in the club when someone shoved a glass in his face and left him badly scarred. He became quite different after that and I don't think we ever met again.'

While an extra, Ollie struck up a friendship with another aspiring young actor, the 22-year-old Steven Berkoff. Then at drama school, Berkoff would take the occasional day off to earn a little extra cash by doing film extra work. 'We met on some movie or other,' remembers Berkoff. 'He had this extraordinary voice, very elegant, and he was rather good-looking, and in the time we were waiting to be called for the scene we'd just hang around the studios and talk. He told me he wanted to be an actor. I said that I was at drama school and a very useful thing to do in acting is improvisation because it gets your mind and imagination flowing. So we did a few little improvisations together, I'd pretend to be a Cockney or a New Yorker, we just played around, and we got on very well and I found him very, very charming. We met occasionally outside of the studios for a cappuccino. I thought he was a bit of a mate.'

One day Reed mentioned that he had an agent and they needed some photographs. Berkoff always carried around with him a camera, and did his own developing, so suggested he could take some pictures. Marvellous, said Ollie. 'So we went to the Embankment and did some poses,' Berkoff recalls. 'The photographs came out really well. He looks fabulous in them. But then when I'd got the prints developed I met him, he was with a girl, and suddenly he was another person, he'd changed. I'd been with him for a month or so, but this person who was sensitive, gentle and well mannered had become loutish. He started complaining that I was charging too much for the photographs. We had a brief chat but I found him to be suddenly repulsive. He'd obviously been drinking and he was arrogant, smug, supercilious, sarcastic – I never saw him again. But I did follow his career and I thought he turned into a fantastic actor. He was a complete natural, with a brilliant intelligence and a wonderful voice. He was remarkable in *The Devils*, perfect.'

Kate

Using her contacts in the advertising industry, Pat Larthe sent Ollie off to audition for a television commercial for Cadbury's Milk Tray. In the room was the usual motley crew of models and hard-up actors, but Ollie felt drawn to one girl in particular, who had devastating eyes and a natural beauty that knocked him sideways. 'The vibes started immediately.' It was the girl who made the first move, introducing herself as Kate Byrne. She'd auditioned already and hadn't got the job. 'They told me I was too beautiful for the girl-next-door type.' Kate had been with Pat as a model for some time and knew all about Ollie, even mentioning his meningitis scare. The two began to chat away idly when there was a sudden commotion in the room and Ollie was distracted, and when he turned back she was gone. He now had a decision to make, go after her or wait for his audition. In the end he opted for both and barged into the office to the shocked surprise of the casting director. 'Listen, you've got to interview me now because a gorgeous redhead has just left and I want to chase her.'

Taking one look at Ollie, the director replied, 'You're not the sort.'

'How do you know what sort she likes?'

'No, I mean for the part. You're not the boy who lives next door sort.'

'Thank you very much,' said Ollie and darted out into the bright sunshine of Oxford Street. Among the crowds of shoppers it was going to be difficult if not impossible to find her, but Ollie got a huge slice of luck when he literally crashed into her as she came out of a department store. They agreed to have a coffee, and as they sipped their cappuccinos Kate suddenly flashed a very expensive engagement ring. Oh bugger! Not to worry, because Kate revealed that all was not well with the relationship. And so it proved, for a few days later she called Oliver in tears: her fiancé had pushed her around and threatened violence. Enraged, Ollie armed himself with a walking stick and went looking for the bastard. Nowhere to be found, so instead he sent out a message that rather than hit on young women this chap ought to take on someone his own size. A showdown was arranged at a local pub, but when high noon struck he didn't turn up 'and I had nowhere to shove my stick'. Instead, standing there was Kate, and out of the tatters of one relationship grew another.

Oliver, however, just after meeting Kate, had become smitten with the sister of a previous flame. Her name was Tina, she was very sexy and impossible to resist, and so Ollie juggled both affairs at the same time. Of course, it ended in disaster when he had to go to hospital again, this time suffering from German measles, and the two women turned up at the same visiting hour. There they stood on opposite sides of the bed staring daggers at each other. Kate crumbled a box of a hundred cigarettes over Ollie's head, while Tina bombarded him with a few well-aimed grapes; it was like a scene from *Carry On Doctor*. 'You can't have both of us,' said Kate finally. 'You will have to choose between us – right now!'

The choice was simple really: he'd known all along Kate was the one, but was rather less enthused with her idea of getting hitched immediately. No amount of, I think it would be better if we both wait a bit, would dissuade her: it was down the aisle or goodbye. Ollie eventually gave in, but it was still a bit of a shock when just a few days later Kate walked into the flat holding a marriage licence. In a 1976 interview for *Penthouse* magazine he put his own predictable spin on the reason why he relented in the face of Kate's marital overtures. 'She was a little spitfire, who wanted me to sign a contract saying I wasn't going to fuck anybody else.'

High on Ollie's list of reasons for not getting married were their precarious finances. Kate did the odd bit of modelling but he'd been out of work for months. So skint would he be sometimes that he'd take half a crown (12½p) out of Kate's purse to go down the pub to drink and gamble at darts, always making sure to replace it by the end of the night. Things picked up by the close of 1959 when Oliver was requested to go out to Bray Studios, home of the Hammer horror films. Stuart Lyons, one of the casting directors there, had seen *The Golden Spur* and thought this new young actor warranted closer inspection. Lyons was to become an early champion of Oliver, keeping faith with him for years, even attempting, though without success, to win him a role in the Elizabeth Taylor/Richard Burton behemoth *Cleopatra*, on which he was casting consultant.

As he waited for the results of his Hammer audition, Oliver's thoughts turned to his planned nuptials with Kate. The ceremony took place on 2 January 1960 at Kensington Register Office and as he was the nephew of Carol Reed the union attracted the attention of Fleet Street (thanks to a tip-off from Pat Larthe), and so for the first time Oliver got his name in the papers. It was a quiet affair, with only a few close friends in attendance, and David the only member of either family to be invited, it seems. 'I remember afterwards we went to our local pub, and the landlord cut a champagne cork and wedged a silver coin inside and gave it to Ollie and Kate for good luck.' Certainly Kate's father wasn't there: Patrick Byrne didn't altogether approve of his good Catholic daughter marrying a struggling actor.

The marriage didn't get off to the best of starts thanks to an almighty row that was allowed to fester for an entire week. It was over the most trivial of matters, David's wedding present of a voucher that could be exchanged for an LP or a night out at the recently opened Talk of the Town. Ollie rather fancied the night out, while Kate wanted the record, and all hell broke loose. Finally Kate got her way, but there were no winners and it was sadly all too symptomatic of what turned out to be a tempestuous and traumatic marriage. 'Kate was very strong-willed, a vibrant personality,' says Simon. 'And because they were both so similar, who was going to back down in that relationship? That was the problem. So the rows were horrendous.'

They were like two peas in a pod, really: Kate was very feisty, great at repartee, could be bitingly awful to people, blunt, honest, very much like Ollie. They were so well suited, equally combustible and fun-loving. 'Kate was a lovely Irish girl,' says Muriel Reed. 'She had a great sense of humour and I can't understand later on what possessed Oliver to leave her. But they were very volatile together, they loved a joke, they loved a fight, they fought like cat and dog, very much like Burton and Liz Taylor.' David recalls one story of when the couple were in Paris and a fight developed outside a bar and there was Kate yelling, 'Go on, get in there, Ollie! Throw him in the bloody river.' Conversely she was also quick to move Ollie out of the way when things got out of hand.

Now a married man, Oliver felt a degree of responsibility to get a 'normal' job since his acting career didn't seem to be going in a positive direction. Just then Hammer got back in touch: impressed by his audition, they wanted Ollie to play a small role in their latest production, The Two Faces of Dr Jekyll. 'That was my first film for Hammer and it saved my bacon.'

Hammer's Bad Boy

People had warned Oliver not to get into horror pictures, because they were seen as low-grade and once you were established in them it was difficult to escape. 'But all I wanted to do was act.' It was only a day's work and paid the less than handsome fee of £25, but he was in grand company. The film was helmed by Hammer's most valued director, Terence Fisher, who had already triumphantly brought Frankenstein, Dracula and the Mummy to life for the studio. Ollie shared his one scene with both the film's star, Canadian actor Paul Massie, and an actor he was to work with frequently over the years, Christopher Lee.

The Two Faces of Dr Jekyll was yet another variation on Robert Louis Stevenson's classic tale and Fisher put Oliver's beefy physique to good use in the role of a pimp in an elaborate scene set in a nightclub. Looking very dapper, Ollie sits with his little harem of spruced-up former backstreet trollops, and when he challenges Massie's Hyde for mistreating one of them, speaking in a clipped voice that is highly effective, he gets a sound thrashing for his impertinence. Sadly the film didn't find favour with critics or the public, becoming one of Hammer's biggest flops, but Ollie had taken an important first step towards stardom.

It was common knowledge within the film industry that powerful people, both male and female, took advantage of young, struggling actors. Oliver was once told to his face that to get on in the business he might have to take his trousers down. When one director, known to be a notorious homosexual, invited him to his house for a private audition, Kate scrawled 'Leave it alone. He's mine' in biro on his cock and 'Get off!' on his back. This didn't stop Ollie, though, from using similar tactics. He wasn't averse, for example, to sleeping with secretaries of casting directors and in the morning slipping them his photograph to put on the top of the pile for their boss to see when he arrived for work. 'I think he wanted to be a star,' argues Simon. 'At no stage in his life was he in love with acting. What he was in love with was being a star – and he was going to be a star whatever it took.'

With no new job in sight, more bad news arrived when Ollie and Kate were turfed out of their flat because the lease had run out. It was David who came to the rescue. He'd recently married Muriel, and Oliver had attended the wedding with predictably disastrous results. Feeling indignant that a Greek guitarist friend of the couple had been best man, Ollie took solace in several pints at the reception before waltzing over to the guy and laying one on him, causing his wig to fall off. With people taking sides and shouting at each other, 'the wedding ended in a bit of a shambles,' admitted Oliver.

David was forgiving enough to invite his brother and Kate to stay at his and Muriel's new two-bedroom flat in Kensington. It's a memory that causes Muriel to roll her eyes heavenward when it's brought up. It couldn't have been easy sharing space with Ollie, especially when David rejoined the army, having given up all hope of becoming an actor, and she was left alone with the pair. Frequently the two women clashed and tempers flared. Muriel remembers having to admonish Kate for always leaving her Tampax lying around. 'And when I came back to the flat after work one day my whole bed was covered in Tampax, forty or fifty of them, packets of the bloody things. You had to laugh.' Oliver boasted that he did his best to keep order by 'putting them across my knee one at a time and spanking them soundly'. In the end things weren't allowed to boil over completely because Muriel left to join David abroad and Oliver and Kate had no choice but to find a new place to live.

It was Kate's parents, having forgiven their headstrong daughter for marrying Oliver, who offered a solution: the couple could stay with them at their council flat in Stockwell, south London, until their prospects improved. That seemed a long way off, with Kate the only one currently earning. She was working as a photographic model, even after she found out she was pregnant, a fact she hid from Ollie at first. By May 1960 the Reed finances were so bad that Oliver contemplated accepting an offer to become a door-to-door vacuum cleaner salesman. That's when Hammer came calling, in the nick of time once again. Michael Carreras, a producer at the studio and son of the company's founder, James Carreras, had seen *Jekyll* and come away impressed by Oliver. With the encouragement of Stuart Lyons he'd agreed to his casting in Hammer's next production, *Sword of Sherwood Forest*.

Arriving in Dublin airport to start work at the newly opened Ardmore Studios, Ollie was reunited with Terence Fisher, who'd directed several episodes of the original fifties *Robin Hood* TV series, of which this was the first spin-off movie. Also reprising his TV role was Richard Greene, a poor man's Errol Flynn who'd brought sexuality and danger to the part. Greene is about as threatening as a cinema usherette with halitosis. Much better is Peter Cushing as the Sheriff of Nottingham. Ollie plays the villainous Lord Melton, a small role but he makes it count, hinting at the character's borderline-psychopathic tendencies and performing with a bewitching effeminacy, complete with a high-pitched, whispery voice. His big moment is the slaying of Cushing's Sheriff, an event the film never really recovers from since it was Cushing's towering personality that was driving the whole thing along. Ollie is also involved in the story's climactic sword fight, hurled across an abbey floor by Nigel Green's hulking Little John and finally dispatched by Robin himself.

Running around the beautiful countryside of County Wicklow, brandishing swords and riding horses, was for Ollie rather like re-enacting his childhood at Bledlow, only he was getting paid for it. 'It was goodies and baddies and damsels in distress, and I was Errol Flynn and every other hero I watched at the cinema.' He had hero worshipped Flynn for years, both the screen image and his don't-give-a-damn attitude to life. When the old hell-raiser passed away the previous October, Ollie was in a pub and immediately ordered a pint of Guinness. Standing to attention, he downed the black nectar in a single gulp.

After his scenes were completed, Ollie shared a flight back home with Terence Fisher's family and the wife of the make-up artist, who Ollie sensed was definitely the nervous type. They had arrived at London airport and were walking towards Customs when he decided to have some fun. Wearing a cloak that Fisher's daughter thought made Oliver look 'fairly sinister', he sidled over to this woman and whispered in her ear, 'Just give me the stuff once we get through Customs, all right,' followed by a highly exaggerated wink. The woman went into hysterics, screeching at the Customs men, 'I've got nothing to hide! I've got nothing to hide!' and acting so suspiciously that she was immediately grabbed and subjected to a search.

Things appeared to be improving when Ollie landed another small film role alongside Adam Faith and Shirley Anne Field in *Beat Girl*, about Soho coffee-bar culture and beatniks. Oliver has only a couple of lines and tries painfully hard to look languid and hip, grooving ridiculously to the modish chords of the John Barry Seven in the credit sequence until he resembles a deranged flowerpot man. The risqué storyline and trashy visuals earned the film an 'X' certificate. It seems desperately tame today, but one can see why Warwickshire Council for one banned it at the time on the grounds that it was 'injurious to public morality'. One reason may have been the scene where the gang play chicken on a railway line by laying their heads on the metal rail.

With money coming in, Ollie now looked for somewhere to put down roots, and the obvious place was Wimbledon. The flat they decided to rent, at 29 Woodside, near Wimbledon train station, was small and airless, but Ollie felt back where he belonged, especially important since he was involved in such a precarious business. 'I needed an environment that was familiar from which to draw reassurance.' Kate meanwhile had been sacked as a model after an astute photographer noticed her bump. It was up to Ollie now to single-handedly bring in the dosh and his agent managed to quickly line up bit parts in a couple of comedies. *The Bulldog Breed* was yet another Norman Wisdom film, almost indistinguishable from its churned-out predecessors; this is the one where Norman joins the navy and ends up getting blasted into space in a rocket. It was just a day's work for Ollie, playing one of a gang of bovver boys who menace poor Norman in a cinema queue. It's quite rough stuff: when Norman is felled, Ollie especially is seen putting the boot in, and his toecaps can't have failed to connect with the comedy institution's gonads. But rescue is at hand, thanks to the timely intervention of a trio of sailors, one of them played by Michael Caine, and for a moment these two future titans of British cinema square off against each other, until Ollie meekly backs down.

Next stop was Elstree Studios, where Ollie joined other young actors Sandor Elès, Paul Massie and Gary Lockwood playing beatniks discussing art in a Parisian bistro. Their passionate discussion engages the interest of the lad from East Cheam himself, Tony Hancock, who has escaped the London rat race to realize his dream of becoming a great painter. It's a pivotal moment in *The Rebel*, one of the best British film comedies ever made.

A huge television star, Hancock was making his first foray into feature films and, taking no chances, he'd roped in his regular writing team of Ray Galton and Alan Simpson. Both men were often to be seen on the set, certainly on this particular day since they can still remember, over fifty years later, catching sight of the young Oliver and definitely sensing something special about him. 'He was mesmerizing,' says Simpson. 'And it was obvious that the camera loved him. But he kept fluffing his lines. Now on a film you have a tight schedule and for one little speech there's a limit to how many takes they're going to do. And he was so good, but he kept fluffing it and the director yelled, "Cut. Go again." I think they got up to seven takes and Reed fluffed every one.' Witnessing all this and shaking his head in dismay, according to Galton, was the film's producer. 'And he kept saying to the director Robert Day, "He's got to go. If he doesn't get it right now he's got to go. We can't waste any more film, it's costing money. Give the line to somebody else." I don't know whether anybody said anything to Oliver because on the next take he was absolutely perfect and it made the final cut.'

By the close of the day the scene was in the can and Ollie offered Sandor Elès a lift back into London. According to Elès, they'd only been driving a few minutes when Oliver pulled the car into a lay-by and 'started crying like a baby. Oliver was convinced he was an awful actor and would never be asked to do a film again.' Elès tried to be positive and suggested a visit to his Uncle Carol. Oliver shot back a glare of hurt pride and indignation that burned away the tears in his eyes. As Elès would recall years later, 'At that time Oliver had a bigger fear of nepotism than he did of failure.'

Far from never being hired again, Oliver was about to land his big break in one of Hammer's most ambitious productions ever and the resurrection of another classic movie monster: the werewolf.

It was all thanks to horror make-up maestro Roy Ashton, who had turned Christopher Lee so effectively into Frankenstein's monster, that Oliver was cast in *The Curse of the Werewolf*. Seeing him around Bray Studios, Ashton was convinced of the young actor's suitability, if purely from a physical perspective. He had dark, penetrating looks, incredible bone structure, 'and already looked like half a wolf when he was angry'. Hammer's management remained unconvinced, though, that Oliver was sufficiently experienced to play so demanding a role.

Terence Fisher had been assigned to the picture and immediately set up a screen test; the results put everyone's mind at rest. 'It was obvious that, experienced or not, Oliver was our man,' said producer Anthony Hinds. 'He was a very powerful actor.' So, from being a bit-part player with just a handful of scenes to his name, Ollie was in a featured role and getting £90 a week. Writing in the film's British press book, Fisher was already picking him for future fame: 'Were I invited to predict sure stardom for an unknown young actor of today, and asked to back that prediction with a heavy bet, the youngster I'd pick would be 22-year-old Mr Reed.'

Less of a shocker than previous Hammer horrors, *The Curse of the Werewolf* plays out more like a Greek tragedy. Oliver is Leon, the bastard child of the vile rape of a servant girl, played by Yvonne Romain, by a filthy, rabid beggar. Taken in by kindly scholar Alfredo (Clifford Evans, excellent in the role but one wonders why Hammer didn't cast Cushing), Leon grows into a fine-looking young man but deep within him lurks a bestiality that each full moon is becoming harder to suppress. Unlike other screen monsters, Leon is not inherently evil. 'He has not sold his soul to the devil, like Baron Frankenstein did,' said Fisher. 'He is more like Dracula, who was a cursed creature as well.' Bringing exuberance and a great deal of physicality to the role, Oliver also exhibits real pathos and it is a performance that far surpasses that of Lon Chaney Junior in Universal's 1941 classic *The Wolf Man*.

It's pretty late in the film before we see Oliver in total transformation but it's well worth the wait, as it rates among the most exhilarating moments Hammer ever put on film. Locked in a jail cell, Leon tears his shirt to shreds as the animal side of his tortured soul is unleashed, and as he turns to face the camera the snarl Oliver manages to emanate is truly blood-curdling. Ripping off the cell door, Ollie was so lost in the moment that it scared the life out of Denis Shaw, a somewhat portly actor playing the jailer. 'I picked up that door and threw it at him. It wasn't a balsa-wood door – it was a real door. And Denis shat himself . . . literally. He shat himself.'

Unleashed, the wolf hurls himself across roofs and bell towers as the predictable village mob descends with pitchforks and flaming torches. Stand-in Jackie Cooper did the more hazardous shots but Ollie was up for doing as much stunt work as possible. 'He was a most courageous bloke,' remembered Ashton. 'There was nothing he wouldn't dare do.' That went for the laborious make-up process too. Ollie would turn up at the studio each morning at seven on the dot to sit for sometimes upwards of two hours while Ashton weaved his magic, and he never complained once. Using a plastic mask moulded from a plaster cast of Ollie's head, dyed yak hair for fur, and wax plugs stuffed up his nostrils to create a snout, Ashton pulled off a masterstroke. By not covering his face completely, he allowed Ollie freedom of expression. Indeed, some of the film's most poignant moments come when Ollie, in full monster make-up, is able to show us the helpless Leon trapped inside the snarling, dominant beast. Sometimes, instead of spending an hour peeling the make-up off at the end of the day, Ollie drove back home with the whole ghastly lot still on. 'It was great fun sitting in the car at traffic lights.'

For certain close-up shots the producers wanted Oliver to wear special contact lenses to lend his horrible visage a supernatural quality, but co-star Yvonne Romain remembers he got a terrible eye infection, 'so they didn't use them, which was much better because Oliver had these extraordinary eyes. He really was very beautiful in his youth and had the most wonderfully cinematic face, and those incredible eyes that stared right through you. I'd never seen anything like them.'

Like Ollie, Yvonne was just starting out in the business, and while they didn't share any scenes in the film they often had lunch together in the studio canteen, 'where they made the best bread and butter pudding; it was all home-cooked food'. Sometimes they'd idly chat on the set or in the make-up room and Yvonne recalls in particular Ollie's interest in the fact that her mother came from Malta and his desire to visit the island one day. 'And whenever I saw Ollie in the studio or playing in a scene there was no sign of him drinking, he was completely professional.'

Filming ended in November 1960 after two months of enjoyable but diligent and hard work. Particularly difficult was the large amount of night shooting, as it rained incessantly and the huge bulbs in the arc lights kept exploding. Ollie loved the friendly but disciplined atmosphere at Bray, which really was a studio like no other then operating in the film business. 'It was a lovely feeling working for Hammer,' remembers Yvonne. 'It was like a wonderful repertory company. They were very loyal to the people working for them, so we all did everything with good humour. There was nobody whinging like they do today: you just got on and did it. There was that feeling of everybody doing their best to make the picture great.'

Ollie also thoroughly enjoyed working with Terence Fisher, not a bad director to have to show you the ropes. 'Terry was a wonderful gentleman who loved a little bevvy. I found him very, very easy. I was a very nervous actor then, who'd done very little, and he just gave me my head.' Fisher himself always looked back fondly on his time with Ollie, singling out his performance as Leon as one of the best he ever gave. Ashton too had nothing but praise. 'He was a really professional chap. I thought he was marvellous. He put everything he had into that role, it was a great performance.'

Which made it all the more unfortunate that when *The Curse of the Werewolf* opened the following spring it was met with public indifference and critical vitriol. 'A singularly repellent job of slaughter-house horror,' lamented the *Monthly Film Bulletin*. Its failure at the box office meant Hammer never attempted another wolfman picture. At least Ollie had been able to make his mark, and indeed his impact was considerable among female fans. Going to see the film with Kate produced an extraordinary scene outside the cinema when he was recognized 'and girls fought for the privilege of touching me'. According to a Hammer press release, after *Werewolf* Oliver received fifty proposals of marriage from complete strangers. 'One girl said I reminded her of James Dean,' he boasted to a reporter. 'Another that she prayed for me every night.' Many of these fan letters came from America, and one said: 'Until recently I revered and worshipped the memory of Rudolph Valentino. But after seeing you in the *Werewolf* I have transferred all my allegiance to you.'

On 21 January 1961 Oliver became a father for the first time when Kate gave birth to a son they named Mark. By design or otherwise, it did seem to be a fortuitous time to start a family, with Oliver having firmly established himself in Hammer's repertory company of actors; in 1961 alone he'd make three films for them. However, there did appear to be a lack of imagination among their casting directors since Oliver would invariably be asked to play villains, no doubt because of his intimidating physical presence. This 'typecasting' did begin to grate after a few years, especially since his performance as Leon had proved he was more than capable of playing a romantic lead. But for now he was happy to play the thug. After all, it paid the rent, and kept Mark in nappies and himself in beer.

The Damned, which Ollie made for Hammer in the spring of 1961, is among the most interesting of his early pictures. *Films and Filming* called it 'undoubtedly one of the most important British films of the year, even, perhaps, of the 60s'. It saw him work for Joseph Losey, a director then blacklisted in his native America by Senator McCarthy's anti-Communist witch-hunt. A clever and intoxicating mix of cold war drama, seaside teddy boy flick and sci-fi drama, *The Damned* is about as bleak as any British film got in this period, with its cautionary tale of innocents stumbling upon a secret government programme where imprisoned radioactive children are being schooled to repopulate the planet after a nuclear war.

Oliver plays King, who is clearly psychotic and harbours an unhealthy obsession with his kid sister (played by Shirley Anne Field), getting her to flirt with older men so his gang can rob and beat them up. A malevolent creation, Oliver performs with such brooding intensity that he practically steals the film from the two main leads. Whistling and swaggering around the streets of an out-of-season Weymouth, King and his predatory cohorts uncannily resemble the choreographed gang violence of Alex and his Droogs in Kubrick's *A Clockwork Orange*. Interestingly, in the late sixties Ken Russell was mooted as a possible director for *Clockwork*, with the inevitable consequence of Ollie playing Alex, which would have been quite something to behold.

The collaboration between Oliver and Losey appears to have been a little rocky but ultimately a fruitful one, with Ollie recalling how the director would take the cast out to dinner and preach anti-bomb stuff to them. 'He was very left of centre.' Losey liked the young actor enormously. 'He had talent but no training at all and he already had a certain arrogance. So he wasn't easy.' Despite that, the two men remained on friendly terms. 'And I think there is a certain mutual respect,' Losey reflected years later.

Within a week of finishing work on *The Damned*, Ollie was required on another Hammer adventure, shot on location in Black Park. Adjacent to Pinewood Studios, Black Park's woods and lakes are as familiar to Hammer fans as gravel pits are to advocates of seventies-era *Doctor Who*, and many a wandering strumpet or rampant horse and carriage has traversed its atmospheric avenues of pine trees. A passable Transylvania then, but by no stretch of the imagination the setting for a pirate movie. Hammer couldn't even afford a boat! With its penny-dreadful title, *The Pirates of Blood River* features Ollie as one of a gang of cut-throats, led by an eye-patched Christopher Lee, who invade a community of persecuted Huguenots in the belief they are storing treasure. In a now infamous scene Lee leads his crew across a swamp; in reality a condemned pond in Black Park. Even the stuntmen refused to go into the water, and yet Ollie, Lee and others were obliged somehow to remain in character as foul-stinking liquid plopped about unerringly near their mouths. So soft was the mud beneath their feet, and the pathway so littered with debris and dead wood, that some of the shorter actors had to be held up by their colleagues lest they go under completely. At one point Ollie does battle with a fellow cut-throat and they both thrash about in the water, so it's no surprise to learn that the experience resulted in an eye and ear infection for Ollie that required hospital treatment. The icing on the cake arrived a few days later when it was discovered that the septic tanks over at Pinewood ran into this very pond.

Ollie's big moment in the film is a sword fight with actor Peter Arne, finishing with Ollie getting run through. Before keeling over, he mumbles an effectively pitiful 'Mama'. Other dimensions were added to his characterization, mainly on a physical level. In one scene a stuntman refused to jump over a high wall. Not only did Ollie bound over the obstacle but did so with a sword in his mouth. Director John Gilling fired the stuntman on the spot. 'From that time on, Gilling thought I was really quite something, because I'd do things that stuntmen wouldn't do. It was only because I was stupid!'

In his memoirs Christopher Lee described how he often picked Oliver up in his second-hand Merc on the Cromwell Road in Earls Court and drove him to Bray Studios. 'He sat in the back seat, thin, nervous and worried, muttering about leaving the industry and how he wasn't cut out to be an actor.' It was during these car journeys that they developed a close friendship. Sometimes Lee would be accompanied by Denis Shaw, who had a small part in the film. Shaw, who'd been the jailer in *Werewolf* whom Ollie flattened with the door, was a character actor specializing in slimy ne'er-do-wells and a familiar face around the pubs and drinking dens of Soho. Lee had no choice but to allow Shaw to tag along, despite his regular condition (pissed) and his habit of chain-smoking in the front seat, which once resulted in the car almost catching fire. What's interesting here is Lee's belief that Shaw was a bad influence on Oliver and that, whenever he picked them up, 'they'd obviously been through Soho the night before'. Lee also believed it was Shaw who got Ollie into most of his pub fights, including 'the one where he got cut up. He'd start the trouble, then push Ollie in.'

In September Ollie started work on his third film for Hammer that year, *Captain Clegg*, based loosely on Russell Thorndike's popular Dr Syn novels and starring Peter Cushing. This too had something of a piratical flavour to it, with its gang of smugglers in an English coastal village trying to outwit the king's revenue officers. Oliver plays Harry, the squire's son and a secret member of the smugglers, in love with sultry barmaid

Yvonne Romain. Their love affair is incidental to the film's more gripping elements of marsh phantoms and mute savages running amok, but it's nicely played all the same and Oliver must have drawn encouragement from being cast as a dashing hero for a change and working with Yvonne, for whom he had begun to develop a crush. 'He was very dashing was Oliver, but he was complex,' says the actress, who was never aware of Oliver's feelings for her. 'You could tell that he wouldn't have wanted to show his feelings. He was very shy about that kind of thing.'

In one scene Harry is shot in the arm during a skirmish and when Cushing helps to take off his bandage Ollie plays the moment for all it is worth, wincing in pain. A few days later he received a letter from his venerable co-star. 'I think you're going to go a very long way, Oliver,' it began. 'But always remember, if you are hurt, you don't have to act hurt. If somebody grabs you, just blink. The screen is so big that even the slightest movement makes the point.' Oliver cherished Cushing's advice and we see it in action in almost every subsequent performance, for the power of understatement is central to so many of his great screen moments. 'To keep things very still and very slow can be extremely effective on screen,' says Mark. 'He was very aware that on stage you obviously had to be very big in order for people sitting at the back to see anything, whereas with a camera stuck up your nose you had to do very little for it to be able to pick up things. Less is more.'

For Ollie, it was advice that came in handy just a few days later while watching Yvonne play a scene. 'It was a very long and intense scene,' she remembers. 'And Oliver was incredibly kind because afterwards I asked if it was all right and he said, "Can I tell you something? You won't be offended?" I said, "No, no, any advice, please." He said, "Just try being more still." Now, I'm by nature quite an animated person. He said, "Remember that movie screen has got you blown up and every move you make is so much bigger, so less is more." I did the scene again and the difference was extraordinary. Afterwards I went up to him and thanked him. He was so helpful. And a wonderful actor.'

The Wimbledon Gang

All this fame and glamour that Ollie was beginning to cultivate left a huge impression on Simon, then attending King's College School. 'No one had a brother who was an actor, not only an actor but one who was starting to do pretty well. So it was a very exciting time for me.' Often Ollie would turn up to see him play cricket for his school, matches that were all-day affairs, going on until seven in the evening. 'So Ollie would go to the pub about noon and very quickly we got into a ritual where I knew around three o'clock he'd arrive with his mates; you could hear them coming down the lane. They'd sit on benches watching and within about five minutes the chants would start. Because one of our players had a very short haircut it was, "Come on, marine!" Then we had Dudley Owen Thomas [born in Kenya and played for Surrey], so they'd shout in a West Indian accent, "Come on, Dudleeey." They'd pretend they were West Indian fans for half an hour for some reason. It was a bit of an embarrassment but also it was very funny.'

Simon was very different from Oliver. He was shy and reserved and, looking back, believes that his father encouraged him to mix with Oliver and Kate in an attempt to put some rough edges on him. 'And I developed a few, not many, but Ollie and Kate showed me a different kind of life.' A place Simon got to know well during this period was Woodland

Wines, an off-licence on the Ridgeway in Wimbledon where Ollie and his mates sat most afternoons on crates in the back storeroom drinking while waiting for the pubs to open again. 'I'd be around fourteen years old and walking back from school I'd pop in and there would be Oliver throwing me a can of very heavy lager.' Something of a regular, Simon was allowed to bring along a couple of mates. 'So I was taking in friends from class and, as you can imagine, I became fairly popular at school. Oliver had a Mini at the time and I remember him driving me home early one night and my mother seeing my feet sticking out of the window. That sort of thing happened. Ollie took on a kind of heroic form for me during that period. It was all good.'

Very early on in his career Ollie cultivated a clique of friends whom he drank regularly with and had fun with, and Woodland Wines was one of their first hang-outs. As Ollie's fame grew over the years his father was to call these people hangers-on; they were anything but. Besides, Ollie could always smell a rat. 'As soon as there was anything artificial about a person or the way they treated him, Oliver would run a mile,' says Simon. 'For the rest he'd treat them as equals. Except financially: he knew he was the earner and he was generous, and so most of the time he'd buy the drinks or buy the meal. But I don't think any of them were there for the freebies. I think they were there for the same reason Ollie was there, to have a good time.' Key among this group were Johnny Placett and Mick Fryer, lifelong friends of Ollie. Placett ran a sign-making business and met Oliver one night in the Swan, where the young actor was playing darts for money. The bond was instant, so similar were they in nature. 'I've never met anyone that was so much like me,' says Placett today. 'That's why I miss him so much. He was irreplaceable.'

It was in the Swan that Mick Fryer first met Ollie, or rather Kate. He'd been training at Rosslyn Park Rugby Club and often popped into the Swan before going home. This particular evening he spied a very attractive woman at the bar. Next to her was a very tall and annoying American, effing and blinding. 'Would you mind, with the language,' said Mick. There was a bit of a stand-off when suddenly Oliver came in and asked, 'What's going on?' Kate smiled and said, 'This guy has just told Lenny to curb his language in front of me.' Ollie burst out laughing. 'Quite right as well. Have a pint.' The two of them got talking. 'You look fit,' said Ollie. Indeed Mick was, being in the building trade. 'Any good at arm-wrestling?' said Ollie. The challenge was on. 'Let's see how good you are.' Mick won. 'And that was the night I met Oliver. I realized he was a lunatic pretty quickly. And so was I. That's what attracted me to him, he was mad. And I was looking for madness, the same as he was. That's why we got on so well together.' They'd do outrageous things, like stuffing a lit candle up their nose for a bet. Another time, on the lash one Sunday afternoon, they ended up in Sloane Square, and right outside the Royal Court Theatre decided to lie down in the middle of the road and stop the traffic. After ten minutes, amid a big build-up of traffic with all horns blazing, they got up and moved off.

Other Wimbledon mates included Raymond Guster, a life-guard and later an entertainments manager at a holiday camp. When Mark was young he remembers 'Gus', who had a suitcase of props, dressing up as a clown at his birthday parties. There was Bill Dobson, who worked in the boiler room of a hospital, and Ken Burgess, who'd been in the navy. Conspicuously absent from this group was any representative of the film business. Throughout his life Ollie rarely socialized with his fellow actors. 'I'm more interested in my barman and the Scotch he's got for me than some actor rambling on about his next film.' It wasn't that he disliked them: he just had nothing in common with them. Instead he preferred mixing with normal, everyday folk, the road diggers, carpenters, builders, people he'd meet in pubs. 'He always used to say, these are the real people,' recalls his daughter Sarah. 'These are the people that make everything work on a day-to-day basis, these are the people I enjoy spending time with. Honesty was very important to him and he felt that these were just good, honest people. There were no different faces to them.' And gradually the circle grew and many of these friendships were to last pretty much Oliver's whole life. He felt comfortable with them, there was no bullshit, they were good at telling stories and joining in with his larks and madness; they refused to get old.

Mick Monks joined Ollie's Wimbledon gang pretty early on. He worked backstage at the Wimbledon Theatre and met Ollie one night in the Hand in Hand. Soon he was sharing jars at Woodland Wines and getting roped into the occasional pub crawl. There was also the 'pissnic', an Ollie invention that was a picnic with booze. The gang would be drinking in the Dog and Fox or the Rose and Crown when the cry would ring out, 'Right, pissnic', and they would disperse around the neighbouring shops to pick up ham, bread and cheese, and booze. 'Then we'd all meet on the Common and stay there until the pub opened again,' says Monks. 'And if anybody was passing that you fancied or looked a bit of fun, you said, come and join us and have a drink.'

If it wasn't pissnics Ollie would always come up with some other way to have fun, usually when he was bored, which was often. He termed these 'Happenings'. 'They didn't have to involve drink,' says Simon, 'but it usually was alcohol-fuelled. "What are we going to do now?" he'd say. "Let's have a Happening." So he'd drive to Wales just for the day, stuff like that. I think the fact that Oliver had an extremely low boredom threshold was a key factor in his life because the big problems arose when the work dried up and he had a lot of time on his hands. Time was a big issue for him, and filling the hours without getting too bored. Boredom was a big thing for Oliver.' This was something else he shared with Herbert Beerbohm

Tree, who once declared, 'Boredom is something to defend oneself against.'

Those long gaps of time that inevitably occur between film and TV jobs might have been more creatively filled by doing theatre, a couple of weeks in rep or the West End, but Oliver had no interest whatsoever in paying his dues by going on the stage. In this he may be unique, as the only British actor to achieve fame in the cinema who never once stepped on the boards in any capacity. 'Most actors want to hear people clapping. I don't need applause,' he once said. Opportunity, even in those early days, was there if he'd wanted it, at arguably the country's most prestigious theatre. According to Catherine Feller, who played the love interest in *The Curse of the Werewolf*, the Memorial Theatre in Stratford-upon-Avon was making overtures to Oliver to join what was soon to become known as the Royal Shakespeare Company, this at a time when Peter O'Toole had just made a huge impact there and the company comprised other young, thrusting talent like Ian Richardson, Diana Rigg and Ian Holm. When Oliver turned down the offer, Catherine told him he was making a terrible mistake, that a season at the Memorial Theatre would stretch and develop him as an actor far better than appearing in Hammer Grand Guignols. Ollie replied, 'No, I shall do these films and become famous. Then I will choose what to do next.' In retrospect he was right: Hammer was the perfect training ground. Even Catherine couldn't fail to recognize his potential. 'He was a very strong personality. He had a lot of confidence and a lot of animal charisma. There was no doubt that this was a man with a future.'

Even if he'd wanted to do stage work, Oliver would not have coped with the task of reciting the same lines night after night for months on end. 'I don't think he had the discipline for theatre,' says friend and colleague Georgina Hale. 'He would have been too pissed, wouldn't he, to come in and do all those hours of rehearsing and then go home and learn the lines. And then would he have arrived at night to be on stage? Theatre work is a discipline, it's a killer. Ollie would never have made it.'

Periodically in his career Oliver would be asked to consider stage work. After his success in The Who's *Tommy* he was inundated with offers to do musicals. In 1968 Jonathan Miller wanted him to play Richard III in a theatrical production he was directing. The approach came when Oliver was making *Women in Love*. 'I said to him, "Oh, you should do it,"' recalls Glenda Jackson. 'But he didn't. He had a very low boredom threshold and the idea of doing eight performances a week would have frightened him to death. It would have bored him. Also, I think he was very clear in his own mind that he was a star. He would always come on the set as though he was in charge of the whole thing; there was that undercurrent all the time, that he was a star, that was his thing, I'm a star. But he was completely unsure that he was an actor.'

Insecurity almost certainly did play a part, the fear that he wasn't good enough technically and would be exposed. 'On the one or two occasions when I took him scripts with the idea of him going on the stage, he chickened out,' reveals David. 'And he couldn't have done it stone-cold sober, he'd have been too shy.' Even as late as 1991, when Dublin was the European capital of culture, Oliver was asked to play Brendan Behan in a one-man play. The concept was for Ollie as Behan to talk to the audience as he sat by the footlights having a bevvy. 'I remember he ummed and aahed about it,' says Mark. 'He'd say to me, "Should I do it?" And I'd say, "Well, it's a great honour to be invited to play one of their heroes." But in the end it was the idea of doing that show for weeks on end, doing the same things seven times a week, I just don't think he could get his head round that, because it lacked the spontaneity of film. I think that's probably what theatre represented to him, it was drudgery, it was repetition, not moving on. At least with a movie you do it, it's in the can, and then you move on to the next thing.'

The physical act of going to the theatre didn't enthral Oliver either, the stuffiness of it and the perceived artificiality of the acting. He much preferred going to the cinema in those early years, devouring sometimes up to three films a week. The actor to whom he found himself especially drawn was Marlon Brando, who spoke – the cliché is that he mumbled – in a brooding, quiet manner which heavily influenced Ollie. He also spoke with the ring of truth, like someone you'd meet in the street, and in a manner redolent of his blue-collar origins; he was one of the masses. Most British film stars of the time were primarily from the privileged classes or projected a clean-cut image: the likes of David Niven, Kenneth More and Jack Hawkins. 'The sorts of actors that always looked like they'd go down with their ships,' joked Ollie. All that was about to change in dramatic fashion.

In the same month as Ollie finished work on *The Curse of the Werewolf*, *Saturday Night and Sunday Morning* opened in London cinemas, creating a new wave in British filmmaking and turning the hitherto unknown Albert Finney into an overnight star. It was the age of 'kitchen-sink' realism and the Angry Young Man, and saw the emergence of a startling generation of new British actors with working-class roots, like Michael Caine and Sean Connery. Now, Ollie was anything but working class: he didn't grow up in a tenement block next to a slag heap. He was, however, perceptive enough to realize that what was beginning to happen around him was of huge significance. 'I thought, gosh, blimey, I'd like to grab some of that. So I immediately started getting into fights in pubs, as I thought it was the thing to do, that I could emulate these angry young men.' He even auditioned for Joan Littlewood, the doyenne of all that was new and experimental in theatre. When he heard she was making a film he turned up all mean and moody, hitting imaginary punchbags, acting the way he thought East End hard nuts behaved. Littlewood wasn't impressed, or saw right through him, and sent him packing.

There may have been another reason why Oliver was so keen to embrace this new acting culture: it was a way of escaping from his own privileged roots. 'You could see that he was well bred and was fighting it all the time,' reveals director Michael Apted, who worked with Ollie in the early seventies. 'In the sense that he wouldn't acknowledge that he was posh. He was a rough boy, he preferred the rough image rather than the other image. But there was no hiding his breeding.' Michael Crawford, who worked with Ollie twice over the years, also recognized that there was something inside him that rebelled against his background and authority in general. 'And also against his natural advantages in life, including his talent. Part of him wanted to tear it all down, and perhaps this is what gave him the air of danger that made him stand out among English actors of his generation.'

Ollie returned to Bray in July 1962 for another Hammer picture, not a gothic horror this time but a contemporary thriller called *Paranoiac*, from the prolific pen of Jimmy Sangster, who'd written the studio's Dracula and Frankenstein movies. He'd also been responsible for *The Pirates of Blood River*, during which he'd become friends with Ollie or, more accurately, a drinking companion. 'But, as in most things, Oliver overdid things and rather scared me off.' The role on offer was the best of Ollie's career so far: Simon Ashby, the most unhinged member of a family that resides in the sort of gothic manor house where you expect to hear eerie organ music at midnight. With his parents dead, Simon lives with his daffy aunt and suicidal sister and is set to inherit the family fortune when his brother, long presumed dead, suddenly turns up. Or is it an impostor? A not very original premise but quite nicely done all the same by renowned cinematographer turned director Freddie Francis.

Playing the sister, and securing top billing, was Janette Scott, a former child star. All these years later Janette can still remember meeting Oliver for the first time out on location in Dorset. 'My memory is of someone who was rather shy, which is amazing when you think of what he became. I was the youngest person on the set and I had never heard of Ollie or seen him in anything, and because he appeared so nervous and shy I felt it was my duty, as sort of the star of the show, to befriend him and relax him a little bit.' This she did on that first day of shooting by sharing her lunch with him and over the course of their time on location they got to know each other well. 'I thought all this was being friendly, I didn't realize how far it was going with him. When we moved into Bray Ollie was much more relaxed. It was then that he started falling for me.'

At first Janette thought it was all very sweet, like one of those crushes you have at school. Luckily it didn't impinge on the working atmosphere and everyone came away thinking they'd made a pretty solid chiller. 'Oliver was very good in the film,' says Janette. 'Slightly over the top but right for what he was doing and for the part he was playing.' Sangster agreed. 'He stole the picture and gave a really great over-the-top performance.' When the film opened in America Hollywood's industry bible *Variety* reported that Oliver played 'with demonic skill'.

On the last day of filming, cast and crew said their good-byes at the wrap party. Janette saw Oliver brooding in the background and went over to wish him luck for the future. She was convinced she'd never see him again. 'Then he began calling me up in the middle of the night. It was getting a little bit out of hand but I thought nothing I couldn't handle.' A little while later Janette started work on another movie at the MGM Studios in Borehamwood. Ollie found out; certainly Janette hadn't told him. 'Anyway he turned up on the set. Of course, we all made him feel very welcome – how are you?, come and have lunch, that sort of thing – but then he came the next day and the next day. I don't know if he was popping pills or drunk but he was in a bit of a state and disturbing the actual scenes when we were shooting them. Sadly it got to the point where the director had to bar him from the set and then from the actual studios; the guards at the gate were told not to let him in.'

Janette had been filming for a couple of weeks when one night Oliver was waiting for her in his car outside the studio and started following her home. 'And he actually forced me off the road. Thank God he forced me on to a grass verge, so although I was really panicky and frightened I wasn't hurt. He said he had to see me, you know, the usual sort of things one says when one is desperately in love. And I was so frightened at that point that I said yes, let's drive into town and I'll meet you somewhere. He followed me very closely in his car, so I couldn't go straight to my home. We went to a pub, I think in Chelsea, because I really didn't know what to do with him and I was afraid. We sat down and talked, I told him I had to get to the studios the next morning, we couldn't see each other. And then I left him in the pub, went back to my car, which fortunately was still working, and drove off. I never saw him again.'

It was only later that Janette discovered Ollie was married. 'And he had a child! I knew nothing of this! Absolutely nothing. He never said anything, and nobody at the studio mentioned he was married. Nothing.' Only now did it begin to dawn on Janette that Oliver was probably making those late-night phone calls to her from the home where his wife and child lay asleep. Or was he traipsing off to use a public phonebox? Both images conjure up feelings of sadness and desperation.

There's little doubt that what Ollie felt for Janette, who was married herself at the time to TV host and songwriter Jackie Rae, was sincere and meaningful and not merely a desire for a quick fling. Janette remembers, while still working on *Paranoiac*, one weekend when Oliver invited her on a nostalgic drive to see one of his old schools. Other times she'd invite him for Sunday lunch at her home, where he made quite an impression on her mother, the actress Thora Hird. All very amiable, but then, during the filming of *Paranoiac*, Oliver had been 'completely courteous and very sweet', confirms Janette. 'He also had a great sense of humour. He gave the impression, and I'm sure it was a true impression, of being slightly timid. I've an awful feeling that it was getting over this fear that he got the Dutch courage with the booze. Watching *Paranoiac* again recently, one of the scenes made me very sad, where his character gets very, very drunk in a pub and the people in the pub are well aware of how drunk and silly he's being. And I thought to myself, wasn't he in Malta in a pub with sailors getting drunk when he died? I thought, oh my God, I wonder if it was like this. I wonder if his last night on earth was something like this.'

Ollie was still working on *Paranoiac* when he tested for a film that promised to tackle the dark underbelly of early-sixties youth culture. Producer Anthony Perry vividly recalls his audition. 'We didn't want stars, we wanted to find new people. And we spent ages interviewing actors. I think it was Mike Stanley Evans, an executive over at Rank, who said, "I saw a guy called Oliver Reed, you should get him." He came to see us and he was bright sharp, and interested, and he'd taken the trouble to find out something about what he was being interviewed for. And we loved him and from that day on we pretty much built the film around him. Clearly he had to be the central character. He had a real presence, it was tangible. Normally, if you're casting a lead, you run a film to see what they look like, but not in Ollie's case: we hired him straightaway.'

The plot of *The Party's Over* concerns a posh American girl called Melina who escapes her domineering father by coming to London, where she falls in with a pack of hedonistic beatnik types led by a highly magnetic Ollie. After a riotous drunken party one of the group, Phil, assaults Melina, believing her to be drunk, only to discover later that she's actually dead. The father arrives to take her body back to America. Meanwhile Phil commits suicide and the pack disperses. It was an interesting and edgy premise and part of the attraction of doing it for Perry and his fellow filmmakers, middle-aged and middle class every one of them, was an opportunity to get down with the kids. They wanted to be 'with it', even though they had little idea of what 'it' was and even less grasp, as Perry freely admits, of the actual subject matter, of these groups of youths who were dropping out of society. 'It was a very innocent and naive time,' he insists. 'For instance, marijuana was called pot, but in fact most people still thought pot was a place you grew flowers in.' As a result, most of the characters in *The Party's Over* come over as rather middle-class dropouts. 'Ollie was the only one who seemed to know about this kind of lifestyle,' says Perry. 'He appeared to have a working-class background and a working-class knowledge. Of course, he didn't really have either – he came very much from our world – but he was quite intelligent and tuned in actually. He certainly did get a grasp of what the film was about.'

Shooting of the film, which was partly funded by Rank, got under way in September, under the direction of Guy Hamilton, in a dilapidated house in Chelsea rented by the production company. Almost from day one a young actress by the name of Katherine Woodville felt herself naturally gravitating towards Ollie; they'd always share their lunch together and chat and joke between takes. 'We felt so comfortable with each other. He was a very sensitive person and yet he was also very bold and confident, and that's an unusual mixture. I saw a man who was truly confident about who he was, he never tried to be something he wasn't, and I liked that a lot about him. It wasn't egotism or cockiness, he was just comfortable in his own skin.

Nor was it necessarily macho. Sometimes the word "macho" implies that somebody is being overly masculine; he wasn't like that. He was such fun to work with and have as a buddy on the set.'

It was a very different story for California-born Louise Sorel, brought over to play Melina. Her first meeting with Ollie was on Albert Bridge at 4 a.m., to shoot a scene, 'and he scared the hell out of me. I thought he was sexy and dangerous.' Theirs was an odd sort of relationship. 'He cajoled me, teased me, and tested me constantly. After I finished my scenes I went to Paris for a little while and when I came back to London I visited the set and finally was able to ask Oliver why he'd treated me so strangely. His answer was that he thought I was an Actors Studio type and didn't like the thought. I set him straight and we hugged.' A misunderstanding had soured a potentially more rewarding relationship since Louise liked him very much. 'Oliver was dynamic and wonderfully instinctive in his acting. He also had an innate theatricality. I did think he was going to make a mark and burst on the scene. He was so very full of life but there was also something vulnerable and sad in him.'

Katherine identified this vulnerability too, and a sensitivity that translated itself into his work. 'And that gave him more facets than most other actors. In *The Party's Over*, Oliver really brought a very strong presence to that character. You could see a thinking person underneath it, which was not dissimilar to himself. He was also very much in the moment as a performer. When you were playing a scene with him he was "there", he wasn't somewhere else.'

Perry also got to know and like Oliver during the shoot, finding him highly professional. But there was one incident that the producer has never forgotten. The house used for the bulk of interiors was in such a state of decay that it had been earmarked for demolition. Most of the party scenes were shot there, including the memorable moment when Ollie enters a room with a spliff a foot long dangling from his mouth, and when told to drop dead by a girlfriend casually jumps out of the window. Perry decided to hold the cast and crew wrap party at the house too. 'We tore walls out and had a bath full of ice and champagne. Anyway, a couple of yobs tried to gatecrash it and Ollie wanted to kill them, and that's the only time I saw this part of his character. I didn't realize there was this violence in him. I did see a man who very much wanted to be violent and I had to stop him because he was going to kill them. These two lads realized this and they were frightened. I told them to fuck off pretty damn quick. He really wanted to do damage to them.'

Incredibly, when *The Party's Over* was submitted to the British Board of Film Classification, the chief censor, John Trevelyan, refused it a certificate, at that time an unprecedented decision against a British film. The main sticking point was the scene where Melina's corpse was sexually interfered with, necrophilia being a pretty racy issue for 1962. In a letter to Perry, Trevelyan (a former schoolteacher) called the film 'unpleasant and rather offensive' and 'a dangerous example to the young'. True, Ollie's character and his cohorts certainly lead a decadent lifestyle of drink, drugs and sex, and while Trevelyan appreciated the fact that the filmmakers had attempted to show this as not being a very estimable way of life, 'In terms of the ordinary cinema audience, *which is not markedly intelligent or subtle* [author's italics], this moral does not seem to us to be nearly strong enough.' Interesting, isn't it, that Britain's chief censor for over ten years believed the average movie punter a moron?

Certainly Guy Hamilton had no time for Trevelyan. 'I always thought that he was the sort of censor who went around sniffing bicycle saddles.' Years later Hamilton revealed that the censors said they could release the film if in the last reel Ollie and his gang all got run over by a bus. 'I couldn't see the point.' The consequence of all this was that *The Party's Over* remained unseen, which didn't do Ollie's career any good at all. Here was a highly accomplished central performance that slipped under the public radar and went unheralded by critics and the industry. Finally in 1965 Rank sold a cut version to an exploitation company and the film was given a limited release before fading into total obscurity. That was until 2010, when the British Film Institute brought it out on DVD to a favourable critical response. Philip French in *The Observer* went so far as to call the film 'of considerable historic interest. It was made at the point when our native cinema was switching from the observation of the northern working class to the celebration of swinging London.'

Perry finds it amusing that his film has been rediscovered as a minor classic, mainly because he doesn't particularly rate it. 'We all wanted desperately to do something different. But we failed. I just don't think we were smart enough to do it really well.' The exception is Oliver, who is utterly compelling, taking control and dominating every scene he's in. Katherine Woodville for one remembers the sensation of watching off set something special emerging. 'Oliver had the sort of presence that would indicate to other people that he was a star in the making, but I don't know how convinced he was about making it in the business. But he had a very strong personality without being in any sense loud or big, just by being, his energy was such.'

Ollie – The Saint

The success of *The Pirates of Blood River* spawned a slew of other costume adventure films from Hammer, including *The Scarlet Blade*. Shot in early spring 1963 at Bray and good old Black Park, this was an enjoyable drama set against the backdrop of the English Civil War and enriched by the company's usual quality production values. A second-billed Ollie smoulders as yet another dastardly fellow, this time a duplicitous Roundhead. One can't help feeling that Hammer missed a trick here, though, for surely Oliver's all too obvious screen charisma would have been better employed in the title role of the Scarlet Blade himself, a sort of steak and kidney pie Scarlet Pimpernel, instead of the rather wooden Home Counties acting supplied by Jack Hedley.

With his finances on an even keel, Ollie moved his family into a much larger flat in the basement of a converted Victorian house. Number 1 Homefield Road was conveniently located near the Dog and Fox, 'so after the pub it was round the corner to the curry house and then all back to Ollie's for a bit of a nightcap,' remembers Mick Monks. It was at Homefield Road that Monks won the nickname he still carries with pride, 'Tractors', when after a party his new shoes left so many scuff marks on the carpet that it looked like a newly ploughed field. Ollie revelled in bestowing often ludicrous nicknames on his drinking crew: John Placett was 'the Major' because he was a good organizer, Ken Burgess, being ex-navy, was 'the Admiral', Raymond Guster was 'Gus', Mick Fryer was 'Mickus'. There was also 'Eddie the Arab', a chap of Middle Eastern descent who ran a flower stall outside the Rose and Crown. Whenever he came in Ollie would pipe up, 'Here comes Eddie the Arab. What are you having?' Eventually this chap got fed up with this and said, 'Do you know, Ollie, I really object to being called Eddie the Arab. I'm not actually an Arab, I'm Armenian. And my real name's Edwin not Edward.' Ollie said, 'Don't worry about that, we'll call you Edwin the Bedouin.'

As for the actor James Villiers, he was 'Old Cocky Bollocks', 'eleventh in line to the throne, dear boy'. Villiers only occasionally drank with the group and Ollie suffered his presence because he adored pricking his pomposity. 'When I was in Henry V part 1 and 2,' he'd go, and Ollie would let him have it. 'He loved baiting old Villiers,' recalls Monks. 'He loved nothing better than, if someone was showing off, to put them down.' It was something that remained a large part of his personality. 'He hated all the bullshit,' says Terry Gilliam. 'If he detected just a whiff from anybody being pompous or bullshitty he would go for them. He'd be like a bullmastiff whenever he felt that.'

Homefield Road is where Mark's earliest memories reside, including one extraordinary incident when aged about four he set fire to his bedroom. 'It was waking up just after Guy Fawkes Night with a box of matches and lighting comics and things, and they seemed to burn quite well, and then when it got a little bit out of hand I didn't really know what to do, so I closed the door and climbed in next to my mum and dad.' Ollie ordered him back to bed but Mark wouldn't leave. 'And I never disobeyed him.' But this time the answer was no. Ollie asked again, and the answer was still no. 'Why not?' asked Ollie. Mark replied, 'Because I've fired my room.' Mark still has visions of his father with saucepans of water opening the door and throwing it in and asking Kate to phone the fire brigade. 'I can't,' she replied. 'I'm naked,' as if they could see her down the phone line. 'The end result was that it badly burned out my bedroom,' says Mark. 'There was a lot of smoke damage.'

In quick succession Oliver won two guest spots on the highly popular TV series *The Saint*, starring Roger Moore. In the episodes 'The King of the Beggars' (transmitted in November 1963) and 'Sophia' (February 1964) Ollie had prominent roles, but it was his appearance in the first of these that left the most lasting impression. Playing a heavy, during the climactic fist fight (*The Saint* always finished with a compulsory public-school-type ruckus, usually in a cardboard box warehouse in Hertfordshire), Oliver lunges at Moore's supremely coiffed Simon Templar, who shoots him at point-blank range. On take one, when the gun fired, Oliver dramatically, and as it turned out ridiculously, hurled himself backwards into the air with such force that he knocked himself out cold on the studio floor. As the scene played on, Moore heard a gurgling noise emanating from Ollie's prone body and immediately assumed it was a spot of play acting, but the gurgling continued. 'I looked down to see Oliver lying spark out, with his purple tongue hanging from the side of his mouth.' Immediately Moore went to his aid.

'What have you stopped for?' asked the director.

'Oliver's concussed,' yelled Moore. 'He's going blue.'

'Oh yes. Fair enough. Cut.'

Johnny Goodman, the show's production supervisor and later associate producer, has never forgotten the incident, indeed has probably dined out on the tale ever since. 'We had to carry him up to the dressing room and call for the doctor. I sat with him for something like two hours. He had mild concussion. I must say, it was the best example of method acting I have ever seen, real Stanislavski stuff. I did like Oliver. He was an amiable sort of chap when he was off the sauce. But when he was drinking heavily he always wanted to take on people; dangerous to be around.'

We are not quite finished with *The Saint*, though. Flash forward to 1978 and the show was resurrected with Ian Ogilvy, who had a most memorable encounter with Ollie. Here it is, told in full by Ogilvy himself:

'In 1978 I was filming the television series *The Return of the Saint*, playing the hero Simon Templar. Several of the episodes were set in the south of France, which is why, on one particular evening, I was in the crowded bar of the Voile d'Or, a fabulously elegant and fabulously expensive hotel in Cap Ferrat on the French Riviera. With me was my episode co-star, the beautiful Gayle Hunnicutt, together with the episode director Cyril Frankel, the series producer Bob Baker, and the creator of the Saint himself, the then septuagenarian Leslie Charteris, who was on a rare visit to the film unit to see how we were treating his hero. A group whose good opinion of me was, in my mind at least, a priority.

'Gayle seemed nervous. She leaned over and whispered in my ear, "Ian, do me a favour and go to the window and look down at the harbour and tell me if there's a Chinese junk there."

'An odd request, I thought, and a "yes" answer highly unlikely, but I looked out of the window anyway and there in the harbour, incongruous among the sleek white yachts of millionaires, was a full-sized Chinese junk in polished teak. I reported back to Gayle. "Oh God," she moaned, burying her face in her hands. "He's here."

'A moment later he was. There was a bellowing noise from the bar's entrance and a large beer barrel dressed in a striped rugby shirt advanced into the room. "HUNNICUNT!" it roared, its arms stretched wide. "GIVE ME A KISS, YOU FUCKING LOVELY TEXAN WHORE!"

'The barrel staggered over to our table, resolving itself on the way into the unmistakable figure of a fairly well-oiled Oliver

Reed. Bob Baker tried to make the introductions. "Oliver, lovely to see you again . . . we're filming the new *Saint* series . . . I think you know our director Cyril Frankel . . . and Gayle of course . . . this is Leslie Charteris . . . and last but not least, our Saint himself, Ian Ogilvy."

'Reed glared at me balefully and silently for five seconds. Then: "YOU? THE SAINT? YOU'RE A POOF! YOU'RE A FUCKING POOFTER!"

'Elegant French heads turned and stared. Gayle and Bob and Cyril and Leslie all looked at me. There was only one thing I could do.

'"Right, Reed. Come on. You and me. Outside."

'I'm not a brave man and have never been in a real fight in my life, but the shame of yielding to Oliver Reed – without even a token resistance, and under the gaze of so many people, some of whom needed to think I was at least a little bit like the hero I was portraying – overcame any fears of French hospitals and French orthopaedic surgeons and French nurses, all of whom were probably very good, of course, but all the same.

'I found myself marching towards the exit, with Reed at my side. Suddenly he grabbed my head and tucked it under his arm in a vague sort of wrestling hold. I got myself out of that with surprising ease and took up a boxing stance. So did Reed. We danced around each other, our arms windmilling away and I found myself thinking, He's not as tall as me, and his arms are a lot shorter than mine, and he's very drunk . . . I might even have a chance here.

'I never got the chance because Reed suddenly lost interest in having a fight and decided to be my best friend instead. "YOU'RE NOT A POOF! YOU'RE ALL RIGHT! COME AND HAVE A FUCKING DRINK!"

'Arm in arm, we returned to the group but, before I got my fucking drink, Reed appeared to experience a sort of epiphany when – through his drunken stupor – he realized he'd just been introduced to the creator of the Saint himself, the legendary Leslie Charteris. Abandoning me, he stared fixedly at Leslie and screamed, "YOU'RE LESLIE CHARTERIS? I CAN'T BELIEVE IT! YOU . . . ARE . . . LESLIE . . . CHARTERIS! FUCKING FANTASTIC! AN HONOUR! JESUS FUCKING CHRIST! LESLIE CHARTERIS! FUCK!"

'Then a wonderful thought occurred to him. He lurched to the bar, shoved aside the bartender, reached over and picked up a very small, slightly serrated fruit knife – the sort barmen use to shave off a slice of lemon peel or spear a maraschino cherry. Brandishing the tiny knife, Reed advanced on Leslie. "WE'RE GONNA BE BLOOD BROTHERS!" he howled. He grabbed the old man's hand and was about to press the sharp edge down on his wrist when it occurred to him that, since it was his idea, perhaps as a matter of form he ought to go first. He dropped Leslie's hand and then made a very small, non-bleeding scratch on his own wrist and held it up for all to see.

"BLOOD BROTHERS!" he bellowed and once again grabbed Leslie's hand.

'A sort of general paralysis gripped all of us and, anyway, I felt I'd done my bit and really shouldn't be required to do any more. Then, to everybody's relief, in the moment before Reed could get round to performing the same operation on Charteris, the captain of his junk arrived – an enormous German sailor, who (I learned later) was hired mostly to keep Oliver out of trouble. The unsmiling and silent captain took Reed firmly by the arm and escorted him – now meek as a lamb – out of the bar and I (with my reputation now up a couple of notches) never saw him again, which I must say was something of a relief, although not, perhaps, as great a relief as the one Leslie Charteris was feeling.'

Winner

Critics had always looked down their noses at Hammer's product and it appeared that the rest of the British film industry did likewise. When a young director by the name of Michael Winner was casting a film called *West Eleven* he wanted Oliver for the lead role. 'But my producer thought he was a B-picture actor, which in Oliver's case was true at the time.' It did appear that Ollie's identification with horror movies was limiting his career choices.

Winner, who died in January 2013, first met Oliver in the winter of 1962 when the actor came to his West End office with a film script he'd written. Eyeing a future as a commercial filmmaker, he found Oliver's story about a man who carried his house on his back up a hill simply too esoteric for his tastes. However, he felt inexorably drawn to him: the way Oliver spoke with passion and was alive with ideas, while at the same time remaining 'very shy and sensitive'.

After *West Eleven* Winner started work on a new film, *The System*. Installed as both producer and director, he could cast whom he damn well pleased, and he wanted Oliver to play Tinker, the leader of a gang of young men preying on female tourists at a seaside town in search of sexual kicks. Winner thought Oliver had it all as an actor. 'He was very good at being still, which is the essence of stardom, not to do too much. He was incredibly handsome and had a great quality of danger. I was convinced he would be an international star.'

Ollie and Winner just seemed to click straightaway and over the course of thirty-five years made six films together. Undoubtedly he was Oliver's closest friend in the industry and perhaps even out of it. 'He loved Michael,' says Josephine. 'They were very close.' Speaking to Winner about Oliver, one can be forgiven for thinking the director is describing a brother or some other close relative, such is the fondness and warmth in his voice, always, though, with a detectable sense of loss that never really goes away. 'I absolutely loved Oliver. He was the kindest, the quietest, and the gentlest man in the world, and the most polite and well behaved, except when he had a drink. But I very seldom saw him drunk on set because he knew I didn't like that. Once or twice he may have had a bit of a hangover from the night before, but nothing remotely serious; not like today, where half of them are on drugs. But he was a menace at night, no question. Utterly professional on the set – in the evening a disaster.'

Winner does not claim to have a fondness for drunks and so always tried to stay away from Ollie during the hours of darkness. 'Drunks on the whole are immensely quiet and dignified when they're sober. But when they're drunk, they're drunk. They're two people; they're Jekyll and Hyde. I remember once I met Ollie in a restaurant and he went out and challenged someone to a fight, he was always doing that, and he always lost the fight. So he went out into Hyde Park in a beautiful Savile Row suit to fight this bloke and came back having been thrown in the round pond; he was soaking.'

The System was shot almost entirely on location around Torquay during the spring of 1963, a halcyon time for its young cast of Ollie, Jane Merrow, David Hemmings, John Alderton and Julia Foster, all of whom clicked as a group, so there was a lot of larks and a lot of laughter. 'We all stayed in the same hotel and there were some mad moments,' recalls Jane. 'There were a lot of drunken parties there. I remember my father came down to visit and one night went into the communal bathroom and found one of the actors drowning in the bath and rescued him.'

The instigator of most of the mayhem, predictably, was Oliver. 'He liked to have physical challenges,' says Jane. 'He was quite into fighting and things like that, manly challenges. I think he was always trying to prove his manhood in a funny sort of way and then he would laugh it off as a joke. And he challenged David Hemmings to hang outside the second-floor window of the hotel, saying he'd hold on to him and not let him fall. And David agreed, which was a stupid thing to do. It was a really dangerous, silly stunt.'

As Hemmings recalled forty years later in his autobiography, he was held upside down sixty feet over a vicious set of spiked railings. 'How do you like this, boy?' Ollie growled. 'Wanna come up, boy?' Hemmings did indeed and was hauled back in. For the rest of his life Hemmings freely admitted to being more than a little wary of Oliver. 'He was never a man you would miss – broad, intelligent, funny, frightening, and deeply unpredictable. He could drink twenty pints of lager with a gin or crème de menthe chaser and still run a mile for a wager.'

This kind of reckless behaviour was more than just larking about, fifth-form high jinks gone bad: there was most assuredly an element of male posturing going on. 'He was like the leader of the pack, always proving himself to be the king,' Jane points out. 'There was a bit of a conflicted personality there with Oliver. He wanted to be the rough boy, but on the other hand he did have a sensitive side to him, which I didn't see very much of if I'm honest because it was predominantly a male cast and there was great competition going on between them all.'

There was the time, however, when Jane got very badly stung by bees and her arm swelled up and she couldn't work for a few days. Oliver visited her, fussed over her, and made sure everything was all right. 'So there was a really gentle, soft side to him. He was two people, he really was. He could be very kind. Then again he could be extremely unkind. For instance, he would get into drinking competitions with people who he knew couldn't drink or shouldn't drink. I think that was unkind. There was a bit of cruelty in that, but then he would have just thought it a very funny thing to do.' Hemmings, too, picked up on this unpleasant characteristic. 'At the time I concluded that Oliver, for all his charismatic, cavalier efforts as an apprentice hell-raiser, was inclined to bully anyone smaller than himself – like me.'

For Jane, Oliver's sensitive side was at its most appealing during what was a potentially stressful scene where she was obliged to run completely nude along a beach with him. 'Oliver was a real gentleman: after we did the shot he covered me up; he was very kind.' This was very racy indeed and caused brief problems with the censor. Indeed, the whole tone of *The System* is fairly daring for a British film of that period with its matter-of-fact depiction of casual sex. It was the same with Julia Foster, another young actress playing one of Ollie's conquests, who in the film had to appear in bra and panties. Again Oliver was nothing less than supportive and understanding, endearing himself totally to Julia, who says, 'My overriding memory of Oliver is that he was devastatingly attractive, just drop-dead gorgeous. I think every woman who came under his eye responded almost in the same way.'

Julia was not privy to any of the destructiveness in Oliver and was genuinely shocked to hear of the Hemmings incident, for this was a side of Ollie she just didn't encounter. 'He had an ability to make you feel you were the only person in the whole wide world that he was talking to. At that time he was a very thoughtful man and very intelligent. And everyone was very excited about him, he was a really exciting young actor who was obviously going to do well, and this film was certainly going to be a part of it.'

Winner, who had sensed this star quality very early, placed the actor right in the centre of his film, bestowing on him a memorable establishing shot. As a train pulls into the resort station, crammed with new holidaymakers and gullible girls ready for plucking, the camera pans along the platform at a series of expectant faces until it rests upon one in particular, staring out at us with a pair of doleful eyes as deep and as mysterious as a lake at midnight, a straw hat deftly tilted on his head – Oliver. At the time of the film's release David was in the Middle East on army duty and remembers going to an outdoor screening. 'When that train pulled in and you got this first sight of Ollie you could hear an audible reaction from all the women in the cinema.' At last a director and a role had captured what Oliver Reed was all about, magnetic charisma and, most importantly, something that you can't create, screen presence. You can be a supremely accomplished actor but screen presence is something you can't be taught or cultivate – you either have it or you don't – and Ollie had it in spades.

'Screen acting is hugely about charisma,' says director John Hough, who worked several times with Ollie. 'That's what you're looking for when you're casting someone, you're looking for on-screen charisma. And you couldn't overpower Oliver Reed in a scene. If Oliver was acting alongside, say, Marlon Brando, it would be like a tennis match, you'd be switching attention between the two of them. Stars like Brando, Paul Newman, Kirk Douglas, Robert Mitchum, I'd put Oliver Reed in amongst that lot because he had the capability, he had the screen presence to be in that company, he had the charisma.'

The System was a modest box-office success, but its value is perhaps greater now as a document of Britain's sixties mod culture, beautifully captured, like a firefly in a bottle, by the stunning black and white cinematography of Nicolas Roeg.

Ollie got noticed, though, that's for sure. 'The role was so perfect for him,' says Julia Foster. 'Which is why it sort of made him, it's what catapulted him to the next level. It's always interesting when an actor plays a role that is close to himself because you never know when the acting starts and when it finishes.'

Over the next few years Julia would occasionally bump into Ollie. And she has never forgotten the time he escorted her to the White Elephant restaurant in Curzon Street, one of the favourite showbiz rendezvous of the sixties, the place to go and be seen. As the years went by Julia began to see less and less of Ollie and then not at all; her only contact with him was the tabloid accounts of his misdeeds. 'My heart did ache when I read stories about the dreadful things he did and the way he treated people and everything, because I used to think back to that rather innocent and joyful young man who did *The System*. He lost his way, didn't he, and I'm glad I wasn't around.'

Reg

The System was an important film for Ollie in another way, too, as it saw the beginning of what would be an extraordinary relationship with a man named Reg Prince that was to last over twenty years. So close did Ollie and Reg become, so intertwined in each other's lives, that they were almost like brothers; blood brothers, in fact, once cutting themselves and sharing blood. 'They were like Siamese twins those two,' recalls David Ball, who worked with them in the seventies. 'It was as if they were joined at the hip.'

Oliver and Reg first met on the set of *The Party's Over* when Reg, then twenty-six, was a movie extra and they just seemed to hit it off right from the start. 'Presumably it comes from the fact that they both lived in and came from Wimbledon,' believes David. 'Years later Ollie loaned Reg the money for him to buy a house down by the football stadium.' It was decided that Reg would work on Ollie's films as his stand-in and occasional stunt double, though it took a year or so to amass the kind of clout to force production companies to hire Reg all the time, starting with *The System*. After that they were practically inseparable on film sets. 'Whenever I was with Oliver on location,' says Jacquie Daryl, Ollie's girlfriend throughout the seventies, 'people used to say to Reg, you must be the contraceptive, because all three of us were always together. But it was a real love/hate relationship, even though there wasn't anything Oliver wouldn't have done for Reg and vice versa. They would have fought to the death for each other. Oliver loathed his wife, though, and Reg's wife loathed Oliver.'

Another of Reg's jobs would be to go on ahead to check out a film's location or turn up at any prospective hotel to check that the room, and most importantly the bar, matched Ollie's standards. Perhaps Reg's most valued job was to watch Ollie's back. If things kicked off in a pub or restaurant, as they had a habit of doing, Ollie was secure in the knowledge that Reg was there to sort things out. According to Johnny Placett, Reg saved Ollie's life on at least two occasions. 'Theirs was a strange relationship,' admits David. 'Reggie was able to cope with Ollie and Ollie saw Reg as his bodyguard just as much as his stand-in, and he was very dutiful in that regard and very protective of Ollie. And Reggie was tough: you wouldn't want to meet him on a dark night, no way.'

Just how tough Reg was is perfectly illustrated by this story from David Ball, who was production accountant on a western Ollie made in Mexico with Lee Marvin. Ball and a couple of the crew were relaxing in a cantina one evening when Ollie and Reg showed up. Ollie was holding a small, heavy stone, about nine inches by four inches; it was rounded, washed and smooth. 'Reg is going to break that.'

'Fuck off, Ol,' said David Ball. 'He's going to hit it with a sledgehammer, is he?'

'No, he's going to break it with his hand.'

'Oh, Ollie, come on.'

'Look, Dave, you do the book and get the money off the crew. Reg is going to break this stone with his hand.'

The word quickly spread and the bar filled up with American stunt men, crew members and locals. As the wine flowed, people laid bets and Ball found himself with a bag full of thousands of dollars. 'Ollie, you're going to have to pay out an awful lot.'

'Don't worry, Reg will do it.' Clapping his hands, Ollie asked for silence. It was show time.

An area was cleared and suddenly all eyes were on Reg. 'And he just looked at this stone,' recalls Ball, 'and made this guttural noise and then he did it and it was like a hot knife through butter. One chop of his right hand and this stone went perfectly in half and I have never ever seen so many jaws drop in my life, mine included. I went, "We won, Ollie." He went, "Yeah, I told you we would." He was so unassuming. 'Well done, Reg. We're up at six tomorrow morning, so good night everyone.' And off they went. Unbelievable. That was the most awesome thing I'd ever seen in my life and I will never know how they did it. Anyone was allowed to study and examine this stone before they made their bet. I don't know how so much mental strength can turn itself into so much physical strength. It's not something I will ever see again.'

What was so inspiring about Reg was that he wasn't particularly imposing physically, he was shorter and of a lesser build than Ollie, which of course made it slightly ludicrous that he was his stand-in. 'Reg was probably five foot five and stocky, with a beer belly,' says Ball. 'He was a black belt, but if you looked at Reg you would not have given him for being strong. But he was lethal. He was a killing machine.'

Exactly where Reg came from before he met Ollie, his background and past history, no one really knew. What is certain is that he must have had some kind of military training, but precisely what and where was never revealed, in spite of stories that he'd worked for British intelligence or the SAS. 'There was a bit of a mystery about Reg,' confirms Ollie's brother David. 'And that lent itself to this sense of, you better be careful, it was very much quasi-underworld.' Oliver liked to intimate that Reg had done time, and whether true or not, rumours that he was associated with the criminal fraternity persisted throughout his time with the actor. 'And that's why Ollie respected Reg because he knew what he was capable of,' says friend Michael Christensen. 'I saw Reggie take care of three people single-handed in this pub one night.' Ollie was in there drinking and these guys weren't going to be placated. Usually Reg was very clever at being able to talk any situation down. 'Look, have a bottle of champagne on the man,' he'd say and that would be the end of it. But these guys didn't want to know and it kicked off. 'One bloke hit the deck straightaway,' says Christensen. 'Then before the second guy could even walk out the door he was down and the third one didn't want to know.'

In pubs people always wanted to try it on with Ollie. It was like the fastest gun in the West: there was always someone who wanted to prove themselves against him. 'I'm really a pacifist,' he once said. 'Yet I'm the most scarred, kicked, beaten-up person I know. The only reason I get into fights is that I'm terrified of violence. The one thing that terrifies me more than violence is my fear of it, so I just have to go out and face it.' Mind you, Ollie did provoke people when he was boozed up. A bloke might come over and say, 'I loved your last film,' and Ollie would give him a withering look and say, 'Fuck off, I'm talking.' And then the guy would get the hump and want to do something about it and Reg would then step in. 'Come on, give the man a break, he's been working, he's an actor, he's an artist. If you want a fight I'll fucking fight you.' Nine times out of ten the bloke would back down. 'If he didn't, Reg would knock him out,' says Christensen. 'Or Sir Percy would come out. He used to keep a cosh in his back pocket. He called it Sir Percy.'

Sod's law, the one time Ollie really needed Reg he wasn't there. The Crazy Elephant was a nightclub in Jermyn Street, in the heart of the West End. Ollie went there one night and, passing a table occupied by a group of rowdy young men, he heard one of them shout, 'Look out, here comes Dracula.'

'Watch it,' Ollie said. 'Or I'll bite your jugular vein out.'

Forgetting the incident, he sat down with his drink. A couple of minutes later one of the men approached him. 'Did you mean what you said?' Ollie suggested he go play with himself and went into the gents' toilet. The man followed. 'Come to help me have a piss, have you?' Ollie said. The next instant a broken glass was thrust in his face and he dropped like a stone. As he lay prone on the floor five blokes started laying into him; feebly he lifted his hands for protection against a volley of fists and boots. Managing somehow to get outside into the street, blood spurting from his face, he hailed a cab. 'St George's Hospital,' he said, unnerved that he could feel shards of broken glass in his mouth.

'What about my cab, mate?' said the driver after taking one look at him. 'You're going to fuck it up, aren't you, with all that blood?'

'Fuck your cab, what about my face? Get me to hospital.'

During the journey Ollie fainted twice and the driver had to stop to prop him up and stem the bleeding with a handkerchief. The glass had gone right through his cheek and shredded part of his tongue and he'd already lost several pints of blood by the time they reached Casualty. Oliver knew it was bad when a nurse caught sight of him and fainted. As he was having thirty-six stitches put in, the police arrived, but Ollie refused to press charges. 'That wasn't going to get me my face back.'

A very meek Oliver arrived late back at his flat and poked his head round the bedroom door as Kate was stirring from sleep. She took one look at him and hollered, 'You stupid bastard.' In pain and feeling groggy, Ollie still attempted the love act that night. 'I had been badly beaten and wanted to prove I was still a man by getting on top.' Kate wasn't entirely struck by the idea, especially when blood started dropping over her face. 'You're bloody kinky,' she said, and pushed him off.

In the morning Ollie looked at his appalling reflection in the mirror. 'Christ, that's it, there goes my career.' Except perhaps for more horror films, this time without the make-up. To drown his sorrows he went out and bought a bottle of whisky and drank half of it, through a straw because he could hardly move his mouth. Next he took the straw with him on a crawl round his local boozers. Mick Monks caught up with him at lunchtime in the South Wimbledon Club and was horrified by what he saw. 'There were these great scars down his face and it was all weeping because it was so cold. "Look what they've done to me, Tractors." Then Kate came in, furious that he'd got out of the house because he wasn't supposed to go out for a few days.'

According to Monks, the culprit was eventually uncovered. 'And a couple of heavies said to Ollie, "If you want us to go and sort it out, we'll sort it out." And Ollie said, "No, if I want to do anything I'll do it myself." But he wasn't that sort of person, he didn't want retribution. But there were people quite prepared to go up and do damage to this guy, there were plenty of volunteers. I think he had to move off somewhere in the end, just in case.'

In a funny sort of way those scars became something of a trademark, like Kirk Douglas's dimple. 'And I have to say, it was lovely when it was red and livid,' says Jacquie Daryl. 'But then it slowly settled down and faded, so you hardly noticed it in the end.' Even so, especially in close-up shots, those scars never truly went away. 'Even in *Gladiator*,' says Jacquie, 'there are moments when you see it.'

According to Mark, Ollie was extremely conscious of the scarring because it couldn't have come at a worse time. 'When you're just starting to climb up the ladder and the next minute you're maimed; it was a real blow to him. But on the positive side it gave him that difference, it made him look moodier and real for the parts he then went on to play.' In the immediate aftermath of the incident, however, Oliver feared that no one would hire a disfigured actor. 'It was an impediment,' says David. 'And he was out of work for quite a bit because of it.' Little did he know that his saviour was just around the corner.

The Enfant Terrible

What Oliver described as the turning point of his career arrived when he made the acquaintance of a director later branded the enfant terrible of British cinema: Ken Russell, who died in November 2011. For years Oliver had battled against the mean and moody looks that had typecast him as Hammer monsters or 'Teddy Boys in leather jackets who whipped old ladies around the head with a bicycle chain and stole their handbags'. Ken Russell changed all that when he cast the actor in his television film about the French composer Claude Debussy.

By a stroke of good fortune Russell happened to be watching television one Saturday evening and caught Ollie as a guest on the panel of *Juke Box Jury*. Russell didn't have the first clue who he was, nor that he had been out of work for months and was currently driving a minicab to make ends meet, but he was knocked out by the actor's striking resemblance to Debussy. On Monday morning Russell called Oliver's agent to arrange a meeting. It took place at the cramped office at the BBC, where Russell had established himself in the past few years as one of the corporation's most original and creatively subversive directors. Pouring Oliver a cup of coffee, Russell asked how much he knew about Debussy; not a lot, came the reply. Russell began to talk passionately about the composer and the film he intended to make about his life and music for the prestigious arts programme *Monitor*. Finished, he stared long and hard at Oliver before offering him the part. Ollie was by far the best candidate. 'He struck me as vivacious, cheeky, and not run-of-the-mill. I remember him being very moody and glowering. I liked his spirit – everyone else I'd auditioned seemed to fade into insignificance.'

But all Ollie could think about were the angry scars on his face and that it was highly unlikely Debussy was ever glassed in a pub. 'You won't employ me with these scars,' he said meekly. 'I don't know what you're talking about,' said Russell, and the deal was done. It was the beginning of Ollie's most important and creative relationship. 'Ken was great for him,' says Mark, 'in having that early faith in him when a lot of people would have been very frightened or put off.'

Co-written by the young Melvyn Bragg, Russell's portrait of the French composer switches between his troubled life and a fictionalized account of a film crew trying to capture the essence of his personality, and thus Oliver is both Debussy and the actor playing him. The conceit works brilliantly as we glimpse this group of actors trying to recreate portions of Debussy's life amid their own dramas and love affairs.

Some of the film was shot in the French town of Chalon-sur-Saône and this is where one suspects Ollie and Ken bonded, recognizing each other as kindred spirits. After a successful first day, Russell invited his cast for a meal at a restaurant. One look at the prices on the wine list prompted Ollie to sneak out to a local shop and smuggle back several bottles of cheap plonk down his trousers. Drunk, Russell took pity on the intended fish course, displayed live in a tank, and handed them through a window to Ollie, who then released them in a nearby stream. Alas, they were discovered and made to pay for the lot.

Another evening, after an equally inebriated dinner, Ollie, Russell and a few others decided to visit the town's famous outdoor light and music show. The place was fenced off and patrolled by security guards stopping people getting in without tickets. 'They behaved like storm troopers,' said Ollie. 'And didn't like the look of us because we were foreigners and drunk.' Russell had a plan to get inside that necessitated the requisitioning of an official BBC staff car. With the car perched on a hill, everyone jumped inside and hid under a blanket, then the handbrake was released and off they went, picking up speed all the time. The guards scattered as the seemingly driverless car smashed through the gates and careered to a halt. Never one to miss a grand theatrical moment, Ollie stepped out, bowed, and said, 'Bonsoir, messieurs.'

'Qui êtes-vous?' asked the guards.

'I'm the BBC,' said Ollie with a smile.

The Debussy Film was broadcast in May 1965 by the BBC and remains an impressive piece of work with plenty of typical Russell embellishments. In a complex role Oliver triumphs, more than justifying Russell's faith in him. He positively smoulders as Debussy, capturing the brooding sensuality and threatening calm that were so characteristic of the man and his music. 'The camera certainly loved him,' says Mark. 'He was a good-looking fella, but he was even better looking in black and white, with that moody soft lighting.' Ann Leslie in the *Daily Express* began to predict great things for him. 'For a start he has one of the most extraordinary and mesmerizing faces ever seen.'

It was without doubt Oliver's most mature performance yet and justly received critical plaudits. The marked contrast he achieved between his sex-obsessed seaside photographer in *The System* (not long gone from cinemas) and his Debussy, and the skill with which he handled both, was clear evidence of his burgeoning range and versatility as an actor. And those reviews did more for Oliver than merely buff his ego. 'They gave me a feeling of immense relief tinged with grateful satisfaction that the grievous bodily harm inflicted on me in the Crazy Elephant had done no more than delay my journey.'

In later years Oliver was to refer to the success of Debussy as 'my intellectual breakthrough'. It was when critics and the business realized there was a genuine ability there and began to take him seriously as an actor. 'For the first time people realized that I was capable of playing something other than a pirate or a werewolf.' Within the space of six months his career trajectory had shifted dramatically, something he was fully aware of and determined to exploit. 'Hammer had given me my start and Michael Winner my bread, then Ken Russell came on the scene and gave me my art.'

It was now that he made a bad misjudgement, accepting the offer to appear in one more Hammer and so landing himself in the worst film he ever made for the company. *The Brigand of Kandahar* is a historical drama set during the British Raj in India, with Ollie playing Ali Khan, leader of a gang of rebel bandits. It's a right royal pantomime of a performance, lots of leering and diabolical guffawing for no apparent reason. And it's no surprise to learn from Josephine that this was the one film from his back catalogue that he never allowed her to see. Even reuniting with Yvonne Romain, playing a sultry princess, failed to lift his spirits. 'We were both moaning and groaning on that one. He was not in the best of moods on it and I don't blame him.'

One morning Ollie was involved in a minor road accident that broke his shoulder. As usual, hoping to avoid a fuss, he arrived on set without telling anyone what had happened. During a fight scene an actor made a grab for Ollie's arm and he let out a huge scream. That's when the director John Gilling found out he had fractured his shoulder. He was turning white with the pain. Asked if he wanted to take a break, Ollie insisted on carrying on, and only when filming wrapped at the end of the day was he taken to hospital.

Turning up the next day with his arm in a sling, he told Yvonne that he'd been driving his car with it hanging out of the window and bashed it against the side of something. 'What were you doing that for, you silly bugger?' she said. 'Were you pissed?'

Ollie looked at her. 'What do you think? I was legless.'

'Well, you shouldn't have been in the car then.'

'Stop moaning at me,' screeched Ollie and walked away.

Yvonne remembers being slightly perturbed by the incident. 'I admired him so much as an actor, but you could just see him going into that brick wall. There was a demon in him, there really was.' And Yvonne wasn't the only one who was becoming concerned about the amount of drink Ollie was consuming and the reasons behind it. The biggest of which was that Ollie drank because of an almost crippling shyness. 'Oliver was deeply insecure, he was deeply sensitive, and he was immensely shy,' says Winner. 'He needed to be pushed to feel in any way at ease with other people. His was social drinking, taken to extremes.'

A lot of people become actors to conceal their shyness; it's a mask they can hide behind. Ollie also used alcohol. 'All through his life he was terrified of being sober and having to act properly,' reveals David. 'He felt he was boring sober. But when he was sober he could argue a point and could be very erudite, but he always feared and fought shy of being challenged intellectually. There was always this thing in his life, and he would never admit it, but he felt he was intellectually inferior because of his dysfunctional education. So he'd get people drunk to bring them down to his level, subconsciously that's what it was about, and he would do that every time.' Is this why perhaps he chose most of his friends from among labourers and workmen, people he felt were on a level that he could accommodate and feel comfortable with? 'Ollie was shy with people of his own class,' says Muriel. 'But not at all shy with road diggers.'

The Brigand of Kandahar was Oliver's last film for Hammer, and although he never went back, neither did he forget the enormous debt of gratitude he owed them, claiming those movies had been 'the best training I could have had'. At Hammer, under the tutelage of fine directors and efficient technicians, he learned the craft of film acting, how the camera works, hitting marks, and how to sustain a performance shot out of sequence: all great preparation for what was to come. Oliver was certainly missed by Hammer. Anthony Hinds, the company's most eminent producer, later reminisced: 'It's a pity what happened to Oliver, but we certainly had no problems with him – a charming, eager young man who wanted to please. We – Hammer – made his career, and Oliver always gave us credit.'

Leaving Hammer had been a momentous decision but already it was paying dividends. Veteran producer George H. Brown had approached Oliver to play the rugged, brawling French-Canadian fur trapper Jean La Bête in *The Trap*, to be directed by Sidney Hayers on location in the mountains and forests of British Columbia. It was Oliver's biggest film to date and its importance to his career was not lost on him. Mick Fryer remembers Ollie calling at his house pissed, clutching a bottle of whisky. 'I've come round to celebrate,' he said. 'I've just got this part, it's going to be the making of me, this is the one I've been waiting for.'

The Trap is set in the mid-nineteenth century. Oliver's La Bête arrives at a settlement to buy himself companionship in the form of a bride, ending up with a young orphaned mute girl called Eve, played by Rita Tushingham. The film follows a rather predictable, if entertaining, course, as Eve must come to terms with both her new life out in the wilderness and La Bête's almost animal-like nature. It's basically a man-against-nature picture and there's a startling sequence where La Bête is struggling to make it back to his cabin at night with an injured leg as a pack of wolves closes in and attacks. Wolves being rather unpredictable animals, the filmmakers made do with German shepherds, though pretty savage-looking ones, and before the scene Ollie took Rita aside, saying, 'Don't worry, I'll look after you,' unaware the actress had already struck up a rapport with them. When the director yelled action and Ollie had to forcibly grab hold of Rita, the dogs thought she was being attacked and pounced, biting Oliver full on the arse.

In another scene Oliver comes face to face with a mountain lion. To get the shot they shoved him into a big bullring surrounded by a high wall overlooked by three Mounties armed with high-powered rifles. The mountain lion was placed on a tree above him and on 'Action' was pushed into the ring. 'The owner told me not to worry because if the lion sprang on me, by the time it actually made contact the Mounties would have shot it. In fact it only missed me by inches.'

Working on the film as a background player was Warren Raines, who hasn't forgotten Oliver, his personable demeanour, and the fact that he treated everyone on the film, from the director right down to the office runner, as absolute equals. He also took his responsibilities as the star seriously. 'I recall Rita Tushingham was getting homesick and wanted to go back to England, but Oliver helped keep the production going by supporting her totally.'

What came as a surprise to many on the crew was Oliver's playful nature, and Raines fell prey to a particularly noteworthy effort. Falling asleep one afternoon on the set, he was scooped up by Ollie and deposited on to the sound stage next door, where a completely different film was being made. 'I awoke inside a church where soft music was playing in the background and I thought, I've died and gone to heaven. After shaking the cobwebs out of my head I realized I had been moved to sound stage B. I went back to sound stage A and demanded to know who the ass was who did this. I noticed Oliver a few feet away and he was breaking up with laughter. Yes, he was a practical joker.' Oliver also spiked Rita Tushingham's husband's drink at a party, 'which rendered him helpless for a couple of days,' said the actress. 'But that was just Oliver's way of having fun!'

For Oliver one of the more fascinating aspects of making *The Trap* was the chance to meet and interact with real native Indians, hired to loiter in and out of the frame to add a sheen of realism. One in particular was the hereditary chief of the Squamish Band in British Columbia, and his name was Chief Dan George. Years later Clint Eastwood would turn him into an unlikely star in his classic western *The Outlaw Josey Wales*. On the negative side, Ollie felt aggrieved by some of the crew's prejudiced notions about Indian culture. Laying a trap, Ollie told one of the crew that he could get a very beautiful squaw for a packet of salt and some beads. Sure enough, this guy got hold of said goods and Ollie drove him to the trading post before then buggering off and leaving him stranded. 'It was a long walk back to the hotel and it was snowing, but he turned up several hours later minus a squaw, with a rather damp packet of salt.'

Ollie drank on the film, of course he did, and Raines often saw him in various states of incapacity brought on by what the Indians call firewater. 'One could not help hearing his husky voice unless the batteries in one's hearing aid had failed. Oliver was a hell-raiser with firewater in his belly, but a perfect gentleman and friend to many when on the set. Good actors of star status come and go, but Oliver in my book was one of the best.'

Back in the familiar confines of Wimbledon, Ollie continued to live it large with his mates. One Sunday afternoon he managed to tag along with Mick Monks and his girlfriend to a party in Esher, even though he wasn't invited. Following them in his new E-type Jag, Ollie overtook Monks and pulled into a pub. 'He didn't know where he was going, so we pulled in with him and had a drink. Then we passed another pub and Ollie pulled into the car park; here we go, we had another pint. So from Wimbledon to Esher I don't know how many pubs there are, but we certainly had a look at most of them.'

They arrived at a grand house and it was obvious this was a very posh do, as fairy lights twinkled in the trees and a small orchestra played in the garden. Monks and his girlfriend, suited and booted, were shown to their designated table, while Ollie stood around waiting for a drink, dressed in his gardening togs. The hostess arrived, looked at Ollie, and said, 'Have you got a place, dear?'

'Well, no, actually.'

'Just a moment,' she said and returned with a mat which she placed on the floor next to a large dining table. 'Don't worry, it's quite clean. My dog uses it.'

Without a murmur Ollie sat down. 'And he had a smile on his face that went from ear to ear,' recalls Monks. Then the girl whose party it was suddenly clocked what was going on – 'Christ, it's Oliver Reed' – and got hold of her mother in the kitchen. She returned and dug an even deeper hole by saying, 'I'm terribly sorry, I believe you're something on television.' Ollie finally got a seat.

One winter's night after closing time at the Dog and Fox, Ollie and Mick Fryer decided they quite fancied a swim and took a moonlight stroll over to Queen's Mere on Wimbledon Common, the deepest lake there. 'It was that cold the grass was crunching under our feet with the frost,' remembers Fryer. 'But we weren't freezing, we were pissed.' Neither bothered to undress, they dived in fully clothed. Halfway across, Mick looked over at Ollie. 'You OK? You can handle this all right?' 'Don't worry about me,' said Ollie. When they got out at the other side they were utterly drenched and began walking home, their clothes like sheets of ice against their skin. They could have died of pneumonia, but then such things never entered their head. Back at Ollie's pad they hung their wet clothes in the kitchen and crashed out. 'I woke up about half past seven,' says Fryer. 'I heard this screaming. It was Kate, she'd come downstairs and gone into the kitchen, which was several inches under water with the clothes that had been dripping all night. She was effing and blinding.'

Drinking with his mates, Oliver rarely, if ever, talked shop. 'Once he walked off the set, that was it,' says Monks. 'He was back to being Ollie Reed again.' He'd never say, for instance, 'I'm doing this Debussy film with that Ken Russell'; they'd all have to find out for themselves. 'He didn't make a thing about bragging that he'd got a really good job,' says Monks. 'If he did start we'd soon kick him into touch. Oh yes, you're getting like Old Cocky Bollocks.'

Over the course of his career Oliver was never to treat acting as an art form, something that had a grand mystique about it: he simply saw it as a job of work. 'Point the camera at me and pay me,' he used to say. 'I don't think he was in love with acting,' admits Simon. 'Yes, he wanted to be a star, yes, he loved the money, and he also loved the professionalism of it, and the work, he was very committed to it, but he wasn't in love with acting.' He never, for example, went to rushes. Because he lacked formal training he perhaps had no academic interest in his profession. 'It was instinctive,' says David. 'Born of an acknowledgement of the heritage that there was acting in the family.'

While the Wimbledon clique remained small there was always room for more members. A new boy was Michael Christensen, born in Denmark, so Ollie immediately christened him Norse. Christensen sank pints with the boys around Wimbledon and also at Woodland Wines, where they still played silly tricks and games. Christensen recalls one in particular. 'I was between jobs at the time, so I was pretty skint, so they thought it might be a good wheeze to bet me £5, a lot of money in those days, that I couldn't drink a pint of milk which had been on the doorstep for about three months. The fat had pushed the top out, it was all congealed and yellow. I had to hit it out like yoghurt. I managed to keep it down and made my fiver.'

Things could also get a little out of hand in the place. Mick Fryer recalls on more than one occasion everyone chucking wine bottles at each other. 'There would be these bottles of wine sailing through the air and smashing on the walls. It was lunacy in there.'

There was also a bit-part actor called Peter who occasionally drank with the group. Out of work most of the time, he had a reputation for being, in one of Ollie's expressions, 'a bit lazy with the shilling'. One day in the Dog and Fox, Ollie took him to one side – 'Right ho, Pete, you're going to be fucking Ollie Reed for an hour' – and they swapped jackets. Peter opened Ollie's wallet and got the drinks in, with some people asking for singles. Going up to the bar, Ollie grabbed him. 'You're supposed to be fucking me. They're doubles or triples, you mean cunt. And it's not even your fucking money!'

It's a story that's indicative of how very often it wasn't solely about getting hammered, but about the fun and games one had in one's local. And what a very special brand of humour Ollie enjoyed employing. 'He was very mischievous,' says Christensen. 'And he made use of the fact he was well known to get away with things. In posh restaurants he'd go up to an attractive woman on the way back from the gents', saying, "Madam, you are stunningly beautiful, would you allow me to buy you a glass of champagne?" It was just to see the reaction of the guy she was with, who's half-flattered, slightly jealous, and a bit pissed off about what's going to happen next, but this was how he liked to play with people's minds.'

A Winning Run

So successful was their first collaboration on the Debussy film that Ken Russell and Oliver were keen to work together again, and for a while it seemed likely this would be a British-made horror picture called *The Shuttered Room*, based on a short story by H. P. Lovecraft and co-starring American actress Carol Lynley and Dame Flora Robson. Only Russell was a no-show. 'Everyone arrived on location and we were going to start the movie the next day but Ken just didn't turn up,' remembers Carol. 'Why, I never found out. So we had a crew, money, the actors, everything in place, but no director.'

Panic broke out. The next morning one of the producers called everyone in for a meeting. 'I'm getting a guy called David Greene, a very good director, he's coming in on a plane right now, as we speak.' There was a lot of mumbling and anxious faces. Carol took a walk with Ollie, not sure what to do. 'Do we trust this guy and go with it? Or do we get out of the movie, too?' Ollie was for staying put and seeing it out. This was in spite of the fact that his role, as leader of a gang who terrorize a young woman, played by Carol, harked back to the thug persona he'd already exploited in films like *The Damned*. Because of his scar Ollie remained fearful that producers would feel inclined to cast him only as villains, although assistant director Stuart Freeman didn't sense this on *The Shuttered Room*, believing Ollie 'played to his looks'. Certainly he is a brooding presence throughout the film, dripping sexual malevolence and adding to the general creepy unease.

Anyway David Greene eventually showed up. 'He had been living in Rome for several years dropping acid,' says Carol. 'And on the first day he threw out the script. He literally threw the script out and said, "Now, Carol, you're gonna make up your part. And Oliver's going to make up his part," and so on. So every morning when we got up, we'd figure out the story and the scene and then shoot it. Considering the mess we were in, it's actually a pretty good movie.'

Shot on location in Norfolk, standing in for New England, the film shows Ollie doing a decent job of an American accent and, according to Stuart Freeman, he was popular with everyone on the set. 'He let his ability as an actor do all his talking. He was one of the most talented actors I have worked with. He was full of life and always challenging the crew. They loved him. In a pub one night, he filled a bowl with every make of alcohol and then passed it around to see who was the last man standing.'

Freeman remembers another incident at a pub when Ollie was challenged to an arm-wrestle by an elderly man and the actor scoffed at the very idea. 'But this old guy shamed him into acceptance and then thoroughly beat him. The elderly man then told Ollie that he was a heart surgeon and had to have strength in his arms and hands to perform his work. Ollie bought him a drink.'

Very early on in the shoot Carol found herself drawn to Ollie. She admits that the attraction to begin with was fairly physical. 'He was very sexy. I noticed right away he was a very sexually attractive man. And very masculine. He made a point of being masculine.' As time went on the attraction grew deeper. Not only did they share the same birth date but Carol recognized that they were not too dissimilar as people. 'Although he was obviously more dramatic than I am. He was also very plain-spoken and very gentlemanly. He couldn't have been nicer.' She was falling in love with him and by the close of filming they'd begun an affair.

Ollie didn't appear to give a damn who knew it either, taking Carol to the London premiere of *The Trap* and also parties and nights out with friends who were well aware that he was married. Those who didn't saw a couple that appeared blissfully besotted. But what of Kate? Certainly Oliver still loved her and Mark remembers their marriage being 'very happy. But I also remember when it became more argumentative. I never grasped the contents of the rows, my mother naturally shielded me from most of it, but I do remember there being a continual sense of friction.' The rows could be colossal. One day they were getting ready to go to a friend's wedding when an argument erupted. Kate was all done up in her finery, when Ollie blasted, 'Go to the wedding on your own then.' Shooting him a hurt look, Kate screamed, 'I will.' As she left the house Ollie tipped a bowl of water all over her from the top window.

'They were young and naive,' says Mark. 'And if you've got one person in that couple starting to ascend it's very easy to see how things do start to divide, especially when there's a lot of pretty women around and everyone thinks you're the best thing since sliced bread and you start to believe a little bit of that. But she was quite good at knocking him back down, tapping him on the shoulder and going, could I have your autograph, please?' But it was tough for Kate, as there would be one crowd of people that he'd meet in the pub, take back home, get them all pissed, and when they staggered off new people would arrive. 'I don't know how Kate stood for it,' is Johnny Placett's view. 'Having people in her place all the time one after the other. He did love her, though. But then again, she wasn't the kind of woman who sat on the sidelines. Kate always wanted to be in amongst the action.'

In the early weeks of Ollie's relationship with Carol he enjoyed taking her to old-fashioned London pubs and touristy landmarks like Covent Garden fruit market. 'He seemed to like to show me very English things, so I got to know London very well. He was very patriotic and he loved the Queen. Whenever I see a picture of the Queen or something on TV about her I always think of Ollie. He just adored the Queen and was passionately proud of England.'

At the time Carol was living in the capital and Ollie would sometimes take her young daughter to school, or they'd all go for long walks in Kensington Gardens. Often he used to turn up unannounced at her flat. One day he appeared declaring, 'I'm going to show you what I used to look like.'

'Fine,' said Carol.

'I was actually quite pretty, you know.'

'Pretty!' said Carol.

Ollie had already explained to Carol how he'd got the scars on his face, 'and when I first met him they were still quite visible.' They went to this rather rundown, seedy movie house to watch *The System*, the film he'd made just before the glassing. 'And I could see that he was indeed very, very pretty. And there was an old lady in the seats in front of us, it was kind of an empty theatre, but people kept coming and sitting next to her and then moving off. Then two bobbies came down the aisle and took the old lady away. She had been giving people hand jobs. She was literally right in front of us and neither Ollie nor myself had noticed it. Ollie thought it was terribly disrespectful to the film.'

Just as memorable was the time Ollie showed up at Carol's flat to tell her that he'd left Kate and wanted to move in with her. Fine, great, she said. The following day Ollie arrived in a car that was loaded with his clothes. 'And he stayed around the house for maybe two days, but he never took the clothes out of the car, so every time he had to change he'd go down and change in the street. He just couldn't bring himself to move his possessions in.'

So it was back to Kate. But Ollie's affair with Carol, remarkably, would continue on and off for the next seven years.

Michael Winner was pacing up and down his office in Piccadilly puffing away on his trademark cigar as he related the plot of his latest movie, *The Jokers*, to his star Michael Crawford. 'It's about these two brothers who steal the crown jewels, dear. It's a comedy.' Circa 1966 Crawford was Britain's hot new comedy talent, launched by Richard Lester in *The Knack*. Such was his kudos at the time that Universal were backing *The Jokers* only if Crawford played the lead. 'So who's my brother in this?' asked Crawford.

'Oliver Reed,' announced Winner proudly.

Crawford's jaw hit the floor. 'You must be bloody joking! Audiences will never accept Oliver Reed and myself as being even remotely related.' Crawford was currently appearing in a West End show and Winner suggested Oliver see it and then they could all meet up afterwards. Crawford's response was: 'Don't bring Oliver Reed to the theatre. I'm telling you right now. If you bring him to my dressing room I'm going to throw him out.'

'If you're going to throw Oliver Reed out of your dressing room, dear,' said Winner, 'you've got about six hours to go to the gym and train, because he's a very fit fella and you're not.'

The meeting went ahead anyway and Oliver turned up with David: a wise move, if it was planned, because Crawford took one look at Ollie's fair-haired brother and announced, 'He could be my double.' So ended any arguments about Ollie's suitability as Crawford's cinematic sibling. In fact, when shooting started the pair were almost inseparable and much of the film's appeal is their on-screen chemistry, dubbed 'The best double act since Laurel and Hardy' by the London *Evening Standard*.

On set there was much mischief-making and Winner's life was quickly made a misery. First they stole his designer sunglasses, which ended up mangled beneath the wheel of a bus, then, with the aid of the crew, jacked his Rolls-Royce clear off the road. The humour reached infantile levels when black boot polish was smeared around the mouthpiece of Winner's prized megaphone and laxative was put in his tea. Nor was Crawford immune to Ollie's japes. He was not a heavy drinker and Ollie sometimes spiked his co-star's feeble half pint of bitter with double vodkas during lunchtime visits to the pub and Crawford would stagger back to work barking insults at a mystified Winner, while Ollie stood in the background tut-tutting, 'How unprofessional, turning up on set drunk, outrageous.' On another occasion Ollie stood outside Crawford's Clapham flat shouting instructions to a heavy goods vehicle. 'OK, back a bit, back a bit.' When Crawford opened the door Ollie's face opened out into a broad smile. 'Oh hello, Michael. I've got that ton of horse shit you wanted.'

Crawford puts the close bond he shared with Oliver during the making of *The Jokers* down to the fact they were playing brothers. 'Whenever we walked about the set together, Oliver always kept a fraternal arm around me and every now and again he'd give me a brotherly squeeze, the kind of squeeze a fruit-extracting machine would give a ripe orange.' The physical side of Oliver was always bubbling away very close to the surface. While not a Method actor, he was nevertheless an instinctive one and 'tended to live the part he was playing,' according to Crawford. In one scene Ollie's character believes he's been double-crossed by his brother and left to the mercy of the police, and so attacks him. 'I was really dreading it because as we shot the scene Oliver took my "betrayal" as something entirely real and completely personal and suddenly my life wasn't worth tuppence. His ham-like hands were fastened so tightly round my neck, I felt the end of my life was imminent.

It took four people to get him off me – and only two of them were scripted.'

If there was one crack in the relationship it was Crawford's perceived tight-fistedness, or, as Ollie put it, 'Michael has very short arms and very long pockets.' At many a lunch it was Oliver's recollection that Crawford always ended up leaving just before the bill arrived. So imagine Ollie and Winner's surprise when Crawford invited the pair for drinks at a flash restaurant. As usual, when the bill was presented Crawford legged it but the pair hunted him down. 'Oliver held Michael over the fountains in Trafalgar Square and threatened to drop him in unless he stumped up,' recalls Winner. 'Oliver was always sensitive to injustice, especially in the way of paying for rounds.'

Yet again, Winner came up trumps for Ollie, for *The Jokers* was a perfect vehicle to showcase his considerable comedic gifts, which sadly were not to be exploited by filmmakers as much as they should have been. It also proved to be his first big exposure in the United States. Cashing in on the swinging London scene, *The Jokers* was a reasonable hit over there. As one critic noted about Ollie, 'The brutal, brooding hulk of volcanic masculinity was beginning to intrude on the dreamland of women both sides of the Atlantic.'

With Winner now a firm champion of Ollie (they were already planning their next feature together), the actor's other benefactor, Ken Russell, came calling. The project was *Dante's Inferno*, another BBC television film, this one about the flamboyant and sensual Victorian English poet and painter Dante Gabriel Rossetti and the Pre-Raphaelite Brotherhood. Again the two men worked seamlessly together. Ollie really was the perfect foil for Russell, who, like Winner, herded his actors along with a megaphone. Russell was never much interested in an actor's motivation, as Glenda Jackson ribs: 'Ken wouldn't have known acting if it came up and hit him in the face!' Like Oliver, he thought all that Method stuff was a load of old bollocks and often made the claim that the two of them quickly devised their own private way of working, labelling it: Moody 1, Moody 2 and Moody 3. Depending on the amount of intensity required for the scene, morose sullenness or outright rage, Russell would indicate, 'I think a Moody 2 here' and Ollie pitched his performance accordingly. It was a form of directorial shorthand that continued for the rest of the time they worked together.

Sheba Gray, whose father Tony was in the film, was nine years old when *Dante's Inferno* was made and appears in some scenes as Rossetti's daughter. She's never forgotten Ollie, who I imagine cut quite a striking figure for a pre-pubescent young girl. 'Oliver was utterly charming towards me and my younger brother. He played a great game which involved throwing half crowns on to the lawn and letting us keep as many as we could pick by the time he counted to twenty. He also took me punting on my own and made me feel like such a lady. I always remember him with the highest regard.'

Oliver delivers yet another consummate performance as Rossetti, managing the feat of making the famed artist both a playboy and a rogue, yet retaining that fatal element of charm that won over friends and lovers. When he reads some of Rossetti's poems he makes you regret that he never did Shakespeare or the classics since his voice was a superbly rich instrument, and his line readings were always extraordinarily good. What a Macbeth he would have made (why didn't Polanski cast him in his blood-soaked 1971 version?) or, had he lived longer, what a wonderfully stately decaying King Lear.

During his time in the industry Oliver was known as 'the whispering giant' and was the bane of soundmen owing to his soft, low, mellifluous voice. It was almost a gentle voice which belied his fierce image. 'I had the misfortune to look like a prize-fighter and speak like a public schoolboy.' Or as one journalist put it, 'looking like an aristocrat's bastard masquerading as a builder's labourer'. It was a whisper that screenwriter George MacDonald Fraser called 'the most menacing in the business, and, unlike many whispers, it was always audible; he would vary it with sudden, unexpected roars'. This was a technique Oliver cultivated quite early in his career. 'I concluded that if I were ever going to achieve anything, I had to pretend to be a volcano, a sleeping volcano always with the threat of eruption.'

As soon as he read the script for Michael Winner's new film, *I'll Never Forget What's'isname*, Ollie knew he wanted to do it, not least because it gave him one of British cinema's greatest ever opening scenes. As the credits roll he walks through the streets of central London nonchalantly holding an axe over his shoulder, drawing looks of bemusement and shock from passers-by. Arriving at his workplace, he takes the lift and, once inside his plush, shiny office, takes the axe to his desk, reducing it to kindling wood in seconds. The man's name is Andrew Quint, an advertising executive, and this is his unique way of resigning from his job and escaping the rat race.

The casting of Orson Welles as his boss was another inducement. Oliver was to describe working with the cinema legend as 'an honour. He taught me a great deal.' He was positively in awe of the man, calling him a force of nature, and out of the film grew an unlikely friendship. They'd meet only infrequently and in the most unlikely of places. Ollie might be in the middle of Greece and hear this unmistakable voice: 'Oliver, my boy, let me take you to lunch.' He'd turn up at the appointed time only to find that Orson had invited what seemed to be the entire local population. 'The place would be packed to the rafters. And the meals! Course after course. Hugely expensive. And, just as the coffee arrived, Orson would rise to his feet and, in that great booming voice, say, "Excuse me for one moment, my friends, I have to pay a visit to the little boys' room." We'd never see him again. He'd nip out the back, leaving some poor sod, usually myself, to pick up the tab. I lost count of the number of times that happened.' Of course, Ollie couldn't stay angry for long, as Orson was a one-off and you always knew that he was going to be good value for money.

The last time Ollie met Orson was in the eighties, when he was stranded at Charles de Gaulle airport in Paris one Christmas Eve, desperate to get back home. Outside the snow was gathering momentum and all flights had been cancelled. Then, behind him, he heard that familiar voice: 'Oliver, my boy! Why don't the two of us hire a private plane and make our own way to England? It's my shout.' And Ollie thought, oh Christ, here we go again.

Winner shot in all the fashionable London places, Mayfair, Chelsea, the Biba shop in Kensington, and it was a brilliant advertisement for the London Tourist Board. For a week his cameras went to Cambridge, where a young actor called Mark Eden (later a regular on *Coronation Street*) joined the cast, playing a private detective hired to follow Oliver's character. Delighted to be working with 'an actor I admired', Eden witnessed first-hand Ollie's close relationship with Winner, which was just as fraught as it was creative. 'They argued an awful lot, although they really did like each other very much. They had blazing rows and disagreements. He stood up to Michael and I think Michael quite liked that, he liked somebody standing up to him.'

Eden highlights one particular incident. Oliver was in a punt gently bobbing along the River Cam, with Winner and the cameraman crouched down at the far end. As usual, Winner was shouting directions, probably through a megaphone, at an increasingly irate Oliver. Eden watched from the bank as there was take after take. 'All of a sudden Oliver threw the pole into the water and stepped off. He literally stepped off the boat as though he was going for a walk. Swimming towards me, he got out and walked back to the hotel. Marooned in the middle of the

Cam, Winner was shouting and screaming and gesticulating so ferociously that he almost capsized the boat.'

That night Eden had dinner with Ollie and asked what had happened. 'Michael wouldn't stop fucking rabbiting on in that grating voice of his, giving me instructions. So I told him, if you don't shut up I'm going back to my hotel. And Michael said, "How are you going to do that, dear, in the middle of the Cam?"' Well, Ollie certainly showed him. On top of all that, the crew didn't have any replacement clothes, so had to send Ollie's costume to the cleaners, and it held up shooting for the rest of the day.

Eden enjoyed Oliver's company immensely. 'He was an enormously likeable man, great fun. Mind you, he did drink an awful lot and he always wanted to have a fight with somebody when he'd had a few. I think he had a bit of a death wish. The way he used to drink was just ridiculous. Funnily enough, the night I had dinner with him he hardly drank anything. I think he had a big scene the next morning. We had some wine but he only had a couple of glasses.'

This was quite often the case when Oliver was working: he'd look at the next day's schedule and if it was a particularly difficult scene he'd lay off the sauce or only partially indulge. If, however, it was a reaction shot or something else minor, well then it was no holds barred. 'He was very professional in that way,' says Simon. 'But he did get increasingly worried and nervous about lines and so wouldn't let the drink get in the way.'

This kind of professionalism was typified for Eden in a scene where their two characters engage in a fierce fight. Ollie choreographed the whole routine himself and Eden found him completely focused and utterly in control; had he not been, then mistakes and injuries could have resulted.

Off set, Oliver generally kept himself very much to himself, racing back home as soon as the day's work finished. 'The impression I got was of a rather shy and quiet man, which surprised me rather,' recalls co-star Wendy Craig, who played his wife in the film. 'He was quite reticent, really. I never knew anything about his private life. I did know he quite liked a tipple but when we were doing the film he was absolutely on the wagon, he never took a drink. And I thought that was highly professional.'

One of the reasons Wendy accepted the film in the first place was the chance to work with Oliver. 'I was mad about him as an actor, I thought he was very good and had the potential to be a huge star. And he was so easy to work with, he had terrific technique and taught me quite a lot just by watching him. It was a real pleasure.' There was also the obligatory love scene, during which Wendy remembers Ollie behaving as nothing less than an absolute gentleman. 'We had to spend a day in bed and he was so polite, bless him, and so concerned that I was comfortable with what we were doing. And I really liked him for that.'

As usual, Ollie liked to have fun on set and played his practical jokes, again mostly directed at Winner. One took place during a lunch break on location when a bag lady walked by and asked what was going on. 'We're making a film, love,' said one of the crew. 'How about giving me some money then?' she replied. Oliver took her to one side and whispered, 'You see that man sitting over there. He's our director and he's a millionaire. He'll give you some money.' Winner was sitting alone under strict instructions not to be disturbed. 'So we all watched with glee as she went over,' remembers Eden. 'But Michael realized immediately what had happened and asked her to sit down and they chatted amiably for a few minutes until Michael, who never carried money, got one of his assistants to give her some cash. Then before she left he made sure that the location caterers put some food in plastic containers for her to take away. And as she walked off Michael gave us all a little smile.'

Other tricks played by Ollie on Winner, such as replacing his beloved cigar with an exploding one, didn't seem to adversely affect their relationship, as Wendy Craig observed. 'They got on tremendously well. It was obvious that Winner held him in very high regard. They were good buddies. They seemed to understand each other very well, and understand the mode of working together.' Yvonne Romain, a close friend of the director for years, says the secret of their success was simple: Winner gave Ollie his freedom. 'Oliver didn't like being told things by directors, because he really did know how to handle himself on the set. That's why he loved Winner so much, because Winner usually just put the camera on him and let him do his thing, which is what you did with Oliver because he was going to get it right anyway.'

I'll Never Forget What's'isname should have blasted Oliver to the forefront of stardom. That it failed to do so did not invalidate Winner's assertion that he was 'going to be the biggest star in the country'. Several controversies surrounding the film may have harmed its box-office potential, notably in America, where the Catholic Church had kittens over an implied scene of oral sex between Oliver and Carol White, slapping a 'Condemned' rating on the film, while the Motion Picture Association of America refused it its seal of approval. As a result, despite good reviews, *What's'isname* was not widely seen Stateside. That wasn't all: it became the first mainstream movie to use the word 'fuck'. Spurned lover number two Marianne Faithfull screams it at Oliver as he leaves her apartment: 'You fucking bastard!' The British censor at first wanted it removed completely but in the end a compromise was reached by partly obscuring the profanity with a car horn. Yet cinema history was made.

By the close of filming Oliver had begun yet another affair, this time with Carol White, the daughter of a scrap metal merchant who caused a sensation in Ken Loach's 1966 television film *Cathy Come Home*. Their affair may have been brief but it was passionate and certainly, as far as Oliver was concerned, serious. Already, though, Carol had problems with hard drugs, something that Ollie had no interest in at all. He'd never touched the stuff, nor expressed a desire to do so, and Carol had to coerce him into trying his first joint. 'But he was so drunk I don't think he even noticed it.' As for the harder stuff, like LSD, which Carol was using, Ollie refused to take part. In the end she spiked his drink with it. 'The effect was awesome,' she told a journalist. 'You could see the trip bubbling behind Ollie's eyes, but nothing surfaced. He was floating, dancing, flying, all in his head; externally he was the same drunken Ollie.' In the morning he felt rougher than he'd ever felt before and learning what had happened renewed his determination never to touch the drug again. One presumes it did little for the relationship either, which eventually petered out and died.

While it's true to say that Ollie quite liked the idea of having Kate but keeping a mistress or two, like good old Herbert had done, he also indulged heavily in casual sex and one-night stands. Joyce Coleman, former landlady of the Dog and Fox, recalls Ollie coming in early one Saturday evening asking if she had such a thing as a weekend case and could she loan it to him till Monday? Yes, she did, and brought it down. Out in the hall there was a telephone with a large stack of directories. 'I'm going to take about three of these as well,' said Ollie. when Joyce asked him why in the world he needed three telephone directories, Ollie replied, 'Because I'm going to a hotel with a beautiful young lady and unless it looks like you've got some luggage, they won't let you in for the weekend.'

The Ferry to County Clare

The sound of hard knocking on his front door woke David up. It was midnight. There was only one person he knew likely to be disturbing him at this ungodly hour and that was Oliver. Sure enough, when David opened the door there he was, accompanied by a hefty-looking bloke you wouldn't want to mess with at a Palais de Dance on a Saturday night.

'Got a map?' asked Ollie.

'I think so,' said David, not bothering to question his brother's motives.

'I want to buy a house,' Ollie announced, as he laid the map out on the floor of the kitchen. 'I promised Pat here years ago that I would buy him a farm.'

The promise had been made, where else but in a pub in Wimbledon, in the days when Ollie was an unknown struggling young actor and Pat Clancy had just left the Black Watch regiment. 'Bastards, that's what they are,' Pat had been muttering to himself while nursing a pint of stout at the bar. 'All bastards.'

Ollie watched this performance for about twenty minutes before curiosity got the better of him and he introduced himself. 'Excuse me, I don't wish to be nosy, but who are all bastards?'

'The army.' The word was spat out with as much Glaswegian

venom as could be mustered. 'Bastards, that's what they are.'

When Ollie mentioned his own army background the veteran seemed to welcome him as an old friend and comrade and out came his whole life story, the twenty-five years of service – Second World War, Korea, Malaysia – and how he'd been pensioned off with a large lump sum that he'd blown on tarts and whisky during a nine-month debauched stay in Dublin.

'That was fairly spectacular,' said Ollie, no doubt impressed. 'Tell me, what would you have done with the money if you hadn't blown it all?'

The ex-soldier looked forlornly into the far distance. 'A little cottage,' he said, his eyes flickering as if it was there now in his mind's eye. 'I'd have kept chickens and maybe a few ducks.'

'Tell you what,' said Ollie. 'When I become a rich movie star, I'll buy you that little cottage and let you live in it as long as you like. Is that fair?'

'Bastards,' said the veteran, going back to nursing his pint. 'They're all bastards.'

And that's how Ollie left him, muttering those same words over and over again. By chance six years later Ollie heard that Pat was back in Wimbledon, drinking in the same pub, the Swan. And, sure enough, there he was, propping up the bar on the same stool, muttering 'bastards' to himself over his beer. Now a successful actor, Ollie bought the bloke another drink and asked if he remembered their conversation from years before.

'Aye.'

'Well, when do you want to start looking for that cottage?'

Hence, after several more drinks, one suspects, the midnight visit to David, who asked, 'And where exactly do you want to buy this farm?'

'How about Scotland?' said Ollie. Though born in Ireland, Pat was raised in Scotland and spoke like it, a voice of thistles, porridge and bagpipes. Ollie scanned the map. 'OK, Pat, you can drive, can't you?' Pat nodded. 'David, buy him a car and send him off to Scotland to find a place.'

Pat came back having found a charming house and David remembers how he was dispatched to buy it. 'This house was attached to a church. It was the vicar's house and it was absolutely idyllic, miles from anywhere. They didn't have estate agents there, it was all done by auction, so I worked with a lawyer and told them we'd beat any other bid. He said, "Och, Mr Reed, we don't do things like that here." So we lost that one.'

In the end Pat switched his search to Ireland and found his dream cottage in County Clare, on the west coast between Kilrush and Kilkee, an area Oliver was to call magical and enchanting, full of real characters, a place where locals poached salmon in exchange for beer. So that's how Ollie came to buy Ferry House for Pat Clancy, becoming a frequent visitor there himself. It was a retreat far away from the hustle and bustle of London and film studios. He'd relax by fishing or duck shooting with some of the locals, always making sure to miss because he hated killing any kind of animal.

During one visit Ollie, David and a reprobate friend of Pat's known as the Dog Soldier drove out to Kilrush. It was a particularly stormy day as they drove along a cliff-top road; below them was an incredible explosion of water as the Atlantic pounded the rocky coastline. 'Come on, let's go down and get a bit closer,' roared Oliver, exhilarated by nature's display. Wearily David followed his brother and the Dog Soldier as they wandered ever closer to the cliff edge. Once there the two men laughed and jumped around like children in and out of the spray, but David was already sensing danger. 'This water was just going straight up past us in the air about fifty feet. So I said, "Come on, guys, you're getting too near," and stepped back. Just as I retreated, this one wave came in and took the two of them and they went down about twenty feet into white, boiling water. Ollie was in a big parka jacket and when he came up struggling I indicated to him to take it off because by that time it was full of water and dragging him down. He did that but I could see he was still fighting for his life out there. Then suddenly this huge wave came in and hurled him into the rock face. When the swell subsided he was clinging on like a stranded starfish.'

Terrified that another mighty wave would pulverize his body and take him back into the seething tempest, this time for good, Ollie began feverishly climbing up the cliff. Reassured that his brother was now safe, David diverted his attention to the Dog Soldier, who was floating out to sea, past the headland. 'I ran over the rocks, he was face down in the water, and I managed to pull him out and push the water out of him. Recovered, we all got into the car and I said, "For God's sake, we've got to go and have a drink." It had been a narrow escape.'

Years later, when Ollie heard that Pat Clancy had died, he and David went over to Ireland to sell Ferry House but were surprised to find Pat had installed a homeless young couple and their two young children there. Ollie was not about to throw them out, so forwent the sale and allowed the family to remain in the house for as long as they wished. It was another example of Oliver's largesse. 'His generosity was so huge,' says his daughter Sarah. 'That's probably why he didn't die a wealthy man, because he played it and he spent it. His philosophy was, I've got it so I'm going to share it; which is lovely.'

Jacquie

When Lionel Bart's landmark stage musical *Oliver!* triumphed on both the London and Broadway stages in the early sixties it seemed only a matter of time before it attracted the heavyweights of the film world. Along with his brother James, Sir John Woolf ran a successful independent production company called Romulus Films and had been in love with the Dickens novel since childhood, and he was fascinated when he saw the stage show. 'I imagined it would make a great film for children and indeed that it would appeal to all ages.' After buying the rights, the brothers next hired Lewis Gilbert, then the hottest director in the country thanks to the runaway success of the original *Alfie* of 1966. It was agreed that James would accompany Gilbert on a casting trip to LA, but late one night James suffered a heart attack and died. 'Lewis rang me up in the morning to say that my brother was found dead,' recalled Sir John. 'He was young, just forty-six. It was a great blow and I nearly cancelled *Oliver!*. But then I decided that I had to go on with *Oliver!* on my own.'

Woolf had already moved into offices at Pinewood in preparation for a start date of June 1967 when news reached him that Gilbert had been forced to withdraw. For the next couple of weeks he repeatedly strolled into the office he shared with art director John Box, offering up names for possible replacements. If Box didn't approve he simply kept silent. One morning Woolf hollered, 'Before you spit in the corner – Carol Reed.' Box looked up. 'I'm not spitting, he's your man.' It was an inspired choice, as Box had worked with Carol Reed before and knew he was quite brilliant with children. There's no better illustration of this in the film than the moment Fagin opens his box of treasures for little Oliver to gaze inside. After several takes Carol couldn't get the required look of wanderlust from nine-year-old Mark Lester, chosen from 2,000 children to play the coveted role. The next day Carol positioned himself behind the camera and said, 'Mark, I've got something that might amuse you,' and produced a white rabbit from his overcoat. Lester's face lit up and that's the shot in the movie.

With Carol installed as director it made things very interesting when Oliver became the front runner to play Fagin's partner in crime, Bill Sikes. For years Ollie had clearly stated in interviews his determination to make the grade as an actor on his own, without assistance from his famous uncle. 'I always said that I would only act in one of his films when I felt I was in the cast because of my ability and not just because I was his nephew.' That time had now come. Simon for one can't recall any doubts or concerns on his brother's behalf about possible accusations of nepotism. 'He was just worried about doing the film well. The nepotism may have been a slight side issue but really he was anxious to just do his best.' In the end it was Woolf who settled the matter: 'Oliver was quite clearly the best actor for the part of Bill Sikes, so I took the decision and the responsibility.'

It wasn't so much nepotism that worried Ollie, but the difficulty of stepping into the unforgettable shoes of Robert Newton, who'd played Sikes in David Lean's 1948 straight version of Dickens's tale. 'I had to watch that I didn't turn out to be Sikes and Long John Silver rolled into one,' he said, referring to Newton's other memorable performance. One night, Mick Monks recalls, Ollie invited a bunch of lads back to his flat, including two huge geezers who worked locally as bouncers. Midway through the festivities Ollie produced a children's Ladybird book and asked the bouncers to take it in turn to read from it. As they struggled with such complex sentences as 'The little duck goes quack, quack, quack,' Ollie turned on a tape recorder. It was only years later that Monks realized his friend was collecting the type of voice he was going to use for Bill Sikes.

Ollie added other little bits of characterization, including one priceless piece of dialogue. He claimed to have heard, while walking along a busy London high street, a couple outside a shop arguing over a pair of shoes. When the man refused to fork out what he thought an inflated price, the girl demanded to know if he truly loved her. 'Loves yer,' he answered. 'Course I loves yer. Fucks yer, don't I?' This tickled Ollie so much that he approached Carol the next day on set suggesting he use the line in a scene where his girlfriend Nancy asks the same question. After momentarily forgetting this was supposed to be a children's film, Ollie altered it to 'Love yer? Course I love yer. I live with yer, don't I?'

Over the years Carol had closely followed the career of his nephew, from his first tentative steps as a walk-on artist to his Hammer roles and his recent successes, often telephoning him to offer his opinion. It wasn't always positive but it was always encouraging and constructive. Ollie also enjoyed visiting Carol at his home to talk over any problems he might be having, 'because he was such a good listener'. Uncle Carol, though, suspected Ollie of arriving most days pissed, as he would stop off en route at various pubs along the King's Road.

But on the set of *Oliver!* Ollie was nothing less than his usual professional self, as witnessed by the film's renowned cameraman, Oswald Morris. 'Oliver was as good as gold. Really the only problem we had was that Oliver wanted to play Bill Sikes with a loud, strong voice and Carol wanted quite the opposite. He felt Sikes was much more powerful if he spoke quietly. And there was a certain amount of friction between the two of them about the way the part should be played, but it was Carol who got his way. And if you run the film you'll see that all the powerful lines are said very, very quietly. Oliver wanted to scream certain lines but Carol said, no, keep it quiet.'

The respect and love Oliver had for his uncle bordered on adoration. While he was making a movie in the early seventies with Geraldine Chaplin, some of their conversations naturally drifted towards famous relatives. 'Your father was great, Geraldine,' he'd say. 'But my uncle was *really* great.' It's one of the reasons Geraldine gives for why she enjoyed such a close working relationship with Oliver, that they had this thing in common, coming from a famous film family. 'And he'd speak with such respect in his voice about Sir Carol. He absolutely adored him.'

Ollie and his uncle remained very close right up until Carol's death in 1976. As a tribute the National Film Theatre on London's South Bank ran a season of his films and Ollie was invited to attend the opening-night celebration. A pre-arranged meeting with a film producer took him first to the Dorchester Hotel, where he liberally partook of the bar, so by the time he arrived at the ceremony he was quite unprepared when the organizers asked if he would say a few words. Bounding on to the stage, there he stood in front of a packed audience of relatives and friends of his uncle. Suddenly he dried. Managing finally to garble some words about feeling humble to be there, he turned to leave and fell clean off the stage. Getting up, he was deeply upset at the thought of having ruined the evening and disgracing Carol's name, but everyone was most sympathetic. David took him to one side and said, 'Don't worry, Oliver, they all loved it because that's what they expected you to do.'

With the obvious exception of *The Third Man*, *Oliver!* is

perhaps the towering achievement of Carol Reed's career. A global box-office hit and winner of six Oscars, including Best Picture, it continues to enthral audiences, its magic refusing to fade. And much of that success is down to Ollie's performance as Bill Sikes, for even when he's off screen his malevolent presence can still be felt, as if at any moment he's about to jump out from the shadows. Much of Ollie's screen image was brooding and rather threatening, almost intimidating, but he knew how and when to use it, that was the skill, and most importantly how to underplay it. Simon remembers his brother telling him that if there was any doubt about what to do on screen, he wouldn't do anything, 'because he had that sense of menace about him it looked great. He was very keen to play that menace. He felt the camera was his fan.'

It was a performance that brought him plaudits and mass recognition; it also scared the crap out of the child actors. Jack Wild, the immortal Artful Dodger, recalled that his overriding memory of Oliver was of total intimidation. 'As kids we were all terrified of him because he was this giant of a man and the only time we ever saw him was when he was in costume and made up for the part.' This was a deliberate and clever move on Ollie's part. 'I kept my distance from the kids. With Ron Moody's Fagin, they kept pulling his beard off and trying to take his pants down, but they kept their distance from me. I wanted Bill Sikes to be a frightening character, and I couldn't have retained that menace if I had allowed them to become too familiar through clowning around with me on the set.'

The only time the youngsters ever saw the 'real' Oliver was at the end-of-filming party, when he turned out to be just as dangerous as his screen alter ego. Mark Lester recalls, 'He got Jack Wild and me completely drunk on vodka by spiking our Cokes. I remember getting home and my mother put me in a cold bath with all my clothes on. I think I was violently ill, but looking back on it, it's quite amusing really.'

Others felt equally intimidated by Ollie's presence. Mark Lester vividly recalls the filming of the scene where Bill Sikes grabs hold of Fagin's throat and spits out a few salacious threats. Oliver had arrived on set heavily psyched up and in character and Lester watched fascinated as the scene was played out. 'I remember looking into Ron Moody's eyes during that moment and, even at my age, seeing real fear.'

Remaining an enigmatic, brooding presence was also good for Shani Wallis, who as Nancy required to be roughed up a good deal by Sikes. In one dramatic moment in Fagin's hide-out Bill smacks her full across the face. 'He scared me doing that,' she later admitted. 'I fell and almost cracked my head open. And I remember getting up from that position and I was trembling.' She does, however, credit Oliver with the success of the film's most shocking scene, when Nancy is clubbed to death by Sikes as the hapless Oliver looks on: the most non-U certificate moment ever to appear in a U-certificate picture. Ollie told Shani just before the take not to hold back when it came to defending herself, to kick and scream and to really go for it. The realism of her reaction was picked up by the camera and the result is truly unsettling. Most of the time, though, Shani did despair of Oliver's carrying on and flirting, although he never once tried it on with the singer, since her husband was a daily visitor to the studio. Most of his chasing around seemed focused on the pretty dancers; well, one dancer in particular that he couldn't keep his eyes off.

The bulk of *Oliver!*'s ten-million-dollar budget went on the huge theatrical sets. The London of Dickens was built from scratch, nothing was shot on location, and art director John Box's aim was to both capture the grimness of the time, for example the rotting stairways spanning a mud-filled canal and leading to Fagin's hide-out, and its elegance, typified by grand houses and exclusive squares. 'Those sets were huge, just massive,' remembers assistant director Mike Higgins. 'Half of Shepperton Studios was taken over and they were used for years afterwards on other films.'

Perhaps the most eye-catching set was that of a beautiful royal crescent, built on the back lot of the studio, where one of the big show-stopping numbers was performed, 'Who Will Buy?'. It took weeks to rehearse and shoot and involved hundreds of extras and dancers. Oliver is only seen briefly towards the end of the sequence but nevertheless was required on set every day in his Bill Sikes outfit because they would switch to shooting his scenes if it rained. 'He'd come down in his yellow E-type and he'd park near the set and just sit there and brood,' says Jacquie Daryl, one of the dancers. 'And you can imagine how broody he was as Bill Sikes. He would just look and watch at everything going on. And we kind of stared at one another all the time, never saying a word, just looked at one another.' This went on for weeks until finally the film's American choreographer, Oona White, had had enough of it. 'This is ridiculous,' she told Jacquie one afternoon. 'The whole set's boiling because you two are just sitting there looking at one another.' They'd still not exchanged a single word. So Oona finally went over to Ollie, grabbed him, and introduced the pair of them.

Jacquie had come to Britain from her native South Africa to join the Royal Ballet School, after which she went into the Royal Ballet Company at Covent Garden, staying there for ten years. She was with the company when Rudolf Nureyev defected in Paris while on tour with the Kirov Ballet, and still recalls the incredible excitement of his first arrival into class at Covent Garden. After that she'd watch from the wings his dazzling performances opposite Margot Fonteyn. Entranced by Nureyev, Jacquie had also fallen in love with American stage musicals; the dancing in them was so modern and vibrant that this was where she saw her future. For the next few years she appeared in West End productions and films. Then came two separate offers, to be in the principal dancing cast of either

Oliver! or *Chitty Chitty Bang Bang*. After much debate Jacquie chose *Oliver!* The schedule was longer, so she figured it would earn her more money. It was a decision that was to change her life.

Finally introduced, Jacquie and Oliver would hook up in the studio bar during breaks or go to the local pub after filming. At the time Jacquie wasn't a drinker and Ollie always joked about the first time he asked what she wanted to drink and she said, 'Orange please,' and Ollie came back with, 'Orange and what?' So no, she didn't indulge. 'It was something I acquired.' These early dates were nothing serious and certainly not clandestine, the whole cast and crew knew about it all, with many of them playing matchmaker. 'Get in there, girl,' some of the dancers were urging, but Jacquie didn't want a fling. 'Hopefully he'll move on to another part of the film and I'll never see him again.' But Oona kept saying, 'This is ridiculous. In my day, darling, one wouldn't think twice.' In this respect the film world is perhaps unique: what happens on a film set usually stays there, and sometimes ends there as well, so people have got terribly involved, broken a lot of hearts, probably broken a few marriages, and then they go their separate ways. But this was different, because the floodgates of emotion had been opened and there really wasn't any way of stopping it. Oliver and Jacquie were not being ruled any more by their heads but by their hearts, and by the end of filming they were lovers. Even Carol Reed got to hear about what was going on and one day his wife came on the set to have a good spy on this girl who was having a fling with her nephew. Afterwards she told one of her acquaintances that there was nothing in it. 'She's just a simple little girl from Africa.'

Looking back, Jacquie regards her behaviour as being that of a lovelorn teenager, confused by the emotions surging through her body, totally unable to control them. 'He was larger than life. He was very magnetic, very charismatic, he was, oh, so like a child at times. It was all of those things put together.' In other words, he was irresistible to her. Of course, she fully understood the predicament she was in, that Oliver was married. 'It was a big problem for him and an even bigger one for me. The whole thing was governed by guilt because both of us felt very, very guilty about the fact that this was going to affect a lot of people's lives. It's not something I'm proud of. But there was nothing I could do about it. He was the most amazing person.' Even the knowledge that Oliver and Kate's relationship had been on shaky ground for some time because of Oliver's womanizing didn't ease the burden. 'Actually you feel worse because it gives someone an option out, doesn't it? And then there was Mark, who was at such a vulnerable age then; not a period I enjoy, really.'

Torn between his feelings for Jacquie and his responsibilities at home, especially his duty as a father, Oliver attempted to stop the affair before it got any more serious. 'We tried to separate, and it didn't work,' Jacquie reveals. 'In fact we tried twice. We suddenly realized, well, this is what we wanted. But it was a big price to pay.' For now, though, Ollie remained with Kate.

The Portley Club

The timing could have been better as Ollie had only recently moved his family into a substantial property in Wimbledon's Ellerton Road. Gate House very much reflected its owner, with its military and hunting prints on the walls, Ollie's growing collection of antique flintlocks, and of course a well-stocked bar. The property also had several balconies and Oliver wasn't averse, at some risk to himself, to leaping down from one to the other, or so he boasted to a reporter.

Back in England after his second stint in the army, David, together with Muriel, had moved into a house nearby and the two brothers rekindled something of the close friendship they'd shared as children and young men about town. One evening Ollie came round and saw a moggy leap across the lounge and out of the door. 'Oh, you've got a cat?'

'Yes,' said David.

'So have I,' replied Ollie. There was a slight pause. 'Is yours a good fighter?'

'Quite honestly, I don't know,' said David.

'Mine's a very good fighter,' insisted Ollie, and rushed round to Gate House to fetch it.

The thing was called Pudding and after the furniture had been rearranged to create some kind of fighting arena the two cats were placed together. 'And Ollie was very disappointed when our cat Twinkle saw Pudding off,' recalls David.

Besides Pudding, Ollie kept two large German shepherds called Scharn and Horst, 'but he never trained them,' says David. 'And they went a bit wild. I think the sixteenth hole of the Royal Wimbledon golf course was just over the fence and one day these dogs escaped and bit the pants off one of the golfers.' When you came to visit Ollie and walked up the driveway, if the dogs were in the garden it was touch and go whether you made it to the front door. In the end both dogs became so unruly that Ollie offered them to the local police force but even they wouldn't take them on.

Gate House backed on to the Common and Oliver often took Mark on long walks or they'd build camps out of dead bracken. And then there were the goblins. 'He had these horrible garden gnomes,' remembers Mark, 'and they'd be hidden and scattered around the garden under rhododendrons and things and he'd say, let's go goblin hunting!' Another game they'd play on the Common was ditch jumping. There was a slope in the middle of the woods and Ollie would pick Mark up after school and he'd jump ditches all the way down. 'I think the idea was to get me as covered in mud as he possibly could. I remember being put in the boot of his car once because I was so dirty and about every ten seconds he'd shout, "Are you OK?" because he was worried about fumes. So it was madness, but it was also care. And it was fun, naughty fun, because you knew you were going to get a bollocking when you got home with your school uniform covered in mud, but God, it was fun.'

It also highlights a strange dichotomy within Oliver. This desire for chaos and misbehaviour co-existed with a fundamental belief in good manners, etiquette and deportment. These he drilled into Mark from an early age. There was the occasion when Mark was going for an interview at a school, and at lunch before meeting the headmaster Oliver noticed that

Mark's nails weren't quite as clean as they could be so gave him some money to 'find a chemist and buy a nail brush'. So there was poor Mark feverishly cleaning his nails over lunch. 'So clean nails, clean shoes, just to be well kept was important. I remember getting lots of bollockings for losing my school cap and him saying, "They don't grow on trees!" It was very much about knowing what was right, table manners, etiquette, manners overall, elocution. I was still being corrected by him when I was twenty years old! Those things were important to him, vastly important. I think he felt it was important that you knew how to be a gentleman. It was as though you had to know all the rules before breaking them. So he could be extremely eloquent, he could be extremely polite, he could be very gentlemanly, and alternatively he could be a complete pain in the arse.'

While at Gate House Ollie continued to drink at his local pubs, and his favourites at this time appear to have been the Dog and Fox and the Castle. Bernie Coleman had taken over the management of the Dog and Fox in the early sixties and Joyce became its indomitable landlady. Ollie adored her and loved drinking at 'the Dog', and the routine was always the same: within minutes of his arrival a large group of people would appear out of nowhere, 'all freeloaders,' says Bernie. 'It was almost like jungle drums and Ollie would buy them all drinks. He always paid for everything. He always had cash on him. It was like monopoly money the way he knocked it out. He was very kind to everyone until somebody tried to get him to have a punch-up, which he never did, certainly not in our pub.' Ollie respected Bernie and Joyce too much to start any aggro, probably because he knew Joyce wouldn't have stood for it. She remembers, 'We used to have a few battle royals, he and I, but I liked him very much. When he was sober he was a lovely, lovely man. But when he was drunk he was a bit naughty.'

George, the landlord over at the Castle, just up the road,

indulged Ollie and his mates and allowed them to drink after hours, in fact any time they wanted. Joyce never put up with that nonsense. 'Sometimes Ollie used to come in and say, "A pint glass, please, Joyce." I'd say, "What do you want a pint glass for?" He said, "I want you to start that end and go all the way along the optics putting some of everything into a pint glass, till it's full." I said, "On your bike, we're not having that here." I mean, if I'd have poured it he'd have drunk it, I've no doubt about that even if it would have killed him. But I didn't want that on my conscience. So we used to have a few battles, but only when he was really drunk. He loved coming to the pub. He should have lived in a pub really.'

There was another occasion when Ollie and eight of his mates had been drinking up at the Castle. It was a Friday night and 'the Dog' was rammed as usual. 'I don't know who dared who,' says Joyce, 'but they came in the front door, Ollie and all these men, totally naked, pushed everybody out of the way, and went down to the end of the bar, where there was a big post, tapped it and then ran out, across the main road, back to the Castle. There was an elderly lady sitting in a chair right by the door and she threw the whole of her drink over the last one's backside and went, "How disgusting that you let people come in here like this, Joyce." I went, "I didn't know anything about it." "Disgusting," she said. "And I hope you're going to replace my drink."'

Joyce could always sense when Oliver had had enough, that one drink that would tip the balance. 'That's enough, Ollie,' she'd shriek. 'You're not having any fights in here or beer thrown all over the place. That's it, out!' And he would always leave, no problem. One night he went to pick up a soda siphon and Joyce said, 'Down!' Oliver had indeed met his match with Joyce, and when she retired in the early eighties he was making a film abroad but still managed to organize a box of roses to be sent to her, along with the message: 'So sorry you're retiring.

You're the only lady that I would never tangle with, because I wouldn't win.'

Bernie and Ollie were close too, often going to big boxing matches at the Royal Albert Hall together. And every Christmas Bernie got Ollie to attend a charity tea dance for the local pensioners, held in the ballroom that was attached to the pub. Ollie would arrive, usually three sheets to the wind, but gladly dance with the old ladies for hours on end. 'He was a remarkable man,' remembers Bernie. 'The saddest thing about him was that he always wanted to drink a lot when he needn't have done. When he wasn't drinking he was the most charming man and tremendous company, you could talk to him about anything. A very, very interesting man to be with.'

In order that he could drink in relative peace, without prying eyes or half of Wimbledon Village turning up, Ollie formed the Portley Club, something he described as his own little 'Bacchanalian society'. The purpose of the Portley Club was, as always with Ollie, to have fun. David was made an honorary member and on occasion Ollie would come round to his house and announce, 'Right, Portley meeting.' This could be at any time of the day or night, 'usually two o'clock in the morning,' says Muriel, bitterly, and one had to obey without question.

It was largely an excuse to get drunk, yet people imagined all manner of wrongdoing and sordid excesses were going on behind closed doors, a reputation that, Simon remembers, no one did much to dispel. 'In fact we would pretend that there was some sort of bacchanalian orgy going on, so much so that David's wife would be outside screaming, "I know you've got women in there!" We created this image of a Hellfire-type club when all it was really was six of us getting wildly pissed and then ordering a Chinese takeaway.'

The Portley Club was a very close-knit thing, the membership consisting of Ollie's closest friends. Perhaps it was an attempt to recreate the male bonding and camaraderie he'd enjoyed in the army. No women were allowed to join. All his life Oliver was to have a strange relationship with women. He was far happier in the company of men. He liked to be with other blokes; women were a rather nice accessory. 'And men almost more than women were like a magnet to him,' says Jacquie. He was perhaps the quintessential man's man.

Another largely male-dominated domain that Ollie gravitated towards was his local rugby club, Rosslyn Park, who played at Roehampton, near Richmond Park. Introduced to the place by Mick Fryer, he became a keen supporter, stumping up something like £10,000 in the early seventies to pay for floodlights which enabled the club to establish the London Floodlit Sevens, a popular tournament which continues to this day. On occasion Oliver would play in the club's B team, as did mates Mick Fryer and Ken Burgess. 'He wasn't very good,' admits Simon. 'He played in the pack. His hand-eye coordination was terrible, so you had to almost plant the ball in his midriff, but then he was difficult to shake off. If he was on a run you wouldn't want to be the guy tackling him because he was immensely strong. Ollie was six foot and his bulk was huge, he had enormous strength.'

It was the earthy humour and lack of bullshit of the people who played the game that Ollie loved, and when he wasn't filming he tried not to miss a match. Some of Mark's earliest memories are sitting in the back of coaches going to away games. 'And on the way back stopping at every pub from wherever they'd been playing, and fifteen fellas getting off to have a pee in the hedge and jumping back on until the next boozer.'

On one memorable occasion Ollie went to Paris with the Rosslyn squad, 'with the idea of drinking a lot and kicking the shit out of each other'. They were all holed up in a hotel, 'passing the time by diving off the wardrobes to see if we could land in the hand-basins', when Kate unexpectedly arrived, hoping perhaps to catch him up to a bit of no good. 'All she found was a load of rugger lads puking their rings up. Fucking marvellous!'

After a few years Oliver was forced to stop playing rugby because insurance companies considered it an unnecessary risk, but he still retained a vested interest in the sport, 'Because a part of rugby is a drink at the bar afterwards.' England international Andrew Ripley was a Rosslyn Park legend, staying with the club his whole career. In 1999 he remembered Oliver in an interview for the *Daily Telegraph*. 'Ollie used to love it down here. He would wander round, get drunk, tell outrageous jokes, occasionally take his clothes off and break a few windows or chairs and nobody would take a blind bit of notice – we'd seen it all before. After a particularly riotous evening a cheque would always arrive promptly the next morning to make good any damage.'

Director John Hough, who worked with Ollie three times in the eighties, heard a tale of when he was making a film in Wales co-starring former American footballer O. J. Simpson. Alas, the money ran out after two weeks and the whole project was shut down, but anyway Ollie and O. J. were drinking in a bar one night and got into an argument about the various merits of American football and rugby and which was the tougher game. 'Suddenly,' says Hough, 'O. J. charged across the room and crashed into Oliver, sending him flying. "That's what it's like in American football." Up came Oliver and charged back and knocked Simpson all across the room. "Well, that's what it's like in rugby." They kept doing it and quickly it got out of hand: they were like two bulls charging against each other.'

Quite unexpectedly this little Welsh fellow, who'd been quietly sipping his pint of beer in the corner, stood up and declared, 'You're spoiling my drink.' 'And with one blow he knocked out O. J. Simpson,' says Hough. 'And with the other blow knocked out Oliver. The film's stuntman, who was supposed to be looking after the two stars and making sure they didn't get into any trouble, jumped in to try and restrain this Welsh guy and he felt his muscles and they were like solid steel. That was one real tough guy.'

Now a household name thanks to his performance as Bill Sikes, Ollie, while he didn't have the pick of the best scripts, was certainly getting his fair share of offers. And none was more potentially career- and life-changing than James Bond. When Sean Connery left the role after 1967's *You Only Live Twice* there was a mildly desperate scramble for a replacement and Oliver's name was bandied about. A popular British movie magazine of the period called *Showtime* even ran a poll, inviting its readers to vote for who they wanted to fill Connery's shoes. The clear winner, beating the likes of Patrick McGoohan and Roger Moore, was Oliver Reed. When informed by the magazine, Ollie thanked the readers but stated no desire to tackle 007. He also revealed that he had been an original candidate for the Bond role back in late 1961, not long after Hammer's *The Curse of the Werewolf*. 'But I was too young. When Harry Saltzman started his 007 search, I was twenty-two. He had me in mind for some time; spent ages trying methods of making me look older!' Are we to believe this story, or was Ollie talking complete balderdash to the reporter from *Showtime*?

How seriously Oliver was considered as the successor to Sean Connery is open to conjecture; certainly he wasn't on the final shortlist of five actors who were officially screen-tested, out of whom George Lazenby eventually emerged. The reason for his omission from the 007 race seems to have been the producers' concern about his growing reputation as a bad boy. Albert R. Broccoli went on record years later to explain that with Lazenby they had a complete unknown whom they could mould into the persona of James Bond, but with Ollie there was more baggage. 'I think maybe they were a bit worried that the image wasn't right,' says Simon, 'because by then there had been a few negative stories and the producers went, I don't think so. But it made sense to me because I always thought Ollie was going to do Bond and he would have been very good. He'd have loved it, too.'

Someone else who thinks Ollie was ideal for Bond is Michael York, who worked with him several times and was a 007 candidate himself in the early seventies. 'Oliver would have been a very good James Bond because he had that class thing that Ian Fleming had and which Sean didn't have at all but made up for in other ways. Oliver would have been a good choice, that dark menace that he trailed around with him, which was so effective in his Bill Sikes, just the way he looked for one thing, and with that scar that added to the menace of his features.' That scar may very well have been one of the reasons why Ollie was a candidate. In one of the few descriptive passages Fleming ever wrote about Bond's physical appearance, from his debut novel *Casino Royale*, is this: 'With the thin vertical scar down his right cheek the general effect was faintly piratical.' A good description of Ollie.

In the end the nearest Oliver ever got to James Bond was being punched in the face by him. Simon tells the story: 'Ollie went to a restaurant with a group of people and George Lazenby – how or why he was there with George Lazenby, God only knows – and someone said, "George is going to be the new James Bond," and Ollie went, "James Bond, don't make me fucking laugh." I think something like that might have happened. Anyway, Ollie then turned round to the girl he was talking to and Lazenby got up and gave him the biggest right hook and Ollie went smack on the ground, because his jaw was slack, he wasn't prepared for it, and Lazenby ran out of the restaurant.' The next thing it was in the *News of the World*, a huge headline, '007 KO's Oliver Reed'. Normally Ollie never gave a damn what was written in the press about him, but this was different. 'Because it was unjust,' believes Simon. 'Here was this bloke who had taken a pot shot at him, run away, and suddenly he's KO'ed him. Oliver was so angry about that.'

Having lost out on Bond, Ollie was approached by Basil Dearden, who'd directed him all those years before in *The League of Gentlemen*, with the chance to star in a sparkling adventure yarn, with a twist of black comedy, called *The Assassination Bureau*. Based on an unfinished novel by Jack London, the film has the fascinating premise of a secret organization that accepts commissions to assassinate people, but only those the members of the Bureau consider deserve to die. Ollie had great fun playing its leader – 'It gave me a chance to play for the first time a dashing, elegant David Niven-type of part' – and he delivers an engaging and self-aware performance. His scenes with co-star Diana Rigg, fresh from television's *The Avengers*, are a delight, even though, according to Oliver's daughter Sarah, 'They didn't get on at all. A strong woman, you see.'

Next Oliver went back to work for Michael Winner. At first the pair were to make an ambitious epic based on the life of William the Conqueror with Ollie in the title role. Alas, the project died when it became clear that the budget would be an unfeasible twelve million dollars. Having turned down the chance to direct *The Prime of Miss Jean Brodie*, Winner was narked, to say the least, but he had another idea up his sleeve.

Hannibal Brooks is a wartime drama with a difference. Ollie plays a prisoner of war working in Munich Zoo who escapes with an elephant after a bombing raid and makes a dash for neutral Switzerland. It was shot in the summer of 1968 on location in Austria, where Ollie's antics found little favour with the local inhabitants, especially when he tore down the national flag from outside the crew's hotel after a drunken binge and urinated on it. Winner was forced to apologize in order to restore the townsfolk's goodwill towards the production. 'We endlessly had to make new hotel arrangements,' he remembers.

'Oliver would throw bags of flour over guests in the dining room, switch shoes outside people's doors. No hotel wanted him for a second night.'

As the Second World War's most unlikely resistance fighter Winner had cast Michael J. Pollard, a hot property after his appearance in *Bonnie and Clyde*. At the time Pollard had a heavy drug problem and Norse remembers Ollie telling him that the American actor was 'a complete headbanger. Doing *Hannibal Brooks*, the guy was out of his skull most of the time.'

Winner even confronted Pollard about it on the set one day. 'You've got a great career ahead of you. Why do you take so many drugs?'

Pollard looked Winner full in the face and told him, 'You don't have to be in a hotel with Oliver Reed.'

'You just won the argument,' replied Winner, who had just one policy when shooting on location with Oliver: 'Never put me in the same hotel.'

Ollie's other co-star in the film was several tons of elephant, two in fact, according to Jacquie, who visited the set. 'And one of them hated Oliver and there was nothing he could do about it, while the other one absolutely adored him. They had this wonderful relationship.' Understandably that's the one they ended up using the most, while the other elephant was employed just for long-distance shots or to give its partner a break. Winner recalls that it was this elephant that always tried its level best to kill Ollie. One scene had them both walking along a narrow mountain path with a two-thousand-foot sheer drop on one side and hard rock on the other, and the elephant tried to either squash Oliver against the rock or flip him over the edge with his heavy tail.

For three nights Oliver insisted on sleeping with his favourite elephant to build up an even greater rapport. Winner wasn't impressed. 'Oliver, the elephant won't give a fuck that you're sleeping with it.' The animal's handler arrived one morning in its stables to see Ollie fast asleep between its giant feet. Often during breaks in filming they'd play together, the elephant sucking up stones with its trunk to use it as a giant peashooter; and whenever they were near water Ollie always got a soaking. If Ollie rubbed up against her and whispered things in her ear, it did appear that she was not only listening but responsive. It was an extraordinary attachment between two living things. 'And I can honestly say when the film was over that elephant cried when it was being led away,' says Jacquie.

Women in Love

It was after a conversation with his father, during which Peter strongly advised his son to get someone to look after his business affairs properly, that Oliver made the decision to ask his elder brother David to be his manager. David, who since leaving the army had been working in radio, happily agreed. 'My job was contracts, looking after money, organizing things, that sort of stuff.' It did seem a perfect arrangement, for after all Oliver trusted his brother implicitly and knew he'd always have his best interests at heart. 'Also from our point of view it went back to our childhood, when it was just me and Ollie against the older generation who were creating all the trouble.'

David immediately got into Ollie's good books by reclaiming a bundle of money he'd been owed. Back in the mid-sixties, when Pat Larthe was still his agent, Ollie had employed his voice in the very first Hamlet cigar commercials: 'Happiness is a cigar called Hamlet, the mild cigar from Benson and Hedges.' These ads, with their signature Bach music, had been running for years in cinemas and on television, yet Ollie had received not a bean. David paid a visit to Pat Larthe to sort things out and eventually managed to secure a large, and long overdue, payment.

The next task faced by David was to raise his brother's public profile. Yes, Ollie had been doing very nicely, appearing in a steady stream of movies in featured roles, but had yet to reach the same kind of levels of exposure and recognition as other contemporary British film stars like Michael Caine, Sean Connery and Richard Harris. So that was the plan, to get him jostling with the big boys. Again, keeping things in the family, David brought in Simon to be Ollie's publicist. Simon had been working in BBC Radio's sports department for a year but had left. 'So I was looking around, wondering what to do, feeling pretty down on life, then David said would I be Ollie's press agent as I had a background in journalism. It was the start of an amazing period.'

Working from an office near Piccadilly, David and Simon set about making Oliver even better known. 'So we engineered stories to bring him to the public's notice,' confesses David. 'And he started being mentioned in the papers. Reporters called him "Ollie" quite quickly. "Dear old Ollie", "Ollie's at it again", the headlines were always Ollie this or Ollie that.' With the gossip columns growing in popularity, it was the perfect time for such a strategy, so Simon didn't find it too difficult getting Oliver press attention. But there was a mighty price to pay for it later on. 'In a way, the hell-raising was part of Ollie's natural personality and character,' says David. 'But he then played on it when he saw it got a reaction. Gradually too the press built on stories of Ollie's excessiveness and I think in the end he embellished what was already there and it began to build up; it was self-generating.' In the end it became a millstone round his neck. 'If I took him to an interview for TV or whatever he always felt he had to do something extraordinary,' says David. Ollie always used to say, let them know you were there. 'That was Ollie really,' says Simon. 'Wherever he was he felt he had to make an impact.'

To some extent Oliver had it easy with the press. Imagine what it would have been like in the news-saturated twenty-first century. 'My God, they'd be around his house the whole time,' laughs Simon. 'They wouldn't need to go anywhere else.' Back then people like Ollie, and also the likes of Burton and Harris, had a much closer and friendlier relationship with journalists and as a result some of their indiscretions were not made public, or with Oliver the general tone of the reporting was, there's Ollie, what a lad. 'Whereas the reality of some of his behaviour was pretty gruesome,' says Simon. 'And the trouble with the press now, they'd have got into the gruesome bits, so Ollie was quite fortunate in the early days.'

Oliver was still on location in Austria for *Hannibal Brooks* when Ken Russell suddenly showed up. Packed in the director's suitcase was a copy of D. H. Lawrence's novel *Women in Love*, which on publication in 1920 caused a storm of controversy because of its sexual explicitness. 'Care to read it, Oliver?' He didn't much, so Russell instead sat him down and went through the entire story, acting out the parts. 'Interested?'

'Sure,' said Oliver.

'There's just one thing, though. I haven't got any money, so you will have to take a percentage.'

'Tell you what,' said Ollie. 'If we can climb up and reach the sun at the top of this mountain, I'll do it.'

Up they went. It was a bloody great mountain and about halfway Ollie came to regret his show of bravado. Russell wasn't enjoying himself much either, wheezing and panting as if he was about to keel over at any moment. Finally Russell took his purple velvet coat off and threw it to the ground. 'I'm not budging another inch,' he announced. It was up to Ollie now, and on he went trudging through glacial snow that reached his kneecaps. When the ascent grew steeper and conditions worsened, 'suddenly, I was frightened'. He turned back and it took three hours to return to the bottom, where he joined Russell for a refreshing schnapps in the hotel bar. 'Sod it, I'll do it anyway.'

Oliver was not Russell's first choice for the role of Gerald Crich, the repressed homosexual son of a Midlands mining magnate; Michael Caine was. When that didn't work out, Russell turned to Oliver, and although it now seems obvious casting it wasn't seen as such by many at the time. Eleanor Bron, playing one of Crich's aristocratic friends, Hermione, was mystified when she first heard that Oliver had got the part. 'My sense that he was miscast may have been based on the fact that he was dark-haired and that Gerald, in my imagining at least, was blond.' She's right: Lawrence describes Crich in the book as 'fair haired' and a 'sun-tanned type'. However, the following passage about Crich's appearance, seen through the eyes of Gudrun, Glenda Jackson's character, may well have persuaded Russell to cast Oliver: 'His gleaming beauty, maleness, like a young, good-humoured, smiling wolf, did not blind her to the significant, sinister stillness in his bearing, the lurking danger of his unsubdued temper.' That's Oliver down to a T.

A highly intelligent actress and light comedienne, Eleanor found herself changing her mind about Ollie as filming began. 'Fortunately, whoever cast Oliver was infinitely more discerning than me. Oliver's performance, I thought, was great, because he conveyed a man who seemed locked in, inarticulate, and prey to mighty passions. A haunted soul unable to express himself. I don't know if Oliver was like that himself, but he certainly understood it. I do think the film is wonderful, based on a script that was so faithful to Lawrence's novel, that is to say, retaining a combination of splendour and absurdity.' It was perhaps those two elements that first attracted Russell to the material, or maybe made him the ideal director for it.

Cast opposite Oliver was Alan Bates, who by the late sixties was one of Britain's most critically lauded actors. In turn sensitive and poetic, then unfeeling and cruel, Bates's character Rupert Birkin also has the hots for Gerald, but this homosexual subtext isn't laboured upon by Russell, so audiences back in

1969 largely missed the elephant in the room. *Women in Love* is notorious for cinema's first-ever full-frontal male nude scene, when Gerald and Rupert undress for a bit of indoor wrestling and go at it hammer and tongs. Both Oliver and Bates were understandably nervous about doing it. 'I was scared stiff,' Ollie admitted. 'And that's definitely not the right word, as anyone who has seen the film will confirm.'

This piece of cinema history, however, may very well have turned out completely differently had it not been for Jacquie. One night Ollie appeared at her flat with the news that Russell had changed the location of the wrestling scene from inside to a meadow by a river at night. 'That's an absolute travesty,' said Jacquie, a fan of the book. 'The most beautiful thing about that wrestling scene is that there's guilt attached to it. There's a library with a fire burning and they both go in and in the book they lock the door, which means they want to be alone. Now, if Ken doesn't do that, the whole film's going to be ruined.'

Ollie grabbed Jacquie's hand. 'Right, come with me.'

Ken was enjoying a quiet romantic dinner with his wife Shirley at his London home when there was an almighty hammering on the door, 'as if all the gods of retribution had finally caught up with me'. Should he ignore it? wondered Russell. 'I know you're in there!' Those dulcet tones were unmistakable. 'I saw your poofy candles through your poofy lace curtains.' It was worse than the gods of retribution, it was Ollie. 'If you don't open up, Jesus [Ollie had taken to calling Russell 'Jesus' because of his long, unkempt hair and preference for sandals], I'll kick your poofy purple front door down!' There he stood outside, resplendent in a black tuxedo and bow tie, with Jacquie. Russell invited both of them inside. 'Jacquie's got something to say to you,' said Ollie.

'Well, I've got nothing to say to her,' replied Russell.

'You're going to bloody listen,' stormed Ollie.

'So I went in really quite heavy,' Jacquie recalls. 'I said,

173

"I think this is going to be the most terrible thing you ever do," and I went into my reasoning. "There, I've had my say and I want to go home now." But Ollie wouldn't let me leave.' He wanted his bare buttocks rubbing against trophies and rhino heads in a posh manor house, manly stuff, not daffodils and daisies. Russell was trying to explain that the whole thing worked better outside, 'When suddenly I was hurtling through the air in a Japanese wrestling throw and crashed to the ground.' It was a most persuasive argument on Ollie's part.

Two days later the phone rang in Jacquie's flat. It was Ollie. 'You've won.'

'What do you mean, I've won?'

'Ken's going to do the nude scene as it is in the book.'

But, as the fateful day drew closer, Russell suspected that his two stars were beginning to have second thoughts. 'Oliver said he'd sprained his ankle and Alan said he had a dose of flu. Both of them said they had doctor's certificates to prove their illness. Oh yeah, I thought, because they'd just done one scene perfectly without limping or coughing.' Ollie confronted Russell, telling him he wasn't going to risk permanent damage to himself just to excite a few birds who hadn't had it yet and a lot of frustrated old spinsters who never would. Then, much to Russell's surprise, the next morning both men turned up on the set in their dressing gowns, ready to go. It was a miracle cure.

In truth, a little Dutch courage had been the saviour. On the morning of the shoot Ollie knocked up the landlord of his local and bought two bottles of vodka. Arriving at Bates's caravan, he saw an actor looking as if he hadn't slept all night, which he probably hadn't. 'How do you feel?' he asked.

'Bloody terrified,' replied Bates.

'Drink some of this,' said Ollie, and they polished off a bottle each.

Oscar-winning cameraman Billy Williams still vividly remembers the moment Reed and Bates walked on to that set for the first time. 'When they stripped off to begin the scene Alan was very cool and collected and Ollie was making a big deal of the whole issue. He said, "Oh, he's got a bigger donger." And we were all falling about laughing. And they sort of sized each other up and then Ollie disappeared into the corner and said, "I'm going to have a quick Jodrell." I suppose he wanted to give nature a helping hand. Then he'd come back for the take. And then we'd have a break and Ollie would say, "I'll have another quick Jodrell," and go off to the corner again. It was fooling around, of course.'

All the time the continuity girl, sitting on a low stool, had a bird's-eye view of Ollie's cock. Giving it a towelling down between takes, he noticed her watching him with ever mounting interest. She broke out in embarrassment when Ollie returned her gaze and went even redder when he suggested she fetch a ruler to measure it, 'Just for continuity, of course.'

The whole scene took three days to complete and was filmed in a magnificent room with a vaulted ceiling at Elvaston Castle in Derbyshire. 'It had this enormous fireplace,' Williams recalls. 'And Ken agreed that we should shoot using the real fire, but it was so hot you could barely stand near it. I recall we shot it with two hand-held Arriflex cameras because we wanted the flexibility of being able to follow the actors. The wrestling took place on this huge rug and all the protection they had was a rubber underlay, so they were risking life and limb in front of this blazing fire and getting very close to it at times. But both Ollie and Alan just entered into it with no holds barred.' By the end Ollie had severe bruising from landing sometimes on the hard stone floor and Bates had dislocated a thumb.

It's difficult today to appreciate just what impact that sequence had on audiences when *Women in Love* opened in the spring of 1969. It was a watershed moment, though now, of course, it's terribly tame, quaint even. Russell described how a friend of his went to see the film in the nineties at a revival screening in a small English town. He was the only person in the auditorium save for two old dears in front of him. When Reed and Bates stripped off and started throwing each other round the room one of the pensioners said to the other, 'Nice carpet.'

Predictably, Catholic countries gave the film short shrift. Italy banned it completely. 'Russell and I were warned that if we ever set foot in the country, we would be arrested as pornographers,' revealed Ollie. A bit harsh from the country that popularized fascism. In some South American countries the wrestling scene was deleted altogether. Audiences saw our Ollie lock the door, both actors undress, and then a vicious jump-cut had them clinched in a sweaty, naked embrace on the floor. It became known as the great buggering scene and filled cinemas for months.

Ollie largely relished the honour of becoming the legitimate cinema's first full-frontal male nude. 'It will be something to tell my grandchildren that I was once seen stark naked by millions of women all over the world.' Certainly the scene played a part in turning him into a household name and a bona fide sex symbol, but conversely may also have had a detrimental effect. Oliver's entry in the BFI's *The Encyclopaedia of British Film* says of it: 'The famous nude wrestling scene got so much attention that it tended to obscure the fact that Reed's was one of the finest performances of the decade – any decade really – in a British film.'

Oliver's tackle wasn't the only cause for alarm: his sex scenes with Glenda Jackson were some of the most explicit yet seen in a mainstream film. Gudrun is really the heart, soul and voice of *Women in Love*, and Russell required an actress of remarkable ability to play her. He found Glenda Jackson, attracted by her stage pedigree and striking, if not classical, beauty. She described her own image as 'varicose veins, piano legs and no tits'. *Women In Love* is the story of sisters Ursula (Jenny Linden) and Gudrun, emancipated young women of the twenties. They live in a depressing coal-mining town where Ursula is a schoolteacher and Gudrun a budding sculptress. Gudrun meets and is drawn to Oliver's callous and brutish Gerald, who appears to be the story's strongest character but is in fact the most vulnerable, the most fragile. They begin an affair that is more a test of wills than anything to do with love, and ultimately leads to tragedy.

It's unlikely Oliver had met anyone quite like Glenda before, and the stories and rumours about their fiery relationship continued for years. Their first encounter was at Russell's home during the first script read-through, a fortnight before filming began. When Glenda arrived, Russell whispered, 'You're going to work with an actress from the Royal Shakespeare Company' into Ollie's lughole. 'Oh, jolly good,' he replied.

Looking back at that meeting, Glenda doesn't think Oliver was at all intimidated by her from a personal standpoint. 'I just think he was slightly unsure about people who had come to film from a predominantly theatrical background because it was something that he had not experienced and he presupposed, which is not the case, that people who came from the theatre tended to look down on the cinema or regard film actors as being somehow lesser. So here I was with mostly a theatrical background and I think his first impression was that I would try to put one over on him or be patronizing towards him.'

Once Ollie realized this wasn't going to be the case he did begin to loosen up but would always keep Glenda very much at arm's length, and the feeling was mutual. The sparks certainly flew on screen and each respected the other as an artist, with Glenda especially impressed by Oliver's grasp of film acting. 'He was very secure on a film set, he knew exactly what he was doing, there was absolutely nothing about the technique of filmmaking that he didn't know. He took the job seriously. It was part of his ethos to pretend that he didn't.' However, on a personal level their relationship was non-existent. 'We were like chalk and cheese,' admits Glenda. 'Apart from the script we had nothing to say to each other and no understanding of each other. He was the antithesis of everything I am.' And it didn't take the actress very long to suss all this out. 'It was immediate as far as I was concerned. It was his attitude to women, it was his excessive behaviour, his endless, endless bravura, all of that.'

Not surprisingly, Glenda didn't go out in the evening with Ollie; nor was she ever asked. 'But these stories were always related to me the morning after; people were only too willing to tell you the terrible things he'd done the night before.' Frankly it bored her, this going out and getting drunk. 'It was a very narrow spectrum of life that he was engaged in and from my perspective desperately repetitive; how he liked the same people around him, and he liked the same activities.'

Nor did cameraman Billy Williams indulge, as he'd heard the same stories Glenda had and so refrained from getting involved. 'But whatever happened in the evening, and it was pretty excessive and went on into the early hours, Oliver seemed to be absolutely fine at the beginning of the day and was up for whatever needed to be done.' How he did it amazed everyone. David remembers going out during the first week of shooting to a Chinese restaurant with Ollie and drinking liqueurs all night until both of them were absolutely plastered. 'Ollie was required early on set the next morning and he got up, went over to the washbasin in the hotel suite, and just put cold water over his face, shook his head, looked at the mirror, and said, "Right, how's that?" And he was ready to go. How he did it, I don't know. I came back shattered.'

Ollie's powers of recovery were one of the marvels of the age. He was never late on set. And whatever he had to do he was always prepared. 'He prided himself on his professionalism,' says Mark. 'He would turn up knowing his lines, he knew what was required of him, he would do the job, and then he would piss off back to his local pub.'

It was Oliver's sheer professionalism that Williams recalls most fondly, that however extreme the conditions or arduous the task, Ollie jumped in with two feet, no questions asked. Take the sequence in *Women in Love* where a young couple drown in a lake and Ollie's Gerald leaps into the cold water in a desperate attempt to find them. That shot had to be done at what filmmakers call the 'magic hour', the final ten minutes of daylight before darkness falls, because there were rowing boats with Chinese lanterns creating an atmospheric effect. 'With this being so long and complex it took three evenings to shoot it,' says Williams, 'which meant that Ollie had to dive into the lake dozens of times and go underwater and it was freezing, yet he didn't complain a bit, he was magnificent. He just got on with whatever he needed to do.'

That went for the location shooting in Switzerland, too, which formed the film's dramatic climax. Driven to utter despair, Gerald almost throttles Gudrun before walking off alone into the snowy wastes. 'Ollie was so brave about that because it was very arduous,' remembers Williams. 'We were underneath the Matterhorn, it was very deep snow, it was quite a long sequence, and he walks a long way. And of course it could only be done in one take because there was no hope of ever doing another one. Everything was perfect, the lights, the camera, the performance, it was a great moment.'

One cannot emphasize enough just how important Ken Russell was to Oliver's career. Both had found they worked together well on the BBC films but *Women in Love* was different: it was a major movie, much anticipated, so the stakes were high. 'Ken had a marvellous relationship with Oliver,' recalls Williams. 'They were like brothers really. They had many similarities, temperamentally. They understood each other. Ollie had a lot of confidence in Ken and was prepared to give whatever Ken wanted.'

Glenda also recognized this, that Oliver put himself

completely into the hands of Russell. 'They were very, very close, on a level of genuine affection. It was something about Oliver's wildness and physical willingness to be in danger, or to endanger, that I think Ken liked. But there was real affection and real respect, I think, on both sides. Oliver would have done anything for Ken, absolutely anything.'

With the film a huge international success, the cast were flown over for the Paris opening and stayed at the prestigious hotel where Oscar Wilde ended his days. When Ollie arrived he was informed that he wasn't staying in the actual building but the annexe. 'No I'm not. I'm staying here,' he blasted and sat down in the middle of reception and started drinking champagne.

The manager arrived. 'Will you please desist from bedding down here for the night, monsieur.'

'Look, mush, if this hotel was good enough for Oscar Wilde to die in, it's certainly good enough for me to sleep in.' A room was eventually found.

Walking up the grand staircase, Ollie spotted the film's associate producer, Roy Baird, up ahead. Manhandling him from behind, Ollie pulled down the guy's trousers, causing him to fall backwards a few steps. Like a big soppy dog he bounded down after him and started landing soggy wet kisses on each cheek. Only then did he discover that the man wasn't Roy Baird at all but a lookalike, a lookalike who just happened to be an important French businessman. He tried to explain that he hadn't pulled down the gentleman's trousers because he fancied him, but this proved rather difficult as he knew not one word of French. Suddenly the real Roy Baird walked in and Ollie gesticulated frantically that this was the man he'd mistaken him for. The businessman finally twigged and broke into laughter.

After the premiere Ollie got really quite dreadfully pissed and, while being driven back to his hotel by Bates and his fiancée Victoria Ward, started to sing bawdy rugby songs. Bates took great offence to this – 'Not in front of my fiancée, Ollie, if you don't mind' – and in the end chucked him out into the street. 'So I ended up singing to a crate of horses' heads in the market.'

Fame

The success of *Women in Love* radically influenced the way critics and the public viewed Oliver Reed. With his performance as Gerald Crich, full of subtlety and hidden depths, he broke real ground as a leading man. It also shot him into the top rank of British stars. He continued to drink in his local Wimbledon pubs but Mick Monks for one noticed a definite change. 'The pressure was starting to build, there were a lot of people starting to get at him, wanting to exploit him. And sometimes he couldn't walk into a bar because he used to get mobbed by the girls.' He had become something of a pin-up, much to his surprise and often embarrassment, and described his sex appeal as 'looking like a Bedford truck but somehow unconsciously giving the promise of having a V8 engine'.

Of course, as he was a permanent fixture in the village hostelries the press always knew exactly where to find Ollie and he started to get regularly stalked by journalists hoping for an interview or a report of some misdemeanour. As much as possible Ollie liked to talk to the press on home turf: his local. Simon had arranged for a well-known Japanese journalist to meet him at the Hand in Hand for an extensive interview. Mick Monks remembers this diminutive woman walking in. 'She was about five foot one and six stone, soaking wet, just a little slip of a thing.' Ollie, with a wide grin on his chops, told her,

'We have this old tradition in England, if you're interviewing me we always have three pints before the sun goes over the yardarm,' or some such bollocks. 'Anyway,' recalls Monks, 'she managed to down the first one, but was struggling through the second one, so the boys decided she'd better not fall over too early, so we took her to the Common for the pissnic. Over there she had about four shots of hard liquor and was in a terrible state; she started giving Ollie a foot massage on his back. The interview had gone completely out of the window. It was an absolute hoot. But being the gentleman he was, Ollie got her a cab back to her hotel and the next day he turned up and she got the best interview she'd ever had.'

On another occasion Ollie horrified a lady reporter during an interview by donning a Dracula cape and leaping about the roof of Gate House. Barry Norman, who once wrote that he 'looks like the kind of man who might be rather nasty when drunk or even, if given provocation, when sober', was showbiz reporter for the *Daily Mail* before his move to television and recalls one memorable encounter with Ollie at his house. It was only about eleven o'clock in the morning but he was well into the beer by the time Norman arrived. Journalists who visited Ollie were invariably plied with unhealthy amounts of drink and staggered home after the encounter with the battle scars of a war correspondent. 'We did the interview and then he suggested that we go off and box each other. At that point I made an excuse and left because he was in much better shape than I was and I wasn't about to be knocked around by him.'

All this fame and press attention did not cut any mustard with Peter: still the son couldn't win his father's admiration. Relations between Oliver and Peter over the past few years had been cordial but hardly close, although Ollie had bought him a house in Epsom, near the racecourse, which he shared with Kay.

Peter had observed Ollie's ascent to stardom with

indifference. He hadn't been against his son becoming an actor, what with Sir Carol and Herbert Beerbohm Tree part of the profession, but in a warped imitation of his disgust at his son winning all those sports day trophies at school, he couldn't bring himself to celebrate Oliver's achievements as an actor. 'He did see Ollie's films when they came to the local cinema,' says Simon. 'But he wouldn't have told Ollie. I'm sure my father was proud of him but he just didn't show it.' Simon can't recall an instance of Peter complimenting his son on a particular film or performance. Not that it didn't happen; Simon just never saw it. And with so much of a child's achieving things being a desire to share that success and impress their parents, it was perfectly natural for Oliver to have wanted some form of recognition from his father. 'But Pete would almost deliberately not give it,' says Simon.

As for Oliver's mother, Marcia, she was an even more remote figure in his life. 'She was out on a limb,' reveals David. 'But Marcia was very, very proud of him, at a distance. But really she didn't have anything to do with him.'

To cash in on his new-found stardom Ollie did a couple of quick, throwaway movies. *Take a Girl Like You* is a sweetly nostalgic, and by today's standards terribly innocent, sex comedy based on a 1960 Kingsley Amis novel and directed by Jonathan Miller. Hayley Mills plays a virginal young primary-school teacher determined to hold on to her virtue at all costs, a situation that comes under threat when she meets Oliver's womanizing rogue. Playing Ollie's best mate in the film was Noel Harrison, son of Rex and still best known for his performance of 'Windmills of Your Mind' from the 1968 film *The Thomas Crown Affair*. Noel got quite close to Ollie during the filming and they often lunched together in the Pinewood restaurant, 'at which we would usually drink a bottle of wine each, if my memory is to be trusted. A most enjoyable man. We thought we held our liquor well, but I think you might be able to tell which scenes were shot before lunch and which scenes were shot after.'

From the rather unglamorous locations of *Take a Girl Like You* (Slough in Berkshire), Ollie flew to the south of France to appear in the bizarrely titled *The Lady in the Car with Glasses and a Gun*. He plays the boss of a Parisian advertising agency whose English secretary discovers a body in the boot of his car – cue an intriguing and stylish, if not wholly satisfying, thriller that someone like Claude Chabrol would have made better use of.

The film teamed Ollie with Samantha Eggar, his old friend and playmate from his childhood days at Bledlow. It was a reunion, however, not entirely enjoyed by Samantha. Awoken one night by Oliver and his friends having a noisy booze-up in the hotel bar, she complained to the hotel manager, who went to confront Ollie. 'Listen,' said Ollie. 'I've got five friends staying at this hotel on my account and a very large bar bill. Miss Eggar is here by herself, and with a very small bar bill. So who's right?' The manager recognized the logic of what was being said to him and Ollie's party was allowed to progress well into the night. The next morning Samantha moved to another hotel.

Being the owner of one of the most recognizable faces in Britain did have repercussions for Oliver, and also for his son. Ollie often used to take Mark to the local swimming pool, but when people started asking for autographs and hassling him they had to stop going. 'It suddenly creeps up on you, fame, and it starts to restrict what you want to do,' says Mark. 'I remember times when people were asking for him to sign things or pose for a photograph, and generally speaking he was very good at doing that, but there were times when you could see he was becoming very irritated, especially after you've had fifty people asking, can you stand next to so and so? I remember him once saying, "I'm not a fucking parrot. What do you want me to do, stand on your fucking shoulder? Leave me alone."'

From an early age Mark lived with not only his father's fame but the inevitable repercussions his profession entailed. Whenever Ollie's mug popped up on television Mark assumed that everybody's daddy appeared on television. However, it didn't take him long to realize that things were indeed very different in his household compared with other families. 'And in some ways I relished the idea of having normal parents, because there was probably a bit more stability in that. He was around a lot and then he wasn't around, he was off working, so there would be long periods of time when you didn't see him at all. But you just got used to it because that's the way it was.'

Mark knew the reason for his father's absences from home. He remembers wandering around the sets of *Oliver!*, in the Georgian square, and peeking into doorways and seeing bits of striped wallpaper and nothing else. No, it wasn't Ollie's job as an actor that caused most of the problems, it was what Mark had to deal with as Ollie's son. 'It was pretty tough for Mark growing up,' says Simon. 'It was tough in a way being Ollie's brother, I had some shit along the way, but being Ollie's son, yeah, there'd be some good times but also there were horrendous times. The way Ollie treated him sometimes was just horrible.'

Take sport: every father wants their son to do well, but for Ollie it was never about the taking part, it was about winning, and winning at all costs, exactly as he'd done. 'I think he desperately wanted Mark to be a real sportsman and play cricket and rugby for England,' says his sister Sarah. 'But Mark wasn't a sportsman at all.' David remembers when Oliver bought Mark a horse and put him on it and told him to go around and jump some fences. 'When Mark failed to get this horse to jump, Ollie screamed at him, "You bloody slug." Poor old Mark.' It wasn't enough that Mark tried his best, he had to be the top at everything, and if he wasn't he'd face his father's wrath. 'Oliver was a demanding father,' says Simon. 'He demanded things that Mark couldn't give and Mark knew he couldn't give, that was the problem, and Oliver would sometimes hurl abuse at him: "You're not the boy I wanted!"'

This was a particularly unpleasant trait of Oliver's, that he could be extremely vicious in the way he expressed himself. 'He had quite a tongue on him when he wanted to,' says Sarah. And because he was both articulate and clever he'd use it as a weapon. 'And he would really go for people's Achilles heel. It was spiteful and he knew he'd win with it. And he did that with Mark and myself at times when we were young, which wasn't particularly kind, but he got his point across. Like everyone, we've all got good and bad in us, but when you're that extreme, as Oliver was, the extreme is better and worse in those degrees.'

Perhaps Ollie saw too much of his father in Mark and wanted to purge that out of him, but all he did was create anxiety and the foundation for a fractured relationship that eventually led to long periods when they didn't speak to each other, a horrible echo of the relationship Ollie had with his own father. 'As a child all you want to do is love your parents,' says Mark. 'And there were times when I didn't particularly love him because he was hard and he was hurtful. There's a saying, you always hurt the ones you love. I think that's almost right, but you always hurt the ones who love you, is probably more pertinent and probably more accurate. You wanted it to be good all the time but he could be very awkward. He could be very dark. And the darker side was challenging for the people who did love him. It was difficult. Worse, if you tried to talk to him the next day about something he might have said or done, he'd just shrug it off. "Doesn't matter," was the usual response. "Water under the bridge, let's move on." And often that wasn't as satisfactory a response as you wanted; it didn't make up for the hurt.'

But then there were times when he could be remarkable, using his spellbinding imagination to enrapture and beguile. 'He could create wonder,' says Mark. One morning, when Mark was six or seven, his father woke him up and together they looked out of the window just as the dawn chorus was starting. Ollie began to describe the various conversations that were taking place between that bird and this bird, as it grew into a cacophony. 'It took you as a kid somewhere else and gave you a completely different aspect of what birds making noise meant; suddenly it became something meaningful. So yes, there were times when he could be absolutely awful, and the next minute he was spreading twinkle dust everywhere and he was the most fascinating, wonderful person to be around. It was almost like he made up for the badness. But as a kid you just want things to be fairly straightforward and sane-ish. You're looking for that stability and it was difficult to find that stability.'

Every so often Ollie would fly to LA and spend several weeks with Carol Lynley at her place in Malibu. It was as if he was living a double life; a triple life actually, when you think he was living with Kate and also keeping Jacquie nicely tucked away; both of whom knew nothing about his liaison with the American actress. The time spent with Carol in California must have seemed like another world and another life to him. They'd take walks on the beach, shop in markets, and dine quietly in restaurants just the two of them. And for the most part there were few outbursts of delinquency or rowdiness. Carol says, 'He would misbehave and then he wouldn't for a very long time, and then he'd misbehave again. But when he wasn't playing the bad boy he was very quiet, he liked to read, he liked there to be quiet around the house, he was very easy to get on with.'

Was part of the appeal of these trips for Oliver the opportunity just to relax and unwind, away from the distractions of his life in England, with just Carol and her young daughter? One also senses that Ollie enjoyed the feeling of being part of a 'family' with Carol. Of course, he had a son back home, but he'd always wanted a daughter, and Carol has never forgotten the tenderness and dedication with which he slipped into the role of almost being a surrogate father. 'Ollie helped me raise my daughter when nobody else would [Carol was divorced from her daughter's biological father]. If he felt that I wasn't doing something right, he'd tell me and I always listened to him because he had wonderful instincts about people, especially children. So he was tremendously helpful, because I knew nothing about raising children at all. I was nineteen when I had her. He was very patient with her, made her laugh, he was just wonderful with her.'

Carol knew all about Mark but Oliver rarely spoke about him or other personal matters: he tended to keep such things to himself, which was his way. Carol does remember one occasion when he raised the subject of his relationship with his father, how poor and difficult it had been because of Peter's decision to be a conscientious objector during the war, although she got the feeling that, deep down, 'Ollie did seem to like his father'.

As for Kate or Jacquie, one feels that Ollie never brought them up either, although Carol knew of their existence. Remarkably it didn't bother her that when Oliver left her house it was to fly back to be with another woman. 'I never interfered with whatever he was doing and whoever he was doing it with and he never interfered with me. But when we were together it was wonderful. He did what he wanted to do, when he wanted to do it, and there was no getting around it, there was no point in stamping your foot or pleading with him. There was never any meanness about it, and there was also no game playing, he just did exactly what he wanted to do.'

Such a cavalier attitude about a man she obviously loved is based on Carol's belief that she knew a normal relationship with Oliver was a practical impossibility. This was perfectly demonstrated the time he visited her when she was staying in Beverly Hills. 'We had dinner and on our way back to the hotel he asked me to marry him. I said, "No, Ol, that will never work." And he stopped the car and he got in front of it and said, "I'm not moving until you give me a definite yes." I said, "Oh, now, Ollie!" We got back to my suite and he asked again and I said, "No, Ollie, I don't think so," and he went out to the balcony and he hung by the ledge. "Now will you marry me?" I said, "Yes, yes, Ollie, I will." I got him back into the room and he seemed very proud that he'd gotten me to say yes. I don't think he actually wanted to marry me, it's just that he couldn't stand the fact that anybody said no to him. Or maybe he did want to marry me, I don't know, but I didn't think it would ever have worked.'

Later that same evening Oliver gave Carol some money to go down to the hotel shop to buy the latest issue of *L'Uomo Vogue*, the Italian men's version of *Vogue* magazine; he was on the front cover. 'I left,' says Carol, 'and I just kept on walking. I didn't get the magazine, I kept the money, got in my car, and drove away.'

Seemingly without much concern about the possible consequences, Oliver had also continued to see Jacquie. She'd visited film sets and been introduced to his friends, even family members. David met her first, going round to see her at a flat in Teddington that Ollie had provided for her. 'I was astounded because I'd hardly known she'd existed and in this room she had this shrine of photos of him in this little alcove.' Muriel seems to remember there being candles there too: 'Jacquie worshipped Ollie.' This arrangement made things precarious for David, who every time he was with Kate had to be very careful not to give the game away.

It was at the same flat that Simon remembers first meeting Jacquie. 'I was playing cricket locally and Ollie came to watch and afterwards invited me back to this flat and I could not believe it. I was polite and everything, and Jacquie was really nice. Obviously it was difficult for her, it was a tricky moment.'

Jacquie didn't stay a secret from Kate for long, and when she found out it led to an even frostier atmosphere at home and more blistering rows, but she didn't walk out of the door, and neither did Ollie. That all changed when Jacquie fell pregnant. 'That was the catalyst for Kate,' says Jacquie. 'I mean, God, it must have been awful for her.' It all came to a head at Mark's sports day. Ollie arrived late, having been to the pub, although he still won the fathers' race. And there was Mark with his plimsolls on, ready to run as fast as he could, watching instead the spectacle of his mother and father tearing lumps out of each other. 'I remember by the long-jump pit my mother whacking him round the head with her bag and then dragging me off. We went back to the house to pick up a few belongings and left. And that was that, we went and lived with her mother. You get told that your mum and dad love each other, but they don't necessarily like each other, so it's better if they don't live together any more. As a kid you get on with it, don't you, although the sense of a family unit was never particularly strong because he was away working so much that I didn't often see him, so in a strange way it didn't feel like a great loss.'

Jacquie's pregnancy wasn't exactly planned, even if Oliver kept pleading, 'You don't love me, you won't give me a child.' The thought of having a baby with Ollie gave Jacquie pause. Before taking their relationship to the next level by bringing a new life into the world, she wanted to be reassured that they were doing it for the right reasons. But it was plain to see that Oliver desperately wanted Jacquie to give him a child, preferably a daughter. For years David, who had two daughters of his own, would gently tease his brother about it. 'You know what they say, don't you, Ollie, that you haven't proved yourself a man until you've had a daughter.' And that really got Ollie's goat. So, when Jacquie gave birth to a girl they christened Sarah, he was ecstatic. 'Oliver thought it was the greatest thing ever,' says Jacquie. And once mother and baby were safely asleep Ollie got in his car and drove up to his brother's, arriving there at two o'clock in the morning. 'He knocked on the door,' remembers David, 'and there he was holding a bottle of champagne and a tin of caviar, and proudly announced, "I've done it!"'

Ollie had attended the birth, and indeed was more there than Jacquie, who by the end was knocked out because of complications. Oliver had frantically hunted down a member of staff, yelling, 'She's in labour,' and they replied, 'No, no, no.' He said, 'She really is.' Just then the baby's head appeared and the doctors all went, 'Oh my God!' It was panic stations and in the confusion Ollie was mistaken for one of the medical team and given a gown and a mask and told to get in there. 'As a normal member of the public he shouldn't have been there because it was becoming a problem delivery,' Jacquie recalls. 'So he was there the whole time.'

Devastated by the collapse of her marriage, Kate had much to feel aggrieved about. Hadn't she stood by Oliver during his years as a struggling actor? And now he'd achieved stardom she accused him of dumping her for a 'younger and prettier' model. Ollie blamed the failure of their relationship on the fact that they'd simply been too young and naive, something he'd told her to her face when she first got the marriage licence. They'd been desperately in love, though, and been a well-matched pair. 'People would say they were a beautiful couple,' says Mark. 'They looked right together and indeed for ten years they were right together.' Perhaps it was the concept of marriage itself that Ollie had problems with, in spite of tossing out proposals to the likes of Carol Lynley. It was, he said, an archaic institution, this promising to be faithful to one person for your whole life. 'I can't believe that it's possible to be sure that you'll live up to that vow.' And, as we know, Ollie didn't, couldn't in fact. For him, the sensation of a new love affair 'was more rapacious than my love for Kate'.

In other words, he had a wandering eye. 'Oliver was very

keen on women,' says Simon. 'Even with all that Kate brought to his life, how alluring she was, she was unbelievably sexy. You see, Ollie wasn't a great picker-up of girls when he was on his way up because he wasn't very good at small talk. Put him in a nightclub or a coffee bar, he wasn't great at that. He got better as he got more famous, but what happened was, he'd go on location with very, very attractive women and – well, you know the history – and so suddenly I'd see him around with what was a who's who of actresses.'

Inevitably Kate found out about some of them, as Oliver wasn't exactly coy about what he was getting up to. Sometimes she would receive a call at home from one of these girlfriends and blast down the phone at them, 'Oliver loves me, not you!' How she put up with it for so long is anyone's guess, especially when Oliver himself didn't see his philandering as an issue. 'To me, when I met a pretty woman, it was the natural thing to want to make love to her.'

Some people did find it hard to forgive Ollie his treatment of Kate. Simon was particularly distraught. As a young boy he'd already bestowed hero status upon his brother, which only intensified when he married Kate, this glamorous model who was great fun to be with, who demanded attention and was a great bon viveur, and a little bit wild. 'She left an enormous impression on me.' As a consequence he found it difficult at first to warm to Jacquie, especially since he remained convinced that Ollie's marriage to Kate was not irretrievable. 'It had a lot of bad moments, but was it over? I don't think so. Obviously Jacquie made it over, so there was part of me that couldn't forgive Jacquie for a little while because Kate was my girl. When Ollie did that to her it was tough to deal with.'

Ollie and Kate weren't divorced until 1971. 'He changed the locks on the house,' confirms Simon. 'It wasn't great.' Kate won custody of Mark and claimed 50 per cent of Oliver's estate, after which he reportedly began sawing tables and chairs in half.

The remarkable thing is that after the divorce they stayed in touch, because something strong linked them, and not just the fact they shared a child. 'But she'd come back from having seen him on her own and go, "He drives me mad!"' says Mark. 'So these encounters often ended in further rows. By the early eighties my mother gave up meeting with him altogether as she found him impossible.'

A year or two after the divorce, when Jacquie was living with Oliver, there was a curious incident. Oliver had gone to Italy to do a film and apparently Kate had got herself into a terrible state. 'And because Kate's family obviously loathed me,' Jacquie recalls, 'Kate's sister phoned me up and said, "You'll never guess where Kate is." I said, "I don't know." She said, "She's with Oliver in Italy."' The time came for him to return home and David was about to drive out to the airport. 'I'm coming too,' said Jacquie.

'I don't think it's a good idea,' David told her.

Jacquie stood her ground. 'No, I'm coming.'

So there they were, waiting for the flight to come in, and standing just a few feet away, having already returned, was Kate. 'Oliver came through Customs,' remembers Jacquie, 'paused, and did a double take. I suppose he couldn't believe it. But actually he went and took Kate's arm and went off with her. I'm a little bit feisty at times and I said to David, "They're obviously going to the Dog and Fox. I think we'll go there for a quick drink." And we did, we walked into the bar and they were all there having a good time. Oliver saw me and came over, kissed me on the cheek, and asked how I was. I said I was fine, how was he? He was fine. And then I left. And he came back a few days later. But that's how he was. It wasn't just Kate, he had many liaisons.'

One is left to ponder why Oliver wasn't able just to sever the relationship with Kate and move on. 'No,' says Jacquie. 'He felt that he owed her something. It was the first serious relationship of his life, they had a child quite quickly. I think if Oliver was alive and here today there would still be a huge concern for Kate.'

While Kate was aware of Ollie's affairs, rightly or wrongly she always viewed Jacquie as the person who destroyed her marriage, and never spoke to her again. A proud and strong woman, even though her marriage was at an end, Kate picked herself up and carried on. But she was never to remarry. 'For her certainly he was the love of her life and that relationship was for ever,' says Mark. 'It couldn't be replicated.'

The Devils

The phone rang: it was Ken Russell, and he was planning something sensational. If the noses of prudes had been put out of joint by a naked Ollie, he was going to outrage them even more with masturbating sister superiors and naked, devil-worshipping nuns. Was the world ready for what Russell was going to give them? The answer ended up being a pretty emphatic no.

Aldous Huxley's book *The Devils of Loudun* was published in 1952 and described the supposedly true events of demonic possession and sexual hysteria that took place in the small French town of Loudun in the 1600s; in other words, perfect Russell material. And the director had no qualms whatsoever about Oliver playing the lead role of Father Grandier, the parish priest of Loudun and its spiritual and political figurehead, constantly railing against the state in his bid to keep the town and its people independent. Yet he's also insensitive and vain, preening himself and dropping pregnant lovers like crumbs from his fingers; he was a most unpriest-like priest. Such foibles and the making of political enemies ultimately led to his downfall. Falsely accused of witchcraft, he was tried and executed. A fascinating figure from the margins of history, Grandier was without doubt the most complex and testing role of Oliver's career and he would rise to the challenge magnificently. 'He worked so hard on that role,' remembers Jacquie. 'He did a lot of research on it, he was totally blinkered. He had a lot of dark moments over *The Devils*, he worried a lot about it.'

As filming began at Pinewood in the winter of 1970 rumours quickly reached the outside world of diabolical happenings on Russell's closed set, of orgies and wanton sexual abandonment. 'I admit there was some naughtiness,' Ollie later confessed. 'And quite a few incidents of one kind or the other, mostly the other.' No one, however, was made to perform any act against their will. Right from the off Russell informed the women what would be required of them, namely scenes of flagellation, masturbation and nudity. 'I mean, there were some of those nuns who couldn't wait to strip off,' says actor Murray Melvin. 'And there were some who were petrified.'

Things did indeed get out of hand during the filming of a sequence that is now infamous beyond measure, the rape of Christ. One afternoon Russell brought on to the set a large prop of a naked Christ upon the cross, a very well-endowed naked Christ, and the female extras went bat-fuck crazy over it. God knows what Russell's instructions were to them that day but they all whipped off their clothes and frolicked about with such wantonness that the plaster phallus split and fell off. Not surprisingly the shock value of this scene was too much and the censor ordered its removal.

Oliver wasn't involved in this sequence but one would be forgiven for thinking that, with a dozen naked women writhing all over one another, he might have paid Pinewood a visit that afternoon. It is a suggestion roundly rebuked by Melvin. 'No, no! He was too polite. He wouldn't have embarrassed those performers more than they had to be embarrassed. It was his upbringing, his breeding. That's why he didn't turn up for those scenes. But that was Ollie, that was the Ollie you loved. It was part of his character that people wouldn't dream was there, but it was and it was a very important part of Ollie, it was his whole background.'

The special bond that Russell had cultivated with Oliver over the years was plain for all to see on the set of *The Devils*. 'Ken adored him,' says Murray. 'There was a great rapport between them. And they often got smashed together.' There was the odd barney as well, predictable given their raw emotional states during what was a tough shoot. Russell wanted Oliver to speak Latin in a couple of scenes, reams and reams of the bloody stuff. For someone who didn't do too well at school and was dyslexic, such a task vexed Ollie, so much so that he told associate producer Roy Baird of his intention to quit the film.

'What are you talking about?' said Baird.

'I am not a scholar,' replied Ollie. 'Had I wanted to be a scholar, I would have gone to Cambridge University. The only reason I didn't go there is that I cannot spell, I cannot add up – and I sodding well can't stand Latin. Now I want off this film because I didn't sign to read a script that was full of Latin and you are in breach of my contract. So tell Ken Russell to piss off!'

A compromise was reached: the Latin was drastically reduced. For the bits that remained, however, Ollie came up with a cunning plan, to secrete his lines in the loaf of bread he breaks during communion. It certainly fooled Russell. 'That was absolutely marvellous,' he roared after take one. But on the second take he noticed one of Ollie's eyes peeping open when they should have been shut in prayer. Ollie was ordered to his caravan to learn the lines by heart.

Co-star Brian Murphy saw the volatile and often playful nature of Ollie's relationship with Russell first-hand. 'He was a great practical joker, Oliver, and it seemed to me that he and Ken played games with each other. I remember one particular scene: Oliver had done several takes but Ken wanted more and in the end Ollie stormed off the set. Everything ground to a halt.'

After a short delay, word reached Murphy that his presence was requested in Ollie's dressing room, along with fellow actors Max Adrian and Murray Melvin. They all sat down and Ollie was grinning from ear to ear. 'We'll have a drink in a minute,' he said.

'Have you got something?' Murphy asked.

'No,' Ollie replied. 'But we soon will have.'

There was a knock at the door and an assistant came in with a bottle of champagne. 'This is from Mr Russell,' he announced. 'And when you feel ready for it, Mr Reed, we'll see you back on the set.'

Murphy and the other actors came away from this episode with the belief that Ollie was up to that kind of thing all the time.

Another cause for heated debate was the film's terrifying climax, in which Grandier had all his facial hair removed before being tortured and then burned at the stake. Ollie was fine with his head being shaved, even his legs, 'although it was a bit embarrassing because it made me look like an ostrich', but he drew the line at Russell's suggestion that his eyebrows also had to go. 'God!' raged Ken, his arms gesticulating wildly. 'We might as well not make the film at all.'

'Don't be so bloody silly,' said Oliver. 'It can't make all that much difference.'

This infuriated Russell even more. 'Of course it's important! They shaved off all of Grandier's bodily hair and then stuck red-hot pokers up his arse!'

Ollie finally relented but only on the condition that his eyebrows were insured (by Lloyd's of London, no less) for half a million pounds in case they didn't grow back properly.

The burning climax was gruelling to shoot, not least the preceding torture scene, where Grandier's legs are pulverized with a hammer by a religious maniac. Ollie's legs were protected by huge oak planks but, even so, poor Murray found it hard to take. 'It just went on and on and on, and there was the screaming and the pounding, something went through you, your whole body was saying, we shouldn't be doing this, this is wrong. Then Ken called the lunch break and I went outside and threw up. It was so horrific. And dragging a weak, bruised, battered, cut Ollie on that cart up towards the stake, God!'

According to Murray, the burning finale took three weeks to shoot on the outside lot. 'And it was freezing. Under my suit I had snow boots because you stood still for three weeks, from eight o'clock in the morning until six or seven at night, you just stood still and you froze. It was a toughie.' By the end of it all, Ollie, already minus his eyebrows, was left with virtually no eyelashes either. It was a dangerous stunt with him tied to a stake and the fire was for real. At least he'd been given a safety device to hold behind his back that turned the gas off if he couldn't stand it any more. 'But Ollie,' claims Murray, 'over and above the call of duty, very often on takes didn't turn the gas off and his face was scorched and the eyelashes all went. It was terrifying.'

It's a tour de force, a screaming, manic crowd and Ollie, raging against his persecutors while his face blisters and boils. With Grandier now a charred husk, nothing stands in the way of Loudun's conspirators destroying its walls, and therefore destroying its independence. It was an important shot, and with the explosives in position and the effects crew waiting for Russell's hand signal to set them off, the director grew anxious. Shouting, 'I'm not having this fucked up!', Russell stormed over to the main camera to take charge himself, but alas his frantic arm-waving was taken as the cue and the walls were blown without a single camera rolling. Ten days later, and the set rebuilt, it was second time lucky.

It all sounds ghastly, a real horror show, but Murray's memory of the shoot isn't all funereal. He adored Ollie and the two of them grew close as shooting progressed. He did see, however, two very different sides to his personality, especially in the way he liked to have fun. After work Murray called into the studio bar for a quick Guinness before going home. Ollie was usually there. 'And he was always arm-wrestling with someone. I'd say, "Oh blimey, look, the fifth-formers are at it again." I always thought that Ollie's playing up was a bit of the fifth-formers, a bit of bravado and a bit of boredom. Anyway, he'd get up and say, "Come here, you," and grab my arm. Now there was no way I could physically compete against Ollie, but he dragged me down on the table and he got my arm right back until it began hurting. I looked at his face, all twisted and red, and I said, "Ollie, when you break my arm I don't think Ken is going to be very pleased tomorrow if I arrive in a sling." He immediately let go. "Thank you, Ollie." I got myself away and let them carry on playing and had my Guinness and went.'

Russell was a stickler for punctuality, so at eight o'clock in the morning you had to be at the studio, ready and dressed, and woe betide any stragglers late from lunch and not on set dead on two o'clock. One afternoon Murray was in the Pinewood restaurant with Ollie and, as usual, lunch consisted of a few drinks; certainly it did for Ollie. 'I was lagging behind a bit and Ken was there. Ollie orders another drink and includes me in the order, and I'm saying, "Oh, Ollie, no." "We've got time," he said. After a few minutes I noticed that Ken had got up and was returning to the set. I looked at Ollie. "It's five to two and Ken is going back." Ollie looked up. "Oh God, come on, let's go the back way." And we ran, in hysterics, him slopping his vodka and tonic, me with my white wine. We ran through alleys and corridors and got to the set just as Ken walked on to it. We calmly strolled up to him laughing and Ollie said, "Oh, Ken, when do you want us?" Not a word did Ken say: he knew what we'd done. And Ollie giggled about it all afternoon. He kept saying to me, "It was a good run that, Murray, wasn't it? Do you the world of good." That was fifth-form, but joyous fifth-form. Silly, daft. And he had that in his personality.'

On that movie Ollie cultivated another friendship, with Georgina Hale, a young actress who'd done plenty of television, but *The Devils* was her first feature and she gives a devastating performance as one of Grandier's mistresses. Georgina has an astonishingly erotic voice; she can read Ryanair's safety instructions and make them sound like a page torn out of *Emmanuelle*. She's also refreshingly blunt and still clearly recalls the first time she ever encountered Oliver: 'I remember this stunning face with piercing eyes that just looked straight through you and I thought, what a fabulous-looking guy. I think we had one or two dinner dates. But we never had a love affair, we never had sex, and never went to bed. On those two dates I was waiting for it to happen and it never did. Instantly you think there's something wrong with you, but maybe that was his conscience pricking him: he was with Jacquie, wasn't he? At the end of the day it didn't matter, because I valued his friendship more.'

As with his other leading ladies, Georgina remembers Ollie behaving like nothing less than a gentleman during their love scenes, sensing perhaps her nerves at having to appear full frontal for the first time on camera. 'We rehearsed with our Marks and Sparks dressing gowns on and then when the time came, and, God, I was dreading it, I whipped off mine, and then when Ollie took his off there he was with his big white underpants on, which I thought was so unfair. But he was completely professional, he was wonderful.'

Relations with his main leading lady, however, were rather stand-offish. Failing to land his first choice of Glenda Jackson, Russell had cast Vanessa Redgrave and it didn't take much to get her political juices flowing. When the trade unions decreed a one-day strike in protest at the Conservative government's anti-union legislation, Vanessa and her brother Corin tried to coerce the acting profession to walk off every set and TV studio in Britain in support. Vanessa's primary mission was to get Ollie on board. 'She knocked on my dressing room door looking very pretty,' is how Oliver remembered it. 'And tried to persuade me to "down tools" – I thought she was being personal at first.' When Vanessa made the real purpose of her visit known, Ollie point-blank refused to have anything to do with it. 'That's typical,' she responded. 'You're so selfish.'

'Don't be so bloody silly,' snapped Ollie. 'And stop involving politics in your profession.'

That statement was like a wet haddock across the chops to Vanessa and they had a barnstorming row that lasted ten minutes. Ollie was vehement in his opposition to such a strike, for, as he made clear, the British film industry was in a perilous state already without people like her making it worse. Ollie also had a personal stake in *The Devils*, taking a percentage of the profits rather than a fee. 'So I'm not jeopardizing the film's success and my income by coming out to support a cause I don't believe in anyway.'

After enough brickbats had been lobbed to and fro, Vanessa burst into tears. 'So I put my arms around her,' said Ollie, 'and gave her a cuddle. Then I slapped her on the bottom and sent her back to her own dressing room.'

When *The Devils* opened in July 1971 it was treated like a soiled nappy by the British censor: they held their noses up at it and wanted to dispose of the bloody thing as quickly as possible. Had Russell gone too far this time? Er, yes, and numerous cuts were made to the film, including shots of Redgrave's Sister Jeanne using a charred bone of Grandier as a dildo. What was left after the hatchet job was still without doubt the most savage film ever released in Britain. The US version was even more heavily cut. Ollie lapped up all the controversy, of course, and even challenged famed American critic Judith Crist to face him on a live TV chat show to explain the reason why she thought the film pornographic and disgusting; she refused. Alexander Walker, film critic of the *Evening Standard*, who denounced *The Devils* wonderfully as 'the masturbation fantasies of a Roman Catholic boyhood', did appear with Russell on live TV and got thwacked over the head with a rolled-up newspaper for his trouble.

The media onslaught had its origins in an editorial in the *Daily Express* which called *The Devils* 'the most shocking film of all' and claimed that at the press show two female journalists walked out in disgust. The *Sun* then barged in and labelled it 'filthy, perverted, degrading and vile', while in America reviewers on *New York* magazine couldn't recall in all their broad experience, wading through something like four hundred movies a year, 'a fouler film'.

While Mary Whitehouse foamed at the mouth at the mere thought of her local Odeon screening the film, Russell's monster was banned outright in Ireland and caused chaos in Italy, where the Vatican condemned it as a 'perverted marriage of sex, violence and blasphemy'. Needless to say, after such an endorsement half the country wanted to see it. 'Why this hypocrisy?' Ollie lambasted a frenzied press conference in Venice, where the city's chief magistrate had slapped an embargo on it. 'Why is it permissible to describe historic events in books and plays, but they must not be shown on the screen?' A good point, and outside crowds of students who agreed with him burned an effigy of the civil servant suspended from a lamppost. *The Devils* was eventually allowed to be shown and its success did much to change the rather antiquated Italian laws on cinema censorship. It also resulted in the lifting of the ban that existed on *Women in Love*, which could now be safely released. 'So we had two films running there at the same time,' said Ollie. 'And I got the Silver Mask award [from Italy] for being a pornographer.'

The Devils is an almost unique cinematic experience, by

turns gross, comedic, tragic, dramatic and shocking: quite an achievement. What stands out today when you look at it are two things. First, the sheer beauty of it, the costumes, the make-up, but especially the production design by the then unknown and untried Derek Jarman. And then there is Oliver. 'It is his greatest performance,' says Murray Melvin. 'And seeing it again recently with some of the gang we were all in tears at the end, saying, God, he was brilliant, why the bloody hell isn't he here to see this now, to really appreciate what he did, because in retrospect it's double the performance that it was when he gave it?' Certainly it was an achievement utterly overshadowed by all the controversy surrounding the film. Ollie felt at the time that his performance was slightly compromised by Russell's operatic visuals. 'There was so much going on that it was difficult to make a performance live. The performances got lost in the tirade of masturbation, flagellation and kissing God's feet.'

It's also incomprehensible to learn that Oliver wasn't nominated for a single acting award for *The Devils*. If a top-class actor gave a comparable performance today, as Murray says, 'He would take the world by storm with it. But don't forget, at that time Ken was persona non grata, of course, and so the film was pushed aside, so unfairly.'

The whole experience of making *The Devils* left Oliver physically exhausted and emotionally drained. Working with Russell yelling and screaming in your ear for four months was akin, he said, to parking your backside on a firecracker. Indeed it was tough on both of them, and their relationship took a battering. 'Ken and I finished up very disturbed by the experience. Relations between us had to lie fallow for a while after that.' But they would be back.

205

Master of Broome Hall

Oliver was making a western, his first, out in Spain, called *The Hunting Party*. Most British actors make a pig's ear out of playing cowboys: they just look false, out of place. Not Ollie, who looked perfectly at home in a western setting and thoroughly enjoyed the experience, practising his draw sixty times a day and borrowing his cowboy's accent from a New York hamburger seller he'd overheard. His dark, menacing looks also suited his character, outlaw Frank Calder, leader of a band of rustlers and thieves who kidnap a schoolteacher (Candice Bergen), unaware that she's the wife of a ruthless cattle baron. Played to the hilt by Gene Hackman, the cattle baron mercilessly hunts down the gang and systematically kills them as if he's on some perverse safari.

It sounds nasty and that's exactly what *The Hunting Party* is. Without doubt it's one of the most savage and nihilistic westerns ever made, and again Oliver found himself having to defend one of his films against accusations of violence. 'But it's not nearly as violent as pantomime,' he said. 'Hansel and Gretel for instance!' An interesting argument, but the film is loaded with brutal slayings, mostly in Peckinpah-style slow-mo, and Candice Bergen is repeatedly raped and thrown about like a piece of hand luggage. She did not enjoy the experience, and in her autobiography, published in 1984, revealed that Ollie stayed in his outlaw character off set as well as on, 'brawling drunkenly and flinging plates of food after fleeing waiters'. But most revealing is Candice's memory of Oliver 'presenting me with an ultimatum that he actually delivered straight-faced. Either we had a sexual relationship during the film or we had no relationship at all. Direct contact would abruptly cease and we would speak no further. After I declined his courtly offer, he immediately imposed a vow of silence, speaking to me only when necessary and then through intermediaries, referring to me succinctly as "The Girl" – "Tell The Girl to get off my mark."'

That is a fascinating insight, especially since Jacquie believes Ollie might very well have had an affair with Candice, 'because he was very taken by her'. Whatever the case, his behaviour does beggar belief, the more so as Jacquie had arrived on the set with their one-year-old daughter Sarah with the intention of introducing her to Mark, who was now ten and also out there and knew nothing of her existence, or for that matter Jacquie's. 'I remember my father had a quiet word with me and announced that I had a sister and that she had blue eyes and that her name was Sarah.' What could have been an awkward moment was instead the beginning of a deep and meaningful relationship that has lasted to this day. 'Mark absolutely adored her,' remembers Jacquie. 'He took over, he was definitely the big brother and very protective of Sarah. There was an immediate bond between them.'

It came as no surprise, making a western, that horses were involved and that Ollie was required to look at least reasonably expert in the saddle, so he hooked up with a couple of horse wranglers. His mount in the film was called Archibald and so deep did his affection run for the animal that after the shoot he offered to buy and ship him back to England. Archibald, as it turned out, wasn't for sale, so Ollie decided the next best thing to do was buy or rent one. 'But like a rented woman, a rented horse doesn't give you a good ride. So I bought one.' Ollie was introduced to the showjumper Johnny Kidd, grandson of Lord Beaverbrook and father of future supermodel Jodie Kidd. He and his sister Jane ran a stud farm in Ewhurst in Surrey and believed they had the perfect horse for Ollie. It was an enormous hunter called Dougal, supremely agile and powerful; Ollie had a ride and the horse almost threw him over a gate. Impressed, he wrote out a cheque on the spot.

It was decided to try Dougal at showjumping, but that proved a bit of a disaster since it transpired he had an aversion to coloured poles. Cursing Dougal, Ollie paid a visit to the Dog and Fox and got chatting with Bernie. The idea was arrived at that what Dougal required was his own little bit of land cluttered up with coloured poles so he could get used to them while grazing. Darting across the road to the estate agents, Ollie announced his wish to buy a field.

'What sort of field, sir?' the man asked.

The question temporarily threw Ollie. 'A field with grass in it.'

The estate agent said he'd see what he could do, so Oliver returned to the Dog and Fox and his pint. 'And it seemed like every hour Ollie ran across the road into this estate agent's office,' recalls Bernie. 'Dodging the buses which come around the corner there quite fast.' By the end of the afternoon the estate agent asked Ollie, if this field he wanted had a house in it, would that be OK? and handed him a brochure for a place called Broome Hall, a Grade II-listed stone mansion, some of which dated back to the mid-1700s. Flicking through it, Ollie was delighted that it had a field – sixty-five acres, to be precise. Back at the Dog and Fox Ollie passed Bernie the details. 'This is what I'm going to buy.'

Bernie looked at the brochure incredulously. 'But you only wanted a small bit of land.'

'Well, this is all they had.'

The next morning, nursing a not inconsiderable hangover,

Ollie was driven down to the outskirts of Dorking, along narrow, winding Coldharbour Lane, and soon, there it was: Broome Hall. Magnificent. It was love at first sight and the sale was agreed. Broome Hall was his and would remain so for the next eight tumultuous years.

The purchase of Broome Hall was in many respects an act of madness. Even Ollie's father tried to talk him out of it, and when Simon was first invited there he couldn't quite believe what he was seeing. 'It was a nonsense in many ways. Why would you have sixty bedrooms? I think there was a sense of grandeur about it, going back to Beerbohm Tree and Peter the Great. He loved all that lord of the manor stuff.'

That's certainly how he saw himself and at first he had no intention of sharing it with anybody else, as Jacquie recalls. 'He was going to live there alone, with me and Sarah in Teddington, Kate in Wimbledon, and be the lord of the manor. Then he came to see me one day and said, "I can't manage sixty bedrooms on my own, you'll have to come and join me."' So they moved in, living in a three-floor section of the house. It was stunning with its ancient oak floors and wood panelling, a big, sweeping staircase, beautiful library and six bedrooms. The rest of the house was left pretty much empty.

For the past twenty years Broome Hall had been in the hands of an order of monks called the White Fathers, missionaries in Africa, who used it as their British Novitiate, with sometimes up to a hundred people staying and undergoing training before taking their vows. 'When Ollie took over Broome Hall it wasn't up to scratch at all,' says David. 'It was very derelict, an enormous wreck of a place.' And so it became a labour of love to restore Broome Hall to its former Victorian splendour. 'He employed a whole gang of people and we had them on the payroll for years because there were constant renovations going on.'

These workers weren't local builders or carpenters. Ollie

had come up with the inspired notion of hiring expert film craftsmen usually deployed in decorating and manufacturing film sets, and they revelled in the job. After all, the tragedy of their normal work was that all their fabulous sets were pulled down after a film was finished. Their work at Broome Hall was different: it would last, it was for posterity. And they were a great bunch of people. Jacquie remembers one chap who went by the name of Jack Sparks. 'He was the electrician and he was a little old man and he used to literally crawl under the floorboards doing all the electrics; quite amazing.'

The work did seem to drag on for years, for which Ollie himself must take a portion of the blame. If he was around and up for play it was, 'Right, chaps, no more work today, we're going wine tasting at the winery in Dorking.' Or he'd fancy a quick one down the local. 'Only for a short time, mind you. You've got fucking walls to build.' Instead they'd usually take up residence. 'David used to turn up on a Friday with his briefcase and his little PAYE envelopes to pay the boys,' recalls Mark. 'By which time they'd done no work and they'd been in the pub for a week on the beer.' David recalls that they used to have a van and as the guys became unconscious, one by one they'd be thrown into the back of it and returned to Broome Hall.

It wasn't just the workers whom David paid on a Friday but also Ollie. So reckless was his brother becoming with money that David had taken away his credit cards, because he simply didn't know how to manage them. Instead he received a wad of notes as spending money. But then Ollie would walk into his local bank and say, 'I'd like some money.' Everyone recognized him, his face was his ID, so they'd give him a counter cheque, he'd sign it, and off he'd go.

At the height of the restoration there'd be around twenty people working at Broome Hall six days a week. 'It was colossal the amount he spent,' says Michael Christensen. 'And it wasn't crap. If he put wallpaper up it was William Morris, hand-printed, beautiful stuff, hundreds of pounds a roll, and some of the rooms were enormous.' Ollie also hated plastic with a vengeance, so everything had to be copper; you couldn't have plastic pipes anywhere. If he wandered into one of his greenhouses and saw plastic pots he'd break them all and have them replaced in terracotta, again at huge cost.

The enormous pride Ollie bestowed upon his home had much to do with the history of the place. During the Great War Broome Hall had been used as a military hospital, while in the Second World War the estate was given over to the Canadian special forces, who turned it into their headquarters for secret training, laying down tons of cement on the gravel drive to withstand the weight of tanks. On the parapet of a bridge that spanned a local stream the names of the long-since-departed soldiers had been left in perpetuity. When Ollie saw it was being damaged by the modern tractors that worked on a nearby farm he rescued the stone and placed it at the front of the house. Every Remembrance Sunday he'd pour a bottle of whisky over this monument and salute it.

From the south-facing upper windows the views were spectacular, with wide rolling green pastures and small copses that gave way to trees and fields, and then in the far distance the outline of the South Downs, an unhindered view that stretched some thirty miles. Outside his bedroom window Ollie had installed a searchlight so he could survey the fields at night. 'He was a real bugger with it: "Get off my land!"' remembers Sarah. There was also a huge lake at the bottom of the hill with a small island in the middle and streams with weirs that ran off it. A small, decrepit boat was moored there for special occasions. 'We're sailing to France,' Ollie might sometimes order, and then he and his mates would all go wobbling down to the lake and get in this silly little boat and they'd reach the other end and announce, 'No, we don't like France,' turn around, and row all the way back again.

This kind of madcap, Outward Bound activity was often the norm with Ollie, who treated the grounds like one giant outdoor activity park. There were war games, for instance. Friends would arrive for Sunday lunch in their finery and suddenly find themselves putting boot polish on their faces and screaming around woodland, or split into two parties, one to attack the boat house, the other to defend it, invariably rat-arsed pissed, and tooled up with .303 rifles. Ollie had a whole stack of them which had been decommissioned. Or they'd swim across to the island and hang a chandelier from one of the trees and then review their handiwork from the house. 'How people didn't die I'll never know,' says Mark. 'Because you took very pissed people and they'd jump into this lake in just a pair of underpants, breaking the ice in winter, swim across and back. Anyone who was associated with it will look back and say, those were days of absolute madness. But they were great fun because they were mad, pushing those limits was really where we all were at that time. So it didn't seem mad, but with your sensible head on, thirty-five to forty years later, you look at it and go, wow, that was really quite out there.'

For the most part, though, the grounds of Broome Hall were a great relaxant, and much of Ollie's free time when he was at home was spent pottering around in the garden. He embraced it and loved being amid its sheer splendour. 'He was very traditional,' says Mark. 'He was quite a square individual underneath all of that macho/hell-raising stuff. For example, he had a fascination for bluebells. On Leith Hill, where Broome Hall was, at a certain time of year you had the bluebells coming out, just this lovely carpet of blue, and he just adored all of that. Absolutely loved it.'

When Oliver first arrived the garden was very rundown, there were lawns with grass eighteen inches high and thistles, and he just set to work on it. As head gardener he installed Bill Dobson, a comrade from his Wimbledon days. 'He was just the most loyal person you could ever come across,' remembers Jacquie. 'And he was magic in the garden. Whatever he touched just flourished.' Bill's wife Jenny was a cleaner and so it made perfect sense for her to become Broome Hall's housekeeper and the pair of them lived on the estate. 'They were very normal people,' says Jacquie. 'And Ollie treated them like his own family.' He even taught Jenny how to drive and then insisted on buying her a car. 'No you're not. I'm going to buy my own car. I wouldn't touch a car that you'd given me,' said Jenny, who was Irish and fiery. 'So they cherished their own little bit of independence,' says Jacquie. 'But I think Oliver could have broken up their marriage if Jenny hadn't been as patient as she was, because he was always taking poor old Bill out drinking and when he was delivered back home he wasn't much good to anyone. God, what Bill must have gone through.' Quite a lot over the years, it has to be said.

Not just a drinking companion and gardener, Bill would be roped into all sorts of other activities; Ollie always made him dress up as Father Christmas for Sarah. And Jacquie has never forgotten one of Sarah's birthday parties when the clown they'd hired cancelled at the last minute. 'I thought, what are we going to do? We had Sarah's entire class from school, about forty children. Ollie said, "Don't worry," and he grabbed Bill and said, "We'll be the funny men." And they entertained the children all afternoon doing stupid things like pulling faces, making silly noises, and giving everybody piggyback rides. The kids loved it.'

With Bill's help the grounds began to take shape and Ollie also installed a walled garden with vegetables and fruit trees. 'And rhododendrons like you've never seen in your life,' recalls Jacquie. 'He also built a terrace in front of the house and put in two hundred standard rose trees; when they came out it was just beautiful. In a sense Broome Hall was his little piece of England.'

Maximum Excess

There really wasn't anything else to do but get drunk every night; that's Geraldine Chaplin's recollection. They were in some far-flung place in Denmark and at night she'd accompany Ollie and Reg as they searched for any bar to get sloshed in. Never once did she feel in any danger, that the evening might get out of hand, as both men looked after her as if she was their kid sister. 'Ollie would always protect me. He was a real gentleman, beautiful manners, beautifully brought up. And the drunker he got the better manners he had, I found.' Ollie misbehaved, of course, walking over to tables and demanding people stand up to join him in a chorus of 'God Save the Queen', which rather mystified these simple Danish folk, but there was no menace about it.

Geraldine is a member of an exclusive club because Ollie rarely invited women to join him on his drinking binges. And it was hard liquor, too, which Geraldine matched. 'I drank what Ollie did, what everyone was drinking, and Reg too. Reggie drank an awful lot. Reg was very protective of Ollie. They always had a good time together and Ollie would make fun of Reg and Reg would take it like an adoring dog.' What was most refreshing for Geraldine was how utterly non-showbiz Ollie was. He didn't seem like an actor at all, and never talked shop. Although if somebody came up and wanted to talk to him about movies, then he was happy to do that. 'One night someone congratulated him on his performance in *Women in Love* and afterwards he turned to me and said, "Well, they've all seen it now, there's nothing to hide, they all know what it looks like."'

The barrenness of the location suited the film they were making, *Zero Population Growth*, a rather ponderous and grim science-fiction tale about a future earth where population control is mandatory and children are replaced by android dolls. Directed by Michael Campus, it was an odd choice, one of many Oliver was to make. He was now entering a phase where he was to take films largely on instinct or to pay the bills for Broome Hall, especially when the energy crisis of the early seventies kicked in and the price of oil hit the roof. 'In heating terms alone Broome Hall could not have been too dissimilar to the cost of running a ship of war,' says David. In *Zero Population Growth* Ollie and Geraldine play a couple who defy the law by having a child and are forced to go into hiding. There wasn't much rehearsal beforehand for the two actors to familiarize themselves with each other and the first thing Ollie said to Geraldine when they met at the hotel bar was, 'Look, we're playing man and wife, so we have to get used to touching each other – so let's dance.' And that's what he did. 'He proceeded to grab me and dance in this absolutely bear-like grip and felt me up and down. It was actually very funny.'

In truth, there didn't seem to be very much direction going on at all, at least in the sense of helping the actors shape their performances. In the end Geraldine turned to Oliver. 'He was very generous. Some actors do it all for themselves, but Ollie was so helpful on the set with your performance. He'd take me aside and say, don't do this, do that, try this, much more help than the director. I don't think Ollie clashed with the director but he knew that he was crap basically. That's why he helped me a lot. But he didn't take it out with the director. I never

215

saw him being rude to anyone, unless they didn't stand up and sing "God Save the Queen".'

Some shooting took place in Copenhagen and Carol Lynley flew there to stay with Ollie for a while. One night they were invited to a very grand house for dinner, along with Geraldine and her partner, the Spanish film director Carlos Saura. Usually Carol had nothing to worry about when going out with Oliver. 'He was good company and most of the time he was very quiet. Once in a while he would misbehave and get banned from certain establishments. I remember when he was in New York at this hotel, I think it was the Sheraton, I had to go with him into the dining room because he'd been banned and they wouldn't let him in without somebody to take care of him.' But generally Ollie would be on his best behaviour with Carol. Indeed, the only time she can remember ever really losing it with him was at this dinner in Copenhagen. 'Halfway through the meal for some reason, I guess he'd been drinking, Ollie got up and stood on the table, dropped his trousers, and tied the napkin around his prick. I was so furious. We were thoroughly thrown out of the house; I don't even remember getting to the car it was so quick. And as soon as we got back to the hotel I was just furious at him. But he would do things like that from time to time. I'm still angry at him for doing that.'

As 1971 drew to a close Oliver was in south London shooting the *Get Carter*-inspired thriller *Sitting Target* with Ian McShane and Jill St John. He liked the hard-edged contemporary subject and his role of Harry Lomart, a violent criminal who breaks out of a top-security jail to kill his unfaithful wife. Ollie always attempted to play these kinds of villains – who in lesser hands had a propensity to come across as one-dimensional – as proper rounded human beings, not totally evil. 'They wouldn't be believable if they were only one colour, with no light or shade.' Lomart was no different, and like most men of his ilk, there was a sad, pathetic side to his nature. 'Evil is not, in my view, an abstraction; it is compounded of some very human flaws.' The result is one of Oliver's most brutal and mesmerizing performances.

Director Douglas Hickox came away from the experience full of admiration for Oliver as an actor and for his generosity of spirit. Late one afternoon three young actresses arrived on the set to test for a small role. Although he'd finished his work for the day, Ollie stayed on for two hours to read the lines for them off camera. 'How many other stars would do that?' Hickox asked. 'They would normally just have the director or somebody else do it.'

Carol Lynley remembers being on the London location of *Sitting Target*. Often she would visit Ollie's film sets, something he never reciprocated. 'He was much too egotistical for that. So I would sometimes go and see him when he was working. Mainly it was just keeping him company, he liked to have company.' Nor was Ollie at all supportive of Carol's career as an actress, and she never discussed with him what roles to take or heard a comment or opinion from him about any of her performances. 'I don't think he really thought about it one way or the other. He was very centred on himself, as most actors are. The only thing that he ever asked me about was, did I really sing the song in *The Poseidon Adventure*? Other than that, he was never particularly interested in what I was doing or who I was filming with.'

Since their meeting back in 1966 Carol had watched Oliver progress from a reasonably well-known actor to an international star. He'd never been at all showbizzy, one of the reasons why she liked him so much, but now Carol couldn't help but be impressed by the way Ollie had not allowed fame to change him. 'He was a very moderate person, he never had a big head, never really ordered people about. He made movies and hung out with movie stars on the set, but most of his friends that I met were just regular people. He didn't change at all, except that his clothes got better.' And it would remain so for the rest of his life: the glitz and the glamour of the business, the premieres, the limos, and all that bullshit just wasn't him. 'He didn't need the fame in order to make him complete,' says Mark. He was about as far from being a luvvie as it was possible to get. 'Ollie wasn't a star in the sense that he frequented glitzy parties,' reports David. 'None of that, he didn't go near them. He was a film star only in the sense that people knew who he was and he was rich. He loved to go into a pub and say, right, everyone a drink, because he wanted everyone to have a good time. But he didn't play the film star. I can't remember him doing that at all. But he would act the part if called upon. If it was a professional thing, then he knew how to make an entrance.'

There was, however, one significant change that Carol noticed about Oliver: his drinking had increased. On the set of *The Shuttered Room* Carol hardly noticed him hitting the bottle but over the past few years it had become more and more of an issue. One evening she brought the subject up. 'Why don't you just drink wine?' she asked. 'It's better for you than hard alcohol.'

'I can't,' he said.

'Sure you can. I'm not saying, don't drink. I'm just saying, have a bottle of wine. Have two. Just don't have a bottle of Scotch.'

'No, I can't.'

'Well, why not?'

'Because I can't feel anything unless it's hard alcohol. I can't feel anything on wine.'

Carol never raised the subject again. Often they'd go to pubs and although Carol rarely drank much herself, Ollie always made sure that she had a shandy. 'Once he saw me take a drink of hard liquor, a vodka and tonic, and he was horrified, absolutely horrified. "Only order a shandy," he said. Looking back, you just wish that he had been able to control his drinking, because that did accelerate. He did try but he never really tried for long enough.'

Simon was another who saw a quite definite shift in Ollie's drinking from the early to mid-seventies and onwards. 'That's when I think the drinking became less fun. He was still after the Happening. It was probably just more difficult to find and it needed more drink, whereas in the early days he only needed a couple of drinks and the Happening would arrive.'

The amount of booze Ollie was buying was startling. David recalls their accountant saying at the end of one year, 'God, how do you spend this much on drink? This would keep any normal family in luxury.' Jacquie recalls Ollie going on a binge that lasted something like three days, 'then even he had to give in and he collapsed on the front lawn and violently threw up – and grass never grew on that patch in my time at Broome Hall.'

Ollie was also a well-known face around the hostelries of Dorking. He'd drink there rather than Horsham, a town about the same distance from Broome Hall, mostly because the police round Horsham, Sussex police rather than Surrey, were a bit heftier when it came to drink-driving. 'They were more on it,' claims Mark. There was the Dorking run, for example, where Ollie and his pals would ask for a quadruple gin and tonic and down it before the barman came back with the change, then dart off to the next pub. The White Hart was where Ollie did most of his drinking in town, though sometimes he ventured to the White Horse Hotel, until he got barred for setting the chimney alight. Seated next to a large, roaring open fire, Ollie kept lugging on log after log until it was a blazing inferno and the fire brigade had to be called. He was told by the management his presence was no longer desired.

He even took Mark to the pub aged twelve and got him pissed. He started the lad on half a shandy. It tasted like shampoo but Mark asked for another one, this time with a small lemonade top. Yuk, still tasted like shampoo. Right, Ollie thought, let's give the little bugger some beer. He drank six pints of their best bitter. 'I remember him driving me back home, and he kept looking at me because he couldn't work out how I was fine – I was shit-faced. Back home I was puking in the bathroom and he was fussing around me giving me a blanket and I just wanted to be left alone to die.'

Jacquie never spoke to or lectured Oliver about his drinking. 'It wouldn't have entered my mind. I would have had a thick ear. In passing I might say, you're not bloody pissed again.' Often she'd join in. 'One just went with the flow and tried to keep up.' Ollie liked to have people around him when he drank, and he'd never crack open a bottle on his own. Nobody from his immediate family ever recalled seeing him do that. 'He never, ever drank alone,' confirms Jacquie. 'He always had to have a drinking buddy, even if he had to pick one up on the way to the pub.' Or drag poor old Bill Dobson out of bed or go round to David's. 'He used to wake us up, sometimes three or four in the morning,' remembers David's wife Muriel. 'He'd break a window if we didn't let him in.' What was it that he was after? He feared being alone, that's for sure, so was it purely for the company, somebody to talk to? Or, as David believes, wasn't the reason all too obvious? 'Most people who drink don't do it by themselves. They always do it in the company of others because it gives them the feeling that they're not the only one. It gets rid of the guilt feeling.'

All this raises the obvious question, was Oliver Reed an alcoholic? Of course, it depends how one defines alcoholism. To Mark it's someone who wakes up in the morning and the first thing they think of is getting a drink down them; certainly that was not Oliver. 'He loved it, had great fun with it, enjoyed the buzz of it, but it had to have a reason. So if there was a good enough excuse, like he had people around and they were up for having a drink, then off it would go.'

Like her mother, Sarah grew up never trying to stop Ollie

drinking, and along with Mark is convinced her father was not an alcoholic. 'Which some people find quite weird, but you never found empty bottles lying around. He could turn it on and off, that was the extraordinary thing, his willpower. I've never met anybody with such willpower as my father. He wouldn't drink for days or months if he had to.' What he'd do, then, was binge-drink, go off on benders, sometimes five days at a time, and then return to the land of sobriety. After these benders Ollie checked himself into what he called 'the clinic'. He'd not leave his bedroom for sometimes upwards of three days, just lying in bed alone watching television and feasting on chocolate, ice cream, sardines on toast, and bottles of Lucozade. Eventually he would venture out, potter around the garden, and walk the dogs. It resulted in a very strange childhood for Sarah because there seemed to be no happy medium. If he wasn't absent through filming Ollie was in drunk mode or being solitary and quiet. 'I was too young to understand or question it, but I knew there was quiet time and there was crazy time, and not a lot in between. That was pretty much the pattern of his life. There were times I was disturbed, probably not by how much he drank, but by how it made him; if he was being unpleasant or embarrassing, then I'd wish he drank less, but I don't think I ever questioned it.'

When he was drinking, it was a case of riding the wave with him. Sarah remembers one morning she and Mark came down for breakfast and Ollie had prepared apple juice; except it wasn't: it was Calvados and apple juice. 'So he was clearly pissed from the night before and that would just be it, you'd keep going. So, ten o'clock the next morning, Calvados, and you were on a roll.' Other times it was best just to get out of his way. Those who lived with Ollie developed this inbuilt radar: they could walk into a room and sense where the energy level was. 'I think both Mark and myself got that from a young age. We could walk in and go, OK, it's a good one, it's a bad one, it's a fun one. Like most drinkers, there's a good drunk and a nasty drunk, and he could be a nasty drunk, and in those cases we would literally go and hide.'

According to Michael Winner, 'There was no greater pendulum swing in any human being that I've ever met than Oliver Reed sober to Oliver Reed drunk.' The transformation when it happened was extraordinary. It was truly Jekyll turning into Hyde. What triggered it? It was like a Plimsoll line, that one drink, that one vodka and tonic too much and then there was this monster. 'Ollie wasn't an alcoholic,' believes Murray Melvin. 'But there was a need, because without it he was lovely. But that one drink and he had to hit somebody. He just had to hit somebody. He really was Jekyll and Hyde. You could almost see the change in him – ohh, that's the one – and you knew to get out or, like a typhoon, you put the shutters down and hoped it blew over and your house was still standing at the end of it.'

Family and close friends could always tell when the switch had gone and Ollie was turning nasty. In fact they coined a phrase: Mr Nice and Mr Nasty. They might be at a restaurant with him and suddenly sense the shift in atmosphere. 'Then Mickie and I would just say bye-bye and go,' says David. 'Because we knew within ten minutes the other character would come out. Oh dear, here comes Mr Nasty. You actually saw the change, it was physical.' As Muriel says, 'He was like Jekyll and Hyde, it was black and white with Ollie, there was no grey.'

In the morning, as with most drinkers, remorse and guilt would set in and he'd go to a florist and buy lots of bouquets and go round depositing them at houses, apologizing with that wonderful excuse 'I'm sorry, I don't remember'. 'There were times when he wasn't lovely and he could be troubled and awkward and stroppy,' admits Mark. 'My grandfather Peter used to come down and visit us and always made sure the car was aimed in the right direction and that he knew where his car keys were should he want to make his exit, because it wasn't fun any more.'

It had become the habit, annually, to pack Oliver off to the Caribbean to get a bit of rest and recuperation. 'I forget why I first did it,' says David, and he doesn't know whose idea it was. 'But one winter, in between maybe girlfriends or wives, I sent him on holiday to Barbados. I put him on a plane and off he went.'

As he walked out of the airport looking for a cab, Ollie's eyes fell on one particular taxi driver. His name was Ivan. 'Right, Ivan, you are my driver whilst I'm here. You work for no one else. You work for me.' That was the first year. The second year David got a phone call from Ollie saying, 'Dave, I'm going to set up a taxi rank for Ivan.' So they bought him some cars. 'Ollie simply loved the man,' says David. 'He nicknamed him Dadi. And Dadi was mad on cricket, so one year Ollie flew him over for the Test Match at Lord's.'

Ollie fell in love with Barbados. 'It was the friendliness,' says Sarah. 'The culture, the rum shops. Just that raw humanity of people, kids playing in the street with a cricket bat.' There was a place called Coconut Creek where he liked to stay and whenever David arrived for a visit the two brothers would swim across a cove to get a drink at a rather splendid hotel. But the water was over a coral reef that was razor-sharp. 'It was one of Ollie's party tricks to swim over this coral reef which, if you dropped down just a little bit, could slice you open,' says David, who has never forgotten those holidays. Coconut Creek was so charming and unspoilt, with its bars on the beach with little straw roofs and houses on stilts to keep the rats out. He went back a few years after Ollie died. 'Now it's all concrete, full of hotels.'

Jacquie went there a few times too, and they rented a house on Gibbs Beach on the west coast. Nothing posh, it was more

223

like a wooden shack with wood partitions dividing the rooms. Outside the door there was almost nothing for as far as you could see. 'We used to walk for miles along that beach. That's why he liked Barbados so much, he felt unthreatened there, relaxed.'

In spite of the island's isolation, Ollie still cultivated a gang of friends he could have fun with. On *The Hunting Party* he had got friendly with a small-time American actor called Ritchie Adams, who'd often stay at Broome Hall while he was looking for work in London. Ritchie had just got hitched to a octogenarian millionairess and they were enjoying a honeymoon cruise. The ship came into Bridgetown, the bustling capital city of Barbados, and Ritchie heard Ollie was around, so left his new bride to have a quick drink. Predictably Ollie and his pals got Ritchie absolutely hammered and dumped him in a wheelbarrow to sleep it off. When he woke up the next morning the ship had sailed on to its next port of call. Panic-stricken, Ritchie got Ollie to drive him to the airport in order to catch it up, but Ollie deliberately bundled him on to a flight that went to the wrong island.

Ollie was sunning himself on the beach when a package arrived at his hotel. It was a script for a film called *The Triple Echo*. The role on offer was only a supporting character but the story was sufficiently intriguing and it also promised the chance of a rematch with Glenda Jackson. Set during the Second World War and based on the H. E. Bates novel, the film has Glenda playing a woman living alone who meets and falls in love with a young army deserter. Determined that he shouldn't be found by the military authorities, she resorts to disguising the lad as her sister, a subterfuge that leads to tragedy when Ollie's bullish sergeant major enters the scene.

As he neared the end of the script something brought Ollie up sharp. 'It said I had to kiss a bloke while feeling his bollocks.' It didn't matter that his character had been deceived by the dragged-up deserter, it still meant wrapping his lips round a fella's whistle. Ollie sent a rather urgent cable to the makers: 'Unless the kiss is out I'm not doing the movie.' A cable came back saying: 'Kiss out. Come in.'

Ollie duly turned up for shooting at a remote farmhouse near Salisbury and, acknowledging the film's modest budget of £200,000, accepted a low fee. Glenda did likewise. It was the only thing the pair had in common, for their relationship, distant in the extreme, had not changed one iota since *Women in Love*. All of which left a young director called Michael Apted feeling very apprehensive, especially after meeting Ollie at a costume fitting. 'He was very nice but clearly going to be a handful, very boisterous, lots of laughing and larking about, and I was nervous as shit about the whole thing.'

It wasn't just the clash of personalities between Ollie and Glenda: the two actors had diametrically opposed ways of working, and Apted was often caught in the middle. 'Coming from the theatre Glenda wanted to rehearse everything and have everything laid down, and then within two or three takes it was done, done beautifully. Oliver, on the other hand, would come in of a morning and not know what scene we were doing, let alone what it was about or what he said. So for me, on my first movie, this was terrifying. My first instinct was to think, well, this guy's just a lazy slob, and some of that might have been true, but he brought incredible life and energy to the thing because he kind of discovered it on the spot, he was able to make use of the location or the set or whatever, he figured it out as we were going along.' Glenda could see what was happening and gave Oliver space to do it. In other words, she compromised. 'And if she hadn't done that I don't know where we would have been,' says Apted.

Later to forge a considerable reputation as a director in Hollywood, Apted came from a career in television and so Ollie was the first pure film actor whom he'd ever worked with. 'And although he was rather extreme he taught me huge amounts about how to prepare as a film actor, how to focus on the moment and be in the moment. That was a huge lesson and I never forgot it. A lot of people that I later worked with were from my school of thought, they liked to prepare things, as Glenda did, but then other people, from John Belushi to Tommy Lee Jones, they had a way of working that was very reminiscent of what I learned from Oliver. So he was profoundly important to me, probably as important as any actor I ever worked with.'

Ollie also left a huge impression on Brian Deacon, the young and inexperienced actor who played the deserter. Often during a scene Ollie would suddenly start improvising and there wasn't a great deal you could do about it except try to keep up. 'I was just out of drama school and weighed less than ten stone, so I don't think this man with a forty-six-inch chest felt particularly threatened by me.' Deacon found Oliver charming and well-mannered, but clearly identified a side to his nature, a dark side, that was fixated on experiencing violence for the sake of it, knowing he had people like Reg around to pull him out of situations if they got out of control. 'Ollie was always looking to fight people. In our hotel one night there was a wedding reception – they must have been Scottish because there was an awful lot of guys wearing kilts – and Ollie got really excited about seeing if he could conjure up some guys from the crew because he said, "We're gonna do the Scots." He was going to go into this wedding reception and just pick a fight with any guy in a kilt. And he was relishing the idea and we had to say, "Don't be ridiculous, Oliver, it's somebody's wedding. You can't just barge in there." That was the less attractive part of his character.'

It was a trait that had begun to emerge in Oliver's teenage years and never really left him, these sudden explosions of pissed aggression. He'd flatten his nose down like a boxer and puff himself up like a peacock. Sarah remembers being in

Dublin once with him in the early eighties and they were at the theatre. 'And for some reason the guy in front of him really annoyed him – he was German, I think that was his problem – and all of a sudden Oliver leaped over the seats and grabbed him and it was like, right, that's the end of that evening. And we literally left after that.'

One of Ollie's favourite haunts of the late seventies and early eighties was Stringfellows nightclub in London's Covent Garden, where he enjoyed a game he christened 'Headbutting'. Each player was required to smash his head against his opponent until one or other of them collapsed or surrendered. A regular victim was The Who's bass player, John Entwistle, who after being knocked out three times pleaded with the club's owner, Peter Stringfellow, to either ban the game or bar Ollie.

Murray Melvin recalls returning with Oliver from a publicity launch somewhere and having a pleasant lunch at the airport while waiting for their flight. 'And there was a chap who was a bit of a wide boy, a bit of a chancer, sitting opposite Ollie. And I don't know what it was he said, I don't know whether he referred to Josephine, but suddenly Ollie was up, grabbing the table, trying to get at this guy. And somebody said to this chap, "Go, just get out." And we restrained Ollie and this chap just disappeared and we calmed Ollie down.'

Jacquie learned to live with these outbursts. One time Ollie had to go to London for specialist treatment on a bad back. 'And because he was such a huge man, they had to have him sedated for three days before they could do anything.' Afterwards Jacquie drove him back to Broome Hall. 'I was terrified of driving Oliver, you can imagine, him shouting and screaming. And I was on this dual carriageway and he said to me, "Go on, overtake." There was someone in front of me. "OVERTAKE!" he yelled. I said, "I can't, I'm on the barrier." He grabbed and pulled the steering wheel and of course we crashed into the barrier. "That's it," I said. "I'm getting out. I'm not driving."

And so even though he was still reeling from all the sedation and should not really have driven, Ollie drove them home.

Strangely, when he was drinking, Jacquie never felt things would get out of control because he'd have friends over and he'd either crash out or go off somewhere else, 'So I never felt threatened.' Carol Lynley is adamant that she never saw Ollie act violently towards anyone, drunk or sober. 'Nor would I have been around if he was violent. I would have been out of there so quick.'

Tales of Oliver's drinking had, of course, reached the ears of everyone working on *The Triple Echo*, Deacon included, of nights out on the town around the pubs of Salisbury. 'One night ended up with some of the women working on the movie having their bras removed, burned in an ice bucket, and nailed to the wooden bar.' As for Apted, he has no recollection of Ollie ever arriving on the set under the influence. 'I may be wrong, but I don't even remember him showing up late. He was pretty professional about the whole thing.' Glenda does, however, remember one incident when perhaps the exertions of the night before had taken their toll. 'We were shooting a scene and, when the director called "cut" Oliver literally fell flat on his face, he was flat out on the floor. But you wouldn't have known it from seeing the shot. He'd delivered his lines and played the scene perfectly.'

After a particularly strenuous day's shoot Deacon walked into the hotel bar and saw Apted, Reg, cameraman John Coquillon and Ollie. 'I went, whoops, and turned on my heels, but before I could get out I was hauled back in by Ollie.'

'What do you want?' he said, throwing his arms round the young actor.

'I'll have a half pint of Guinness, please.'

Ollie turned to the barman. 'Right, half a pint of Guinness and then we'll have five triple whiskies, please.'

'Oh, I can't drink that,' said Deacon.

'Come on, get it down you.'

It was a command intended for everyone to heed. 'And it was so intimidating we all drank them,' says Deacon. The drinking continued at a fearsome pace until Oliver insisted on taking everyone out for an Indian. Reg was driving the Roller and they all got in. At the restaurant Ollie ordered the meal and several bottles of wine. 'He sent the wine glasses back, asking for half-pint tumblers, and was just tipping it straight in: "Get it down your neck,"' remembers Deacon. 'And we were completely smashed.'

Back at the hotel, Deacon got out of the car and walked straight into some glass doors. 'I'm picked off the floor and hauled up to Ollie's room because now we're going to smoke some joints.' Suddenly Ollie realized Apted and Coquillon had gone AWOL and went storming around the hotel looking for them. Deacon turned to Reg. 'I'm going. I'm outta here.'

'Ollie will be really pissed off when he comes back and doesn't find you here.'

'Reg, I've got to go.'

Deacon just about managed to drag himself back to his room and collapsed on the bed. The next thing he knew his alarm was going off; it was five o'clock in the morning. 'I got into the bathroom and within about thirty seconds I was like a baby, it was projectile vomiting, made a complete mess of the place. I got in the shower and tried to get cleaned up, and shaved my face and made a real mess of it, cut my chin, hopeless.'

Arriving at the location, a couple of the crew took to marching Deacon around a car park in an effort to straighten him out. Half an hour later a car came screeching to a halt outside the make-up caravan. 'Michael Apted got out,' says Deacon. 'And literally crawled inside, on all fours. I don't think he'd been to bed at all.'

Glenda was furious when she found out, grabbing hold of Deacon. 'You stupid, stupid boy.'

'What?'

'Do you think it makes you more of a man going out and getting drunk with Ollie? Is that what a man is?'

'Glenda, I had no choice. I was hauled . . .'

'Of course you had a choice!' And so it went on. She really tore into Deacon, who was left scratching his head about why he'd been singled out when both Apted and Coquillon could barely stand up. And there was Ollie, as bright as a button and walking about with a huge Cheshire-cat grin on his face. He'd certainly left his mark, which of course had been the whole point of the exercise. 'That was in a sense my rite of passage with him,' believes Apted.

Despite *The Triple Echo* failing to find an audience, Ollie remained enormously proud of it. Making his entrance in a tank churning up farm fields, he is the epitome of the macho army lout, and plays the role with just the right degree of humour, testosterone and menace. 'I think *The Triple Echo* is a very under-recognized film and I think Oliver is particularly good in it,' says Glenda. 'I thought that he brought a lot of personal touches to his character, which were his own. I thought it was immensely layered.'

The film's most memorable scene is the deserter's near rape at the hands of the sergeant major during an army dance, shot in a real barracks. Both actors weren't relishing shooting it, least of all Ollie, who, Deacon was told, had a bottle of vodka stashed away and had already downed half of it. Getting the snog removed had been a small victory, but Ollie was still required to throw Deacon hard up against a wall and get quite friendly: 'Come on, girl, don't you mess about, give us a little feel, eh.' It was an incredibly brave scene to try, especially for an actor with a highly macho public image. 'But that's what was so appealing about Oliver,' claims Apted. 'He went for it 100 per cent. Despite all the bluster and the larking about, he did take the work seriously, he took the story seriously and in those scenes when he realizes he's been duped he was truly terrifying. I really thought he was an incredibly interesting actor. And he clearly loved what he was doing. This was a small film, he was probably making hardly any money, but he really got with it.'

It was at a press conference for *The Triple Echo* that Ollie's most infamous party trick, that of taking out his dick in public, or as he cosily described it, 'My snake of desire. My wand of lust. My mighty mallet', first drew attention. It was something he was still doing as late as 1996, by which time he was referring to it as 'a national institution'.

The questioning had turned to Burt Reynolds's recent decision to pose naked in *Cosmopolitan* magazine. Ollie revealed he'd turned down a similar opportunity and when asked why replied that it was because his dick was too big to fit on the page. 'Prove it,' demanded an elderly female journalist on the front row. Without hesitation Ollie dropped his pants and flashed the end of his knob. 'Why have you stopped?' the woman demanded to know. 'Madam. If I'd pulled it out in its entirety, I'd have knocked your hat off.'

Foreign Assignments

Living it up as lord of the manor at Broome Hall, Ollie hadn't forgotten his old stomping ground, and if he ever had any business in London he would always head back to Wimbledon to drink and catch up with old friends. In the Dog and Fox one day he recognized a familiar face: it was Norse. They got chatting and Ollie asked how he was getting on. Christensen had joined the police but was not enjoying it, as the hours were long and the money crap. 'Look, I've a proposition for you,' Ollie said. 'I've got this big pile in the country. Why don't you come down and see what you can do with the market garden and anything else you fancy? I promise you it will be fun.' Norse thought, fuck it, I'll never get another chance like this.

Christensen didn't know the first thing about market gardens, but got tips from the local farmer, bought machinery, and started from scratch. Soon they were producing vast quantities of vegetables and the excess was loaded up in the car and taken down to local pubs and restaurants, and Ollie got credit, so for weeks after he ate and drank for free. 'And he was very hands on, if he felt like digging he'd dig or he'd be on the mower. He was involved 100 per cent.' Ollie truly loved his market garden and always kept a salt cellar just standing inside the greenhouse so he could walk inside and pick a warm tomato right off the plant, put salt on it, and say, "How can you beat that?"

After moving into a cottage in the stable yard Christensen pretty quickly sussed out the regime at Broome Hall, which was pretty full on, especially at weekends. It hadn't taken Oliver long to cultivate a new gang of mates, principal among them Paul Friday and later his wife Nora. Friday was partner in a television aerial business and met Ollie one afternoon in his local. Not a keen cinemagoer, Friday didn't have much of a clue who he was, but was told he'd recently bought Broome Hall and wanted TV aerials put up. 'Of course, it was one of the longest jobs we ever did because every time we started to do something Ollie dragged us back to the pub, so this two-day job took about three weeks.' The result was they hit it off almost from day one and Friday became another lifelong friend.

If Ollie wasn't filming, weekends were indeed special occasions at Broome Hall. It would be down to the pub on both Saturday and Sunday and at lunchtime everyone would pile into cars to go to the Curry Garden in Dorking, and then back to Broome Hall for games. These usually took place in the cellar bar. 'The games there could get quite raucous,' remembers Christensen. 'Ollie had a collection of military helmets and some of the games used to entail breaking bottles of wine over people's heads wearing the helmets. All you had to remember was to sink your head into your shoulders so you didn't get a crooked neck. There would be wine and glass flying all over the fucking shop, and poor old Jenny would be cleaning it up the next day.'

The cellar bar was deep in the bowels of Broome Hall, near the huge, noisy boilers, and women were barred from the place. 'You were very honoured if you were allowed inside to have a drink with the boys,' recalls Jacquie. Sarah remembers it as a particularly scary place for a young child. 'I was allowed in there but it was more of a man's domain. I didn't like it, it was dark and dingy and there was a hole in the wall as you walked down to it where dad put this skeleton. I think it was a real one, so that wasn't particularly appealing.' Taking pride of place in the cellar bar was the Thorhill Glass, which held the equivalent of a bottle of wine. At dinner Ollie would announce, 'All Thorhill members be upstanding.' Those remaining seated had the chance to become members if they so desired. 'This entailed Oliver filling the glass up with red wine, right to the top,' remembers Paul Friday. 'And you had to drink it down in one, the whole bottle, and then put the glass on top of your head.' Things got even sillier when Ollie introduced a system of Thorhills 1, 2 and 3. Friday, along with Oliver's son Mark, qualified as a Thorhill 2, which required drinking two bottles, straight down, over the course of a meal. Invited over one evening, Friday knew that he was going to be cajoled into doing a Thorhill 3. This called for some clever scheming on his part, since Ollie would go round all the toilets after dinner making sure there were no splashes of red wine on any of the pans. Friday came up with the perfect plan. Just outside the back door Bill Dobson had left a wheelbarrow full of grass cuttings, and if he could get to that and dig a hole, he'd be OK. 'And that's what happened,' recalls Friday. 'So Ollie and myself were the only members of the Thorhill 3, but I actually cheated. Although he never knew I cheated.'

There was also the Penicillin Glass. 'That was probably the safest thing to drink out of,' says Christensen. 'Because it was literally thick, crusted penicillin lining this V-shaped crystal glass, and whatever alcohol was drunk from it the glass was never cleaned, just left to dry, so it had this thick scab which took up almost half the volume of the thing.'

At Broome Hall Ollie resurrected the Portley Club, which had its origins in Wimbledon. If Ollie called a meeting members were obliged to turn up, and if they failed to do so, the meeting would go on regardless, in an extremely expensive restaurant, and the missing member was obliged to foot the bill. Sometimes meetings took place in the cellar bar, sometimes in the beautiful 'grand dining room'. Again games were played. 'Somewhere along the way Ollie had acquired this huge assegai spear,' remembers Christensen. 'It was so long that if you held it upright it could clear the floor by an inch and clear the ceiling by an inch. And the members had to drink a bottle of port down in one, including all the sludge, because Ollie liked vintage port, and then carry this spear round the dining-room table without touching the floor or the ceiling. If you could do that then it was the next person's go. If you failed you had to drink another bottle of port down in one and do it again.'

The Cricketers Arms, in the nearby village of Ockley, quickly became Ollie's local pub. The landlord was Ray Figg, and quite often in the mornings if he felt under the weather from the exertions of the night before, Ray opened his bedroom window and dropped the key down for Ollie and his pals to open up themselves. Should a customer stroll in fancying a quick drink, Ollie would seize the opportunity for a bit of fun. Seeing no one behind the bar, they'd begin to chunter a bit and jingle their change. 'Didn't you see the sign outside?' Ollie would say. 'It's a free house, you just help yourself.' So you had these people going behind the bar to get a gin and tonic, with Ollie directing. 'Well, the gin's there and you'll find the tonic on that shelf.' It was pure mischievousness. 'It was about seeing people's reactions to the unconventional,' says Mark. 'People expect routines and conformity and things to work in a certain way and when it doesn't that's what he found was fun.'

It was the Cricketers that played host to one of Ollie's most amusing deeds. Drinking with friends one lunchtime he suddenly decided to climb up inside the chimney for a rest, and at once fell asleep on a ledge. 'At five o'clock in the evening they changed the pub over to a restaurant,' relates Mick Monks, 'and there's a couple sitting having their soup, just arrived, and down comes Ollie, down the chimney. Frightened the life out of them. Banned for a week, I think. They daren't ban him for any longer: it's half your trade gone.'

Another time at the Cricketers, Ollie heard the landlord had been refused a one-off extension to his evening licence. After thinking for a moment, he suggested Ray do it the other way round instead: get an extension to open early in the morning and have an insomniacs party. That evening Ollie told his usual crew to arrive the following morning at 7.45 a.m. wearing their night attire. Ollie showed up in his pyjamas, slippers and a dressing gown. 'It was hilarious,' recalls Christensen. 'But a darn sight more funny when the pub opened properly and people on their way down to Bognor Regis for the weekend stopped in at lunchtime and there's thirty pissed people in their pyjamas. And, knowing Ollie, he liked his baggy old stripy pyjamas with everything hanging out at the front.'

One of Christensen's other jobs was to look after the horses. Broome Hall came complete with a stable block, except there were no horses in it, save for good old Dougal. That quickly changed when Ollie took the decision to start breeding a new line of large, fast horses called heavy hunters, which were produced by mating thoroughbred stallions with shire mares. 'People thought he was mad until he started winning stuff at Hickstead. Not jumping, but at showing,' recalls Christensen. The things were popping out each and every year. 'The fields became full of little foals running around,' says David. 'They were very sweet.'

Soon the stables became a hive of activity as several grooms were taken on to help with the breeding programme. 'He was passionate about whatever he got into,' says Mark. 'And he was passionate about breeding horses. I remember at one time they had twenty horses there, at vast expenditure.' It became a dream of Ollie's to breed a horse that would go on to win the

Horse of the Year Show. That, alas, never happened; indeed, according to David, he rarely even rode them. 'It was just an indulgence. He was playing, in his mind, the country squire.'

An indulgence of an altogether different kind of horse power was cars. Oliver had always loved driving and the sensation of a good motor car, but not in the technical sense: you wouldn't catch Ollie slaving away under the bonnet on a Sunday afternoon. No, it was more the ownership, and when the money started rolling in he totally spoiled himself. Around the time of *Women in Love* Ollie saw a yellow Jaguar in a car showroom and bought it. Christened 'the Banana', it was followed by a Jensen, 'which he thrashed up around the fields,' says Muriel. There was also an open-top Rolls-Royce which, according to David, Ollie drove into a bridge on his estate. Then another Roller, purchased from Michael Winner. It was in this, in the early seventies, that Ollie was caught drink-driving while going over Battersea Bridge. David was at home when he got a call from the police.

'Are you the brother of Oliver Reed?' said a faintly ominous voice.

'Yes,' said David, dreading what might be coming next.

'We've got him in a police cell.'

Off David went to collect Ollie and learned that he'd also given a sample of blood, which after analysis came back borderline. David felt they had a case and it went to the High Court. 'It turned out that the judge had only just been sworn in, so this was his very first case. Our barrister, who was very famous and experienced, wrapped the police case up in knots, and with a bow on top. The prosecution counsel didn't know whether he was coming or going and the judge was losing the plot too.' Calling a halt to proceedings, the judge ushered Ollie's barrister and the prosecution into a side room for a conference. An audible rumble went around the court room, everyone assuming the case was being dismissed.

The Chief Constable had been the last witness on the stand and, stepping off, he walked over to Oliver. 'Well done, Ollie. Would you like your blood sample as a souvenir?' he said, and handed over a small plastic container. Back at Broome Hall, Ollie kept little mementoes on display in the cellar bar, and this would make a fine addition. Just then the judge returned and, banging his gavel, announced, 'Right, back on with the case.' It wasn't finished, after all. The prosecution stood up. 'May I present to the court a sample of Mr Reed's blood.' Everyone stared at the Chief Constable, who had turned bright red with embarrassment. 'I'm sorry,' he said. 'I've just given it to Mr Reed.'

In the end Ollie was found guilty, despite the fact he was only 1 per cent above the legal limit. 'Not enough to get a newt slightly merry,' he complained. The judge fined him £5 and disqualified him from driving for a year. When Ollie went to pay the fine, the clerk said, 'I've never seen such a low fine in my life.' To which Oliver replied, 'I've never seen such a travesty of justice in all my life.'

For a while David took to driving Ollie around, though sometimes it was Muriel's task. Then one lunchtime Oliver was in the Hand in Hand and this enterprising guy showed up. 'Mr Reed, I understand you're looking for a driver.' Ollie threw him the car keys. 'Take the Rolls round the block and if you bring it back without a dent you're hired.' And he did. Ollie gave him a job on the spot and Martin came to live at Broome Hall. Jacquie remembers him as 'really quite sweet, a public school chap, but very bumbling, and he had a terrible habit of picking his nose and wiping it on parts of the car while he was driving'. One day Martin got a clip over the head from Ollie. 'If I ever see you doing that again, you're out!' From then on he was always known as Snotter Martin. Ollie also thought he looked 'more suitable as the driver of a sewage wagon than the chauffeur of a smart new limousine'. In the end he was made to wear a uniform. The union lasted less than two years. After several bumps, scrapes and near-misses, Snotter resigned by throwing the car keys at Ollie. Ollie hit him. 'You are very rude, Snotter. You're fired.'

'No I'm not,' the chauffeur said. 'I resign.' Ollie hit him again. 'I was never in the army, but I look upon my eighteen months with you, Mr Reed, as my National Service.'

Ollie continued his love affair with cars, which included the purchase of an Aston Martin. David had treated himself to one too. 'Second-hand, I hasten to add, and I collected Ollie at Gatwick airport and he went, "Bloody hell!" He had a Rolls at the time that did eleven miles to the gallon, and I was the agent and mine did nine. So then he immediately went off and bought a second-hand Aston Martin, but this one was the James Bond type, a DB5.'

Another time Ollie bought a huge American jeep with roll bars and began testing it out in the fields with a view to using it somehow in one of his military games. One afternoon he was driving the thing around in ever tighter circles. Christensen was sitting in the front passenger seat, with old Bill Dobson in the back, and getting rather agitated. 'You ought to be careful, Ollie, as the circles get tighter you wanna reduce your speed or you're going to roll it.'

'Don't tell me how to drive my own fucking jeep,' roared Ollie.

Bang – he rolled it. 'And we got thrown out,' recalls Christensen. 'Thank God the vehicle rolled away from us. I wasn't seriously injured, nor was Ollie, but Bill was lying there saying, "I can't breathe. I can't breathe." He'd broken his ribs. Luckily they hadn't punctured his lung. But he was out of combat for a while.'

But by far the peak of Ollie's car-buying mania was his Panther De Ville, which cost an absolute fortune and was hand-built. 'I remember he was away filming,' says David.

'And he'd ring me and say, "Oh, I want a fridge put in." That was so he could have chilled champagne and lager or whatever. So I'd keep having to go round to the factory giving them all these instructions. He also had a licensed shotgun at the time, so we put a pouch for this gun along the front end of the back seat.'

The bodywork of the De Ville resembled a Bugatti, and the bonnet was seriously long, which made driving, especially in crowded cities, difficult, if not hazardous, according to David. 'If you were coming out of a car park you had to be terribly careful because the nose would arrive on the pavement first and you didn't know who or what was there. It was a very difficult car to drive, but Ollie loved it.' The car was finished in gold over brown, and as a final touch Ollie had his National Service commission number inscribed on the filler cap.

Note that the cars mentioned – Jaguar, Rolls-Royce, Aston Martin, Jensen, De Ville – all have one thing in common: they're British. Ollie's patriotism even extended to the car he chose to buy. It was reported that when a friend turned up one day at Broome Hall in a new Mercedes, Ollie tried to urinate on it.

Bulgaria circa 1972 wasn't the most exotic location to make a film in: it was grindingly poor, regimented and depressing. Into this flew Ollie. The film he'd come to make was *Days of Fury*, a bleak and savage historical drama from the pen of British playwright Edward Bond. Ollie plays Palizyn, a tyrannical eighteenth-century Russian landowner, who allows a stranger, played by John McEnery, to enter his community and become his servant, treating him worse than a dog. But the stranger has an ulterior motive, to avenge the death of his parents at the hands of Palizyn and to stoke up revolution among the people. This sad and desolate period of history is brilliantly recreated on screen, with an almost documentary realism, but as entertainment the film is a bit of a slog to watch. Ollie's dark looks are again a terrific bonus in his portrayal of Palizyn, and he gives an assured performance, pulling off the feat of making the man appear brutish while retaining an air of nobility. And, as with all Oliver's villains, there's more than a hint of vulnerability and insecurity.

Based in Sophia, the Bulgarian capital, Ollie and the rest of the cast and crew were transported the hour's drive into the desolate countryside where the sets had been built. Between takes he was determined to teach an eighteen-year-old French actress named Carole André how to speak cockney rhyming slang. Poor Carole never really got the hang of it but did grow enormously fond of Ollie. Having recently worked with Visconti on *Death in Venice*, she had been cast as Irene, Palizyn's foster daughter, for whom he harbours lustful thoughts that lead to her traumatic rape. It was obviously a difficult scene to shoot, especially for such a young actress, but Oliver made sure that before a foot of celluloid was taken Carole was fine with everything. Unfortunately something went wrong. The Italian director wanted it very realistic, saying, 'So Oliver is going to really rip your clothes off, but when you don't feel comfortable any more just say stop in Italian so that I understand.' As Carole recalls, because of some miscommunication Oliver didn't know this, 'And so he's ripping my clothes off and I said, "OK, all right, this is enough," and I started shouting, "Stop, stop," and obviously [it] being a rape scene Oliver continued and the director didn't stop filming either. It ended up being a very awkward and embarrassing situation and Ollie was absolutely as adorable as he could have been about it, he was so apologetic, saying he had nothing to do with it, and I totally believe that he didn't. He was so protective of me, he really looked upon me as a child.'

For Carole, on her own in Bulgaria and feeling extremely vulnerable (her mother died during filming and she had to go back for the funeral), Ollie took on the persona of a big brother. 'He knew that I was very lonely and I think people that drink always have a very sensitive part to them, as crazy as they can get under the influence. I think this need to lose yourself in alcohol stems from people that are insecure, very sensitive, and need friends, and I was in a similar situation in Bulgaria, where I felt very tender and lonely and alone, and I think Ollie hooked into that. I thought he was terrific and it was so nice to have somebody you felt was on your side.'

As luck would have it Oliver's next film, a spirited comedy drama called *Dirty Weekend*, also co-starred Carole, so their friendship easily picked up again on location in Italy. 'It was great working with Ollie again, it was fun, it was cool. I was quite a shy person back then, quite reserved, so it was not easy for me to feel comfortable on the set, but with Ollie I did, always. Since that relationship we had in Bulgaria, where I felt that he would never hurt me in any way, either physically or emotionally, I would have done anything for him because I did feel like there was somebody that was looking out for me. Although for some reason – because in Bulgaria he kept it more hidden – that's when I noticed he had some issues with drinking.'

It wasn't difficult to miss. Reg was around, and a few other chums, and in the evening there was the usual trawl through unknown streets for a place to drink. One press story had them fighting some Mafia types. Outside one particular bar Ollie and Reg were approached by a vicious-looking local bastard. Fearing he was going to be attacked, Ollie pounced and bit his nose. Just then two cars pulled up and some other sinister chaps got out. 'I think there's going to be a little bit of trouble here, Reg,' said Ollie. 'It's the local syndicate.' Suddenly gunfire rang out and Ollie and Reg hit the deck, only to realize it was the sound of a television set somewhere. Relieved, everyone tore into each other but seemed to spend most of their time chasing each other around parked cars. Later it was revealed that one of the Italians did indeed have Mafia connections, but instead of putting out a contract he ended up buying Ollie and Reg drinks and spaghetti.

Carole can recall only two incidents when she saw Ollie get out of hand through drinking. At breakfast one morning in her hotel she was told by a crew member that Ollie and his gang had made quite a mess the previous evening. 'They'd had a lot of fun and thrown things around in the hotel bar. And then another day I remember Oliver coming on to the set and he didn't look great, he looked really hung-over, in a bad, bad way. We tried to shoot but it just wasn't working. We could all see that it wasn't going to look good on the screen, his face was puffy, his eyes were bloodshot, so the director decided to shoot something else. "Oliver, go, just go, and when you're better we'll finish you up another day."'

Ollie's drinking certainly wasn't Marcello Mastroianni's cup of tea. One of the biggest names in Italian cinema, Mastroianni was his co-star in *Dirty Weekend*, playing a wealthy industrialist on holiday with his lover, played by Carole, when he's kidnapped by Ollie and his gang of bank robbers. So it's no surprise to learn that Oliver and Marcello didn't exactly bond. 'They were respectful to each other,' remembers Carole. 'But Ollie was just running wild at that time, so I think it probably wasn't easy to even try to socialize with him.'

It was on *Dirty Weekend*, David recalls, that one of the Italian actors fancied himself a bit of a boozer and challenged Ollie to a drinking contest. 'They drank for two days solid and on the third day this Italian bloke said to one of his assistants, "For fuck's sake, get me on a plane out of here, I can't stand the pace." He just couldn't keep up with Ollie, who just had this incredible capacity, he had this limitless ability to drink.'

Of course, such behaviour has always been frowned upon on the Continent, where they have a much more cultured approach to alcohol consumption. They drink, of course they do, in some cases prodigious amounts of wine or beer, but the loutish boozing that Ollie seemed to excel at is much less prevalent. 'For them it's like acting like a wild man,' says Carole. 'But you know, when somebody behaves bad with everybody else but is sweet to you, it makes you feel even more special. Ollie could be rough and even just by showing up you were scared of him, but to me he was absolutely adorable.'

In the early seventies very few British actors were working in Continental cinema, and certainly not in starring roles. Dirk Bogarde was the most high profile, but then he was a very English-style actor; Oliver, in looks and mood, was much more European. 'He could be Italian, he could be Serbian, he could be Russian,' says Carole. 'He came across as much more than just English.' Ollie had found himself immensely popular and in demand, especially by Italian filmmakers, because films like *Women in Love* and *The Devils* had become causes célèbres. He was very much a hot box-office proposition in Europe, much more so than in America. His performances in these European productions, for which he was paid well – the main reason for taking them – were largely ignored by critics back home and the films themselves little seen by the British public. Maybe they thought he was slumming it, but this was an unfair accusation, especially when levelled against his next Italian-made film, *Revolver*. For not only is this movie a superior crime drama (with a great Ennio Morricone score) but it features one of Oliver's best performances as a no-nonsense prison warden whose wife is kidnapped by the Mafia and the only way to get her back is to spring a criminal from jail.

What's even more remarkable about this performance are the circumstances under which it was delivered, namely that Oliver was knocking back lethal doses of booze every day. He's clearly intoxicated in many of the scenes. Usually he was highly professional when it came to not drinking on the set, but for some reason this went completely out of the window here, as his co-star Fabio Testi and director Sergio Sollima revealed in a documentary for the film's 2004 American DVD release. 'Oliver was a very lovely person until two or three in the afternoon,' he said. 'Let's say around the twenty-fifth or twenty-sixth bottle of wine. He could hold his liquor, no problem, then after that it would get more difficult. Therefore, we had to shoot his scenes during the early bottles.'

Testi got to like Oliver a lot, finding him amusing and likeable, but a real handful. 'When he came on the set drunk, he had the tendency to become violent. I was the only one able to restrain his violence because I was always humouring him.' During the filming of a scene where Ollie was required to release Testi from handcuffs and drag him out of a car, he found the key too small and couldn't fit it in the lock. After several takes Ollie got so frustrated he threw the key into the road, where it fell into a drain and down into the sewers. Testi was left handcuffed for two hours while a replacement key was found.

Not only did Ollie zero in on his director, with the intention of getting him hammered, he also challenged Testi to several drinking games, but, like a good Venetian, Testi could match him drink for drink. 'And Oliver couldn't stand the fact that he couldn't get me drunk. So at the end of the drinking, as a final challenge, he would break some light bulbs and eat them.' As strange as it may sound, this was not a one-off incident. Wendy Kidd, the wife of showjumper Johnny Kidd, from whom Ollie had bought Dougal, recalled one dinner party at their London apartment where Oliver was a guest. He sat at the table drinking incessantly but not uttering a single word, and refusing to eat any of Wendy's carefully prepared cuisine. Suddenly he stood up, removed a lampshade hanging over the table, and unscrewed the light bulb. 'The next thing I knew he put the glass bulb to his lips and, without taking his eyes off me, proceeded to eat the end of it!'

Eating light bulbs was one of Ollie's favourite party tricks. Mark recalls a couple of visits to restaurants when his father couldn't resist calling the waiter over and, even if the food was great, saying, 'Excuse me, this food is shit, in fact I'd prefer to eat one of those,' before unscrewing a light bulb and munching away. 'You've got to chew the glass very finely before you swallow it,' he'd caution. 'It was to shock people and a demonstration of physical prowess,' says Mark. 'He also had this thing for a short time of putting cigarettes out on his tongue. It was shock value.'

Ollie also liked to make people squirm. Sarah remembers going out with her father one evening in London when she was in her late teens. Before heading off, Ollie said, 'Right, you've got to pretend that you're my lady of the night.' Arriving at a very posh restaurant, he went up to the doorman. 'Good evening,' he said, and then, pointing to a decidedly awkward Sarah, 'This is miss, er . . . this is my niece.' Nudge, nudge, wink, wink. 'Er . . . actually no, it's not, she's a lady of the night.' Poor Sarah would be standing there not carrying it off at all. It was just to see how people reacted. It was mucking about. 'I hate being bored, you see,' he once explained. 'And, most of all, I hate it when I'm boring myself. So I pull faces. I dance around a bit. I act the goat. If I'm sitting in a pub and nothing is happening, I'll climb up the chimney and pretend to be Father fucking Christmas. Anything to get a reaction.' When he arrived on location in Italy for *Dirty Weekend* Ollie showed up unshaven and dishevelled, then fell out of his car and lay motionless, apparently unconscious, on the road. No one noticed, or cared, so he got up and went and had a coffee.

Ollie's behaviour on the set of *Revolver*, however, did not go down at all well with the majority of the Italian crew. So badly in fact that Sollima sensed something might happen and took precautionary steps, as Testi recalled. 'The crew was told that Oliver would finish four days later than he actually did because some people were waiting until the end of the shoot to settle scores with him.' Testi was the only person of the entire cast and crew that Ollie said goodbye to when he left.

All For One, and One For All

The origins of what would prove to be one of the most popular and entertaining movies of the seventies date back to a dinner party held by the father-and-son producing team of Alexander and Ilya Salkind, later responsible for the Superman movie franchise. It was Ilya's girlfriend who mentioned that Alexandre Dumas' classic novel *The Three Musketeers* would make a great movie. Both Ilya and Alexander seized on the idea, and from the very outset had in mind a comedic take on the much-filmed tale and the bizarre notion of casting the Beatles as the musketeers. They even hired Richard Lester, who'd made his name directing *A Hard Day's Night* and *Help!*, but the American filmmaker wasn't keen on the idea, telling them, 'The Beatles have such huge personalities, they are so well known that they will take away from the characters of the musketeers. If I'm going to do this I want to find great actors.' He wanted not just great actors but big stars, to help sell the film on the international market. Ilya firmly believes that it was Lester's involvement that encouraged the participation of some of Hollywood's biggest names. 'Richard was an absolute magnet for actors and when I look at that cast now it's possibly one of the most perfect in cinema history.'

The first star to be approached was Charlton Heston, who was offered the plum role of Athos. Heston loved the script but thought he was a bit long in the tooth to jump off horses and wave a sword around, so opted to play the Machiavellian Cardinal Richelieu instead. This still left the producers with the task of finding the perfect Athos, who is really the group's heart and soul. Drawing up a list of actors that included the likes of Alan Bates, the Salkinds returned to Dumas' description of Athos as a man who 'lives hard and drinks too much'. There was only one candidate, surely. 'Unanimously we thought, Oliver is the one,' says executive producer Pierre Spengler. 'Simply because he was a great actor and we figured this was a role that required great acting. And when you watch the film, Oliver brought so much depth to that role. You can feel the past of Athos.' Oliver did like to claim that Athos was 'probably the nearest to myself that I've ever played. I identify with his drinking habits, his playing habits, his suspicion of women.'

The other musketeers fell relatively quickly into place. For D'Artagnan Lester wanted Malcolm McDowell, while the Salkinds preferred and got Michael York. As Aramis, Lester cast his friend Richard Chamberlain, and then Frank Finlay was brought in to play Porthos. The rest of the cast was filled out by other top acting talent such as Faye Dunaway, Christopher Lee, Simon Ward and Raquel Welch.

An essential part of the film was going to be the sword fights, which Lester wanted to be both realistic and exciting. Very quickly Ollie and his fellow musketeers bonded as a unit, largely because of all the rehearsal and time spent together on set. 'We were also totally involved in Dick Lester's vision for this film, which was highly physical,' says York. 'We were doing crazy, crazy stunts, riding horses without stirrups and jumping this way and that, and all the fighting that we had to do. We just got caught up in the heat of the moment. Without doubt it's the most physically demanding thing I've ever done.'

At the grand age of fifty Christopher Lee was the most disadvantaged of the swordsmen, because, playing the villain, he was involved more than most in the duels. 'You've got to remember we all had costumes on, boots, hats, capes, wigs, beards, moustaches . . . now you try and move fast with a real rapier. They were real swords, they weren't fake, it's not easy.' William Hobbs, the fight arranger, had gone for total realism, not the hokey sword fighting of the Errol Flynn days. And because everyone was using real blades rehearsal was essential – except, that is, for Ollie, who just went hell for leather when the cameras rolled. 'Oliver sometimes would go totally berserk and start to really fight 100-per-cent real,' recalls Ilya Salkind. 'And we'd have to say, Oliver, it's just a movie!' Such was his, shall we say, exuberance that the forty-strong stunt team drew lots to determine who would fight him. 'He terrified the stuntmen,' Lester recalled, 'who would be seen retching in the corner.'

The problem was, Oliver was good at picking up a planned routine, but then, when the cameras whirred and Lester cried 'Action', he would often lose himself in the moment. 'Oliver did nothing by halves,' confirms Christopher Lee. 'I remember during a fight scene he came at me with both hands on the sword, like an axe, and I parried it and stopped totally. I said, "I think we'd better get the routine right." Then I said to Oliver, "Do you remember who taught you how to use a sword?" He said, "You did." And I said, "Don't forget it." You see, I made *The Pirates of Blood River* with him for Hammer and he was a bit of a menace in that, quite frankly. People leaped out of the way when he had a fight, because he went at it absolutely flat out. Nothing wrong with that, provided you stick to the routine.'

In the end Oliver received a sword injury. 'He was always going at them like a maniac,' says Ilya. When it happened Ollie halted the scene and clutched himself in pain, saying, 'The sword went through my arm.'

'It's not possible, Ollie,' said Lester. 'These swords are not sharp enough.'

'I'm telling you, that's what happened.'

Everyone decided to humour Ollie, no one wanted to contradict him, and after the scene was finished he was taken to the local hospital for an X-ray. 'And the sword had definitely gone through,' reports Spengler. 'But thank goodness only half of it had gone through the muscle so there were no real consequences.' Save for a spot of blood poisoning that resulted in a short stay in hospital. After Ollie complained about the food, Reg climbed through the window every night with a plate of pasta and a bottle of red wine.

It may have been disconcerting for his co-stars and the stunt team, but Ollie's madcap sword-fighting style in *The Three Musketeers* was later to bring praise from an unlikely source, director Quentin Tarantino. 'Oliver Reed is just fucking GOD in this movie. Oliver Reed owns the film. During the fight training Reed threw himself into the fighting so much he made all the other musketeers work twice as hard. They knew if they didn't, Reed was going to own the movie completely. He was that good. You've never seen sword fights the way Reed fights them in this movie.'

An arduous twenty-week slog, *The Three Musketeers* was shot in Spain, which, then under General Franco, was a very conformist country. Still, the production managed to land unprecedented access to sundry royal palaces and other locations, which helped lend the film a real sense of time and place. This attention to detail is one of the reasons why it has endured as a movie classic. 'If you look at the Gene Kelly version of the story, it was so Hollywood of the 1940s that you can immediately place when that film was made,' says Spengler. 'I don't think our *Musketeers* are actually placeable, because they are so authentic.'

The cast and crew mostly stayed in Madrid, with Ollie put up at the illustrious Hilton Hotel, the only member of the cast staying there. 'We deliberately kept him a little bit aside from the others,' admits Spengler. Pretty soon the pranks began, including one of Ollie's all-time best. The centrepiece of the hotel's foyer was a large fish tank replete with very expensive goldfish. In the dead of night, when the building was asleep, Oliver crept down, removed the fish, and took them back upstairs to his room, placing them safely in his bath. The next few hours were spent whittling large carrots into the shape of the fish, and then popping them into the tank. Come morning, when the foyer was thronging with tourists and guests, Ollie announced himself loudly, then walked casually over to the fish tank, grabbed the 'goldfish', and started munching on them, to the horror of everyone. The hotel manager called the police and Ollie was hauled off the premises, bellowing, 'You can't touch me! I'm a musketeer!'

It sounds like one of those apocryphal tales, so preposterous does it seem in the telling. Only there is a witness to it, as Michael York happened to be arriving for breakfast and saw the whole thing. 'It was such a great prank. I really applauded it. Oliver could be pretty wild sometimes, though. Unfortunately this was now his image with the press, and I think he rather lived up to this wild, carousing, sort of latter-day Errol Flynn tag. This is what they expected of him and he duly delivered.'

More problems followed. Drinking one night in the hotel bar, Ollie started challenging his fellow guests to tests of strength. 'I am the greatest. I'm a British true blue and will take on anyone.' When no one obliged he started overturning tables and smashing glasses. Again the police were called and he was dragged away. It took five officers to bundle him into the interrogation room. 'Oliver, God rest his soul, was incredible,' remembers Ilya Salkind. 'He could go out and get totally smashed until six in the morning and show up on the set at seven and be ready to go. That was pretty fantastic.'

In court the hotel manager revealed that this skirmish wasn't the first problem he'd had with Señor Reed: there had been several insulted guests, broken chairs, and a hole punched through a bathroom door. As a result Ollie was ordered to leave the hotel. 'So I was thrown out on to the streets with my bags,' he explained a few months later on Russell Harty's ITV chat show.

'All life seems to be a kind of adventure to you, doesn't it?' said his host.

'I think it should be,' Ollie replied, smiling. 'I think that everybody would like that. It's just that very few people have the opportunity.'

'But thank God there are people like you through whom we can actually live vicariously,' Harty wound up the interview.

It had got to the stage in Ollie's life where his reputation preceded him and his invitations to come out drinking were met with either trepidation or a 100-yard dash in the opposite direction. 'If you wandered into a restaurant or a bar and Ollie was there you spun around and hoped you weren't seen because you could become his captive all night,' says Quinn Donoghue, publicist on *The Three Musketeers*. 'If you wanted to go home at 11.30 p.m. or midnight he would not have that, and at two o'clock in the morning he and Reg would start arguing or would pick a fight with somebody and a scene was made. I was there frequently in the beginning and realized, nope, don't want to do this much any more. That's the dark Ollie and everyone's seen that at one time or another, and that's not the good side. Ollie was fun to be with until, let's say, drink number eight or whatever it was. When he wasn't drinking, though, he was a pleasure.'

Certainly none of the cast went out on the lash with Ollie. Chamberlain, for instance, classed him as 'A terrifying presence, an extremely dangerous man. He could be very sweet, but if he turned on you, he could make life terrible for you.' This attack would normally take the form of a vicious verbal assault, during which he'd play on a person's weakness. If he found you had a weakness he'd home in on it. 'But he'd admire you if you stood up to him and stood your ground,' says Paul Friday.

Because of the tough schedule and early starts, most of the actors retired to their hotel rooms at a respectable hour anyway, and behaved themselves. 'The only one that was always carousing was Ollie,' says Donoghue. And, as always, news of his excessive behaviour would filter back on to the set the next morning. 'And he relished this,' adds the publicist. 'He was like the little boy getting his wrist slapped but never really being chastised. He was regarded fondly among the crew as somebody who got into trouble.' But all this had personal repercussions for Ollie's driver. The poor man was taking him to parties and clubs and bars, and God knows what else, at all hours of the night, so he was hardly ever home and his wife asked for a divorce.

Incredibly, over the course of the shoot, Spengler can only recall possibly one day when Oliver turned up drunk. 'The rest of the time he would be extremely tipsy between 7 p.m. and 7 a.m., but he was showing up knowing his lines and knowing his stuff. He was a great pro. I had a real soft spot for him.'

Because the film was so star-laden, acting heavyweights were popping in and out of Madrid all the time. Geraldine Chaplin, Ollie's co-star a few years back, had been cast as the Queen and recalls, when she arrived in Spain, coming down the steps of her hotel and there was Ollie, bowing reverentially to her. 'Your majesty,' he said, and kissed her hand. Invited up to his room, Geraldine was fussed over even more and served champagne. 'He treated me as the Queen, he was already in his part. It was very funny. During that whole film I was the Queen. He absolutely wouldn't give up, on set, off set, I was the Queen, it was relentless.'

The arrival of Raquel Welch and Faye Dunaway on location was a hotly anticipated event. Playing the devilish Milady, Faye didn't have very much to do with Ollie, as they shared only a couple of scenes. One of these, however, where Athos threatens to shoot her in the stomach if she doesn't hand over a compromising document, is easily the best acted scene in the movie and one of Ollie's finest screen moments, truly electrifying. Relations were much better with Raquel, and they even went out drinking together a few times. Simon was in Madrid, as Ollie's press agent, and got drunk one night with Raquel's hairdresser. 'She was out of her head because they'd been drinking vodka all day. Getting up to leave, she told me to follow her up in five minutes. She was beautiful. "Thank you," I said. Reg was opposite me and winked, "You've scored there, sunshine." I got up, grinned at Reg, then I realized I'd forgotten her room number. Fuck it. Apparently she collapsed outside the lift on the wrong floor anyway.'

Early the next morning Simon was sitting outside a Winnebago when Ollie came out with a cup of tea. 'Raquel wants to meet you,' he said. Just then a door opened. 'And out came this unbelievable vision. I'll never forget, she had "No 1" written on her T-shirt, and if anybody looked like the No 1 in the world she did. She walked straight across to me, obviously her hairdresser had said something, looked me right in the eye, and said, "You must be Simon, I've heard so much about you." I remember thinking, fuck me, wait till I tell my mates about this, it's just ridiculous. But it was that kind of life. From living in Raynes Park to suddenly handling Ollie's press stuff and doing all this, it was just amazing.'

Simon also sensed that something was going on between his brother and Raquel. 'She was after him, no question. David was having to field calls from her.' Much to Raquel's frustration, Ollie didn't seem remotely interested. 'She just couldn't understand it,' says Simon. 'Because anywhere she went everyone wanted to get inside her knickers and all of a sudden here's this guy ignoring her. So I don't know if she was really attracted to him or she was merely curious, what's going on here?, why doesn't this guy want me? kind of thing.' Not long afterwards Ollie was back at Broome Hall with Johnny Placett when the phone rang. Jenny Dobson picked it up. 'It's Raquel.' Ollie took the phone. 'Hello, Raquel, how are you?'

'I'm staying at the Savoy. I'd like to invite you up for lunch.'

'Oh, Raquel, I've already prearranged to go out and have drinks with the major. You see, he's a good friend and he's come round, so we're going out to have a few jars.' Ollie glanced over at Placett. 'You have a word with her.'

'Hello,' said Johnny, in his best phone manner. 'I can't believe what he's saying, Raquel. To get the chance to take such a beautiful woman like you out to lunch, but he's decided he wants to see me. There's something wrong in his head.'

Raquel laughed. 'Well, you sound interesting, why don't you come along?'

Johnny put his hand across the receiver. 'She wants me to come along, Oliver.'

'Give me that,' said Ollie, snatching the phone out of his hands. 'It's no good, I heard all that, I'm going out for drinks with the major.' And then he hung up.

Was all this an elaborate joke on Ollie's part, to snub a woman who was every hot-blooded male's wet dream? 'It could have been a bit of that,' says Simon. 'Also, don't forget at that stage Ollie was drinking.' And the drinking is perhaps where the answer lies.

In the sixties Ollie had been something of a boozy ram. Johnny Placett is convinced he knocked off Princess Margaret. Ollie went off with her on some social engagement but was uncharacteristically coy about discussing what may have happened on his return. He sort of left the possibility dangling. However, by the early seventies his sex drive had gone. 'The wandering eye finished probably after his mid-thirties,' claims Simon. 'He wasn't that keen on it any more.' What had been a flood now resembled something approaching a trickle, because of either a lack of interest or the booze. 'I think he preferred the drink rather than the sex,' says Georgina Hale. 'If you're pissed all the time I don't really see you having a lot of sex.' David believes that the drink did indeed play a part and had begun to effect him physically. 'Ollie was a very virile person, but later, either through drink or whatever, he was probably not able to perform always. My very firm belief is that by that time he found it very difficult.'

Jacquie does admit that booze had now become the all-consuming component in Oliver's life and that the physical side of love no longer held much attraction for him. 'It was too much fuss.' And while it's true to say that drinking does have an effect on a man's libido, she denies that he was physically incapable. It was more that the desire had gone. 'And I think a lot of it was the drink.'

He still kept his relationship going with Carol Lynley, but it remained a curious relationship in that it didn't seem to be going anywhere constructive. Sure, when they weren't together he'd sometimes write letters to her, send telegrams or call. But if Carol began a new love affair with someone, Ollie wouldn't display an ounce of jealously, 'because they didn't exist for him,' she says. 'I only existed when I was with him. Outside of that I didn't exist and the other people in my life didn't exist.' Still, she dutifully flew into Spain for a time to keep him company on the *Musketeers* picture. 'And he was so very excited about doing that film. He just seemed to be having a really good time and kept his musketeer hat with him everywhere he went.'

Sadly for Carol, it proved the last film set of Oliver's she'd visit. Just a few months later he flew out to break the news in person that he couldn't see her any more. Their parting was amicable: there was no storming out, no screaming, no arguments, he just gave his reason, that he had a young daughter to look after, got on a plane and left. 'And you can't argue with anybody who says that. You can try and say, no, I don't want

257

you to, but in the end you have to let them do what they think is best.' And looking back some forty years later, Carol has no regrets about the relationship. 'It was a wonderful seven years. I remember good times, and how very, very attractive he was. And I remember the fun and the originality of him. He was just so original.' They never saw each other again.

For years Oliver referred to *The Three Musketeers* as one of his happiest times on a film set. Much of that was down to Richard Lester, who instilled in his company an atmosphere of collaboration. 'If you came up with something creative and better, it often made the cut,' remembers York. And Lester fair galloped along, too. His style was to use multiple cameras, as he loved spontaneity. If he got what he wanted in the first or second take, he'd move on, no messing about. That was something Ollie could appreciate and invest in.

Imagine, then, having put all this effort into the movie, you found out that the producers had sliced the thing right down the middle and intended to release it in two separate parts, but somehow forgot to tell any of the actors about it. According to Christopher Lee, the deception was unveiled at the Paris opening. 'When the lights came on at the end everybody started leaving the cinema. We just looked at each other and said, "Wait a minute, it's only half the movie." Then somebody came up and told us, "Oh no, there's another film to come out, it's called *The Four Musketeers*." Well, you can imagine the reaction. What in effect we'd done was make two films and we'd only been paid for the one film!'

A feeding frenzy ensued, with lawyers and agents claiming their clients had been royally shafted. In the end the Salkinds came up with a financial deal that appeased everyone. The rationale behind the decision was that a family audience would be unable to sit through a three-and-a-half-hour movie, so it made better sense to release them over two successive summers. It was a point of view the actors pretty much agreed with, as the alternative would be to lose a whole bunch of great material. 'I'm glad they did it,' admits Michael York. 'Because there's not a dud sequence and there's no sense of padding in either of those films.' Indeed, of the two, Oliver much preferred *The Four Musketeers*. 'In my opinion it's a better film, not only because I'm in it more, but because you get more into the characters.'

Ollie's Athos ranks alongside his Bill Sikes, Gerald Crich, Father Grandier, and Proximo in *Gladiator* as one of the finest achievements of his career. So good is he in fact that you can't see anyone else coming close to matching him. 'Oliver was blessed with that rare quality that is beyond mere acting: style,' claimed the film's screenwriter, George MacDonald Fraser. 'He had it by the bucket. Flynn and Fairbanks never swept a cloak or threw out a challenge with greater panache.'

There is something else about Oliver. It may or may not have been a throwback to his 'alleged' Peter the Great heritage, but he seemed just to fit perfectly into historical settings. 'He had a face that looked real in very many centuries,' says actor Stephan Chase, who worked twice with him. 'And there aren't many people that you can cast like that. If you see things on telly or in movies that are meant to be medieval, most of the faces don't look right. I think Ollie had a quality where you could put him in a film set in the time of William the Conqueror, or earlier or later, or even possibly a future film, and his looks would have worked, you would have believed he was a person from that time.'

It wasn't just the bombastic elements of his performance as Athos that are memorable, for Oliver also brings softness and vulnerability to the role, especially in his relationship with the young D'Artagnan. 'I think the affection between Athos and D'Artagnan is certainly there,' says York. 'And during filming I got very fond of Ollie. I had to look up to him. He was a sort of role model, but not off the set.' York also counts himself as one of Oliver's biggest fans. 'He's one of the icons of the British film industry. There were performances like his Bill Sikes, which used his physicality and that dark, dangerous energy that he seemed to carry around with him. He used it triumphantly. And the great thing about his Athos, and why he made the part his own, was Oliver was raised in the middle class, if not quite the aristocracy, so I think some of that came through. He may have been pretty wild and rough, but there was something that tempered his personality that he couldn't help, that was in his upbringing. In short, the class system.'

York raises a fascinating point about class because the musketeers themselves were a cut above the average French soldier, having been founded by King Louis XIII and becoming a popular fixture at court. 'And certainly Oliver was an aristocratic sort. I knew he had a house in the country and I could see him as the country squire type, wearing tweeds with his gun dogs. He fitted in perfectly with that kind of image. He'd been brought up in good schools, with good manners. Oliver wasn't run of the mill. He was like an aristocratic ruffian, a complete contradiction in terms.'

Hollywood Calling

Back at Broome Hall, Oliver did indeed continue to play at being the lord of the manor. However much of a folly the place was, bought on a spectacular whim, as a home it was an extension of his personality and played host to some great parties. One of the most memorable occurred in the winter of 1974, after a home win at Rosslyn Park, when Ollie celebrated with twenty-five squad members, including star player Andy Ripley. The evening started off at the Cricketers when everyone sang 'Get 'em Down, You Zulu Warrior' and crammed fifteen of their party into a single cubicle in the ladies' lavatory. They all arrived at Broome Hall after midnight, and that's when the real fun began. Jacquie remembers it well because Ollie insisted she and Jenny dress up like little serving girls. 'The rugby players thought we were the hired help. We also had to give them a few whacks over the head with French rolls because rugby players get ideas after they've been drinking.'

To keep everyone's strength up, a local chef made huge bowls of chilli. 'Very hot,' remembers Christensen. 'And fucking inedible.' Meanwhile Ollie made pints of hot buttered rum, a bygone coaching drink that drivers used to keep themselves warm, consisting of butter, rum and Demerara sugar poured into boiling water. 'We drank gallons of that until everyone was nice and warm,' says Christensen. 'And then Ollie suggested a follow my leader. Everyone stripped off to their jockstraps and underpants and ran round and round the grounds, culminating in a swim across the lake, which was madness really because everyone was pissed and it was freezing cold. Everyone came back blue with their teeth chattering.' By morning sixty gallons of beer had been consumed, thirty-two bottles of whisky, seventeen bottles of gin, four crates of wine and fifteen dozen bottles of Newcastle Brown.

After these booze bashes little Sarah got quite used to going down to breakfast in the morning and finding lying on the floor various bodies, which she'd have to step over to reach the kitchen. 'People would just come and get drunk, keel over, be sick, and I'd go, OK, that's so and so there, and this was just completely normal.'

For a time Ollie hosted a spate of dinner parties, even though he usually abhorred such social occasions. 'He got bored very quickly with people,' says Jacquie. 'So he would never go to a family cocktail party or dinner party, it would bore him to death.'

But the grand dining room, with its huge stone fireplace, seemed to be going to waste, so several dinners were arranged, though only for very close friends. Ollie also had a huge dining table built from an oak tree – it could seat almost thirty people – and everyone who came to dinner was encouraged to carve their name in the wood.

It's unlikely that Oliver's father was ever a guest, although he did visit a number of times. Sarah remembers him as 'a bit of a cold fish' and notes that David and Simon were much closer to their father than Ollie was, and had a very good relationship with him. 'My dad didn't. I think Pete never felt that my dad fitted. He didn't understand where my father had come from.' When Ollie was best man at Paul Friday's wedding to Nora he played a dastardly trick on Peter. Showing up at his father's house in Epsom on the way to the wedding, he intimated that it was in fact he who was getting married. So poor old Peter turned up, in his gardening clothes, convinced that it was Ollie and Jacquie, sitting happily in front of the registrar, who were the ones tying the knot.

As for Marcia, in the eight years Jacquie lived at Broome Hall she only ever remembers her visiting on one occasion. Looking round the place, all she had to say was, 'What a waste of money. Such an extravagance.' It was also the only time Jacquie ever met Oliver's mother, but her memories of her remain strong. 'She was very formidable and very beautiful; that's obviously where Oliver got his beauty from. She was just incredibly beautiful, with blue eyes and black hair.'

For one memorable dinner party Ollie invited an elderly couple whom he'd only met a few weeks before in the Cricketers. 'For some reason Oliver used to suddenly take to people,' says Jacquie. You could say he collected people. Once he was returning from visiting Mark at school and some Welsh kid was thumbing a lift. 'Where are you going?' asked Ollie. 'London,' said the kid. 'I'm gonna get a job.' Ollie had a think. 'Well, I need a butler.' So he drove this kid back to his house, where he was a butler for a week. 'But he never did any butler duties,' recalls Paul Friday. 'All Ollie did was get him pissed for the week, then give him £200 and put him on a train and off the kid went.' Jacquie also remembers the time he picked up a band of road diggers who were carrying out roadworks outside the Cricketers. 'They didn't go home for a week.'

Beryl, the woman of that elderly couple from the pub, was nearly eighty when she first joined the club, so to speak. Ollie's dinner parties nearly always began with the main course, since he couldn't abide starters, or, as he called them, ingy-pingy this and ingy-pingy that. He also liked to make a grand entrance when everyone else was seated. 'And he loved gravy,' says Jacquie. 'But we didn't have it in gravy boats, I had huge jugs of gravy. So he'd come in and he'd hack at the meat. He didn't carve, he'd take it with his hands and put it on the plate. Then he'd pour a whole load of gravy over his dinner and then he'd say, "I can't eat this shit," and he'd sling the plate into the fireplace, where it shattered, or against a wall. And poor Beryl was sitting next to me, well she nearly had a heart attack.'

Was this yet another instance of Ollie play-acting for shock value? 'Who knows?' says Jacquie. 'Because then he'd storm out and we wouldn't see him for a day. And there was everyone else politely eating their puddings.' Simon remembers being told a story by Ken Russell about when he was invited to Broome Hall for dinner and there was just such an occurrence, Ollie screaming at Jacquie that the food was inedible and hurling the plate against the wall. And Ken being Ken, with that director's eye, he looked up and said, 'Hold on, there's about ten other gravy marks like that one there. I think this has happened at least nine times before.'

Another social occasion at Broome Hall took place in the summer of 1976. There was a drought and a hosepipe ban on and the local council refused permission for Ollie to fill up his outdoor swimming pool, so he decided to have a party in it instead. There were loudspeakers, flashing lights and dry ice, the works. He started the evening dressed in a red silk dressing gown, holding a sword and with a knight's helmet covering his face. 'And he just stood there with this sword absolutely still for half an hour,' recalls Mark. 'Absolutely dead still as people were arriving, not quite sure whether it was him or not. Every few minutes he'd open the visor and a big gin and tonic would go in.'

When the party was in full swing Ollie decided it would be a good idea to jump off the edge of the pool on to one of the trestle tables covered in plates, bottles and glasses. Wham! 'The table collapsed,' Mark remembers. 'Glass flew everywhere, and you thought, fuck, he's got to have hurt himself. It was literally a starfish dive straight into this table. He got up without a mark on him.' They say some people are untouchable, and Ollie really was. He'd do things, usually on impulse, where you thought, God, that's fucking madness, but he got away with it; talk about a cat with nine lives. 'I don't know how you can get away with as much as he did,' says Sarah. 'He did a lot of these things for the sheer effect. He'd go, right, let's jolly this up a bit, let's just do it because I can and I want to.'

Life wasn't like this all the time at Broome Hall, of course. When Ollie wasn't filming or drinking he enjoyed peace and relaxation, spending time in his garden and going for long walks, usually on his own. He wasn't someone who liked going out much, and Jacquie can't remember even one occasion when they went up to London to see a play in the West End, for example. Why? 'Because he wasn't interested.' Nor did they go out very often as a couple or a family to the cinema. 'He wouldn't go to see a film or anything like that. He'd probably only sit through half an hour of it and then walk out. He would watch a little bit of television, but there was no specific programme he liked. The television was in the library and if he happened to be wandering in and something caught his eye he might watch it, but again he would very rarely go through a whole programme. He was most unusual in that way.'

Much of Ollie's social time did seem to gravitate around the Cricketers and other nearby hostelries. 'As soon as he was up he'd grab someone to go and have a drink,' says Jacquie. 'If he couldn't find anyone else, I'd do. Although if I ended up behaving in a drunken fashion I would be sent to bed, so to speak, or sent to my room. He didn't like women behaving badly.'

One of the reasons why Ollie loved pubs so much was because the 'real' people whom he identified with drank there. It had been the same during his National Service, when he'd never have thought of drinking in the officers' mess. 'He'd go to the ratings' bar,' says David. The same applied to film sets, where he was much more relaxed chatting to the chippies and the props men than the producer or studio bigwigs. Take the time he was shooting an episode of *The Saint* at Elstree. Across the road was a pub where everyone went for a drink after filming, and you'd always see a horde of parked cars outside with their chauffeurs. Ollie himself had a driver on that show, but always invited him in for a swift one. David remembers that Tony Hancock, filming at the same time, did likewise, but everyone else left their drivers outside. 'I thought that was quite revealing. Both Ollie and Hancock didn't like being aloof from the driver, to them the driver was an equal.'

Nor did Ollie socialize much with the local gentry where he lived. The exception was David Hunt, a rich businessman who lived a little bit farther up Leith Hill from Broome Hall. Ollie occasionally drank at Hunt's place and together they inaugurated the Leith Hill Flying Club. Hunt had a huge games room-cum-bar in his house with a long beam that spanned its width. Ollie and the boys took to leaping off the end of the bar and grabbing hold of the beam. One night Muriel was there and decided to have a go, fell down, broke her knee, and was in traction for three months. Another victim of the Leith Hill Flying Club was Paul Friday, who fell awkwardly once and was in bed for a fortnight in a terrible state. 'There was a bang on the door at three o'clock in the morning,' Paul's wife Nora remembers. 'It was pouring with rain. I opened the door and there was Ollie in a pair of blue jeans and a denim jacket with nothing else underneath and he'd put all these safety pins through his skin and said, "I'm a punk rocker. Can I come in?" How can you be mad with the guy? He came in and saw Paul was in extreme pain, so the next day we carried him to the car, took him out for a beer, and laid him on the floor of the Indian restaurant and gave him a meal. Then Ollie took him to the best back surgeon in London and paid for all the treatment.'

Ollie and David Hunt were invariably sparring or challenging each other. One bet Ollie made with Hunt in the Cricketers was that he could pee three pints of piss. All the boys went out to the gents' toilet, milk bottles were produced, and one pint, two pints, two and a half pints, then the flow suddenly stopped. Hunt thought he'd won the fifty quid, as there was Ollie straining, but as soon as Hunt declared, 'I've gotcha, you bastard,' Ollie went, whoosh, and filled it up – three pints of piss.

They even clashed when it came to their flagpoles. Ollie flew a Union Jack outside Broome Hall on what he always boasted was the highest flagpole in Surrey. That was until David Hunt got one just that little bit higher. Ollie retaliated by making his flagpole twenty feet higher, so Hunt added six inches to his. This kind of thing went on all the time. 'Ollie was outrageous to poor old David,' recalls Michael Christensen. And just as bad to other big knobs living in the area whose company he tolerated rather than enjoyed. One afternoon Ollie and Christensen were having lunch in the kitchen of Norse's cottage when this chap turned up and invited himself in, sitting at the head of the table with his back to this flight of stairs. 'It went a bit quiet,' recalls Christensen. 'Ollie looked at me and then went upstairs to the loo. Coming back down, he stopped halfway on the stairs, got his dick out and pissed on this guy's head. And for a few seconds he was trying to work out what this sudden warmth on his head was. He was absolutely outraged – how dare you! – it was splashing all down his back, and I was biting my lip from having fits of laughter. Anyway he got up and flounced out – "I've never been so badly treated in my life. How dare you!" – got in his car, and fucked off. Ollie said, "Well, you did want to get shot of him, didn't you?" I said, "Yeah, but not by pissing on him." He came back a few days later.'

As with Wimbledon, there was a core group of friends whom Ollie hung around with and then a larger group of people who wanted to get in on the action. Ollie was always happy to accommodate them, but many exploited his generosity. Take a typical Broome Hall Sunday. Ollie would be holding court down the Cricketers, buying everyone drinks as usual. Then if he didn't want the mob around him he'd shoot off early and drive to the curry house in Dorking. 'There'd be Jacquie, Sarah, Ollie, a couple of others maybe, and me,' says Christensen. 'Then within half an hour there'd be forty people sitting with us and the bill would arrive and he'd pay for everyone. It's not that he couldn't afford it but he hadn't actually invited them. You'd see people order lobster bhuna when they'd normally have a chicken curry, and bottles of Nuits-Saint-Georges wine when they used to drink a half of Carlsberg.' This annoyed Christensen so much that he brought the matter up with Ollie. 'But what can I do?' he said. 'I don't want to suddenly start going, who's had what? It's too embarrassing.' Christensen suggested that next time he ask for a separate bill.

The following Sunday it was drinks at the Cricketers again, then off to the curry house on their own, and within fifteen minutes the crowd barged in and started ordering. Later the waiter quietly slipped Ollie the bill: it was £20 instead of the usual £200. He paid, got up, and announced, 'I'll see you all later if you want to come up for a beer,' then left. Their faces fell, and suddenly the arguments started. 'I only had one rice.' 'Who ordered the naan bread?' Whether it solved the problem Christensen doesn't know, but it was just saying, I'm not stupid, please don't do this.

A lot of interviews were conducted at Broome Hall, such was Ollie's pride in the place. Sometimes the invitation came with the instruction to bring a change of clothing. 'You're going to be pushed in the pond or the swimming pool,' it warned. Simon

ROKEBY, WIMBLEDON.

Xmas Term, 1949

Name _O. R. Reed_	Class _5B_
Age _11·7_	Number in Class _18_
Final Order _18_	Average Age of Class _11·3_

Subject	Order	Remarks.
LATIN	18	He has made practically no progress although he seems to try hard. _T.S._
FRENCH	18	Lamentably weak. He seems to lack the energy to make an effort to improve. _J.E.J._
SCRIPTURE		His work generally is very inconsistent. Fair. _T.S._
HISTORY		Tries hard but needs to settle down. Has made some progress.
GEOGRAPHY	11	Very much better. Has made good progress in this subject and I hope he will keep it up. _T.S._
ENGLISH	18	His English is very careless and extremely untidy. He tries hard but has made very little progress. _T.S._
MATHEMATICS	18	He is very confused and makes little or no effort to conquer the elementary work – such as 'Tables' and the four Rules. _J.E._

HEADMASTER'S REPORT:— His extremely poor standard of work has been a great disappointment, as it had been expected that he could hold his own in this form. There have been complaints of his stubbornness, amounting to a refusal to accept advice. At this rate of progress, he could not possibly reach Common Entrance standard in the required time.

Next Term begins _January_

" " ends _April_

H.D. Fisher.

School report from 1949. *(David Reed)*

Oliver, aged three, wearing the light top, with his elder brother David. *(David Reed)*

Dear Peter Kay and simon.
I hope you are all very well.
Thank you very much for the letter
you sent us. The school is a
verry nice one but some of
the boys are rats. What does
Simon think of us going to
Shool? send him a big kiss from
me wont you.? The Masters are
verry nice to us. I am in
Castlemain house It was the best
house last year. It has bean
very damp hear. The school is
a very big one inside. I am
getting on o.k.. I hope to see you
all very soon
        Love Oliver
        XXXXX X X X X

Letter home from boarding school. *(David Reed)*

Very early publicity shots. 'Oliver was extraordinarily good looking when he was young,' says David. 'There was a mystery and a roughness.' *(Steven Berkoff)*

Reed's breakthrough in Hammer's *The Curse of the Werewolf*. The make-up artist suggested him for the part convinced, 'He already looked like half a wolf when he was angry.' *(© Rex)*

Working for acclaimed director Joseph Losey, Oliver gives a malevolent performance as a street thug in *The Damned*. *(© Rex)*

Fooling around between takes on the BBC Debussy film. *(Mark Reed)*

On a night out with his wife Kate Byrne circa 1966. As a couple they were well-suited, equally combustible and fun-loving. *(Mick Fryer)*

As Bill Sikes in *Oliver!* Reed terrified the child cast members both on and off camera. The film was directed by his uncle Sir Carol Reed. *(© Rex)*

In *Women in Love* Ollie and Glenda Jackson smouldered on screen, but privately their relationship was non-existent. 'He was the antithesis of everything I am,' says the actress. *(© Rex)*

Oliver and his 'friend' the elephant from *Hannibal Brooks*. *(Mark Reed)*

Filming *The Devils* with Ken Russell and co-star Vanessa Redgrave. Its depiction of religious hypocrisy caused huge controversy, obscuring a commanding central performance from Reed. *(© Rex)*

Getting his hair cut for the fiery climax of *The Devils*. *(Mark Reed)*

Lord of Broome Hall, the magnificent manor house in Surrey that was Ollie's own little piece of England. *(Sarah Reed)*

Oliver attends *The Three Musketeers* premiere with Jacquie Daryl. Their relationship lasted for the whole of the 1970s. They were similar personalities. Oliver liked women who were tomboys, girls that would muck about and indulge his playmaking. *(Sarah Reed)*

Mark with his father on the Spanish set of *The Hunting Party*. (Mark Reed)

On location with his daughter Sarah who remembers: 'When you had his attention it felt like the sun was shining on you.' (Sarah Reed)

The hard-edged thriller *Sitting Target* features one of Ollie's most brutal and mesmerising performances. (© Rex)

(above) Competitors in the 'Slippery Pole Contest,' which involved knocking your opponent off with a heavy cushion into manure covered straw. Ollie is flanked by his gardener Bill Dobson and friend Paul Friday. *(Paul and Nora Friday)*

(right) Coming off second best at another slippery pole contest. *(Paul and Nora Friday)*

The Three Musketeers, with co-stars Richard Chamberlain, Michael York and Frank Finlay. Reed threw himself so enthusiastically into the sword fights he terrified the stuntmen who would be seen retching in the corner. *(© Rex)*

The cat that got the cream: Oliver and Claudia Cardinale on the set of *Days of Fury*. *(Mark Reed)*

Oliver and Beano in the bluebell wood at Broome Hall. To Sarah, 'This photograph epitomises the gentler side of my father. Animals and nature.' *(Sarah Reed)*

Oliver with Reg Prince, the actor's stand-in, drinking pal and bodyguard; their relationship lasted over 20 years but ended in tragedy. *(Mark Reed)*

Sarah's birthday party at Broome Hall. Oliver loved children, 'He just didn't know how to cope with them,' says brother David. *(Sarah Reed)*

(above) Toasting The Queen on her Silver Jubilee from Ockley Pond. *(Paul and Nora Friday)*

(left) Oliver aboard his Chinese junk the *Ding Hao*, moored at Cap Ferrat where it stood out like a sore thumb among the shiny yachts of millionaires. *(Sarah Reed)*

In Barbados, a regular holiday destination, with mates Norse, Paul Friday and Ivan, a local taxi driver. *(Paul and Nora Friday)*

Oliver in the library at Broome Hall. *(Mark Reed)*

(above) Oliver with his son Mark and daughter Sarah at the launch of his autobiography in 1979. *(Sarah Reed)*

(left) Ollie, Mark and friend Mick Fryer dressing up in period costume at an old time portrait studio in Dublin 1980. *(Mick Fryer)*

Before his career went into near total decline Reed gave one of his best performances in David Cronenberg's cult classic *The Brood*. (© Rex)

Mugshot following Ollie's arrest in 1981 after wrecking Ye Old English Pub in Vermont.
(Lamoille County Sheriff's Department)

Ollie plays the clown at a charity cricket match. *(Mark Reed)*

Oliver's friends and family reacted with shock when he began dating 16-year-old Josephine Burge, but their relationship lasted until his death.
(Josephine Ryan-Purcell)

(*left*) With co-star Amanda Donohoe in Nicolas Roeg's *Castaway*. Ollie was in a near intoxicated state for the shoot in the Seychelles, once so drunk he attacked an aeroplane landing at the island's airport. *(© Rex)*

(*below*) With two of his beloved dogs. 'He found animals easier than people,' claims Oliver's daughter Sarah. *(Sarah Reed)*

Relaxing between takes on location in Montana for the TV mini-series *Return to Lonesome Dove*.
(Josephine Ryan-Purcell)

At home in Ireland Oliver enjoyed pitching his gardening prowess against other local enthusiasts in an annual vegetable growing competition.
(Josephine Ryan-Purcell)

His last role as the slave merchant Proximo in *Gladiator*. Reed was chosen for his larger than life quality, 'That he could send men to their deaths with a twinkle in his eye and you'd forgive him for it,' says producer Douglas Wick. *(© Rex)*

With *Gladiator* co-star David Hemmings watching a local football match on location in Malta. Just a few weeks later he was dead.
(Josephine Ryan-Purcell)

Oliver's grave in Churchtown, County Cork. Note the beer, cigarettes and money, items regularly left at the graveside.
(Mark Reed)

ROBERT OLIVER REED

1938 — 1999

He made the air move.

remembers taking Barbara Walters there once. At the time she was America's top female broadcast journalist, but when she arrived Ollie refused to come down. Oh shit. This dragged on for half an hour, with Simon sweating buckets and Barbara looking agitatedly at her watch. Just as she was about to leave, Ollie arrived, all smiles and charm; just another of his japes, or had it perhaps been a power game: how long can I keep Barbara Walters waiting?

Other interviews took place in the pub. In these circumstances the journalist was under an obligation not just to drink, but drink to excess. Midway through one grilling, Ollie stood up and pulled open his shirt to reveal his stomach. 'Do you know what I am? I'm successful, that's what. Destroy me and you destroy your British film industry. I'm the biggest star you've got.' An accusing finger was wagged at the bewildered hack. 'But it took years for it to dawn on you that I was worth writing about, pig, didn't it? I'm Mr England!'

Declaring himself to be the biggest star in Britain was actually no idle claim. Ollie had indeed established himself as an international star and was now in that select band of actors termed 'bankable', names that, once attached to a project, not only guaranteed its financial backing but also drew in the punters. 'I remember going into Leicester Square and seeing three out of the four cinemas there showing Oliver's films,' recalls David. 'It was amazing.' He'd also amassed a legion of fans and admirers, mostly, it must be said, female. Some of them used to send photographs in of them chained up, in handcuffs, or standing with whips all dressed up in rubber and leather. 'It was unbelievable,' says Johnny Placett, who remembers Oliver showing them to him. 'It was a real eye-opener. He was getting sackfuls of letters.'

Christensen recalls two girls in particular who lived up in Yorkshire and worked in a factory. Once a year they saved up enough money to come down to Ockley, booked into a local hotel, and visited the Cricketers every evening for three or four days hoping Ollie might be around. 'And a couple of times he was, and he was absolutely charming, he'd buy them drinks, he posed for photographs, he had them sitting on his lap with a big smile on his face, and then they'd be off again.'

Of course, there was a downside to all this. Being in demand as an actor meant Ollie was away working for much of the year and so for Sarah her own father was like a stranger for much of her early years. 'He used to come back as a different character: more facial hair, less facial hair, orange hair, black hair, moustache. I never knew who was coming back into my life.' There was also always a big fuss made when he did return from filming, especially if he had been away a long time. Everyone would make an effort, the garden would be spruced up, the horses cleaned, and a banner placed on the bridge saying, 'Welcome home'. 'It was like the wanderer returning to his kingdom,' says Sarah.

And then when Ollie was home he invariably wanted to go off drinking with his friends. One of Sarah's most vivid memories from childhood is of Sunday afternoons sitting on her own outside the pub for hours on end with a packet of crisps and a bottle of Coke. 'And then it was on to the curry house, and if I got tired I just went to sleep under the table. He wasn't a bad father, he just wasn't very good at playing the family man.' That went for birthdays and Christmases too. 'That whole standing on ceremony thing didn't work with him. He was great at preparing Christmas, but, once you got to it, it was horrible because it meant family and ritual and formality.'

Some Christmas moments do stand out. One year it had been snowing and Ollie got Bill to dress up as Santa and walk across the lawn carrying a huge sack of presents. Ollie burst into Sarah's bedroom and got her out of bed, and hiding behind the curtains they watched the spectacle from the window. 'So for me Father Christmas was real until I was about twelve because

I really believed it.' Another Christmas Eve he told Sarah to shout 'hello' and there was this booming reply coming down the chimney. He'd got someone on the roof to shout down to her. 'That whole make-believe thing was lovely. Also, normally you'd just leave out a tangerine and a glass of brandy for Father Christmas but no, he had to make sooty footprints, he had to leave orange peel all over the carpet, and open the brandy bottle because Santa had helped himself to it. When he had those moments they were really, really magic.'

This was the sensitive side of Ollie that was largely hidden from the public, the gentle side that, when it emerged, was a delight and a wonder. 'He'd want to talk to you about a piece of lavender for hours,' remembers Sarah. 'Or why that plant grows like that and why your dog's nose is wet and cold. It was lovely. He'd say to me, always be inquisitive, about what you look at, what you read, what you listen to. We used to go off looking for fairies in the wood. He used to tell me they lived in the bluebells, so we'd literally get down on our knees and look inside them. There were those extraordinary moments, but the reason you really remember them is because they didn't happen that often because he was away or he was in the pub.'

Flying high as he was, feeling fairly invincible, now seemed the perfect time to take Ollie's career to the next level, to get him into that A-list category among the Newmans, Redfords and McQueens, and to do that he had to conquer America, more precisely Hollywood. Ollie had yet to make an American movie, one either fully financed or made in Tinseltown. He didn't really see the point. 'As long as we make exciting films here, there is no real need to go to Hollywood,' he said. 'So I have no desire to rush off there just because of what Hollywood is supposed to represent.' Simon puts his brother's feelings about the place more succinctly: 'He felt that he would be prostituting himself by going there.'

Yet all the big British stars had already made the move now

that the British film industry had gone into serious decline, thanks to a slump in ticket sales and lack of funding for home-grown movies, and on many occasions both David and Simon tried their best to persuade their brother to follow suit. Ollie would always shake his head. 'I don't think I can do it. I don't really want to do it.'

There's a scene in *The System* where Jane Merrow's character asks Oliver's Lothario of a seaside photographer why he stays in a small town, thinking him to be the type who would have moved on to a bustling city long ago. Asked if he likes living in the town, he replies, 'No, not particularly.'

'Then why stay?'

'Perhaps I'm a little nervous of going anywhere bigger.'

Recalling that exchange today, Jane sees it as being quite revealing. 'That really was close for him. Oliver never quite became the massive star he could have been and it was sort of relative to the industry in England at that time. Turning Hollywood down was part of his problem because had he gone out there I think he would have become very big because they would have known what to do with him and how to make the best of him. Maybe the problem with Oliver was his ambitions didn't go beyond having fun doing films where he was safe and comfortable amongst his mates.'

Michael Apted agrees. 'He was too comfortable. He had his lifestyle, which was hilarious, and he had his mates. I think not choosing to go to America was a mixture of comfort and fear; he didn't want to make that break.'

All the time pressure was building. Big, powerful American agents were making overtures. 'Look, he needs to come out here.' It would have meant a massive commitment, of course, and almost certainly it would have meant Oliver moving out to Los Angeles for a couple of years. Did he perhaps fear losing Broome Hall as a result? David was quick to put his mind at rest on that one. 'Look, I'll wrap Broome Hall up and put everything in mothballs. You don't have to lose it. Just go over there, for goodness sake, it's big money and it's where you need to be.' Still the answer was no. 'He just didn't like Hollywood,' says Mark. 'He didn't like what it stood for. He just wanted to be in his little local boozer, do his movie, and be out of there.'

A couple of years after they made *The Devils* together, Georgina Hale remembers Ollie saying to her, 'You know, Georgie, I could have gone to Hollywood but I chose life instead.'

Only much later, in the nineties, did Oliver admit that he should have made the switch to Hollywood when he had the chance, when he was at his peak. 'It might have made all the difference.' Much more of a calamitous mistake was turning down two Hollywood blockbusters, since the parts on offer were real game-changers. Both heralded from the same man too, Hollywood producer Richard D. Zanuck. The first was the role of Doyle Lonnegan, a crooked gangster swindled by con artists Paul Newman and Robert Redford in *The Sting* (1973), one of the most popular films of the decade. The second was to play the grizzled shark hunter Quint in *Jaws* (1975), which went on to become one of the most commercially successful films of all time. In an email Zanuck confirms that Ollie was indeed offered both of these roles and rejected them. In reference to *Jaws* Zanuck says he approached Ollie after Robert Mitchum and Sterling Hayden had already turned Quint down. One can only speculate where Ollie's career might have taken him had he accepted either of these films, especially *Jaws*. One can quite easily visualize him playing Quint, shouting and screaming at Richard Dreyfuss and Roy Scheider on his rickety old fishing boat while downing bellyfuls of whisky. In a strange quirk of fate both roles ended up being played by Robert Shaw, quite brilliantly too. But what a shame Ollie didn't do at least one of them. 'Certainly had Oliver done *Jaws* he'd have been a big star,' says Michael

Winner. 'A serious star, not sort of wobbling about headlining British films. But he was nervous about going to Hollywood, he was nervous of being where he didn't feel secure.'

Oliver had already had a 'taste' of Hollywood, which predictably ended in disaster. Steve McQueen flew into London to meet him with the intention of talking about their making a film together. Ollie invited McQueen to Tramp nightclub, where he got quite dreadfully drunk and vomited over the American superstar. The manager found some new jeans for McQueen to wear but, alas, couldn't offer him replacement shoes. 'So I had to go round for the rest of the evening smelling of Oliver Reed's sick.' Needless to say, the film project died a death.

Having spurned his chance of Hollywood fame and opting instead to remain in Britain to be the biggest fish in a small pond, however tepid and stagnant that pond was, Ollie stood exposed to the vagaries of his native industry's death throes. David continued to field offers for his brother, some good, some indifferent and some just plain bizarre. Into that last category one must place *Blue Blood*, a British film made for the staggeringly low cost of just £55,000. Ollie agreed to take part, for a very low fee, provided the film could be shot over a two-week period when he was free. Based on a novel by Lord Alexander Thynn, 7th Marquess of Bath, and filmed at his palatial home, Longleat, the film has Ollie as a malevolent butler who uses satanic means to replace the master of the house, played by a very young Derek Jacobi. Esteemed film critic Leslie Halliwell wasn't wrong when he wrote that the film 'plays like a Grand Guignol version of *The Servant*'.

With only a fortnight to make the film, speed and efficiency were of the essence. But, according to producer Peter James (now a best-selling author of thrillers), 'Ollie was, to put it mildly, a nightmare.' It didn't take him long to organize a crawl of the local pubs. Everyone piled into their cars – Ollie was then driving a rather beautiful Bentley Continental – and off they went. 'In those days one wasn't so worried about drink-driving,' says James. 'I remember we were completely and utterly pissed and ended up in a restaurant where this po-faced maître d' approached our table and said, "Anybody here has a Bentley Continental?" and he gave the registration number. Ollie said, "Yes, why?" The maître d' said, "It's just rolled into the wall of the conservatory, sir."'

Later that same evening everyone ended up back at the hotel propping up the bar. At around one o'clock people started slipping off to bed. 'The next morning,' James recalls. 'A waitress was taking somebody up breakfast and she saw Oliver naked and fast asleep in the corridor, curled up around a radiator. What had happened, he'd gone into his room, taken all his clothes off, and gone into the bathroom, except he hadn't gone into the bathroom, he'd walked out the door into the corridor. Of course, the door locked behind him, he didn't know what to do, so he just curled up and went to sleep.'

Midway through shooting, Ollie approached one of the producers, a nice chap called John Trent. 'I've got a problem, John,' he said. 'There's this absolute cunt in London I've fallen out with, he's part of an underworld gang and he's threatened to come down here and duff me up.'

'Oh shit,' said John. The last thing the crew wanted was Ollie getting a black eye or even a cut, anything that would delay shooting. 'For Christ's sake, if he turns up just let me know.'

'Don't worry, I will,' said Ollie, walking back to his caravan.

About two days later John was on the set when Ollie sidled over to him. 'You know that bloke I was telling you about?'

'Yes,' John said.

'Well, he's just driven into the car park.'

'Right, who is he?' Two men, behemoths in suits, were walking purposefully forward. John told Ollie to get lost and went over to confront them. 'Yes, can I help you?'

'Who the fuck are you?' one of the guys said.

'I'm the producer.'

'I want to see Oliver Reed,' the thug replied, his face impassive but deadly.

John stood his ground. 'I'm sorry, he's on set at the moment.'

The thugs pushed John out of the way and carried straight on towards a visibly shaking Ollie. 'We want a word with you.'

'You cunts,' yelled Ollie. 'Fuck off.'

About to see his star seriously pummelled, John gallantly dived in between the two goons. 'I said, get off the set!'

One of the men picked John up by the lapels as if he were a twelve-year-old and hurled him to the floor. Getting up, John rammed into them again and a fist fight broke out. After several right hooks had been thrown, John became aware that the entire crew were standing in a circle watching and grinning. 'The whole thing was a set-up,' says James. 'Ollie had arranged it all. John got a bloody nose, loosened teeth. It was a nasty prank.'

In spite of the pranks and pub crawls, James confirms that Oliver was utterly professional when it came to the actual work, mindful of the incredible time constraints on everyone, and the film was finished on schedule.

Next Ollie flew into a pre-revolution Iran to take the lead role in an all-star adaptation of one of Agatha Christie's most famous and often told tales, *And Then There Were None*. He stayed with the rest of the cast at the glamorous Shah Abbas Hotel (now the Abbasi Hotel) in Isfahan, which also stood in for the film's location. In Christie's novel ten guests, all with a guilty secret, are invited to a lonely mansion on a deserted island by a mysterious host who then proceeds to kill them off one by one. Producer Harry Alan Towers had shifted the action to an abandoned desert hideaway more in keeping with the cosmopolitan cast he'd assembled, the likes of Richard Attenborough, Elke Sommer, Stéphane Audran and Charles Aznavour.

At the helm was Peter Collinson, best known as the director of *The Italian Job*. Collinson and Oliver took an instant dislike to each other, which probably explains the reason for the violence and carnage that followed. A witness to it all was the actress Maria Rohm, wife of Towers, and her evidence seems to point to the fact that Collinson was a disagreeable presence to just about everybody. 'I don't believe anybody liked Peter Collinson. He was very rude and crude to everyone.'

Unwarranted rudeness had always rankled with Oliver, as it smacked of bad manners and lack of professionalism, but his anger boiled over when Collinson turned on Maria one evening when she and Ollie were innocently dancing in the hotel's nightclub. 'Collinson made rude remarks about me which set Ollie off and they got into a fight. Ollie was not very precise with his punches but Reggie was. The crew was mostly Spanish and sided with the director: it's an honour thing. The whole situation got way out of hand and some crew members got really hurt. There were knife wounds, hospital visits and stitches. The actor Adolfo Celi took care of me but I felt rather guilty for having been the initial reason for the altercation. It was all very traumatic.'

Just a couple of days later Maria witnessed something else that chilled her blood. 'The hotel had a beautiful courtyard and I saw Peter and Ollie walk towards each other with broken bottles. I was truly concerned and ran out into the courtyard and together with some of the crew managed to keep the two men apart.'

Elke Sommer also found Collinson 'crazy and horrible' and she and Ollie spent much of their time bitching and moaning about him. One morning on the set Ollie confided to her, 'Don't worry, sweetheart, we're gonna take care of him.'

'What are you going to do?'

'You'll see,' said Ollie, grinning.

That night there was another massive ruckus in the hotel between the Spanish crew and the Brits working on the film. 'One of the Spaniards took a pop at Ollie when he wasn't looking,' recalls Simon, who witnessed the whole thing. 'And within about six seconds this guy had been laid out by Reg – bang – and another guy had been laid out who'd come in to follow up. Everyone who saw it said it was one of the most impressive things they'd ever seen. The way Reg reacted was unbelievable.' Then it all kicked off with tables and chairs flying everywhere. 'And the next day Collinson came on to the set and he had his arm in a sling,' recalls Elke. 'And Ollie just looked at me and winked and said, "I told you. I told you."'

In the end it was left to Richard Attenborough to attempt to calm things down by organizing a kind of court hearing where people could thrash out their disagreements without resorting to violence. 'We always called Dickie the judge after that whenever we met,' says Simon. So a room was hired and all the Spaniards sat on one side and the Brits on the other, with dear old Dickie in the middle presiding. One gets the feeling it didn't work. 'It was a very nasty atmosphere after that,' says Simon. 'Because I think the Spanish lot were after Reg and Ollie.' Indeed, Maria confirms that Ollie and Reg had to move to another hotel.

In spite of all the problems, Maria was very fond of the enduring double act of Ollie and Reg. 'If I'm honest, I was somewhat afraid of them to start with. But Reggie turned out to be the nicest of people and I learned to love Ollie despite both of them looking and acting rather intimidating at times. And there was the drinking. Yes, Ollie was drinking rather heavily, yet he was always a complete professional on the set. I remember once Ollie and Reggie had a drinking contest with one of the film's Iranian backers. Very much a gentleman, he could not decline and he did not know how to handle the situation. His manners did not allow him to leave and he ended up very drunk. He couldn't stand up by the end of the evening. I was very concerned and felt sorry for him but I am glad to say he survived it all OK.'

Elke, too, had a soft spot for Ollie, and in spite of his temper problem she got along with him very well. 'We had fun together and we laughed. I liked the fact that he was intelligent but he was always a little proletarian in his behaviour, in his looks, actually in everything, very down to earth. We became good friends.'

As a souvenir from his time on *And Then There Were None*, Ollie brought back with him a hookah which he gave to Christensen as a present. 'And we used to get a half ounce of roll-up tobacco and to make it more fun he poured a bottle of gin in the hookah instead of water and a couple of rose leaves and a shot of Angostura bitters.'

Moon the Loon

Early one morning the peace of Broome Hall was shattered by an ear-piercing roar that seemed to be coming from overhead. 'What the bloody hell is that?' yelled Ollie. Outside, a helicopter was making several sweeps over the house looking for a suitable place to land. Adjacent to the terrace and the rose garden was an open field and the whirring machine deposited itself on it. Oliver stormed out of the house, ranting and raving, then suddenly the door of the helicopter opened and out stepped Keith Moon. 'And Oliver's face was a picture,' says Jacquie. 'They ran up to each other and they hugged and they kissed. "I've come for lunch," announced Moonie. He ended up staying a week.'

The helicopter was a spectacular show of ostentation and Ollie was suitably impressed. Grabbing Moonie, he took him on a guided tour of Broome Hall and its grounds. Afterwards Moon suggested they play a game. As Ollie remembered it, 'I was supposed to run round the fields while he chased after me with the car to see if he could hit me.' Exhausted but still alive, Ollie suggested they head off for a liquid lunch at the Cricketers, where Moon failed hopelessly to keep up with his host. Victorious, Ollie proceeded to take his clothes off but was hauled back home before exposing himself to the local punters. How had all this madness come about, this merging of the film and rock worlds? Blame Ken Russell.

Since their fraught experience on *The Devils* Oliver and Russell had patched things up, with Ollie appearing very briefly as a railway guard in the director's recent *Mahler* for the princely sum of three bottles of Dom Pérignon. More importantly, Ollie wanted Russell to direct a project he was working on about the four knights who murdered Thomas Becket in Canterbury Cathedral. Oliver had helped write the script and also expressed an interest in producing and starring in it. Invited round to Broome Hall to discuss the film, Russell must have twigged that something was up when Ollie opened the door dressed in his Athos costume, bowing and donning his hat with theatrical absurdity. 'Welcome, your eminence.' Russell should have bolted there and then. 'I knew I was going to be put to the test again.' But no, professional curiosity won out.

Instead of discussing the project, all Ollie seemed to want to do was re-enact his musketeer heroics, walking about the great hall swishing a rapier with one hand and holding a glass of brandy in the other. 'Shouldn't we talk about this film of yours, Oliver?' Russell asked, exasperated.

'I'd clean forgotten about that,' said Oliver, throwing the sword to the ground and walking across to the grand fireplace, where an ominous-looking broadsword hung on display. 'The man in the shop swore this was a thousand years old.' Carefully, with love almost, Ollie lifted down the sword. 'I'm sure it's authentic.'

Russell looked the thing up and down, all six foot of it. 'It's certainly very rusty.'

'Blood, dried blood, that is.' The devilish merriment in Ollie's eyes was enhanced by the flames flickering in the fireplace. 'A sword like this killed Becket.' Ollie raised it up as if he were holding Excalibur itself. 'Priest or no priest, Becket was quite a swordsman. He must have put up a hell of a fight before they killed him.' Ollie threw the lethal weapon at Russell, who just about managed to catch it. 'Imagine you are standing on the altar steps, Jesus, and I'm coming at you, coming to spill your guts and rub your sanctimonious nose in them. It's you or me, trying to split each other in two.'

Russell looked at the sword in his hands. 'Where's yours?'

'My what? My sword? You don't imagine I've got two of those big bastards, do you? I use the rapier.'

'I rather see Becket defending himself with a crosier,' said Russell hopefully. 'I don't suppose you . . .'

'Bullshit, Jesus!' yelled Ollie, practising a few lusty swipes. 'Now get up on the altar steps.' Russell had no choice but to obey. 'Prepare to meet thy maker, heretic.' With those words Ollie lunged at him.

As Russell was later to recall, 'I knew that I'd have to fight him properly otherwise he'd kill me. So we were duelling and I brought the blade down with all the force I could muster. It crashed across his chest, tearing open his shirt.'

There was silence. Ollie dropped the blade to the floor and ripped open his costume to see a gash in his chest. 'Excellent!' he roared. 'Now we're blood brothers.'

Removing a stuffed parrot from a Victorian glass dome on the fireplace, Ollie threw the creature on to the blazing fire and replaced it with his bloodied shirt. It remained there for years as a memento. The Becket film fared rather less well and never came to fruition. In the meantime, Russell had become attached to a film that would prove to be one of the most striking cinema experiences of the seventies.

In 1969 Pete Townshend, the John Lennon of The Who, wrote his rock opera *Tommy*. Inspired by his own scarred upbringing by warring parents, *Tommy* deals with the alienation of the post-war child. 'I was trying to show that although we hadn't been in the war we suffered its echo.' It was musical impresario Robert Stigwood who saw *Tommy*'s movie potential and secured Russell's services, no doubt influenced by his skill in marrying images to sound. The director insisted Oliver be cast as Tommy's stepfather, Frank, a surprising decision considering the entire film was to be sung and Ollie confessed that he possessed the vocal dexterity of a rugby forward. So David was called into Stigwood's office to do the deal. 'It was a very imposing office,' he remembers. 'I always had unimposing offices.'

The canny Stigwood was pushing David to agree to a fee for Ollie out of future profits from the movie soundtrack. David said no: Ollie wanted cash up front. Stigwood tried another tack: Ollie could have a fifth of a per cent of this and that and whatever. David wasn't having any of it. 'So in the end, which I invariably did as a theatrical gesture, I put all my papers in my briefcase, said thank you very much, and walked out.' Unbeknown to David, he'd played an absolute blinder. 'It wasn't just Ken who wanted Ollie, so did the money men. The financing was totally dependent on bringing Ollie on to the project. I didn't know this, so in the end Stigwood had to give in to our terms.'

Before a foot of celluloid was exposed, the entire album score had to be re-recorded for the film at The Who's private London studio. When Ollie arrived for his first rehearsal, a disturbed Townshend was pacing up and down, swigging neat brandy from a beer mug. Russell was waiting in the control room. 'OK, Ollie, grab a mike and start singing.'

'I don't know any songs, Ken.' Then, turning to Townshend, he said, 'Listen, Peter, all I can give you is "The Wild Colonial Boy".'

Townshend's face was vacant, as if a 'To Let' sign had been hung up on his forehead, but he was game and sat down at the piano. Clearing his throat, Ollie gave it his all but still sounded like a prop forward singing 'Nellie Dean' in a pub toilet. Townshend stopped playing, downed the remainder of the brandy, and announced, 'Are you fucking joking?'

Ollie was dispatched home, along with a tape of the musical

score, and ordered to learn all of his songs by heart. David remembers driving his brother back up to the studios a few days later with the music of *Tommy* blasting out of the car stereo's speakers and both of them singing along to it. In the end Ollie approached his role rather like Rex Harrison did with Professor Higgins in *My Fair Lady*, in that he performs the songs rather than sings them. This led to a highly endearing but also a broad comedic performance, and initially Russell was worried that it was straying into the realms of caricature. Confronted about this, Ollie yelled, 'Me, over the top? Have you ever seen any of your films?'

Keith Moon wasn't present at Oliver's recording session. Nor was their first meeting his notorious helicopter landing at Broome Hall. They had first bumped into each other at a hotel in Weymouth on the south coast during *Tommy*'s first week of shooting in April 1974. 'We were shown into Keith's room,' Jacquie recalls. 'And we were only there about fifteen minutes when he started complaining that he couldn't get his television to change channels. He phoned down to reception, who of course had never come across anyone like Moonie before. "I can't change channels, bring another television set up here." And the guy said, "We don't have another telly." And Moonie picked up the set, opened the window, and chucked the television out and it smashed to pieces. Can you imagine that poor hotel?'

While Jacquie was dismayed by such behaviour, Ollie immediately responded to it. Curiously, of all of the members of The Who he might have befriended, Jacquie thought the most obvious candidate was Townshend, a man of equal intelligence. 'But no, Oliver gravitated straightaway towards Moonie. He was another child to play with.' And very quickly Jacquie sensed that she was no longer welcome on the *Tommy* location. 'I was only there for a very short time because obviously Oliver wanted me well out of the way so he could play with Moonie.

And it wasn't until the film was over that I really saw him again.' And play they did.

In order to prevent global catastrophe, Ollie and Moonie were separated and housed in different hotels. The plan backfired because Keith and his entourage simply decamped over to Ollie's hotel, and within a few days, as word spread of the drummer's wild all-night parties and groupies, the rest of the crew moved in with them. It was like Sodom and Gomorrah. 'The place was full of crumpet,' recalled Ollie. One night he was besieged in his bedroom by six bunny girls pressed up against the glass fire escape door, all waving dildos at him. When Ollie had to go away for a couple of days he invited Keith to use his room if he wanted. On his return he walked in the door and there was Keith with girls attached to every orifice and he just stood up, 'Hey, Ollie boy, make yourself at home.' As Oliver later told his brother David, 'I knew right there that things are very different in the music world.' Indeed they were and Keith was a very different kind of hell-raiser, heavily into drugs. 'Ollie only dabbled in drugs very, very infrequently,' claims David. 'But Keith did drugs in a big way.'

About the only thing Ollie dabbled in was smoking weed. He used to grow it in the greenhouse at Broome Hall and dry it out in the attic. 'I grew up around marijuana constantly,' admits Sarah. 'I knew how to toast marijuana before I knew how to toast bread. I was rolling joints for them all at quite an early age, not very well. It was completely normal.' Mark got into trouble at school once for bringing in weed. When the teacher asked where he got it from, he said, 'From my dad.'

As for that Weymouth hotel, it did seem to have a pipeline running from the Playboy mansion in Beverly Hills. David recalls visiting Ollie there and going out together for the evening. On returning, they discovered a party of dolly birds in Ollie's room brazenly ordering champagne. 'Good evening,' said Ollie. 'What can I do for you?' They told him in no uncertain fashion. Slamming the door shut, Ollie and David went down to reception, only to be told, 'Look, it's not our responsibility.' So they trudged along the passageway to Keith's suite, knocked on the door, went in, and there was Keith in bed with two of the most stunning blondes you've ever seen in your life.

'Hello, Ollie, what's up then?'

'We've got all these birds in our suite.'

'What's the problem, then?' replied Keith.

'What do I do?'

'Oh, for fuck's sake, Ollie.'

Keith got out of bed stark bollock naked and strutted down the passageway, opened the door and yelled, 'Right, you lot, OUT! Out! Go on! Get away with you!' All these girls stopped doing whatever they were doing and said, 'All right then, we'll go and see Reg,' and they all trooped out. God knows what Reg did with them. 'There must have been twenty of these girls,' recalls David. 'Ollie and I ended up hiding downstairs under the reception desk out of sight in case any of them came down.'

During a break in filming, Ollie retired to Broome Hall and a temporary respite from the insanity of Moon's universe. It didn't last long: Keith arrived for the weekend with a new girlfriend, Joy Bang, a ditzy blonde American actress who made quite an impression on the young Sarah. 'She used to go into my mother's wardrobe and help herself to anything and I admired her, she was a complete hippy. I remember I used to jump into bed with her and Moonie in the morning and sit in between them and we'd just laugh, all three of us, like children, because they were probably high by that stage. That kind of thing was my normal as a child, so I would go to school on a Monday morning and the teacher would ask, "What have you done this weekend, Sarah?" And I'd say, "Oh, I jumped into bed with Keith Moon from The Who."'

Filming continued on *Tommy* in the Lake District and at

Southsea, where Ollie and Moonie almost killed themselves when they pinched a boat and went off in it, no doubt trying to row to the Isle of Wight to see Gus, who was entertainment manager at a holiday camp there. 'Well, it capsized,' remembers Mick Monks. 'And they both somehow managed to swim ashore – pissed. Amazing they got back alive, just terrifying.' Interiors were completed at Shepperton Studios, where Monks was working, and he'd often meet up with Ollie to talk over old times. Driving home one night, he saw Ollie's car parked outside a pub near the studio and went in. 'He was in there with Moonie. "Tractors, come and join us." And Moonie asked for this exotic type of liqueur but the barman didn't have it, so Moonie just picked up a chair and threw it through the optics and screamed, "You better fucking get some in then." A lot of people wouldn't stay the course. If Ollie said, "Come on, we're going out on the piss", they'd run away because they couldn't keep up. Not Moonie.'

During another journey home from the studio, Bill Dobson, Christensen and Reg were in the car when Ollie announced that everyone had to make up a dare for each other. It couldn't be dangerous but they all had to do it. 'Should liven the journey up a bit,' he said. The first dare was for Reg. Stopping outside a normal suburban house, he had to go and knock on the door and insist on a cup of tea and a biscuit and be seen from the window partaking. Sure enough, a couple of minutes later there he was at the window. Next up was Christensen. His dare was to go into the saloon bar of a pub, order a pint of whisky and pour it over his head. This he did and his eyes stung like mad, and there was Ollie and the others sitting in the next bar saying to the customers, 'Is he some sort of fucking nutter or something?' Bill was up next. Just by chance Ollie's chauffeur had a pair of yellow washing-up gloves in the boot that he cleaned his car with. Bill had to put one of these on his head, go into a pub and walk around in a circle clucking like a chicken. So successful was his performance that this became something of a party piece for old Bill. Ollie even got him to do it naked once in a crowded pub.

Back in the car, Bill turned to Ollie. 'Right, your go.' Knowing they were going to drive past a golf club, where a four were usually teeing off somewhere, Ollie had to run on to the course and go up to the bloke about to tee off and say, 'No, no, no, you're holding it completely wrong,' take the club off him and drive his ball into the rough somewhere, then bugger off. And it happened exactly like that.

Tommy marked the last time Ollie and Russell worked together for sixteen years, not counting an uncredited walk-on in Ken's very next movie, *Lisztomania*, a gloriously ripe biopic of the Hungarian composer starring Roger Daltrey and with Ringo Starr as the Pope. Again payment was in the form of champagne, this time a whole case. Working with Russell nearly always produced Ollie's best acting, and the reason for that was simple: Ollie believed in Ken. 'And there were very few people that Ollie believed in,' says Simon. 'He tolerated some, didn't tolerate others, liked some, but he really did rate Ken and trust him.' There was a shared lunacy and sense of the ridiculous that came across in the work they did together and also in life. Here's a good example. Dropping into a pub on the way back to his hotel after a day's filming, Russell ordered a bottle of wine and a plate of whelks. 'I'm sorry, sir,' said the landlord, motioning his head across the saloon bar. 'We've just sold the last whelks to Mr Reed.' Ollie raised his glass, a big soppy grin on his face.

Annoyed, Russell left and got back into his car. He was about to drive off when an object hurled itself onto the bonnet – it was Ollie. Undeterred, Russell revved the engine and manoeuvred his way onto the main road, with Ollie still lying spread-eagled before him. 'Since when do you refuse to take a drink with me?' Oliver screamed through the glass.

'Since you ate all the whelks,' Russell shouted back, nursing the car up to forty miles per hour.

'You want whelks,' Ollie roared. 'I'll give you whelks. Turn back.'

Now approaching a roundabout, Russell went round it and returned to the pub. There, as he hit the brakes, he watched Ollie shoot off the bonnet, fly through the air and land in a heap in the car park. 'You want whelks,' said Ollie, dusting himself down and marching over to an estuary that adjoined the pub. Open-mouthed, Russell saw his leading man dive into the water, fully clothed, to emerge seconds later with a fistful of seaweed and undetermined gunk. 'Here's your fucking whelks.'

'Thank you, Oliver,' said Russell as he examined the rather unappetizing shellfish that had been hurled unceremoniously on to the bonnet of his car.

'Now, what'll you have?'

'Half of shandy,' said Russell, borrowing a knife to prise open the shellfish. As he later recalled, 'It was worse than swallowing two globs of phlegm soaked in sump oil.'

Boxing Clever

With *Tommy* in the can and destined to become a great success, Ollie and Moonie drew up plans for another collaboration, a theatrical venture that, had it come off, would have been among the most unusual shows ever to hit the West End. It was called 'The Dinner Party', and that's exactly what it was going to be: Ollie and Keith having dinner on stage with some of their celebrity friends popping in. There would also be a snooker table on stage, so Alex Higgins could play a quick game when he felt like it. During the meal, catered by the best restaurants in London in exchange for a credit on the programme, all manner of topics and conversations would take place, all impromptu; every night would be different. Ollie also planned that five members of the audience would be invited to join them on stage for each performance. The poster would ask: 'Have you been to the Dinner Party?' It was an inspired idea, but just how successful it would have proved is another matter.

Having reached the pinnacle of his profession, Ollie was now considered a suitable candidate for that doyen of broadcasting institutions, *Desert Island Discs*. It proved to be a troublesome recording. He arrived at the BBC's Broadcasting House with his gardeners, having insisted none of them change their clobber of jeans and dirty wellies. 'There were quite a few raised eyebrows when my agricultural entourage traipsed after me, swigging gin straight from the bottle and depositing mud and horse shit all over the carpets.' Again it was Ollie aiming a swipe at convention, putting two fingers up to what he called 'po-faced traditions'. His musical choices ranged from Frank Sinatra to Claude Debussy, but, when asked what luxury item he'd take with him, he chose an inflatable woman. Afterwards the normally placid host, Roy Plomley, was heard to mutter, 'The only island that man should be cast away on is Devil's Island.'

After the broadcast Ollie took his gardeners to the White Elephant in Curzon Street for a slap-up meal. As a joke he got the filthiest gardener to go in first and ask for a table. Of course, the maître d' told him to fuck off. In walked Ollie wearing a big smile. 'Ah, Mr Reed, I should have known it was you. But can they leave their boots by the door?' Christensen remembers ordering tournedos Rossini, a portion of fillet steak on toast with pâté, and when it turned up Ollie stared at the waiter. 'What the fuck's that?' The waiter began to get nervous. 'It's what the gentleman ordered sir, it's a tournedos.' 'I know what it is,' said Ollie. 'But look at the size of that steak and look at the size of that man. Go and get another five.'

As a rule Ollie preferred his local curry house in Dorking to posh restaurants, and always sat with his back facing the room, as he didn't like facing out because people would recognize him. There he often played the 'hottest curry' game. Ken Burgess, aka the Admiral, an old rugger bugger from Rosslyn Park, loved his curries, the hotter the better, and was a regular visitor to Broome Hall. One lunchtime Ken ordered the hottest curry on the menu but when it arrived a look of disappointment flooded his face. 'This is pathetic, Ollie. It's not nearly hot enough.' Oliver called the waiter over. 'Excuse me, this man likes a hot curry. What you've presented here a girl could eat. Take this plate of food away.'

Ten minutes later the waiter returned with a new plate

of food, all swimming in red and shit. Ken took a couple of mouthfuls. 'That's better,' he said. By the third mouthful he started choking. But he ate the lot. Christensen was there and when he put his finger in the curry it physically hurt, and it burned his lips. 'They'd obviously just ground up some chillies and said, "Right, have that on us, clever bastard." Anyway Ken was sitting in the back of Ollie's Roller, moaning and groaning and farting. We got to the bottom of Ollie's drive – it's a long, long drive going up to Broome Hall – and Ollie shouted, "Right, get out of the fucking car, Admiral, I'm sick of your moaning and farting. Sit on the bonnet and hold on to the lady." So Ken was sitting there and as we got to the bridge there was a speed bump, we hit it and old Ken went flying off the bonnet. Ollie just managed to stop in time. After that Ollie renamed Ken "the Tumbling Admiral".'

Moonie was by now a regular visitor to Broome Hall and Christensen met him on several occasions, arriving at the opinion that if such a thing were possible the drummer was even crazier than Ollie. One afternoon they'd been drinking in Dorking and had come back, and Moon said to Christensen, 'Hey, Norse, do you happen to have such a thing as a twelve-bore shotgun?' He had several. 'Could I have one, please, and some ammunition?' Christensen answered, 'No fucking way. I'm not giving you a gun under any circumstance, pissed or sober.' Moon looked at him and said, 'Don't be such a spoilsport.'

Usually Moonie arrived with a new girlfriend in tow. 'He always had these Swedish blonde bombers with him,' recalls David. 'And he got girls walking naked round Broome Hall.' On one memorable occasion Ollie and Moon dressed up as clowns and cavorted around the gardens and boated on the lake for hours. Ollie adored clowns, owning a huge collection of watercolours of them bought from a Wimbledon artist. 'I think he saw himself as a clown,' says Jacquie. Ollie's humour wasn't so much telling jokes as physical comedy, pulling funny faces and doing silly things to make you laugh. 'There's also the pathos and the crying, the tears of a clown,' notes Jacquie. One of the very few things she still has from her time with Ollie is a painting called *The Clown and the Dancer* that he bought for her. The picture must have spoken to him the second he saw it, because the faces of the two figures are almost identical to the way he and Jacquie looked when they first fell in love.

Jacquie has also kept some of the poetry Oliver wrote for her. 'He wrote lovely poetry. They were very strange and whimsical, much like Lewis Carroll. A lot of them were love poems, to me.' Much later Oliver wrote poetry for Josephine. 'It wasn't necessarily very good,' she admits, 'but he did enjoy writing poetry. Often he'd say to people, give me a word, any word, and then he'd make up a poem using that word.'

Mark also used to come down to Broome Hall, mainly on weekends and school holidays, and spent much of his time there driving the Land Rover and tractors. Oliver did up one of the mezzanine floors like a disco, with music and lights and a glitterball, and Mark would have his mates round for parties. At the time Mark was at Millfield, a top public school in Somerset. Perhaps remembering how he was abandoned in such places by his parents, Ollie was determined not to make the same mistake with his own son. Mark remembers, 'He used to come down from time to time, arriving in a jet ranger helicopter that he'd chartered, and we'd go off for lunch somewhere, or he'd pick me up at the end of summer term and we'd fly back to Broome Hall.'

Growing up, Mark was conscious of the fact that his father was keen for him to do well academically, helping him with his homework whenever he was around. 'He recognized that he'd probably had a chequered past with his education, so saw it as important. For my sister it wasn't – she would be swept off her feet by some rich young landowner and live happily ever after – whereas boys had to go out and do their bit. So he

293

always thought that academia was important, but not hugely: he thought the university of life was of greater worth.'

It was during these visits to his father that Mark built up an understanding and a friendship with Jacquie, who was both kind and supportive to him. And she would defend him, too, if Oliver was being awkward. 'She would stand in my corner. Good woman, Jacquie. She probably had more of the challenging times with him than my mother did, or later Josephine. I mean, he'd bring all his mates back from the pub and suddenly she'd have to make fifty-eight fried-egg sarnies. It wasn't an easy life to share.'

For Mark, Broome Hall was like an adventure playground for grown-ups, and being a young lad he was the perfect age to enjoy it. 'There were always antics going on. Because of the way he was he would have people round and it got fun and outrageous. Then they would go because they'd had enough – they could hardly see or walk or talk, most of them – and then someone else would knock on the door and go, "Hi, Ollie." It was continuous.'

Sarah, of course, was much younger and has always said that at Broome Hall there was play time but it wasn't child's play time, it was the big boys' play time. Off went her dad and his mates to the Cricketers and when they came back they were going to be silly. 'In which case I was usually removed, or you were around until it got overly silly or loud and leery. My mum says there was an occasion where my dad was playing with a shotgun and it went off and I was quite close by, so you always knew something dangerous could happen, but I was removed as soon as it got too much. But I do remember being very envious that they looked like they were having such fun and I wasn't included. It was play time but not for me.'

It must have been strange for a young child to watch her father behaving in such a fashion. 'But he liked to do silly things,' says Jacquie. 'He'd play hide and seek in all those bedrooms.

He liked to jump out on people.' He'd also get Bill Dobson and others who worked on the property to be in his gang. 'We're on parade,' he'd announce, and they'd all stand to attention on the gravel driveway at the front of the house and he'd put paper hats on their heads. 'Can you imagine these people, a bit pissed, marching up and down?' says Jacquie. 'They fell in the roses and everywhere, screaming with laughter like children.'

Sarah hits the nail on the head when she says that her father never really grew up. He was the Peter Pan of hell-raisers. When Space Dust first came out he bought boxes of it and was going up to people in the pub and shoving it in their mouths. 'It's that real childlike quality: he would just go, "Wow, this new thing's really exciting", and he'd get all waggy-tailed about it. He also had this thing, "I want to play – now. I've got to play." It was that intense and immediate. So he'd walk in at four o'clock in the morning when you're asleep, he'd be stoned or pissed, and want to tell you a story or show you something. I remember he came back from the pub one night with these glowsticks and shoved them down my duvet cover and woke me up, yelling, "Look, look, spacemen are coming." And I'm half groggy, going, "What are they?" He was so excited by it. Then they all faded and he went away and I couldn't get back to sleep again. He was so maddening at times. Looking back, though, I really wish I'd appreciated it more.'

All this, of course, tallies with the fact that Ollie had a supremely low attention span. 'He grew bored easily,' says Jacquie. 'He liked new adventure all the time.' Once he decided to take Sarah and Mark to Her Majesty's Theatre in London to show them its connection with Herbert Beerbohm Tree. A revival of *The Sound of Music* happened to be playing, so he bought tickets and they went to see it. Half an hour in, Ollie was bored and buggered off to the bar. Sarah also remembers the occasion Ollie and Keith Moon heard there was a circus coming to Dorking. They were like a pair of kids, let's go to the circus, so they took Sarah and off they went. 'We walked along endless fields and crawled up the bank of this hill and finally got to the circus and it was like, no, don't fancy it now, and we came back. I said to Mum, "How could you leave those two men in charge of me?" And she said, "Joy Bang must have been with you." I was like, "She was no good, she was never any good."'

It was almost like the idea or the planning was sometimes better than the actual event. One time when Mark had friends over, Ollie got an empty bottle from the cellar bar, all cobwebby, and put a handwritten note inside and told them it was a pirate's message. 'So he had this amazing childlike imagination when he really wanted to,' says Sarah. 'But just as you were getting into the game or the story he'd go, "I'm bored now, I'm off," and he'd disappear. He'd want to go and play with the big children.'

All this couldn't have been anything other than tough for Sarah growing up. She remembers Jacquie saying once, 'Most people's lives are fairly mundane, with the odd up and the odd low, whereas ours was always up or down, with the odd mundane.' And she has never forgotten what her father used to say to her when he sensed that maybe it was all getting a bit much for her: 'Would you prefer a daddy that goes to work with a side parting and a briefcase and a suit or would you prefer me?' And of course she always used to say, 'Oh, I prefer you, Daddy', but sometimes deep down she'd think, I would love just to be normal for a little while. 'He used to occasionally turn up at my junior school and flirt with the mums and blow kisses. He used to embarrass me terribly. Unless he was in his quiet mode he would never go anywhere quietly, it was always a performance and there'd be a commotion. Now I look back and think, wow, isn't that great? But at the time it wasn't: it was, please, can I just be normal, I really want to be normal, and we never had that. I just wanted him for me. Everyone always wanted a bit of him, and he was good at giving out bits of himself, and sometimes you just felt, actually, what's left for me? I just want it to be me and my dad. And that didn't happen very often.'

For some time Ollie had been regularly going to see fights at the Royal Albert Hall. Boxing was never going to eclipse rugby as his main sporting pastime, but it was something he enjoyed watching and knew quite a bit about. 'Ollie did love his sport,' says Simon. 'He watched a lot of sport on TV. He followed horse-racing to a certain extent and football a bit, also golf, but rugby was always his big love.'

When John Conteh fought the Argentinian Jorge Victor Ahumada for the Light Heavyweight crown at the end of 1974, Simon was part of the BBC radio team at the Empire Pool, Wembley. He'd been asked by the producer if he could persuade Oliver to be a ringside guest. Ollie agreed and a car was booked to pick him up at home at 4 p.m. The bill started at eight, with the main fight on at 9.15 p.m. 'It got to eight o'clock and Ollie hadn't arrived,' recalls Simon. 'They contacted the guy in the car and he said, "Look, we've stopped six times in pubs, he keeps taking me this way and that way. He's Oliver Reed, I can't do anything." Eventually he turned up five minutes before the fight. Typical Ollie: the timing was perfect. And he did a decent job; he was pissed but he did what he had to do. So he did like his boxing. He was a big fan of Conteh and Alan Minter.'

Back in the late sixties, when he still lived in Wimbledon, Oliver even sponsored his own boxer for a while. 'Suddenly I was asked to start feeding this gentleman with steaks,' remembers David. 'Ollie said he was going to be the next best thing since sliced bread. Then I started getting these bills from this butcher and they got bigger and bigger until in the end I was saying to Ollie, "One man can't eat all this meat." So it was obviously feeding half of Bermondsey or wherever the guy lived. I do remember we used to go to watch this guy box and quite famous underworld characters would be seated in the prime chairs round the ring.'

When Ollie heard that in his next film, the Richard Lester-directed *Royal Flash*, he was going to spar on screen with one of his heroes, Henry Cooper, he could barely contain his excitement. 'It was like going to the pantomime and meeting Jack and the Beanstalk for real!' Oliver had been cast as the famous nineteenth-century German statesman Bismarck, while Cooper was playing the real-life John Gully, an English bare-knuckle prize-fighter and politician. As the two men started trading punches for the camera, Ollie admitted to getting carried away with the glory of the situation and deviated from the rehearsed routine. The next thing that happened was, he was lying on the floor with Cooper standing over him. 'Sorry, Ollie, I felt that one sink in.' As he was helped to his feet, Oliver's head was throbbing. He'd just been stung by Henry's Hammer, 'his famous left hook that had spread-eagled Ali across the canvas'.

Simon, however, recalls events a little differently: that Ollie aimed a swipe at the former heavyweight champion, 'just because, I think, he wanted to tell me and others that he'd knocked Henry Cooper out. It wasn't a very good move. I think Henry handled it very well.'

Revenge may very well have been on Ollie's mind when the two met again in 1985 on a television show called *All-Star Secrets*, hosted by Michael Parkinson. Henry Cooper was the subject of this particular episode and celebrity guests were brought out on to the stage to reminisce in that cringe-making way celebrities are very good at. Ollie had been booked to make a surprise appearance at the end and was psyching himself up in his dressing room, jabbing away in front of a mirror, reducing it to so many broken shards with swift left hooks. Already out on stage were Roy Kinnear and *EastEnders* actress Wendy Richard. They knew Ollie was coming next and were expecting him to make his entrance from the side, but instead he punched a hole in the set. 'I thought it was part of the programme till I saw Michael's face,' said Wendy.

Ever the pro, Parky took Ollie to the side of what remained of the set and began discussing his bout with Henry in *Royal Flash* and asking how many rounds did he fancy going with the ex-champ now. Ollie was supposed to have said the scripted line, 'As many as he will buy,' but instead his face was blank, unresponsive, dead like the far side of the moon. Suddenly there was movement, a powerful but hopelessly misdirected swing aimed at Cooper's head, who ducked just in time, but the end result was almost Ollie's fist smashing into Wendy Richard's face. 'I swear my eyelashes sort of fluttered, he was that close. What a night!' As one of the production staff said later, 'Oliver was like a hurricane that blew through but did not kill anyone.'

Michael Parkinson had other encounters with Oliver, 'and lived to tell the tale'. He once played cricket with him, a charity game at the Oval during which Ollie walked to the wicket wearing a turban and a sarong and carrying a tray with a pint of bitter on it. 'The man next to me sighed at the spectacle,' Parky recalled. 'I said, by way of polite conversation, "I suppose he belongs to someone." My companion said, "As a matter of fact, he does. I'm his father."'

Royal Flash concerned the exploits of Harry Flashman, a Victorian military bounder of the highest order, played to perfection by Malcolm McDowell. It was based on a series of enormously successful books by George MacDonald Fraser, who also wrote the screenplay. Fraser liked Oliver a great deal and thought that as Bismarck he was far and away one of the best things in *Royal Flash*. In lesser hands Bismarck might have come across as a bit dour, since it's he who has to set up the rather clunky plot, but Ollie gives him gravitas and his own usual aura of malevolence. 'As I discovered later,' said Fraser, 'Ollie was unusually proud of his performance. When we met again years later he hailed me with a cry of, "Not a bad

Bismarck, was I?"' Until his death Fraser kept a card bearing Oliver's sketch of a rapier and plumed hat labelled 'Ath' and a top hat and moustache captioned 'Bis', signed 'Ollie Reed'. It was sent to the writer in 1982 'and it's a remarkably neat piece of work, considering that he did it, according to the messenger who brought it to me, in an advanced state of inebriation.'

Ollie and Lee

In the autumn of 1975, when Oliver agreed to appear in the comedy western *The Great Scout & Cathouse Thursday*, he faced the challenge of sharing the screen with a man whose hell-raising and boozing matched his own: Lee Marvin.

'You know, Oliver, that Mr Marvin enjoys a drink.' The voice belonged to the film's English producer, Jules Buck, who was in the limo with Ollie that was taking him to Los Angeles airport to catch his flight to Mexico. 'Could I ask you as a great favour to calm it down, because Lee's terribly difficult?'

'Of course. I quite understand,' said Ollie, stifling a burp. 'You can count on me to do all in my power to keep Mr Marvin away from that disgusting liquor.'

'Oh, and may we ask you to do the same?' said Buck.

Ollie puffed himself up with fake indignation. 'What do you mean?'

'Well, er, I understand that you have a certain reputation for, well, how can I put this, you know, for having a few drinks at night and, you know, getting into fights.'

Ollie's face was one of alarm and bewilderment. 'What! How dare you! Stop the car! Let me out – I'm going back to England.'

A volley of profuse apologies followed. Buck hadn't really meant what he said, oh no, and yes, of course he trusted him completely, oh yes. Ollie must have revelled in watching his producer squirm in his seat. It was only later, talking to Marvin, that Ollie heard that Buck had told him exactly the same thing.

The car pulled up outside the airport hotel and Ollie walked inside. Marvin hadn't arrived yet, or so he thought, then someone pointed to an object asleep outside on a bench which stirred when prodded by an assistant. Wearing a baggy pair of jeans, mangy shirt and shabby sports jacket, Marvin strolled into the Departures lounge, looking like a crumbled wad of ten-dollar bills. And there was Ollie, dressed in a smart Dougie Hayward suit. 'How do you do? Pleased to meet you, I'm sure,' he said, in his best *Brideshead Revisited* voice. Marvin was genuinely taken aback. 'I was expecting to meet up with this actor who was supposed to be Britain's hell-raiser and what do I see but this tailor's dummy in a pinstripe suit looking more like a fucking banker.'

During the flight Ollie and Lee were as good as their word and declined offers of beer and spirits, instead drinking orange juice. Things changed when they hit Durango. High up in the Sierra Madre mountains, the city of Victoria de Durango had long been acknowledged as a perfect location for making westerns, despite its remoteness. Back in the seventies there was just one flight a day to Los Angeles; that was the only means of getting there and the only communication with the outside world. 'It really was a hick town,' recalls David Ball, the film's accountant. 'There was no tarmac on the street and there were potholes that you could lose a car in. It really was a funny old place and very much bandit country. Our member of the secret police allocated to us by the Mexican government, who we made our transportation captain, gave me a gun on my first day out there. "What am I going to do with this? I'm from England," I said. "You are best to have this, señor," he replied. "Because down here banditos."'

Ollie considered Marvin 'Mr America' and claimed to have 'crossed the Atlantic to challenge him for his crown'. It didn't take them long to decide to have a drink one evening, once the producer was safely tucked up in bed. 'Well, what are we going to have?' asked Ollie.

'We're in Mexico, we'll drink fucking tequila,' Marvin replied.

'Let's not waste time, then,' said Ollie as he poured himself half a pint of the stuff, took a handful of salt and a lemon, smeared the glass with it, and drank it down in one.

Marvin watched this, said, 'If you're just going to fuck around, I'm not playing,' and went to bed.

When the drinking contest proper was finally arranged, co-star Strother Martin was elected referee. 'Marvin was the champ and had the privilege of calling the shots,' said Ollie. It was to be vodka on the rocks, and they were knocked back, line after line, until Ollie emerged victorious after a reported ten hours. 'He was as proud as punch about that,' remembers Simon. 'And he rang me about three in the fucking morning, slurring, "I want to tell you that Lee Marvin's given me his drinking cloak, and he's now under the table. He's under the table as I'm talking to you now, and I've got his cloak." So they'd obviously had a monumental session. Getting Lee Marvin's drinking cloak was almost like getting an Oscar for Ollie.'

Respectful of his drinking prowess, Ollie was also a fan of Marvin the actor and had seen all his films. He was the prime reason for taking on what turned out to be a disappointing film in which, for some reason, Ollie was playing a whisky-soaked, gonorrhoea-ridden Indian. It's a marvellously inventive and funny performance but you can't help thinking while watching it that Ollie was miscast. The plot has him and Marvin's grizzled frontiersman out to reclaim a lost gold mine from villainous Robert Culp.

David remembers just how thrilled his brother was about working with Marvin but couldn't help feeling at the time that producer Jules Buck was 'very, very mad' to team the two of them together in the same movie. Incredibly Durango survived – look it up on Google Earth, it's still there – but it was touch and go for a while. The crew were housed in a hotel called the Campo Mexico, a series of chalets on the northern edge of the city. Ollie and Marvin, though, were allotted houses, but most evenings Ollie ventured to the Campo to drink with the crew. 'And Ollie's drink was six bottles of Domecq, Mexican white wine,' recalls David Ball, who along with Ollie was one of the few Brits on a crew largely made up of locals and Americans. Ball is a chief witness to the shenanigans and wildness that went on in Durango with Ollie. 'As people came into the bar he'd invite them over, so the table would just get bigger and bigger, and Ollie would order six bottles of Domecq and, irrespective of what you drank, if you were sitting with Ollie you drank Domecq white wine. And they couldn't chill it fast enough.'

One night Ball's girlfriend arrived from London and they were part of Ollie's table, cracking jokes and having a laugh. Six bottles of Domecq, please. Then suddenly Ollie turned to Ball and said, 'Goodnight, Dave.'

'Oh, goodnight, Ol. You going? See you tomorrow.'

'No, I meant you. Off you go.'

Ball grew anxious. 'Listen, Ol, we're all having a drink here, we're all getting a bit lathered. If I've said something that may have upset you, it was certainly not intentional, so please forgive me.'

'Oh no, no, no, no, you're all right, mate. The thing is this, I'm going to smash this fucking place up in ten minutes and I wouldn't like your good lady to get hurt. So better go.'

'Good night, Ol,' said Ball, and he and his partner left. 'And he did: he fucking threw a table through a plate-glass window. And they had to board it up.'

The following evening Ball was sitting there with his girlfriend and in walked Oliver. Pleasantries were exchanged. And then this little waiter came up to him. His hands were shaking and he was holding a small piece of paper. 'What's this?' asked Ollie. 'It's probably the invoice for the damage, Ollie, you did last night,' said Ball. Ollie looked at the bill – it was something like a couple of hundred dollars – pulled out some money, gave the waiter an extra $50, and ordered six bottles of Domecq. 'That was class,' says Ball. 'Pure class.'

Ball first met Ollie at Los Angeles airport, but it was Reg he got to know first, both being cockneys. Ball saw first-hand exactly how Reg operated in the evenings with Ollie, how he kept him out of trouble and also indulged his excesses. If Ollie wanted to smash a place up, Reg wouldn't stop him. 'If that's what you want to do, you want to let off steam, fine,' he'd say. And then when Ollie was done, Reg was on hand if there were any repercussions. 'Reg knew that Ollie was a leery git sometimes when he went out on the booze. Reg was the safety barrier.' It was needed sometimes, because in bars or clubs there would be a bit of a fracas to start with but then things quietened down and they'd be left pretty much alone. 'The word went out very quickly,' says Ball. 'Ollie and Reg roll into town, they put their stamp down and that's it, you don't fuck with them, you really don't fuck with them. I mean, Ollie was strong, but Reg was something else. But you'd always find that, if they did cause a bit of damage, there would be a couple of hundred bucks over the bar to sort it before they left.'

Ball was also privy to the playfulness that existed between the two men. One day on the set Reg bought Ollie a piglet and left it in the bathroom of his location trailer with a pink bow tied around its neck. Ollie kept it as a pet in his rented house, even teaching it how to play hide and seek. 'At three o'clock in the morning you could hear Ollie and this little piglet running all around the house together,' remembers Ball.

One afternoon news reached the crew of a terrible accident. A production driver had to collect someone at the airport and, passing through a village, inadvertently ran over a little boy and killed him. Ball was asked to get a thousand dollars in an envelope, which he did, and give it to the associate producer. 'What's it for?'

'This has got to go to the chief of police to hush it up.'

'But it was an accident,' said Ball.

'Yeah, but this is how it works down here.'

The next day at lunch Ollie announced they were holding a collection for the dead boy and threw a couple of hundred bucks on the table. 'Right, Lee,' he said. 'You give me two hundred, come on you've got it, give me the fucking money. Come on you, Strother, give me two hundred. Robert, come on, come on, everybody.' By the end Ollie had a bundle of cash and as a result the Americans on the crew, instead of giving a dollar or two dollars, were handing over tens and twenties. Ball reckons the dead boy's family received something like the equivalent of twice their annual income. 'And Ollie was the one who kicked it off. He was the one that forced people to dig deep into their pockets. That's how big-hearted he was. Because if you animated Ollie to do something for you he would do it 101 per cent. That's what he was, Mr 101 Per Cent.'

Amid all this a film did actually get made and the chemistry between Ollie and Marvin is terrific, even if Lee was pretty much pickled most of the time, according to Ball. 'His wife Pamela had to physically restrict the amount he could drink because he only needed to sniff the bottle and he was gone, more or less.' This isn't to imply that Marvin had reached a point in his life and career where he was a walking coma patient, but Ball does remember Ollie sometimes goading the veteran star to get a performance out of him. 'He'd push him, he'd say, "Come on, Marvin for fuck's sake, can't you do better than that!" Those were great days. You looked forward to going on the set because you didn't know what Ollie was going to do. He did something new every day. Wonderful, wonderful man. And probably the most professional actor I've worked with in forty years in the business, and I'm putting him up against people like Burt Lancaster and Rod Steiger. He would always, always get blind drunk with Reg but in the morning would be on the set at six and do the scene in take one while Marvin was still learning his words. They don't make 'em like that any more.'

Mayhem at the Beverly Wilshire

During the winter at Broome Hall nothing very much went on in the garden, especially in the market garden. 'It's freezing, the ground's solid, so nothing's growing,' Christensen told Ollie when he enquired one morning on the state of play. 'Fancy a bit of heat then?' Ollie said. 'Wanna come out to Barbados?' Christensen grabbed his passport and off they went. As they arrived at the hotel Ollie took Christensen to one side. 'The barman at the restaurant knows who you are, you're staying with me, you pay nothing here.' And the holiday lasted three weeks. 'I went out to Barbados with £45 spending money and came back with £55,' says Christensen.

Paul Friday came along too, and Ollie boasted one night to the locals that he and Friday were top-notch darts players, foolishly as it turned out, because somebody set up a darts match with the island's champions. Thinking it would be a few drinks and a bit of a laugh, they got a shock to see three hundred people and a local TV crew waiting for them. By a complete fluke they won, 'Only because they were more pissed than us,' said Ollie. The next day Christensen and Friday were told to be 'on their best fucking behaviour' because they'd all been invited to a barbecue. Ivan, Ollie's driver on the island, took them to a beautiful villa that was discreetly tucked away and had a guard on the gate who was quite obviously wearing a piece. Christensen started to get a bit worried. 'Anyway, we were let in and introduced to this middle-aged man, who was very pleasant. We had traditional food, it was a very nice evening. I was on my best behaviour obviously. And driving back with Ivan I asked, "What's all the big deal about being on your best behaviour?" and Ivan replied, "I wouldn't want you to insult the Prime Minister."'

Another day Ollie took the group for a treat to Greensleeves, a very upmarket private estate fronting the beach. Almost immediately Oliver started to misbehave, climbing on to the flat roof of an outbuilding that overlooked the pool, while waiters tried to pull him down by one of his legs. Finally he got on to the diving board and, fully clothed, pretended he was going to jump in. Sitting nearby eyeing him up was an immaculately dressed woman, probably in her late fifties. When he saw her she said, 'I will if you will.' That was a red rag to a bull and Oliver leaped into the water. With that the woman stood up and executed a perfect swallow dive. 'Give that woman a bottle of Dom Pérignon,' Ollie announced. But the fun and games weren't over. 'Because then everyone else started to dive in too,' remembers Paul Friday. 'They were jumping off the diving boards. Nearly everyone in the restaurant ended up in the water. One broke his leg, a girl broke her ankle, another broke his arm. It was complete mayhem.'

During their stay HMS *Fearless* came into port and here Ollie executed one of his great wind-ups. The victim was Paul Friday, who always told Oliver that he could see his wind-ups coming a mile off. With the ship sitting in Coconut Creek, all the officers frequented the local bar and immediately recognized Ollie. Asked if he was on holiday, he replied that he and his men were diving for Sam Lord's treasure. Now, Sam Lord was the island's most infamous buccaneer in the early 1800s and lured ships laden with gold on to a reef where he and his men slit their throats and stole their booty, much of which, legend has it, still lies on the seabed. Without any prior warning Ollie introduced Paul Friday to the officers as one of the best divers in the Royal Navy, presently AWOL because Ollie was paying him so much. Invited aboard HMS *Fearless* and into the officers' mess, Friday grew ever more anxious putting on the old naval act as he was subjected to numerous questions about this fictitious dive. 'Then suddenly I've got this bloody diving officer coming on to my shoulder asking what sort of gases I'd be using to go down to this depth. And I'm thinking, what have I got myself into? Ollie's going, "Oh, it's top-secret, experimental stuff." The evening went by, we had quite a bit to drink. The next thing, these two heavies come in and I'm grabbed hold of, taken out, and locked up. I'm in this cell all night thinking, I've talked myself into this. The next morning the door opens and there's Ollie and Norse and Ollie says, "Gotcha!" The whole bloody lot of them on that boat knew what was going on apart from me!'

After Barbados Ollie flew alone to Los Angeles, where he booked in at the Beverly Wilshire. There he awaited David, who was flying over to negotiate some business; it also happened to be David's fortieth birthday. Driven from the airport, David arrived at the Beverly Wilshire, where grand steps led up to the entrance, but there was no front door, nothing at all. 'I thought, well, obviously the weather's so good here you don't need front doors. Only to find out later that Keith Moon had come visiting and driven up the steps and through the doors, smashed them, and his car ended up in the foyer of the hotel.'

On the morning of David's birthday the two brothers met in the hotel bar. 'What do you want to do then?' asked Ollie.

'I really don't mind.'

'I'll tell you what, we'll go out for a meal tonight.'

'That sounds good.'

For the rest of the day they stayed in the bar, slowly making their way through several bottles of liquor, chatting, laughing and telling jokes. At one point David just happened to glance down at the end of the bar and thought he saw Keith Moon walk past an open door. He turned to Ollie. 'Keith's just come in.'

Ollie looked blankly at David. 'No, no, Keith left days ago, he wouldn't be here.'

Evening descended and remarkably both brothers were still standing, quite compos mentis actually. 'OK, let's go out,' suggested Ollie. 'I know somewhere to go. Let's both have showers and meet down here in twenty minutes.' David was in his room when the phone rang. It was Ollie. 'Where are you?'

'Ollie, it's only been ten minutes. I'm in the middle of having a shower.'

'For God's sake, hurry up.'

At the allotted time David showed, only to see a huge banner spread across the bar: 'Welcome to David's 40th Birthday Party.' Ollie had organized a huge surprise party in the main dining room, an opulently furnished space with flock wallpaper, chandeliers, the works. And there was Moonie, grinning from ear to ear. Ringo Starr was another guest. 'I sat down at a table,' recalls David, 'and a very pretty girl was put beside me, so I started talking to her. She was at some university. About halfway through the meal she disappeared. Never mind, I thought. Then suddenly there was a fanfare and these huge doors opened and six chefs pull in this cake, which is almost up to the ceiling, about nine foot tall with layers going up and candles all round it. I was given a sword to cut it but as I approached the lid of the cake exploded and the girl who had been sitting beside me came out stark naked.' It was Ollie's idea to have the girl in the cake. He'd always heard about these girls jumping out of cakes, but never seen one.

Moonie, one surmises, had probably seen plenty of naked girls jumping out of cakes, jumping out of all sorts of things probably. But the sight of this particular girl set him off. What happened next David has never forgotten. 'Keith leaped up the

311

layers of the cake and tried to grab the girl, who made a run for it. At that point Keith started going mad: he got the sword and slashed at one of the chandeliers, which came crashing to the floor. Women were screaming, running out of the room, and goodness knows what. Then Keith got hold of this enormous great tablecloth and pulled the whole thing off and the crockery and soup tureens and everything were smashing on the floor. In doing this he'd cut his hand rather badly and blood was pouring out. The next minute he's gone, with Ollie chasing after him. So I ended up talking to Ringo and he was telling me about how your nose gets delicate after you've been snorting for so long, when suddenly the doors opened and the police came in with truncheons and Ringo went, "Oh dear, here comes trouble."'

It was at this point that David decided he'd better find Ollie. He was in the kitchen attending to Moonie, who was lying stretched out on the floor, blood everywhere. Ollie was holding his arm up, trying to stem the flow of blood, while balancing a whisky and soda. Then the paramedics arrived and got down on the floor by Keith's head to ask, 'Where does it hurt?' And there's Ollie spilling his Scotch over Keith, who's going, 'Aarrgghh!' And the paramedics go, 'Where's the pain?' After about ten minutes they realized this was a total fiasco and left. David ended up outside helping put Keith in his car and then watched it drive off. Meanwhile the kitchen door had slammed shut behind him, so he had to walk back in through the foyer. 'By that time hotel security were in great evidence. I went back into the dining hall and there was Ollie sitting round a mountain of broken chairs, tablecloths covered in red wine, and shattered chandeliers. "That was quite a party, wasn't it, David?" he said.' Quite a bill too: Ollie had to pay £10,000 for the damage.

But Ollie and Moonie weren't finished yet. Their next stunt was kidnapping David Puttnam. The British film producer had just arrived in LA and was stepping out of the Beverly

Wilshire on his way to a business meeting when Keith's Rolls-Royce slammed on its brakes in front of him, a door burst open, and he was grabbed and thrown into the back. The next thing Puttnam knew he was being driven fast along the Pacific Coast Highway. 'It was mad,' he later recalled. 'They were laughing, it was stupid and it was edgy. I knew I could handle Keith [Puttnam had recently worked with Moon], but the two of them together I certainly couldn't handle.'

In comparison with their antics on *Tommy*, Ollie and Moonie's escapades in Los Angeles seemed to have a much darker tone to them, a result no doubt of Keith's mental state at the time. Not only was he fighting alcoholism, but he was increasingly withdrawing into himself. Ollie was one of only a select few Keith allowed to visit him at his LA pad. They'd spend hours in the evening just sitting and listening to music, often in silence, not talking. Ollie was only too painfully aware of the change in his friend, that things were flat-lining, the clown's make-up had smeared.

Sometimes the old Keith would resurface. One evening Oliver was attending a film premiere downtown, something he despised, but he had two lovely ladies accompanying him, so things weren't all that bad. Resplendent in a dinner jacket, he walked out of his hotel to get into a limo, a multitude of flashbulbs exploding around him, when – thwack – something hit him in the face. It was moist and tasted of lemon: it was a custard pie. After removing the mess from his eyes and noticing that his lovely lady friends had suffered collateral damage, he then had a card pressed into his hand by a man. It read: 'Pie In The Face International – you have been selected by Mr Keith Moon to become a member. Here is your certificate.' Ollie burst out laughing.

Film director Peter Medak recalls standing outside the Beverly Wilshire when a limousine pulled up, the door opened and somebody on all fours backed out on to the pavement on his hands and knees. 'And it was Oliver. He'd arrived at the airport at four o'clock that afternoon and he'd stopped at every bar, and now he was checking into the hotel. We fell into each other's arms and he said, "Come on, let's go to the bar, they'll take the luggage upstairs." We go into the bar and within two seconds he had the bartender by his neck. They threw him out of the hotel before he could even check in. Oliver was the darkest of those hell-raisers. Oliver for no reason would start a fight. If he didn't like someone's face or someone said the wrong thing – boom.'

Ollie also bumped into Yvonne Romain and her husband Leslie Bricusse, who had a house in LA and often hosted Sunday lunch parties for Brits working in Hollywood. Ollie, who hadn't seen Yvonne since their Hammer days, was invited and found himself among a who's who of British film stars. 'It was amazing,' remembers Bricusse. 'There was Ollie, Roger Moore, Mike Caine, Sean Connery, you name it. Sadly no one took a photograph.'

Bricusse recalls another memorable Sunday. He was just on his way to have lunch with Timothy Dalton at a famous pub on Sunset Boulevard called the Cock and Bull, when Ollie called and asked if he could tag along. Bricusse was only too happy, so called the Cock and Bull and the manageress told him, 'I'm sorry, Mr Bricusse, but Mr Reed is barred. The last time he was here he threw the barman through the back of the bar and destroyed it. So he's not allowed in here. I'm sorry.' Bricusse reassured the manageress that both he and Timothy Dalton would be responsible for Oliver and she finally relented. 'So we had lunch, it was very nice, and Oliver was very well behaved. I had a four o'clock business meeting, so I left Tim to look after Ollie. When I got home later that day the phone rang, it was the manageress of the Cock and Bull. He did it again, three minutes after I left, knowing the circumstances – and it was the same barman!'

The reason for Ollie's lengthy presence in LA was that film offers had all but dried up in Britain and he now had no choice but to go where the work was. David had managed to get mega-agency ICM to put one of their best agents on to the job of looking after Ollie. 'And bless her, she came home with the goodies.'

Ollie's first Hollywood-based movie was *Burnt Offerings*. Shot early in 1976, this adequate haunted-house chiller did modestly well at the box office and was from writer-director Dan Curtis, best known for his cult TV series *Dark Shadows*. Ollie was teamed with Karen Black, a hot actress at the time after roles in *The Great Gatsby* (1974) and *Nashville* (1975), and the legendary Bette Davis. His admiration and respect for Miss Davis were unqualified, and on screen it's a joy watching them bounce off each other and share some choice barbed dialogue. Off set, things were a little different, with Miss Davis declaring Oliver 'possibly one of the most loathsome human beings I have ever had the misfortune of meeting'. An overreaction for the press perhaps, since at the close of filming she presented him with a signed pen and ink drawing of herself which he proudly displayed in his study. What's true is that Ollie did send her round the bend a few times. Miss Davis used to have her evening meal sent up to her hotel room on a food trolley. Returning from a drinking session one night, Ollie deployed the trolley as a skateboard, hurtling down the corridor and waking her up. She also complained to the producer about his nightly drinking ritual and said that he would arrive on the set in the morning the worse for wear. 'That man seems to be perpetually on a hangover,' she blasted.

Karen Black refers to Oliver as 'a guy's guy' and remembers one morning having to do a scene where his character is attempting to drive away from the house during a torrential rain storm. 'And these rain machines can drench you in thirty seconds. I don't think Ollie had slept all night, so there he was in the car completely drenched with the wind machines howling outside and he was shaking, he was visibly shaking. But he kind of used that for the scene: his character was supposed to be distraught. It was very bewitching to watch, it was quite brilliant.'

Often before scenes, Karen remembers, Ollie would 'get seriously wired-up', but she also found that sometimes when he fluffed a line he'd very subtly and nervously chastise people for standing in his eyeline. 'But the truth was, in my perception, he just forgot his lines and he didn't want to say, sorry, let's do that again, so he would blame the first person he saw standing there.' That insecurity again: Oliver was desperate to make a good impression on his first American movie. Karen saw it more as being childish, a trait that jockeyed for space with his chauvinism in her estimation of Ollie. Her description of a chauvinist is a man who can't tolerate it when a woman takes a point of view and can't be moved off it, not because she's stubborn but just because that's her position. Karen remembers one scene with the two of them swimming in an outdoor pool and Ollie had placed his face on the camera side of hers. On the next take she said she was going to put her face at the forefront of the camera this time. During the shot Ollie did everything he could to prevent her. 'But I held my position, and he got up right out of the swimming pool and he had to take a very long walk because he was so infuriated. But I must say I liked him, he made me laugh. But I don't think he paid much attention to me at all. I think if I asked him the colour of my eyes he never would have known.'

That chauvinism reared its head in spectacular fashion during a memorable appearance on Johnny Carson's *The Tonight Show*. Carson had steered Ollie on to one of his favourite subjects, women, and good ol' Ollie didn't hold back, going into misogynist overload and elaborating on his theory that, underneath all the political beliefs and talk of equality, women really wanted to be in the kitchen with their pots and pans. Fellow guest Shelley Winters, a staunch women's libber, could contain herself no longer and poured her drink over Ollie's head. It's a great television moment and Ollie handles it perfectly, not rising to the bait but behaving like the perfect English gentleman. Carson's face throughout is a picture.

Reporters always knew they could get good copy out of Ollie by asking him to discuss his attitude towards women, because invariably he came across as a male chauvinist pig of the Jurassic era. Of course, most of the time he knew exactly what he was doing by suggesting that a woman's proper place was on her hands and knees scrubbing the floor. 'In return I feed them, wine them, make them laugh and give them a punch on the nose and a good kicking when they need it,' he wrote in his autobiography as if it was some kind of manifesto. Such statements were nearly always intended to get a reaction, and to his mind it was great if at the same time they also pissed off the dreaded women's libbers, a breed he genuinely despised. 'I don't like to sit around listening to these stupid women's libbers, who are anyway eventually going to be fucked to death by some big marine, and enjoy every moment of it.' But, as Simon admits, this horseplay wasn't wholly an act. 'I think fundamentally this chauvinism was there and then he would use it as a weapon to shock.' Jacquie agrees. 'As far as women were concerned he genuinely thought he was superior.'

At Broome Hall Jacquie time and again wished she could join in the fun with the boys more often, but instead she was usually consigned to the kitchen with the other women drinking Blue Nun round the table. 'It really was quite Victorian when women disappeared while the men went to smoke their cigars in the drawing room.' Ollie was old-fashioned in other ways, demanding Jacquie give up her dancing career, which she did. 'His mentality was, you don't work, you're here twenty-four hours for me.' She was also forced to drop some of her friends or he made it awkward for her to see them. 'My father was quite controlling,' admits Sarah. 'He did tend to control the women in his life and he did like to control his children.'

This level of control reached absurd heights during Jacquie's time with Ollie. On holiday, for example, she wasn't allowed to wear a bikini: it had to be a one-piece. All this derived no doubt from Ollie's own insecurity. Often he was guilty of misinterpreting situations, especially when he was drunk. 'I might be talking to someone,' says Jacquie. 'And it could be a friend, a person he knew, and they'd make a joke or something and I'd laugh. Well, that was like a red rag to a bull. He'd go, "Leave her alone" or "Get out!" And the poor guy hadn't done anything. He was very, very possessive. He had to possess someone completely.'

It's amusing to discover that Ollie once confronted Carol Lynley, complaining that he'd been referred to as a misogynist in a magazine article. 'You don't think I'm a misogynist, do you?' He seemed genuinely surprised by the notion. This in spite of the fact that he regularly came out with gems like: 'Clever women make me apprehensive. Women are not thinking vessels. They are vessels for a man's sex and his children.' Or this description of his ideal woman: 'A deaf and dumb nymphomaniac whose father owns a chain of off-licences.' The BBC was once bombarded with angry phone calls from housewives after he took part in the Radio 4 chat show *Start the Week* and suggested a woman should behave like a nun by day in the kitchen and a whore at night in bed.

Such trivializing of women appears at odds with the impeccable manners he always displayed when in their presence. 'I may be a bastard but I'm a polite bastard,' he once said. If a woman came into the room he always stood up, always, and that was with him right the way throughout his life. 'His manners, when he was deciding to act in that way, were outrageously correct,' says David. 'He would exaggeratedly get up, he would make an absolute feature of getting up.' It was the same if a woman left or returned to a table at a restaurant. 'And if it was a table of twenty people he was standing up every five minutes, a bit like a yo-yo,' jokes Mark. Sometimes he would open a door and a woman would walk through and he'd say, 'I beg your pardon,' and she'd say, 'I didn't say anything,' and he'd reply, 'I'm so sorry, I thought you said, "Thank you."'

These gentlemanly characteristics and good manners, harking back to a bygone age, added immeasurably to Oliver's personal charm and were part of what Mark believes made him so endearing to the opposite sex. 'Women like a naughty boy, but Ollie had that very smooth, gentlemanly veneer that had a naughtiness underneath it which crackles, which is exciting, which is attractive.'

It's undeniable that Ollie was far more comfortable in the company of men than of women, but he was capable of both affection and great love for a woman. 'He certainly loved me,' says Jacquie. 'Women as a whole, though, I don't think he liked them as a species. But, in a funny sort of way, he needed a companion of the female kind, both physically and emotionally.' Carol Lynley believes it runs much deeper and that, rather than a general dislike of women, he felt anger towards his mother. Certainly Oliver blamed Marcia for the break-up of her marriage to his father. 'And he held a score against her all his life,' says David. The fact that she was never around much during Oliver's childhood may also have contributed to his insecurity and to his lack of trust of women. Carol Lynley remembers only a few instances when Oliver brought up his mother in conversation, and when he did the anger was tangible. 'I got the impression he didn't seem to like her very much. So I don't think Ollie disliked women, I think he was still angry at his mother and it came out like that.'

Madness in Budapest

Straight after *Burnt Offerings* Oliver made another American film, *The Ransom*, but this was a distinctly average thriller in which he played a law enforcer brought in to capture a renegade native Indian threatening to wipe out the well-heeled residents of a town unless he is paid a million dollars. The cast met up for the first time for a read-through of the script in their hotel in Arizona, where the film was shot. Paul Koslo, hired to play the deranged Indian, arrived early and was astonished to find Ollie already resident in the bar. 'He had this goblet, as big as a fish bowl, full of booze. This was, like, six o'clock in the morning.' The read-through was scheduled for 10 a.m. and Koslo was in for another surprise. 'Oliver didn't know just his own lines, he knew every character in the film by heart. To me, that was totally amazing. I've never seen a man drink so much and still be rock solid. He could drink a gallon of gin or whatever and you wouldn't even know that he'd had anything. We don't know how he did that. Everybody said, you've not only got one hollow leg, Ollie, you've got two hollow legs.'

The sheer amount of drinking that Ollie was doing was as troubling as it was impressive, and he didn't care who saw it. 'He did it out in the open,' recalls Koslo. 'And the director, Richard Compton, he was a young guy and this was a big movie for him, he got real concerned about it. But after the first few days, once he saw that Ollie was a total professional, he dropped his concern a little bit. But Ollie was so out of left field sometimes, he was so unpredictable that his behaviour definitely kept the director on the edge.'

The heat was intense too, as it was summer, with the temperature soaring. Unbeknown to Ollie, Georgina Hale was staying in the same hotel as a guest of Koslo and was in the habit of relaxing beside the pool in the afternoon. 'All of a sudden Oliver arrived and he just picked up the sun chair I was in and was about to throw me in the swimming pool when I screamed, "Oliver!" He looked at me and suddenly recognized who it was and immediately put the chair down. It was great to see him again but he was drinking and always you felt like you had to join him. In the end it was like one of those movies where, every time he filled up my glass, when he wasn't looking I'd throw it over my shoulder. I was very fond of him. But he loved his drink, loved to be at the bar with the guys. And that was his life.'

Ollie must have known when he read the script of *The Ransom* that it was garbage, but he still approached his role with dedication and enthusiasm, particularly when it came to the accent. He prided himself on his American accent, a skill many of his fellow British actors couldn't master. He had it perfectly and could do different pitches and different dialects. 'And he was so riveting that you knew you had to be at the top of your game because he could play a scene five different ways and every one of them was brilliant,' says Koslo. 'Obviously he always played Ollie Reed, but he had so many facets to him that he could actually make anything believable and compelling.'

The Ransom proved to be Ollie's last American movie for several years. He and Hollywood hadn't really taken to each other and the top ICM agent assigned to look after him, in David's words, 'didn't know how to cope with him'. It had nothing to do with Ollie the actor: it was his behaviour, perceived or otherwise. 'The Americans are terribly cautious about drinking and rudeness,' says David. 'They're quite puritan about it actually. You go out to dinner and if you take more than one glass of wine you're looked upon as a drunkard.'

As a place Los Angeles didn't excite Ollie, either. It was bearable when Moonie was around and he could lark about at the Beverly Wilshire, but as somewhere to settle down or to work in for long stretches, forget it. 'I don't think he actually disliked Los Angeles as much as he was so very English that he was just like a fish out of water,' believes Carol Lynley. 'He didn't really want to fit in and always wanted to go home.'

Admittedly Oliver had lost his best chance of succeeding in Hollywood by not succumbing to its overtures a few years before. Now the impetus was lost and the big offers that had been available to him were no longer on the table. For the next few years he actively sought films well away from Hollywood, working in Canada, South Africa and back in Britain. But first stop was Budapest, for *The Prince and the Pauper*, another all-star costume drama, brought to the screen by the Salkind brothers in the hope of trading on the success of the *Musketeer* films. 'And like with Athos,' says producer Pierre Spengler, 'when we talked about who should play Miles Hendon, the film's swashbuckling hero, Ollie was the obvious choice. He was perfect for the role: all the nuances and the depth and the humour was there.'

In the 1937 version of Mark Twain's famous historical tale about a prince and a pauper who are virtually identical and decide to exchange places, the role of Miles Hendon was taken by Errol Flynn, so Ollie was delighted to be stepping into the shoes of one of his screen heroes. In fact he'd been wearing the man's shirt for some time. Oliver claimed that he was dining in a restaurant when an American approached him and said, 'Like to make a swap? Your leather jacket for my shirt.' Ollie laughed, 'You must be joking.' The guy took the shirt literally off his back and revealed the laundry label with Flynn's name just about legible and the studio number. The deal was done. Remarkably, given Ollie's forty-six-inch chest, the shirt fit snugly enough and he began to wear it regularly. 'Although Errol seemed to slow me down, or perhaps his ghost couldn't stand the pace.'

World-weariness and outstanding swordsmanship weren't the only similarities between Athos and Miles Hendon. Hailing from the landed gentry, both are also street brawlers and supreme quaffers of ale, and in both cases Ollie's portrayal trades heavily on his gentleman-thug image. In both films he is seen drunk or waxing lyrical about the virtues of the grape. And drinking is what Ollie did a lot of on location in Budapest, nearly getting himself deported and killed by eastern European gangsters in the process. According to George MacDonald Fraser, who'd written the screenplay, Oliver was installed at the luxuriant Gellert Hotel with the rest of the cast and crew but after making a continued nuisance of himself was sent, in disgrace, to the Intercontinental. 'Apparently he changed hotels, not by taking a taxi across one of the bridges, but by wading and swimming the River Danube in the middle of the night, arriving in the Intercontinental lobby clad only in mud and waterweed. It says much for his persuasive powers that the management allowed him to stay instead of throwing him back.'

The Prince and the Pauper reunited Ollie with his *Oliver!* co-star Mark Lester, now all grown up, and also Murray Melvin. When Melvin flew into Budapest a couple of weeks into shooting, he walked into the lobby of the Gellert Hotel holding his suitcase and there, sitting on a sofa, were Ollie and Reg, 'looking like two naughty school boys who'd been found out'. Murray greeted them from across the foyer, and Ollie looked up. 'Oh, Murray.'

'What's the matter, Ollie?'

'Umm . . . well . . . I've . . .'

'Oh no, Ollie, what have you done?'

323

It had started out as a pleasant evening in a local restaurant, but then the Bull's Blood began to flow. 'A few bottles, I think,' says Murray. 'And there had been a Hungarian family who were obviously celebrating something and were rather boisterous. Ollie took exception to this and threw a bottle of Bull's Blood at this man's head, which hit him and put him on the floor. Pissed as he was, good shot. Ollie was arrested and his passport taken away. Now he was about to be deported and had been ordered back to the Gellert to await the verdict. All the producers were there with the hierarchy, the police and the immigration service making this decision; and they still had a lot of filming to do.'

Ollie's little indiscretion having been smoothed over, filming carried on without too much disturbance. That was, until the night of Mark Lester's eighteenth birthday, a seminal moment for any young man, and, to celebrate, the producers laid on a huge dinner. All the cast and crew showed up save for Ollie, who made his grand entrance later in the evening, much to everyone's shock and horror. 'He'd brought me a present from the streets of Budapest,' Lester recalls, with all the affection of someone reminiscing about their first tooth extraction. 'It was a Hungarian hooker.' There she stood, wearing a tight T-shirt that barely kept control of her ample knockers, with the words 'Mark Lester – Private' emblazoned across it. 'Ollie, who was completely paralytic, dragged in this poor girl, who took one look at everybody, gasped in fright and then legged it. Fortunately for me, because Ollie didn't have the best taste in women. I think he had his beer goggles firmly on at that time.'

Ollie then joined in the festivities by jumping atop the main table and throwing a cake into one of the producers' faces before falling backwards on to the floor. For his pièce de résistance Ollie poured a bowl of chocolate trifle over his head and goose-stepped out of the room. 'When he worked Ollie was completely straight and very professional,' reaffirms Lester. 'But there was this other side to him. It was more than just naughty schoolboy-type pranks, it was actually things that were so embarrassing you wouldn't expect the local rugby team to behave in such a manner, jokes not appreciated by everybody.'

More antics followed, much of which, according to the film's publicist Quinn Donoghue, was instigated by Reg rather than Ollie. Entrusted with the job of keeping Ollie out of trouble, Reg became a cohort rather than a protector, especially after six drinks, when his protective sense got skewered and he either joined Ollie as a partner in crime or they started fighting among themselves. 'Then the police would come but they'd be bought off,' says Donoghue. 'One night Ollie and Reg gate-crashed a party and it was full of cops and secret police, and Ollie was pissed and calling them all cunts in English. Luckily they couldn't understand and when they were eventually thrown out Ollie asked who were they and was told, "That was the cops, and not the sort of cops you want to mess with."'

Another evening Ollie rounded up several of the crew, along with Mark Lester, for a meal with a difference, the difference being that each course would be served and eaten in reverse. 'So we started off having brandy and a cigar,' says Lester. 'Ollie was drinking all the time this Bull's Blood wine, but we were all fairly merry. Then, when the chocolate pancakes came, one of the camera crew lobbed his pancake across the room, and within minutes there was this huge food fight and everyone was just covered in chocolate, and the manager came over and just threw us all out. We were literally thrown out into the street.'

Joining Ollie and Lester was a supporting cast almost comparable in star power to the *Musketeer* films: Ernest Borgnine, Raquel Welch, Rex Harrison and Charlton Heston. The gruff American George C. Scott also featured. A fearsome drinker himself, George MacDonald Fraser was instructed to rewrite a key scene to ensure that Scott and Oliver would not be called upon to perform together. Some risks are just too great to run.

There was also a role for David Hemmings, who'd last worked with Ollie on *The System*, when he was hung upside down from a window over spiked railings, something you don't forget in a hurry. After that he'd become something of an iconic figure in late-sixties British cinema as a result of his role as the trendy photographer in Antonioni's *Blow-Up*. But as the seventies rolled on, good parts dried up and there was also a chronic problem with alcohol which eventually devastated his youthful looks. According to Spengler, Hemmings and Ollie were practically inseparable while Hemmings was on the film. 'They got on very well and went out drinking together all the time.' Their big scene together was a dust-up in a horse-drawn carriage, where, Hemmings recalled, he was 'beaten to a pulp on the pretext of making it look real'. When director Richard Fleischer called 'Action' the next thing he knew he was out of the carriage and sprinting off the set with his trousers falling down and Oliver in hot pursuit, his sword out of his scabbard.

Raquel Welch was due on location towards the end of the shoot, but news reached Spengler that she had been held up in America and it was going to be another four weeks until her arrival in Budapest. Since Ollie had now completed all his scenes, save for those with Raquel, this meant that by the time she arrived he would be over his stipulated schedule, thus triggering a penalty clause costing about $20,000 a week. Spengler put in a frantic call to David to explain the situation and to seek a solution.

'Let me talk to Ollie,' said David. Later that afternoon David called Spengler back. 'I talked to Ollie and it's going to cost you something.'

'I imagined that it would. Have you got any thoughts?'

'Yes,' said David. 'Ollie told me to tell you that he needs a sofa.'

And that was it. So instead of $80,000 the producers bought him a sofa for Broome Hall. Ollie was nobody's fool and he knew full well that he was entitled to that money by virtue of his contract. It was a gesture that Spengler has never forgotten. 'Oliver was incredibly generous.'

With a month's free time Ollie took himself off to the south of France, where he often holidayed. He'd rent a fabulous villa and invite all manner of friends to stay. 'We arrived one day,' says Paul Friday, 'and Ollie moved out of the main bedroom and into a cupboard downstairs. It was literally a cupboard with a single mattress that curled up at the end because it was so cramped, and he'd moved in there because he'd given all the bedrooms to his friends.' Upon arrival these friends tended to split into two separate groups to go off drinking, exploring, and having fun with Ollie. 'We had to take turns,' confirms Nora Friday. 'We had to do night shifts and day shifts. You couldn't do a day and a night with him because you wouldn't survive.'

During this particular visit Ollie acquired a Chinese junk. Mark seems to think that it was a part payment for a film that went down the tubes. Called *Ding Hao*, the boat was built in Hong Kong in 1959 for a trade fair in Montreal, after which it spent several years in the Caribbean before ending up in the south of France. 'Ollie didn't know how to sail it,' says David. 'He didn't know how to get it out of the harbour. So he had this skipper who'd hire a crew on the day. It only went out infrequently. Basically it was a houseboat.'

Ollie kept the thing moored at the marina at Cap Ferrat, where it stood out like a sore thumb among the bright, shiny yachts of millionaires. David Niven came aboard one afternoon and, hardly impressed, wrote in the logbook, 'This is not a film star's yacht.' But Mark, who lived and sailed in it, remembers the *Ding Hao* as a beautiful craft. 'It was sixty-five foot long and had a master cabin with a seven-foot-square bed in it. The thing was full of old Chinese antique carvings and had marble bathrooms. It was just a delight.'

The plan was to hire out the *Ding Hao* whenever possible,

so in the end the thing paid for itself. 'He used to charter it to the Monaco Grand Prix,' recalls Mark. 'And James Hunt used to come on board, and there'd be lots of girls in tennis costumes serving canapés and champagne. For a sixteen-year-old it was great.' After he'd taken his cut, the idea was for the skipper to reinvest any profits into the upkeep of the vessel, but it didn't quite work out that way as each season the thing looked tattier and tattier. Mark was on the boat one day when Oliver came down and just looked at the state of it and went, 'That's it, I'm out.' He didn't want to play this game any more. After just three years Ollie sold the junk. It then promptly sank, not in a storm, but in the middle of the Mediterranean in fine weather. A suitably confused Lloyd's investigator came to see David, asking about water-tight bulkheads and things like that. Lloyd's simply couldn't understand how a boat could sink on a calm day.

Oliver returned to Budapest two days before the arrival of Raquel and immediately got into a spot of bother. A newspaper had published an interview in which he'd fired a slingshot in the direction of fellow bad boy Richard Harris. Boasting of his forthcoming love scenes with Miss Welch, Ollie announced that he was offering Harris a job as his stand-in, providing his wig didn't fall off in the clinches. 'What with his toupée and her falsies they would be perfect for each other,' he said. When Spengler read this he was furious; what if Raquel saw it? Ollie protested his innocence. 'I promise, I swear to you, Pierre, I never said that.' In the end a statement was put out on his behalf denouncing it all as tabloid bullshit, and when Raquel arrived everything seemed fine. 'Then one night,' remembers Spengler, 'I was sitting at the bar at the Gellert Hotel and I hear these loud voices. I look and it's Oliver and Raquel screaming at each other, really going at it. I started to get extremely nervous but when I approached them they both burst out laughing.'

Three days later Spengler was at the hotel's very chic

nightclub. Oliver was sitting at a private table with Raquel having drinks. A guy, who, it later turned out, was a black marketeer, came over to them. 'Would you like to dance, Miss Welch?' he said. 'No thank you,' came the reply. The guy walked away. Two minutes later he returned. 'Now would you like to dance, Miss Welch?' Raquel again declined. He walked away. A few minutes later he showed up a third time, only now Oliver took charge of the situation. 'Hey, listen, fella, the lady says she does not want to dance with you, so enough.' He walked away. Spengler describes what happened next: 'Two minutes later the guy comes and jumps over Oliver, attacks him. Raquel runs towards me shrieking, "I promise Oliver did not start this." Then we had a fight like in the western movies, we had tables and chairs flying in the air, just unbelievable. The entire nightclub was fighting, because there were about seven of these black marketeers and most of our crew was there. The result was that the nightclub was pretty much upside down, quite destroyed. The manager wanted to call the police. I said, don't call anybody, I'll pay for the damage.'

The next morning Spengler returned to the nightclub, which had been put back into some semblance of normality. It was completely deserted except for the solitary figure of a drunk Oliver fashioning an improvised weapon of really quite menacing quality. He had taken a fork and twisted the metal teeth so that he could fit it into his fist like a ninja fighting device. A shiver went down Spengler's spine. 'What are you doing, Oliver?'

'I'm waiting for the Germans.'

'What are you talking about?' The guys from the night before had in fact been Yugoslavs but probably, in Ollie's befuddled mind, villainous Europeans were all Germans.

'It's my honour, Pierre,' said Ollie. 'I cannot let this go by.'

'Oliver, you really mustn't do this. Let's go back to the hotel.'

'No, Pierre, this is my honour.'

329

Just then Spengler remembered something Ollie had said to him when they had dinner together before shooting began. He'd grabbed Spengler's hand and looked him straight in the eye, saying, 'Anything you want from me, you can always ask.' Spengler composed himself. 'Oliver, now I'm asking. Give me that fork.' Ollie gave him the fork. Spengler went outside and threw it into an alleyway. When he came back inside, Ollie was preparing another one. 'Ollie, please.'

'You really want me to go back to my hotel, don't you?'

'Yes, Ollie, I do.'

'All right, I'll go.' Spengler walked him back to the Intercontinental.

Really, at moments like this, dealing with Ollie was akin to dealing with an errant child. 'It's true,' says Spengler. 'But that was also the reason why you'd have so much affection for him, because there were some childish aspects about him. He really was like a child, with the outbursts of a child but also the forgetfulness of a child, so that even if he would have an outburst, the next minute he'd be in a good mood again, happy and all smiles.'

As he'd done on the *Musketeer* films, Spengler watched Ollie's drinking from a safe distance. Not once was he tempted to go out on the town with him. That path led to ruin. There was a party Oliver held after filming that everyone was invited to, and it said on the invitation: 'Starting at 8 p.m. until crash-out.' Spengler declined. 'I heard it lasted something like three days. Madness.'

Certainly Murray Melvin had grown concerned that Ollie's drinking wasn't merely tipping him over into the depths of oblivion but might also have more short-term personal repercussions. For he'd heard stories that on his days off Ollie would go boozing in Budapest's roughest nightspots with Reg, expeditions that usually ended in brawls. One local who'd been beaten up came back for revenge the next night, only to be knocked out again by Ollie. The police intervened and Ollie and the other guy spent a night in the cells. Murray remembers taking his friend to one side and saying, 'Ollie, you do have to be careful because time's creeping on and one of these nights you're going to hit somebody and he's going to be the equivalent of a nineteen-year-old Oliver Reed and he's going to hit you back harder and quicker than you'll hit him.'

For the rest of the filming Ollie remained something of a handful, so much so that reinforcements were sent for. A huge press call had been announced, with Fleet Street's big hitters flown out to the location, but Oliver stubbornly refused to go unless Simon was there. Arriving in Budapest on the first plane from England, Simon was taken straight to the hotel, where he expected to meet Ollie, but his brother was nowhere to be seen. He'd disappeared. It was now lunchtime and the press call was scheduled to start at eight that evening. So where to begin the search? Simon tried Ollie's room first. No answer. Next he went into the hotel bar. No sign. He asked the barman where Ollie normally drank and was directed to a watering hole in the centre of town. 'I'm sitting there,' says Simon, 'and it's gone six o'clock and it's getting dark. Suddenly the barman comes over and says there's a note for me. I take it and read it: "Meet me under Elizabeth Bridge in twenty minutes." Elizabeth Bridge divides the two sides of Budapest. So I'm on this bridge and it's enormous. I walk from one end to the other and there's no sign of Ollie. Suddenly I hear, "Psssstt", and there underneath the bridge, hanging by the rafters, it's Ollie. And he's had a few drinks. "What's the story?" he asks. "They want you to come to this press thing, they'll all be there, Raquel's dressed up to the nines," I said. He said, "Oh fuck, what do you think, do you think I should go?" I said, "Yeah." He went, "All right then." So he climbed up and we both went to the press conference. Amazing.'

It would also prove Simon's swansong as far as handling

Ollie's press was concerned. It had been fun and, he recalls, probably the easiest job in the world in the early seventies, when Ollie was at his peak. 'Everything I did looked like it was genius. Trying to sell Ollie to the press, you'd have to be an idiot to get it wrong. It was a fantastic time.' But Simon had always been ambitious to get back into broadcasting and in 1973 began doing television work. With his services being more frequently required he was having to squeeze Ollie's stuff into his busy schedule until he made the decision to leave. Ollie completely understood and was a keen follower and admirer of Simon's work over the years as an accomplished sports presenter and journalist.

Where Ollie's antics had been previously confined to after hours, and on set he had been nothing but patient and cheerful throughout long and difficult days, his last two weeks on *The Prince and the Pauper* represented something of a fall from grace. According to George MacDonald Fraser, Ollie often turned up drunk, once so far gone that he began loudly telling Fleischer how he was going to perform a fight scene, waving his sword wildly in the air and throwing himself about the set, and not hearing when the director said, 'But, Ollie, we've shot that fight, remember?' Fraser recalled thinking at the time, 'Plainly booze is going to be the ruin of a fine but undisciplined actor.' As for Fleischer, he was adamant that he would never work with Oliver again.

The Hurricane

To mark Her Majesty's Silver Jubilee in June 1977, Ollie decked
out Broome Hall with Union Jacks and held a giant garden
party. In the middle of the festivities he went down on one
knee and proposed to Jacquie. It wasn't unexpected, as Ollie
was always saying things like, 'You don't love me, because you
don't want to marry me.' Jacquie would tell him he was being
ridiculous. Deep down she believed that being married again
would only make him unhappy. But, looking at him now, on his
knees, holding a bouquet of long grass because there were no
flowers handy, gave her pause. In those few seconds of silence
before she replied, her mind must have been bursting with
conflicting thoughts. Finally she answered. It was no.

Jacquie never regretted her decision. She didn't feel the
need to make it 'official', as things were working fine the way
they were, even though, as she admits, 'we were never really
a proper couple. I was there at Broome Hall, he would go off
on a movie, I would stay there, he would come back. It was
extraordinarily strange. It was almost like we were best friends
stroke lovers.' Surely then, in such a situation, it made sense to
tie the knot. Didn't she feel, with Ollie away for long periods of
time, a sense of insecurity? 'Not really, because I wasn't in the
relationship for what I could gain out of it, I was there because
of him. It didn't enter my mind that if it ended I might have

to go and dig potatoes in Ireland or something. I didn't think of things like that. We really did have an extraordinarily good relationship. People used to say we were the mirror image of one another.'

In many ways they had very similar personalities. 'So when it was good it was good,' says Sarah. 'But when it was bad it was horrid.' Ollie liked women who were a little bit like boys, tomboys, girls who would muck about and indulge in his play-making; 'women who didn't have too many airs and graces,' says Jacquie. Take the time they were holidaying in the south of France and went out to sea with a few friends on a motor boat. After a couple of hours they were running dangerously low on booze and the captain decided to head for shore to get fresh supplies. Ollie turned to Jacquie. 'We're not going back. Jump over the side.' After grabbing the last few bottles and sticking the corks back in, they hit the water as the boat sped off. 'So we bobbed around in the ocean, having a cocktail party at sea. We'd take the cork out, have a swig, and put the cork back. Just treading water until the boat returned. Bloody mad, but that's the sort of thing we used to do.'

Undoubtedly what also helped the relationship was Jacquie's tolerance, for she wasn't the sort of woman who had the sulks and took umbrage at Ollie's antics. 'I think that's probably why there weren't that many rows; what's the point?' So life at Broome Hall carried on much as before. Unfortunately, the place also continued to haemorrhage cash. It had got to the point where Ollie was having to take movies just to pay the bills, which did nothing for his long-term career prospects. 'When you think about it, no one in their right mind would have taken on Broome Hall and do what he did,' says Mark. 'He just threw money into it.'

Ollie was caught in a trap of his own making. It seemed pointless having a beautiful house with fantastic gardens and horses and everything else if he was away so much of the time working on up to three films a year. There was also a prohibitive tax regime, put in place by the then Labour government, whose Chancellor Denis Healey's battle cry of tax the rich 'until the pips squeak' had resulted in a large exodus of top earners from the worlds of film and music. Because Oliver fell into the top tax bracket, being required to pay 98 per cent tax on income, his financial advisers had to develop very sophisticated arrangements to minimize his liability to UK tax, and this meant he needed to spend time abroad, usually in Ireland or Guernsey.

Sometimes Jacquie and Sarah joined Oliver, but for the most part he was holed up alone, a prisoner in a luxurious hotel suite. One time Mark and Mick Fryer visited him when he was staying at the Gresham in Dublin. 'But if Ollie gets shitty, I'm straight on the plane back,' warned Fryer. 'Because that's the way he used to go,' says Fryer. 'After a few days he could turn into a different kind of man. As it turned out, we stayed five days and he was lovely the whole time. And when we left he started crying.' Fryer had with him a new pair of shoes and asked Ollie, 'What do you think?' Ollie nodded his approval. That afternoon they went on the piss and Fryer drew attention more than once to his new shoes. 'What do you keep on about the shoes for?' said Ollie. Back at the suite, Fryer fell asleep. 'All of a sudden I felt this shaking. "Mick, wake up." It was Ollie. "Look at the fire." My fucking shoes were on the fire. He said, "Fuck you and your shoes. Don't talk about them no more."'

This enforced solitary existence of living in hotel rooms for long periods was something Ollie deeply resented, and a strange price to pay for success, but it was either that or leave the UK altogether and become a tax exile, which he wasn't prepared to do. His patriotism wouldn't have countenanced such a move, for after all this was a man who had a collection of Churchill's wartime speeches on LPs and only backed horses if they had a royal name or connection. So he continued to spend heavily and be taxed heavily, cursing the name of Healey whenever the subject of income tax was raised.

Leaving Jacquie and Sarah, Ollie flew to Montreal to start work on another movie, *Tomorrow Never Comes*. He was playing a police detective about to retire who is suddenly thrown into a deadly hostage situation. The props department had given him a police badge which had his full ID and photograph, the only difference between it and the real thing being that it was signed by the producer of the film rather than the chief of police. Mark had flown to the location with his father and they were arriving back at the hotel after a day's shoot when Ollie noticed a couple of teenagers smoking a joint outside and indicated he'd seen them. When they asked if he had his badge on him, he smiled and got out of the car. Flashing his badge, he said in his best Canadian accent, 'You guys smoking a joint?' Nervously they replied, 'Yes, sir, yes, sir.' Ollie said, 'Good on you, carry on,' and walked back to the car. Only then did they go, 'Wow, Oliver Reed!'

Ollie is in good form in *Tomorrow Never Comes*, though the film barely rises above the average, looking too much like a TV movie. But it did reunite him with his co-star from *The Ransom*, Paul Koslo, playing the policeman taking over from Ollie's veteran cop, and it was on this movie that the two men really bonded. Often that meant lavish lunches in fancy restaurants, to which only a select few were invited. 'And of course everything had to be top-notch,' remembers Koslo. 'And Ollie would literally spend two or three thousand dollars for lunch; today that would be something like fifteen thousand bucks. It really was incredible. I mean, bottles of wine that cost a few hundred dollars each.'

And then there were the dinner parties Ollie held in his three-room hotel suite, where guests could number between twenty and thirty. Extra tables would be laid on and waiters would serve food. At these parties he would recite from Winnie the Pooh, his favourite book. 'That was like his bible,' says Jacquie, whom Ollie nicknamed Tigger; Sarah was Roo. 'I think he almost memorized the whole book from cover to cover; he could bring out quotes at the most extraordinary times,' Koslo recalls, adding that Ollie would jump on the table and act out every character and the food would go flying. 'He would be so funny, so entertaining and so loud.' One evening things got a little out of hand and when complaints were made about the noise, the hotel's security staff went up to the suite. Ollie threw them out. 'And when I tried to calm him down,' says Koslo, 'he actually tried to throw me out of the window. Reggie was downstairs trying to pacify the management, so he was not there to protect me, and I was literally hanging on to the ledge and the side of the wall so he couldn't throw me out. I was terrified. We were something like three or four floors up. And he was so strong, he was a lot stronger than me, he was built like a warthog. Finally I got him in a headlock: if I was gonna go I was going to take him with me. And he started laughing like a crazy person and dragged me into this closet. He knew the shit was gonna hit the fan and yelled at me, "Now, you say one fucking word in this closet and I swear to you I'll fucking kill you." So he locked us both in this fucking dark closet with no light. Nobody could find us for a couple of hours until everything had quietened down.'

Someone who refrained from attending any of Ollie's wild nights was John Osborne. The renowned British playwright, who, with the ground-breaking *Look Back in Anger* had instigated the Angry Young Man acting movement that so heavily influenced the young Oliver, had a very small role in the film, and Koslo remembers how much in awe of him Ollie was. 'A group of us would sometimes go to dinner and I saw how much Ollie would listen and behave himself when John was there. It was a totally different scene, it was very cordial, almost monastic. I remember vividly how much he thought of John Osborne. He respected the hell out of him.'

The rest of the cast was filled out by a host of distinguished actors such as Raymond Burr, who took an instant dislike to Oliver, and the feeling was mutual, Susan George, and Donald Pleasence, whom for some reason Ollie targeted for ridicule. 'He'd send him up all the time,' says Koslo. 'At the read-through Ollie would act out everyone's part. Of course, everybody thought this was hilarious, except for Donald. Ollie told Donald that he was a fucking idiot actor and he couldn't fucking act his way out of a wet paper bag and this is how it should be played, and Donald had no fucking sense of humour, Donald was very serious about his work. He was kind of a strange bird, like he didn't really fit in. But I wonder if there wasn't a bit of competition there between the two of them, I'm sure there was.' Or was it Ollie just being his old mischievous self? 'Who would ever think of memorizing everybody's part and acting it out?' offers Koslo. 'But he did that because it was fun, he did it to get reactions, to see where people were coming from and who they were. He had that much fun inside of him and that much adventure and that much talent.'

Halfway through shooting, Mark had to go back to England to start a new school term. Before his son had to leave for the airport Ollie invited him to the hotel bar for a beer and said he'd go and fetch his passport. 'I've already got it,' replied Mark. Silence. Then, 'What! You've been into my room.' It all kicked off. 'We had a phenomenal row. The next minute the concierge was involved and then the manager of the hotel. We used to have these sorts of arguments and, looking back, they were silly and about nothing really, but at the time they were very big.' They were also symptomatic of where their relationship was at. Mark was now sixteen and starting to become independent, and as a consequence Ollie felt his role as father growing increasingly marginalized. 'Because a lot of him was based on physical prowess and strength, probably he felt that that was being contested,' is Mark's belief. And one event had been the catalyst.

Going out to Hungary to see Ollie shoot some of *The Prince and the Pauper*, Mark had met his father at the airport. There, Ollie followed Mark into the toilets to wash his hands and, looking in the mirror, suddenly realized his son was taller than he was. 'It changes the complexion slightly,' says Mark. 'OK, you might be taller than me but I'm still tougher than you. So it was quite often a contest between us, me the young buck and him still asserting his seniority and strength and prowess. It was, so you think you know it all. You know fuck all. We spent a lot of time through my teens and into my twenties contesting each other and there were times where I just didn't want to invest any more of me because I found it too sapping. So we did fall out, sometimes quite magnificently, sometimes for a number of years where we just wouldn't talk. And then when we got back together it was as though nothing had happened and we'd carry on from where we were. If I look back I could have perhaps been easier, he could have been easier, I could have taken things slightly less to heart and been more understanding, but then I was a young guy trying to work out who I was within all of it.'

At the helm of *Tomorrow Never Comes* was Peter Collinson and it didn't take long for open hostilities to resume. They erupted on a night shoot featuring Koslo and Susan George, naked save for a very thin negligee. It was something like three in the morning and colder than hell. Collinson was shooting from about a block away and during breaks Koslo wrapped a coat round Susan to keep her warm, but several times the director made no effort to tell them he'd stopped shooting, with the result that Susan was repeatedly standing there freezing when there was no need to. Boiling with rage, Koslo let fly at Collinson, who fired him on the spot. After frantic phone calls to the studio, Koslo was rehired the next day. Later he heard that Oliver had given Collinson an ultimatum: 'Listen, if you fucking fire this actor, then I'm gone!' Reggie told Koslo this, 'because Ollie would never have told me that himself'.

Koslo is a member of a rare group, an actor whose company Ollie enjoyed off set, and, even rarer, an actor whom Ollie invited to his home. Whenever Koslo was in England he would contact Ollie and they'd meet up. He remembers going to Broome Hall at least three times. 'The first time I got there, he had this dining-room table that must have been fifty feet long and he gave me this big carving knife and told me to carve my initials where I was sitting. Then he showed me around. It was absolutely unbelievable.'

Koslo also remembers Jacquie. He liked her a lot, calls her a sweet lady, but got the impression that she didn't like Ollie drinking. 'She knew that he could get wild and crazy, and so did everyone else in the county of Surrey, including the police.' During his last visit Ollie took him on a pub crawl that took in all the local hostelries. 'And every time Ollie walked in anywhere everybody stood up and applauded and cheered. We finished off at this five-star restaurant and I swear to you, we were swinging off the chandeliers. Ollie said to me, "You ever do this?", and he got up and jumped off the table on to this chandelier and he started swinging. So, of course, I had to do the same thing. The management totally lost it and they called the cops, so Ollie decided we'd better get out, but the police later pulled his car over and arrested both of us.'

It's no surprise to learn that Oliver was well known at the local police station, and he got his usual reprimand and talking to. 'Ollie, you've got to stop this. You're going to hurt yourself or you're going to hurt somebody else.' Because Koslo held a Canadian passport, the police didn't quite know what to do with him until Ollie started raving, 'If you're releasing me, you're releasing him. If you're not going to release him, I'm not going anywhere, I'm staying here and I'm going to make your fucking life hell.'

Koslo has never forgotten Oliver. In spite of the fact that he tried to throw him out of a hotel window, he classes him as 'A special kind of man. He had that wonderful charm and forcefulness. I've never met anybody like him, never met anybody that had so much talent and had so much strength and gentleness all at the same time. And he was a great judge of character. He could sense what kind of person you were in an instant. He could analyze you with his eyes, look right into your soul, look into your heart to see whether you had one or not. That's how I felt about Ollie, and of course you just give yourself up to a person like that because he's so powerful.'

Another celebrity who was becoming a very frequent visitor to Broome Hall was Alex Higgins, especially since Ollie had put in a billiards room. Higgins was one of the first people to play there. Intrigued by the Irish snooker ace, Ollie had engineered a meeting, sending his driver to collect him from Dorking railway station. When the car pulled up outside Broome Hall, Oliver greeted Alex warmly. 'So you're "the Hurricane". I shall call you Hig the Pig.'

When Higgins was shown into the opulent billiards room, the décor certainly met with his approval, as did a lemon tree planted nearby that allowed players to pick fruit to freshen up their drinks. Having only recently taken up the sport, poor Ollie was obliterated, but afterwards invited Higgins to the cellar bar for a drinking contest. The snooker star drank like he played, fast, and soon got very drunk and was thrown out. But Ollie was certainly intrigued by the man and they remained matey for the rest of his life. 'I think Ollie liked him because he was Irish and he'd come from nowhere to be a success,' believes Christensen. 'He was dedicated to what he was doing and was fantastically good at it. I saw a few exhibition matches on Ollie's table and even pissed out of his head the bloke was phenomenal.'

In many ways it was a relationship that parallels the one Ollie still shared with Keith Moon. 'I think Ollie was attracted to kindred spirits,' says David. 'People who broke the rules and didn't lead a conventional life. Although Hurricane became more dependent on Ollie than Ollie was dependent on Hurricane.' When Higgins was in trouble with the press or having women or money problems he often rang Ollie, who was always willing to give him shelter and help. There was the occasion when Alex was breaking up with his wife and Ollie arranged for him to stay at David Hunt's villa in Majorca until he'd sorted himself out. 'Well, he wrecked the joint,' reveals David. 'And this Hunt chap wasn't very happy. So it was a relationship very similar to Keith: they gravitated towards each other. Both Keith and Alex were destructive characters and I think that's what attracted Ollie to both of them.'

But, according to Christensen, Higgins often wore out his welcome and was not a happy influence at Broome Hall. 'I never saw Higgins buy a drink, ever. Ever. In the pub he'd sit there and Ollie would fill him up.' The thing with Ollie was that he always bought his mates drinks. He didn't expect you to return the favour but was always appreciative of the gesture when you did it.

Famous for his own terrifying behaviour, Higgins did admit that Oliver was more than capable of frightening the shit out of him. After a particularly hectic afternoon in the pub, Higgins passed out in an armchair back at Broome Hall. He was rudely awoken by a sword jabbed into his ribs. 'Get up,' growled Ollie. 'How dare you fall asleep in my company. For that insult, sir, I require satisfaction.' Higgins was thrown a rapier. 'Now, sir, prepare to die.' Ollie attacked with a series of mighty blows and Higgins did all he could to defend himself. On another visit Higgins made the mistake of falling asleep again in Ollie's presence and this time was hunted down with an axe. When Higgins bolted the door of his bedroom Ollie started chopping at the solid oak like Jack Nicholson in *The Shining*. 'I was terrified,' Higgins later admitted. 'I honestly thought I might be about to breathe my last if he got through.'

Bye-Bye, Moonie

Oliver got a call from Michael Winner offering him a small but pivotal role in his all-star remake of the Raymond Chandler classic *The Big Sleep*, jockeying for space on screen with the likes of James Stewart, Joan Collins and Sarah Miles. His first instinct was to refuse, until, that is, Winner revealed the name of the actor playing Chandler's anti-hero Philip Marlowe: Robert Mitchum. Hooked, Ollie signed on. Sharing scenes with an actor he considered one of Hollywood's 'biggies' was too good an opportunity to miss. 'It was his reputation,' Ollie explained. 'Tough. Uncompromising. Son of a bitch. I had to see how I measured up to him.' He also admired Mitchum's relaxed acting style and screen presence, one not too dissimilar to his own. Here was another actor who 'made the air move'. As Eddie Mars, a London casino owner you wouldn't want to cross, Ollie shared a number of scenes with Mitchum and they positively crackle with electricity.

Winner hadn't worked with Oliver for almost ten years and noticed that his old friend was drinking more than ever. He still never drank on set but sometimes would arrive for work a little wasted. Famous for his gourmet lunches, Winner invited Ollie and Mitchum to a very prestigious London restaurant. Booze was not on the menu, given Winner's aversion to it. Mitchum whispered in Ollie's ear what his tipple was: 'Gin and tonic.'

344

Clicking his fingers, Mitchum got the waiters to bring over two bottles of gin, one of whisky, another of brandy and all the mixers. Winner was just tucking into his lunch when they arrived. Straightaway, his eyes fixed accusingly upon Ollie. 'Who ordered these?' he said.

'I did,' went Mitchum.

'Oh,' said Winner, clamming up.

The next day on set Winner, in a foul mood, accosted Ollie. 'You mustn't encourage Robert to drink, Oliver. You've no idea of the terrible trouble we had with him last night.'

Mitchum then arrived, having heard every word. 'What do you mean?'

'It was because you'd been drinking,' said Winner. 'Do you know you drank a whole bottle of gin at lunch?'

'It wasn't the gin,' said Mitchum. 'It was the whisky I chased it down with.'

Ollie remained in London to play a tyrannical and scheming headmaster at a school for unruly teenagers in a low-budget British film called *The Class of Miss MacMichael* and co-starring Glenda Jackson. It was shot during the winter of 1977 in a disused Victorian school in Bethnal Green in the East End. Ollie was happy to make a film he knew had little international appeal, calling it 'Home-grown for home-grown audiences. We don't get paid a lot of money for these films, but we make them because we want to make them.' He baulked, however, at the cack-handed way he perceived it was being done. 'They cheapskated it. Even in the most complicated scenes there was no time for rehearsals. It was just, turn on the lights and fucking shoot it.'

Because Ollie hardly ever socialized with the film set, it was perhaps as an act of revenge that he invited *Miss MacMichael*'s director, Silvio Narizzano, and its producer, Judd Bernard, to Broome Hall for dinner, giving them an evening they'd never forget.

Jacquie was instructed to put on a posh dinner. David and Muriel arrived, Bill and Jenny were there too, as was Ollie's mate Gus. Everyone now waited for the guests of honour. Through the window came a flash of car headlights. Moments later in walked Narizzano and Bernard and dinner was served. Almost as soon as the soup arrived Ollie began the entertainment, starting off by bending some spoons. When that didn't get enough of a reaction he got up and went over to the wall and pulled down a huge Scottish broadsword. 'I tell you,' recalls David. 'It was as tall as a man, it had a huge long blade, and Ollie said, "Do you know what this is?" And the two film people said, well it's a sword, Ollie. There were these candlesticks glinting on the table. "You watch that flame," said Ollie and he started swinging this broadsword across the tops of our heads and these film guys were ducking under the table. And of course he missed the bloody thing and went, damn! So he had another go. And that got them really worked up.'

Nothing, though, quite prepared them for what happened next. Ollie went off into the library and came back with an old flintlock pistol and threw it into Gus's soup. 'Gus simply put his hand into the soup and brought it out,' continues David. 'But the look on those two guys' faces was unbelievable. By this time Muriel, who normally didn't put up with much from Oliver, said, "Ollie, this isn't really good enough." She got up and led Ollie out of the room and into the library and you could hear off-stage Muriel saying, "Ollie, put that gun down. Put it down, for God's sake." And these two film people are nearly in shock. Then suddenly we hear bang!, followed by Muriel's voice saying, "He's bloody shot me." And she came out of the room clutching her arm and these two guys leaped up and ran for it. Amazing. We didn't even get to the main course. We got as far as the soup.'

Paul Friday remembers a similar occasion when Rick Parfitt of Status Quo came round to Broome Hall 'and Ollie got this bloody shotgun out and blew a hole in the dining-room table and Parfitt freaked out completely'.

Anyway, Muriel lived to tell the tale, as the pistol had in fact been a starting pistol and it was the wad that hit her arm, leaving a nasty bruise. But it was perhaps indicative of her relationship with Oliver over the years, which can best be described as cool, largely because Muriel was one of the very few women who stood up to him. 'And, funnily enough, he respected her because of that,' says David. 'And another funny thing was that Ollie could never understand how Mickie and I endured. As a couple we were a constant, and to him that was alien.'

Quite often, though, Muriel and Ollie didn't see eye to eye and she always resented the fact that he kept David out drinking. 'It's sad because he was such fun in the early days,' Muriel says. 'We always laughed. There wasn't this aggression; later on there was always this aggression. You went out with him and you didn't know how the evening was going to end. Sometimes Ollie was very dangerous to be with, very dangerous.'

One Christmas Muriel bought Ollie a cuckoo clock which he naturally hated so kept in the kitchen where it wouldn't be seen by anyone. 'We're in the kitchen one day,' remembers Christensen. 'And I'd just got back from doing some shooting and I had my gun but it was unloaded. Ollie said, 'Give me that one second.' So I gave it to him and out of his own pocket he took two cartridges and he blasted this clock off the wall, blew it to fucking pieces. Not the safest thing to do because there were people in the kitchen and bits flying everywhere. 'I've fucking always hated that clock,' he went.' Sarah is also pretty certain her dad once pissed into Muriel's cooking sherry bottle during a party and then put it back in a cupboard giggling like a little school boy because he knew the next time she made a trifle . . .

The Class of Miss MacMichael was the last time Oliver worked with Glenda Jackson. Their personal relationship had not improved in the interim; in fact it had stayed exactly the same: non-existent. Professionally it was an entirely different story and Glenda still has great admiration for Oliver the actor. 'Even at his worst, be it exhausted, or hung-over or whatever, he was immensely professional in front of a camera. And he had great energy as an actor. On *Women in Love* Ken used to like to shoot a lot, and Oliver was never, ever not with that energy. And I think the performance he gave in *The Triple Echo* and again in *Miss MacMichael*, which were essentially comic roles, I thought he was marvellous.' Ollie does a wonderful job with his headmaster, all mock prissiness to important visitors but treating his charges like so much flotsam. It's an outrageous comic turn, skirting dangerously close but never falling into outright farce. 'He had a capacity for being funny,' confirms Glenda, 'which he was not aware of, I don't think. So when he tried deliberately to be funny or do stupid things to make people laugh, it wasn't at all funny, but he had a real comic flair as an actor that I don't think he recognized in himself.'

Back at Broome Hall, Ollie heard the news that Christensen was leaving and going back into the Metropolitan Police, where he was to have a distinguished career, retiring in 2010. They kept in touch and often met up for further antics, but it's the Broome Hall years that Christensen looks back on with the most fondness, though by no means with rose-tinted glasses. 'There were times when Oliver was in a foul mood and you'd think, what the fuck am I doing down here? I'm not trying to gild it and make out he was a saint, because he wasn't: there were times when he was horrible. I got fired five times. I'd say, "OK, fine, I'm off. But do me one favour: re-fire me tomorrow morning when you've slept on it." And come the morning it would be, "sorry, Norse".'

On the whole it's the good times Christensen prefers to remember, and Ollie's zest for life and appetite for fun, especially when it came to practical jokes, such as the time he rubbed Boursin garlic cheese into his hair instead of the usual hair tonic when he was introduced to Princess Anne. As he bent to kiss her hand the stink rising from his head was just ghastly. Another time he was invited to a posh dinner do by an old Ewell Castle classmate he happened to bump into in the Cricketers. 'But I warn you, Oliver, it's formal dress, penguin suits.' Driving home, Ollie was already regretting agreeing to go. 'Why don't you call a theatrical costumiers and get a real penguin suit?' suggested Christensen. Ollie smiled and said, 'Fuck it, I will.' When the outfit arrived it had a huge beak, enormous stomach, feet about five foot long, and wings. Turning up at this big, mock-Tudor mansion, Ollie could hardly walk up the gravel track, the feet were so big. Wobbling up, he rang the bell and a flunky opened the door, took one look and started smirking. Of course, this bloke had told all his City dealer mates that his old friend Ollie was coming. 'It was just hilarious,' recalls Christensen. 'He pricked this guy's pomposity.' When the host complained, Ollie just answered, 'You did say it was penguin suits.' There was also the time he hired a British Rail uniform and strode through the compartments on the Victoria to Dorking train asking passengers to identify their bags and briefcases and saying, 'That's not a bomb in there, is it?'

One time Ollie bumped into John McNally, singer and guitarist in the famous Merseybeat group the Searchers, in the Royal Oak in Rusper. They got chatting and McNally was invited up to Broome Hall. Ollie was between films and revealed his plans to become a pop star and asked McNally to join a band he was putting together with a few mates. Ollie was after a hard-looking image and over the course of a few days they'd written a song called 'Everybody's Gonna Be Butch'. Then suddenly Ollie turned to McNally and said, 'There's only one thing wrong, John, you're not butch enough. You need a broken nose.'

'There's nothing wrong with my nose,' said McNally.

'There is,' insisted Oliver. 'Look, I've got a busted-up nose and if we're going to sing, "Everybody's Gonna Be Butch", you've got to look butch, for Christ's sake!' Ollie took McNally to one side. 'I'll tell you what I'll do. I'll give you a quick whack now or we'll get it done professionally.'

'You're not touching my nose,' reiterated McNally.

A few days later he was persuaded to meet Ollie in the Cricketers. They were drinking together when Johnny Placett, obviously in on the wind-up, walked in. 'Hello, Mr Reed,' he said and went over and began examining his nose. 'Ah yes, it's come on well, hasn't it?' After a few gentle prods of the Reed hooter he said, 'Who's the patient?' Ollie pointed at McNally. Placett walked across and gave his nose the once-over. 'I hope you don't mind, Ollie wanted it done privately but I thought the best thing locally is, we'll do it on the billiards table up at Broome Hall. There are nurses up there. I've got everything ready for you.' You've never seen anybody move so fast. McNally was gone, never to return.

Inevitably some of these practical jokes went too far, such as the time Ollie invited Simon to a house and suddenly threw himself out of the top-floor window. Ollie had reconnoitred the joint beforehand, so knew there was a ledge below, and was hanging by his fingertips. 'I thought that was the last I would see of him,' Simon confessed. There was also the episode when Ollie threw shotgun cartridges into an open fire, and when they exploded David and Simon leaped from their chairs and ran for their lives.

Christensen's own favourite Ollie jape was when Ollie's American actor friend Ritchie Adams came to Broome Hall for dinner one night. Before he arrived Ollie took Christensen to one side. 'I want you to pretend that you're my bodyguard and you're carrying a gun,' he said, handing him a toy pistol that looked pretty realistic and a shoulder holster. 'And can you wear a black polo neck and a black jacket. And say very little, just be in the background.'

Adams arrived and after dinner he and Ollie walked into the study and started talking. After a few minutes Ollie gave Christensen the nod, then turned to stare straight into Adams's eyes. 'Rich, you don't really suppose that I'm just an actor, do you?'

Adams looked a tad nervous. 'What do you mean, Oliver?'

'Do you really think I fund all this and have ex-special services bodyguards if I'm just an actor. Norse, show him.' Christensen deftly opened his jacket to reveal the gun. Adams's eyes widened. 'I've been working for Her Majesty's government for a long time now.' By this point Adams was shitting himself, wondering what the hell he'd got himself into. 'I can have you killed at any time,' Ollie continued, completely straight-faced. Then, relaxing, he said, 'Enough of that now. What were we talking about?' He looked over at Christensen. 'Norse, you can go now, thank you, unless I need you.' So Christensen drifted out of the room. The next morning, after Adams had gone, Christensen said to Ollie, 'How did he sleep?' And Ollie replied, 'I don't think at all.'

Shot in Zambia, Oliver's next film was a political comedy called *Touch of the Sun* that remained virtually unreleased, so abysmal was it. It reunited him with his old Hammer stalwart Peter Cushing, but the film is irredeemable in every department and Ollie simply mugs his way through his role as a US Marine captain sent to a despotic African nation to retrieve a lost space capsule.

About the only good thing to come out of this disaster was a safari holiday with Jacquie and Sarah, followed by a trip to Victoria Falls. Sarah remembers this holiday as one of the very few she enjoyed with her father. As a family they never really did holidays, because Ollie was away working so much that any free time he had he preferred to spend at home. Occasionally, on school holidays, Sarah would visit him on a film set, 'which was quite exciting. But then after a bit you just got bored sitting and waiting, and I remember him saying to me, "This is what I do, this is my job, I sit around and wait a lot." And you couldn't communicate much with him, either. He just wanted to be in his trailer thinking and going over his lines.'

In the town of Livingstone, near Victoria Falls, Oliver befriended a white farmer, who invited him back to his home. The whisky pretty quickly made an appearance and the two men got steadily pissed. It just so happened that this farmer used to be a hunter of big game. 'Oh really?' said Ollie, fascinated. 'I used to be in the army. As a matter of fact, I was a marksman.' Ollie's porky pies knew no sane boundary. 'Her Majesty keeps me in her special file in case there's another war, you know.'

This bullshit impressed the farmer so much that he produced a rifle and pointed to a washing line at the end of the garden. 'Do you think you could hit one of those clothes pegs? The second one from the right.'

Ollie picked up the rifle, took aim, and fired through the window. To his utter amazement he scored a bull's-eye.

'Wow, man, that was fantastic!' the farmer hollered. 'I've never seen shooting like that.'

'That's nothing,' said Ollie, milking the moment.

'Do you think you could shoot this cigarette out of my hand?' asked the farmer, considerably upping the ante.

Ollie figured that since he could hit a clothes peg from forty yards, a fag a few feet away would be a doddle. 'Easy,' he said. 'Just hold it up.' He took aim, fired, and shot the farmer straight through the hand. The man just stood there, blood pumping from the wound. Ollie was about to leg it when the farmer announced, 'That was fantastic, man. You were only about an inch out.'

*

Oliver was in Cap Ferrat in the south of France, taking a short break, when he heard the news, on 7 September 1978, that Keith Moon had been found dead in his London flat. 'He was inconsolable,' remembers Jacquie. 'I've never seen anything like it. He couldn't believe Moonie had gone and deserted him and left him to play on his own.'

Moon's spirit, however, lived on at Broome Hall in the shape of two quite different objects that the musician had bequeathed to Ollie when he went to live in the USA. One morning a removal lorry drove up to the house. 'We've got a delivery for Mr Reed. It's a dog and a rhino.' Yeah, very funny, was the first reaction. 'No,' said the removal man. 'It's a real dog and a fibreglass rhino.' The rhino was life-size and Ollie called it Hornby. It was an incredible thing to behold, but for days he wondered where to put the damn thing. Finally its home was in the middle of the rhododendron bush at the top of the driveway, with its face just poking out, always with fresh grass in its mouth. 'The trick was,' says David. 'That people arrived at night in their cars and their headlights would come up the drive and they'd pick up this rhino charging out of the bushes, which caused a wobble or two.'

The dog was called Beano, a huge Harlequin Great Dane that Moon had been devoted to since it was a puppy. It had a nasty habit of headbutting doors and smashing windows to get to its food. Another trick was to lead guests by the sleeve and bash open the back door, which was on a spring, and walk them into the kitchen. Nicknamed 'the Pink-Nutted War Dog' because of its huge pink balls, Beano was employed by Ollie in some of his army games, or they'd play together in the bluebell woods. Ollie would whistle and then hide and Beano would sniff him out. Over time some of Beano's more deranged Moon-induced habits were erased and he lived to a ripe old age. 'He was very much part of our family,' says Sarah. 'He was a great dog, we all loved him.'

Ollie never truly got over Moon's death, so closely were they linked spiritually, so closely matched as individuals. Their lunacy was inspired. They really were like kids, and one would set the other one off. 'My father really loved him,' says Sarah. 'Because they were so alike. But Moonie would get on his nerves towards the end because Moonie really was like a child, he needed looking after and he didn't know when to stop at all, whereas my dad could stop. Moonie was magic and mad.'

Ollie said this once of his friend: 'I knew the way to the bar, but not to the bizarre. His shadow is always on the sunny side of the street with me, always, because of that path he showed me.'

A Date with Cronenberg

Oliver had been sent a script that he called the best thing he'd read since *The Devils*. It was from a cult Canadian director called David Cronenberg who'd been responsible for a pair of highly controversial horror films, *Shivers* and *Rabid*. The part on offer was that of an egocentric and slightly mysterious psychiatrist conducting experiments at a private institute where he encourages patients to externalize their rage. Unfortunately his prize patient, played by Samantha Eggar, has taken to 'hatching' homicidal mutant children. The film was *The Brood*, considered today to be one of Cronenberg's finest works, certainly his most personal, written when the director was undergoing huge personal trauma as a result of a divorce and a battle for child custody.

Whenever Ollie received a script of the quality of *The Brood* it was always difficult to contain his excitement and he'd be raring to get started. Whether a film was good or bad, though, he always approached it in the same methodical and professional manner. Around six weeks before a job he'd pack the circus away, not see his friends or drink, and start learning the script. When he thought he'd got it, then he'd start to play again. 'But he'd be in a local pub like the Cricketers,' says Mark, 'and suddenly start spouting these lines and people would say, "What the fuck's he talking about?" He would always try out bits of dialogue to see what reactions he got from people.' Then, maybe two weeks before cameras rolled, he'd put the blinkers on again and totally focus on it, and that included staying off the booze. 'I'm on the dry,' he'd announce. It was like an athlete in training. Jacquie would always sense when an important film was pending, 'because he became quite morose and into himself, so obviously he was getting involved with what was coming'.

Ollie arrived in Toronto in the winter of 1978 to begin shooting *The Brood*. Neither Cronenberg nor his producer, Pierre David, had ever worked with a mainstream star before, certainly never one like Ollie, and the experience was to be a massive learning curve. 'We were pretty naive at that time,' admits Pierre. 'And we didn't really know what we were getting into with Ollie. But the fact of the matter is *The Brood* was one of the most entertaining movies that we ever did because Oliver's adventures at night were pretty amazing.'

Take the time Oliver was enjoying a drink with some of the crew at a bar in the city centre. At the height of the revelries he announced an outrageous bet, that he'd take all his clothes off and walk back to his hotel in the buff. Don't forget, this was winter in Toronto, so it was not particularly warm. 'I got a phone call saying Oliver Reed is at the police station,' remembers Pierre. 'He'd been arrested for walking up the street nude. Somebody from production went to get him out. Nothing came of it, in fact everybody found it pretty funny. He was at the police station for about an hour delighting all the cops.'

That was the first thing. Then he threw a party one night in his suite at the Four Seasons Hotel and began hurling his bedding from the window down to the street below: sheets, pillows, you name it. Pierre called Ollie's agent. 'Guys, this is crazy, we never know what to expect from him. What's gonna be the next thing?'

'Don't worry,' they said. 'There is only one solution to your problem: fly in his brother.'

So that's what happened: David was flown in from London. 'And it was much calmer after that,' says Pierre. 'We had no more crises.'

Oliver thoroughly enjoyed making *The Brood*, a movie that is creepy and unsettling. And, sensing in Cronenberg a director of huge talent, he upped his game accordingly to deliver an exceptional performance, beautifully understated. 'However drunk Oliver would get at night, he would be perfect on the set the next day,' confirms Pierre. 'And in terms of performance he was great on every level, he got it, he understood what to do, he was perfect. Ollie really was an excellent actor, but it was, like, oh my God, what's he going to do tonight?'

Make-up artist Steve Neill was relaxing at home when he took a phone call from colleague and friend Rob Bottin. 'I've got a job for you, Steve. It's going to be a bit of a tough one for you, but I think you'll have a good time, you're just the right guy for it.'

'What is it?' asked Steve, already curious.

'You're going to work with Oliver Reed and do his make-up.'

'Oliver Reed! Oh my God, that's incredible.' Neill was a huge Hammer fan and of course knew Ollie from *The Curse of the Werewolf*.

'But you're going to have to be a bit more than a make-up artist,' cautioned Bottin. 'You're also going to have to keep an eye on him.'

The film in question was *Dr Heckyl and Mr Hype*, directed by Charles B. Griffith, who'd made the original *Little Shop of Horrors* for Roger Corman. It was a tired comic variation on the well-worn Robert Louis Stevenson story, with Ollie playing a hideously deformed scientist who turns into a handsome but evil pervert. The prosthetics involved were fairly extensive: coloured eye contacts, false teeth, big ears, a fright wig, talons and skin pieces, and required Ollie and Steve Neill to be on set at something like four o'clock. A week into the shoot a crew member came storming into the make-up trailer demanding Oliver's presence on the set. Neill had been working on him for just an hour and explained that he'd been given four hours to do the job. 'No, we've got to have him now,' pressed the assistant. 'Do whatever you can do, just get him on the set.' Neill refused: it was impossible to get Ollie ready that fast. Then the assistant turned nasty. Ollie, who had been observing all this, looked at Steve and waved his hand. 'Let me deal with this.' Getting up, he grabbed the assistant by the scruff of the neck and lifted him off the ground and bellowed, 'Steve's an artist. Leave him alone.' Then he threw him backwards out of the door of the trailer. Slamming the door shut, Ollie settled back in the chair and said, 'Steve, you may continue.' From that point on Neill knew he and Oliver were going to get along just fine.

Part of the monster make-up was a set of false teeth, and to get them to fit Ollie's mouth Neill made some dental impressions. Looking at them, he could see clearly that at some point his jaw had been broken, rather badly too. 'Shush,' said Ollie. 'Never tell anyone, that's your secret, you're the only one who knows.' Neill guessed the injury must have happened when he was glassed all those years ago.

In the make-up chair Ollie was perfectly compliant and tolerant of the whole process and paid close attention to everything Neill did, sometimes during the day pointing out where the make-up was coming loose or needed a touch-up. This was totally refreshing for Neill, because so many actors he has worked with over the years would let things like that go or just not care. 'He was the most incredibly professional actor I've ever worked with in my whole career and I worked with a lot of big stars. All through that production he was always on time and never once missed a line.' That said, at two each afternoon out came the Stolichnaya and Oliver always insisted Neill have one too. 'Of course, after a while it got a little difficult for me to do my job, so I started leaving the vodka out and then one day he grabbed the glass from me and smelt it, then poured me this huge tumbler. "Naughty, naughty." Needless to say, we got a little tipsy, but we never got out of hand.'

That was usually reserved for the evenings. 'He was always hard to escape from at night,' says Neill. 'Because he always wanted to go out partying.' Most memorably on Neill's twenty-eighth birthday. Ollie got to hear about it and asked what his plans were. Nothing much really, a quiet night in with the girlfriend. Ollie scoffed at that. 'No you're not. I'm taking you out. Call your lady and tell her you won't be home tonight.' It all sounded rather ominous. Ollie was staying at the Montage Hotel in Beverly Hills and its world-renowned restaurant was their destination, except they were hardly dressed for fine dining, having just come from the set. As they went up in the elevator, a man recognized Ollie. 'Oh my God, you're Oliver Reed. Can I have your autograph?' Ollie smiled. 'Sure, can I buy your shirt? I need a clean shirt.' He took out a wad of cash and the exchange was made. That still left Neill looking in a bit of a state and, sure enough, the maître d' barred their entrance. 'A bit of money later and a lot of talking from Oliver, we were in,' recalls Neill. 'And everybody was staring at us. We sat down and had a great dinner with lots of drink. Later on I looked over and saw Gene Hackman, who I'd worked with before. I could see that Gene recognized me, but I also could see the horror in his eyes of, oh God, don't let Oliver see me. Of course he did and up he shot and ran over and grabbed Gene and brought him back to our table.'

As the evening wore on it turned into something of a drinking contest, slightly soured when Ollie wanted to start a bar-room brawl. Neill managed to talk him out of it. 'Over here, Oliver. They'll come and get us and throw us in jail.'

'Yeah, I know, won't it be great?'

'No,' said Neill. 'We have to be on the set tomorrow.'

'Yeah, you're right.'

The night ended at Ollie's penthouse suite. 'Do you like to box?' Ollie asked, shoving another drink in Neill's hand.

'I'm not much into boxing and brawling, Oliver.'

'It's great, let me show you some moves.'

The pair started sparring, little jabs at first, then Ollie launched a haymaker that accidentally caught Neill in the face and down he went. 'I was practically out cold.' Hauled up by an apologetic Ollie, Neill dusted himself down and then noticed he was alone. His host was gone; where the hell was he? He started a search, ending up outside, and there was Ollie hanging off the balcony. 'All I can see are his hands on the railing, and then he leaps back over and shouts, "That makes me feel so alive!" And I'm thinking, this guy could have fallen to his death. But of course he didn't because he's Oliver Reed.'

It was at that point of the evening that Neill decided it might be a good idea to try to go home. After easing his sports car out of the hotel car park, his next memory was of waking up in bed the following morning not knowing how the hell he got there. 'I went to work and got in the trailer and there was Oliver sitting in the chair giggling and pointing. I don't know what he's laughing about and he tells me to look in the mirror and I've got this black eye. I consider that something to be proud of. I got a black eye from Oliver Reed.'

Neill counts his experience working with Oliver as one of the best of his career, which later included stints on *Ghostbusters* and *Fright Night*, and often thinks of him. 'He was someone who really becomes a friend to you, it was a relationship that was more than just, you're the make-up guy, I'm the actor. We were buddies.' Neill remembers an occasion when a gang of people were in Ollie's trailer. 'Everybody wanted to be close to him, he was very charismatic. He drew people in because he was a fascinating person and highly intelligent. You could speak to him about almost any topic. He was extremely well read.' There was this female assistant on the set who was overweight and one of the production team said, 'Look at that fat chick. Why doesn't she lose some weight?' Ollie went through the roof and threw the guy out. 'He was always a man of the people,' says Neill. 'He was always on the side of the underdog. And he always hung with the crew, not the money people. He was really quite unique. When I saw *Gladiator* it really drew a tear because that was the real guy. It was a fitting last picture.'

End of an Era

After spending several months in the Libyan desert, it was nice to get back to the green, rolling hills of Surrey and Broome Hall. Ollie had been there for months on end shooting *The Lion of the Desert*, an overlong if historically accurate epic about Omar Mukhtar – played by Anthony Quinn – who led guerrilla resistance to Italian rule in Libya until his capture and execution in 1931. In the movie, filmed on a lavish scale and bankrolled by Colonel Gaddafi, reportedly to the tune of thirty-five million dollars, Oliver plays the fascist General Graziani, appointed by Mussolini to crush the rebellion. It's a noble performance, full of the required gravitas, and it was a film he was justifiably proud of, in spite of its eventual failure at the box office.

There was always something special about coming home to Broome Hall for Ollie, his own little piece of England, especially from such an alien and far-flung location as Libya. 'He aspired to be what he probably always wanted, that was to be an English squire and a gentleman, and he was,' says Christensen. 'He loved all that bullshit about being related to Peter the Great. It was a great source of pride to him. To sit on that ancestral pile and to look across the land as far as you can see, and the woods and the lake and the horses and the croquet lawn, and that half-mile drive going to the huge gates, he just loved it.'

But the place had never stopped being a millstone round

Oliver's neck and by the end of the seventies it had finally brought him to his knees. He simply couldn't afford to keep it running any more, a stark reality that broke his heart. It must have been awful to watch all his belongings being packed into tea chests and the large furniture sold off, the stables cleared out and his beloved horses going, to see his personality totally erased from a house that had so often played host to the sound of laughter and marvellous antics until it was completely empty and soulless. 'I remember when the whole thing was starting to fragment and Broome Hall was going,' says Mark. 'And being down in the cellar bar with him, a place that was a shrine to fun rather than a shrine to alcohol, it was his play place. I remember him breaking the place up almost, breaking pictures, the Thorhill Glass got broken and the Penicillin Glass was smashed. There was a sense of finality about it all, that mould was being broken, because it was time for a transition. He was moving on.'

Worse, his gang of loyal workers had to be dismissed. Too upset, Ollie couldn't face them himself, so it was left to David. 'I got them all together in the hall and gave them a speech about our problems and they took it well. Some of them had been there years.'

Although leaving Broome Hall was, as David puts it, a 'huge wrench for Ollie', for about a month now it had ceased to resemble a proper home. The reason: Jacquie and Sarah were no longer living in it. It hadn't always been happy families between everyone but the last year or so had been particularly rough and Jacquie had walked out on Ollie several times. 'They'd have a big old barney and then we'd go and stay with my grandparents or somewhere else for a few nights,' recalls Sarah. 'Then we'd go back home again. But obviously it was just getting to the stage where it wasn't manageable any more.'

That Christmas was particularly miserable. On New Year's Eve Oliver sat sullen in the kitchen, imploring the clock to reach midnight. Unable to wait any longer, he changed the hands to twelve o'clock and shouted, 'Now it's midnight! Now it's New Year,' and, taking out his shotgun, he blasted the timepiece off the wall.

Just ten years old at the time, Sarah couldn't help put pick up on the changeable atmosphere in the house. 'I was aware that it was quite volatile. They tried to hide a lot from me, but there were moments when they couldn't and there were occasions it got quite physical as well. My mum did have the odd black eye.' Jacquie even turned up at Millfield once to visit Mark with a rather obvious shiner. 'By helicopter. Can you imagine it? The things I did. But it wasn't that often. Maybe it was my fault: I provoked him too much. It would be a complete sudden outburst and one just happened to be in the way. If you have a really awful row, sometimes it reaches a point of no control and also no return. But it happened so seldom.'

Such incidents can't be so easily dismissed or swept under the carpet, especially coming from a man who all too often embraced violence. 'Jacquie had a horrific time,' says David. 'I wasn't there but Bill and Jen were and there are stories of Ollie pulling Jacquie along the passageway by her hair. Towards the end it was gruesome. Jekyll and Hyde again.'

Still, Jacquie was more than capable of sometimes giving as good as she got. 'She tried to stab him once,' reveals Sarah. 'He always used to show me these marks. "Look at this scar on my arse, girl! That was your mother with a carving knife." I don't know if that's true or not, but he used to show me this scar on his bum. I wouldn't put it past her, she was very feisty.'

Then one night Jacquie grabbed her daughter, put her in the back seat of her car and drove off, this time never to return. She'd finally had enough. A few days earlier they'd all been at the pub and after returning to Broome Hall Jacquie was as usual dispatched to the kitchen to cook Ollie and his mates dinner. 'I had a great big bowl of pasta sauce that I'd heated up and was ready to serve and he just tipped it all over me. I didn't react, I just went on serving it out, I didn't do anything, I didn't go and clean myself up, I just sat there for the rest of the evening covered in pasta sauce. It had come to a stage where I thought, I don't think I can take any more of this.'

Jacquie was under the impression that Ollie wanted things to change anyway. 'I think he needed to move on and I think I was wise to go.' She'd suspected, or knew, that he'd been seeing other women. 'And, looking back, I think in a sense he was trying to make it so that I would be the one to leave rather than him; which I did in the end.'

By walking out Jacquie knew exactly what she was doing, that by not being married to Oliver she had no legal right whatsoever to his property or wealth, not that it bothered her one jot. 'Even if we had been married I would never have gone to a solicitor, it just isn't in my nature. When I took Sarah and left I expected nothing in return. I was with the man because I loved the man, I wasn't with him because of what he had.' In any case, without having to raise the issue Oliver made sure that Sarah was provided for, and that included continuing to pay for her education. 'That's what he was like,' says Jacquie. 'He was supportive of everybody in his past, Mark, Kate, everyone.'

Broome Hall was eventually sold to a property developer and Sarah remembers spending a final day there with her father, saying goodbye to the place before it was carved up into apartments. They walked around the grounds and in and out of empty rooms, finally coming to rest in what had been Ollie's bedroom. 'We both stood there and just looked out of the window. It was a view he'd always loved. As a ten-year-old you don't really understand what's happening, but there was this sense of sadness. Broome Hall had been his dream and it had gone.'

Ollie moved into a seven-bedroom Grade II-listed sixteenth-century farmhouse called Pinkhurst Farm, just outside

Oakwoodhill, near the Surrey–West Sussex border. Jacquie meanwhile moved to Guildford, close to where Sarah was attending boarding school, and found a job working for a medical magazine. For the first time in her life, aged nearly forty, she took out a mortgage, the first step towards independence and trying to build a new life for herself. Every weekend she drove Sarah to Pinkhurst to stay with her father, dropping her off halfway up the drive, not wishing to get too near the house. She'd do the same when picking her up, and there would be Sarah waiting alone near the bottom of the driveway. 'One time I came and he was there with her. "Why don't you come to the house," he said. So I did, and we had a couple of glasses of wine. Sarah had a bedroom there and while she was upstairs Oliver said, "Why don't you stay?"' It was a difficult position to be put in and Jacquie was tempted. Of course she was: they'd had a great life together and shared a child. 'But then it flashes back: do you really want to go through all that again?' So in the end the answer was no. And after all these years Jacquie still thinks she made the right decision. 'Do you ever know if you've made the right decision? I so very nearly did say yes, but I didn't, I said no. And that was the last time I saw Oliver.'

Ollie vs Klaus

Before Ollie had even moved into Pinkhurst he was planning his new garden. Would it ever match the majesty of Broome Hall? Ollie was determined to give it his best shot. He had around fifteen acres at the back of the property to play with, but it was all pretty uninspiring, just your typical English country garden with very flat lawns and symmetrical rose bushes. There was also a small lake but it was fairly dull. Ollie's plan was radical. 'I want hills,' he said, and they were to surround the lake. In came tractors and diggers and tons of earth were excavated and dumped on to the lawn. When out of the country Ollie would call David to direct operations. He'd be on the phone asking, 'How big is the hill?' and David would tell him and Ollie would go, 'No, no, I want it higher than that. Higher!' In the end, Mark believes, thousands of tons of earth were used before Ollie's vision was realized. 'Everyone thought he was crazy. And he got old lumps of York stone and dropped those in and had semi-mature trees and wild flowers put in there, and half-built brick walls that looked like they'd been there for a hundred years. Within three years of doing all this people used to wander round going, "Wow, this is just the most amazing garden." It looked like it had been there for ever.'

Much to the chagrin, however, of a lot of the farmers whose land surrounded Pinkhurst. As he'd done at Broome Hall,

Ollie delighted in letting the fields grow wild, but this became a problem now he had a much smaller acreage. 'The farmers used to ring up because Ollie's fields were full of thistles,' says David. 'And of course on a windy day these thistles would be blowing over their newly seeded fields and the bloody farmers were going berserk.' Ollie didn't care, though. 'He didn't care because he thought that there needed to be a haven for wildlife not to be persecuted,' says Mark. 'Just to be able to get on and do what it does.'

Few people did get it, and when the time came to sell Pinkhurst the new owner couldn't understand why the garden looked like a wilderness. As for Ollie's huge mounds and hills, bulldozers were brought in to flatten it all again.

During those first few months of life in his new home, Oliver missed Broome Hall terribly and also admitted to being lonely. 'Things were a little bit lost for him for a while,' says Mark. 'It must have been a dark time. But Pinkhurst was a stunning place, just beautiful. The interior was lovely, it had these old beams that ran through all the rooms.' And he wasn't entirely on his own, as Bill and Jenny came with him, living in a bungalow on the estate, although this didn't stop Ollie dragging poor old Bill out for a drinking session at all hours. Nor from tampering with the couple's home. Ollie thought their bungalow rather lacklustre, so built a Sleeping Beauty-style tower with a pointed roof that sat on the corner and called it 'the Sky Rocket'.

Changes were also made to Pinkhurst itself, but not on the same dramatic level as Broome Hall. For starters, the entrance to the house was on one side of the building and Oliver felt that it should be at the front. So a grand porch was planned. 'That was a labour of love,' says Mark. 'And very expensive.' A new kitchen was put in, and given that extra Ollie touch when all the handles of the drawers were shaped to look like penises. Generally, though, he just liked there to be workers hanging around the place, like at Broome Hall, company for him to go out drinking with. Their presence saved his life on one occasion. Mucking about, Ollie dived head first into a large barrel that was kept underneath a drain to collect rainwater. It was full and he managed to wedge himself in with his hands behind his back, so he'd no leverage to clamber out. Luckily a gang of workmen saw his flapping legs, tipped the barrel over and dragged him out before he drowned.

Ollie was very loyal to his workers, organizing a Christmas party for them every year at the local pub. One story illustrates this loyalty. Oliver was invited to play for the Lord's Taverners at a charity cricket match and brought along his workmen for a day out. He was marching up to the grandstand with them, when the organizer blocked his way. 'You can come in, Oliver, but your friends can't.' There was a slight pause before Oliver replied, 'Then you can stuff your cricket match up your arse.' So off they went and Ollie commandeered the beer tent, along with his friends. After the match, when Nicholas Parsons and the like had about three urchins asking for their autograph, a thousand people surrounded the tent trying to get Ollie's.

At Pinkhurst Oliver also connected some of the outbuildings to the main house and converted a barn into a pub which had a snooker table, a disco, and a bar made out of the long table from Broome Hall. He christened it the Bark and Hornet. One afternoon Ollie, Paul Friday and a few others got too raucous at the local pub and the landlord chucked them out, so it was back to the Bark and Hornet, where Ollie pranced up and down, declaring over and over again, 'You can't get banned from the Bark and Hornet. You can't get banned from the Bark and Hornet.' 'With that,' recalls Paul Friday, 'this guy got up on to the bar, unzipped his flies and pissed all over Ollie's head. It was a whole bladderful, and Ollie just wiped it off, downed the whisky he was holding, and said, "You can't get banned from the Bark and Hornet."' Paul saw the guy two days later and he was in floods of tears. 'I can't believe I've done that,' he said. 'I admire Ollie so much. He's actually changed my life because I was a bit of a hooligan and his values I've taken onboard myself, so I can't believe I did that to someone I respect so much.' Paul gently patted him on the shoulder and said, 'I wouldn't worry about it.'

Then there was the cider shed, which was much more rustic than the Bark and Hornet, with peat on the ground, an oil lamp hanging up, and a wind-up gramophone that played records of the old newsreels from the war and sirens going off. Ollie loved making his own cider. It was lethal stuff, as Sarah remembers. 'It was weird because it went to people's knees before it went to their heads, so people literally would collapse. They'd be walking and then their legs would completely go.'

Christensen made many a visit to Pinkhurst and invariably ended up in the cider shed with Ollie. 'He had a proper old-fashioned cider press in there and made different varieties of cider, all in big barrels. One would have a bottle of rum poured in it, another would have a bottle of vodka or Scotch, or gin, just to see how it developed by the time it was ready to drink. It was potent stuff. Alan the poacher went mad in there one night and Reg had to knock him out.'

Even more bizarrely Ollie built a two-storey tree house next door which had a diving board in it. 'So you came out of the cider shed after drinking cider all day,' says Sarah, 'climbed up a ladder into the tree house, and then jumped off into this field. It was so stupid: limbs could have been broken and God knows what.'

Paul and Nora Friday often visited Oliver at Pinkhurst, and when they had their daughter Louise, Ollie took it upon himself to be the child's godfather, grandfather and guardian all rolled into one. 'He dressed up in a three-piece suit, with hat and opera cane, and dragged me off to the hospital on the first night,' remembers Paul. 'We'd had a few drinks and I was pretty pissed, so he marched in and saw the baby before I did probably.' Oliver arrived carrying a bunch of Michaelmas daisies with a banana hanging out, and a rose. He tossed the rose into the cradle and Nora got the daisies and the banana. It didn't end there because he turned up over the next five days, each time delivering things like potatoes, cabbages, and goodness knows what. It was like a harvest festival. 'I had a Chinese nurse and she thought it was some sort of strange sexual rite, all these vegetables arriving in droves,' Nora reveals. It got to the stage where she had to plead with her husband: was there a chance she could see him on his own without Ollie?

As Louise grew up, Ollie continued to dote on the child. Returning from foreign locations, he'd toss her a banknote, a high-denomination rand note from South Africa, say, or a hundred-dollar bill, which infuriated Nora. 'Ollie!' she'd rage. 'Louise is three, for God's sake, she's not to have paper money like that. You can't give it to her.' One day Nora was about to go out Christmas shopping when Ollie arrived with a large carrier bag. 'Louise,' he said. 'Your mummy says I'm not allowed to give you any notes,' and he handed her this bag of silver coins he'd been collecting for a year – there must have been a small fortune inside – then he turned to Nora, beaming, and said, 'You can't complain now.' Louise bought the biggest doll in the toy shop and it took an absolute age to count out the money.

Girls of a very different nature were often to be found coming in and out of Pinkhurst, quite a few actually. 'He wasn't a man to be on his own,' says Sarah. But they didn't stay very long. Muriel remembers that these brief liaisons tended to all end the same way: 'with their clothes thrown out of the window on to the lawn'. Then there was the time Ollie went down to visit Gus at his holiday camp. 'He came back with a little totty girl of seventeen,' says David. 'And she was installed at Pinkhurst and ended up terrified, the poor thing.' And the reason, according to Muriel, was that Oliver 'tried to stuff bread down her throat'. David attempts to excuse this mad behaviour by describing the girl as very thin and waif-like, 'so obviously Ollie thought she needed feeding and when she said no did it anyway. You see, the one thing Ollie didn't like was women telling him what to do or what he couldn't do. He wouldn't stand for that.' It was indeed a stupid and crass thing to do. 'She honestly thought he was trying to kill her,' says Muriel. 'She had great weals round her neck. Anyway she managed to get away and shut herself in the bathroom and slept the night in the bath. She was so frightened. And early the next morning she went over to Bill and Jenny's cottage and she left.'

A regular visitor to Pinkhurst was, of course, Sarah. She would turn up and always wanted to visit the local stables, while Ollie just wanted to go to the pub. 'And that's what we'd do: he'd drop me off at the stables and then go to the pub. Afterwards we'd have these awkward dinners where we'd sit there and have no conversation. It was just an awkward relationship.' It was not helped by Sarah's chronic shyness. Ollie used to say to Jacquie when Sarah was young, 'Why won't she talk to me?' The reason was simple: she was terrified of him, a situation that lasted well into her teens. It wasn't helped by the fact that he'd come back after two months away filming and just want to embrace his family. 'I have this recollection of this huge great bear of a man coming back and cuddling me with bristles and it being really overpowering. He just wanted affection and love and I didn't know him. He'd been gone for months, and he scared me because he was so imposing and such a personality. I was scared. Plus I was a naturally shy child. We always had this awkwardness with each other.'

Family relationships didn't fit easily with Oliver, whether it was with his parents or later with his brothers. And, Sarah believes, also with his children. 'He loved us but I don't think he knew how to deal with us. I never felt unloved and he would tell me that he loved me but I don't feel that he really understood us sometimes.' Nor was Sarah made to feel that she was the most important thing in her father's life. Ollie never felt that was necessary, or had the capability to express it, because he had other things going on in his life: his partner, his work, his playtime and his friends. 'I think his friends were his family, they were the people that didn't challenge him on an emotional level. He couldn't take being challenged on an emotional level. We weren't a close family. It's weird to me when I see families that are really close, because we never had that.'

And there was the drinking. Often when Sarah arrived at Pinkhurst Ollie's friends were there and the booze was flowing. On one occasion they'd all been out for a long, late lunch and sent her back to school pissed, at the age of fifteen. 'And I had a music concert that night, so I had to go and do my piano solo half-cut.' Another time Sarah brought her best friend from school to stay for the weekend. She was Russian, so not unreasonably in Ollie's mind he wanted to drink vodka with her. 'He literally made her sit there and drink vodka with him. It was, you're Russian, you must drink vodka. I mean, she was fifteen and in his charge, but it was, like, you have to finish this bottle of vodka with me.'

Of course, Sarah had grown up surrounded by alcohol and heavy drinking. She remembers the first time she got drunk, at the age of eight, at David Hunt's house with her dad, and they made her traffic lights: crème de menthe, apricot brandy and cherry brandy. 'I woke up feeling not the best. I think that was my first hangover.' Generally Ollie never encouraged it. He never said no either. 'So it wasn't the normal thing of have one glass at Christmas time, it was more of a free-for-all. I don't remember raiding the drinks cabinet because I didn't need to, it was always there.'

Another visitor to Pinkhurst was Sarah Miles. 'She just couldn't leave him alone,' recalls Jacquie. 'I'm not sure if he ever returned the affection; she wasn't really his type.' The pair of them were currently working on a picture together called *Venom*, under the watchful eye of director Tobe Hooper, of *Texas Chainsaw Massacre* fame. Ollie was offered the film after a Screen Actors Guild strike delayed the start of another job, playing Bo Derek's father in *Tarzan the Ape Man*, a role that eventually went to Richard Harris. Then, just a week into filming *Venom*, everything was thrown into turmoil when Hooper unexpectedly departed, for reasons that have never been entirely clear. The entire production was put on hold while the producers set about searching for a replacement.

Their choice was Piers Haggard, largely a television drama director, who had Dennis Potter's *Pennies from Heaven* for the BBC under his belt. Like Ollie, Haggard was intrigued by *Venom*'s premise, that of an escaped venomous snake inside a house where a hostage situation is being played out, but in hindsight he regrets ever going near the damn thing. Up he ventured to Elstree Studios to meet the cast, who'd been hanging around for nearly two weeks. 'That's when I first met Oliver, in the canteen, and he played a trick on me, pretending to throw a moody fit, that he was going to walk out and leave the film because I'd insulted him by saying something completely spurious. But it was just a hoax. He was testing me.' Things went rapidly downhill after that.

The problem was Ollie's relationship with co-star Klaus Kinski. They detested each other at first sight, which was a bit difficult since they had most of their scenes together. By the close of shooting Haggard declared the black mamba the nicest thing on the set. 'Oliver was clearly goading Klaus, who unfortunately had no sense of humour. Oliver, on the other hand, had a fabulous sense of humour, very wicked, he definitely liked a laugh, and he definitely liked a laugh at Klaus Kinski's expense. Ollie took the most exquisite pleasure in winding him up. That was the main cause of the problem.'

Oliver used to amuse himself by going over to Kinski's trailer and shaking it violently, yelling, 'Come out, you fucking Nazi bastard!' Kinski would emerge trembling with rage and screaming back at him as best he could. Actually Kinski was born in Poland and was an immigrant to Germany. 'But he passed for a Nazi in Oliver's eyes,' says Haggard.

So what caused this feud? A clash of personalities, obviously, but also professional rivalry? Kinski was an imposing figure, and with both of them playing the bad guys in the story Ollie knew it was going to be a battle royal to see who would make the bigger impact. 'There's no question there was a testosterone-fuelled competition between them,' confirms Haggard. 'Lots of ego, too. Klaus had the more obvious ego. He was quite clearly an egomaniac.'

Round one, which took place quite early on in the schedule, was an innocuous scene that required both actors merely to walk down a corridor and enter a room. 'One of the things that got Ollie's goat was that the Kinski character was his boss in the script,' says Haggard. 'He was the brains behind the baddies, so he had to have precedence and Ollie did not like that. Even though he'd read the script he really didn't like that.' When the time came to do a run-through Ollie nudged ahead of Klaus in the corridor and when he arrived at the room rested his arm on the door frame, essentially blocking Kinski from entering. Haggard called for another run-through, and again Ollie stopped by the doorway, his arm blocking Kinski's path. 'What happens?' pleaded Kinski. 'What I do?'

Haggard saw the problem. 'Ollie, do you think that you could just ease over a little bit and maybe Klaus could come through?'

'No,' said Ollie casually. 'I think I look good here. I feel comfortable here.'

Kinski looked hard and long into space before saying, 'No problem. We shoot.'

'OK, let's roll this,' ordered Haggard. 'OK, ready, stand by. Action.'

The two actors approached the door, and it was like a pair of thoroughbreds straining to get their necks over the finishing line first. Ollie took up the same position as before, except this time Kinski came right up from behind him and with a vicious uppercut cracked Ollie's arm out of the way, came into the room and began the scene. 'They were so determined to upstage each other,' Haggard remembers, 'they didn't give a fuck really.' It very much seems like there was some one-upmanship going on, almost some game. But, says Haggard, 'Klaus wasn't playing a game. Ollie was. Ollie was a prankster. He just loved winding people up or having a laugh. And I grew rather fond of him. He could be a bastard, but he did have a sense of humour. Their behaviour, though, was completely unprofessional and childish. Disgraceful.'

Most evenings Oliver retired after filming for a drink at the studio bar. One time he was joined by pal Mick Monks. Next to them were five stools around the edge of the bar, all occupied by young men. 'Who are they?' asked Ollie.

'They're the lads that do the voices for Kermit and co,' said Monks. 'You know, the Muppets.'

Ollie went, 'Muppets!' And up he got, pushed the first chap, and like dominoes they all went down, one after the other. 'You're not bloody actors!' he roared.

Venom was funded by the Guinness family, and early one morning producer Martin Bregman informed Haggard that at eleven o'clock the money was paying the set a visit. Sure, he said, and clean forgot about it. The crew were setting up a scene in the three-storey set of the house when suddenly there was an almighty rumpus from right at the top. 'The whole thing trembled,' says Haggard, 'and down the stairs came Oliver, laughing hysterically, and Kinski running after him, shrieking, "You fucking English cunt." And at that moment, with the studio resonating to the furious screams of Kinski and the maniacal laughter of Oliver, in through the studio doors comes Lord Guinness and his fragrant wife and fragrant children, along with Marty Bregman. And, I can still remember it, Marty saw Oliver and Klaus and herded the Guinness family away, saying, "I think we'll come back later."'

The film did seem to be deteriorating into something resembling a battleground. 'It was an extraordinary and very unpleasant experience,' says Haggard. 'An accumulatively unpleasant experience because as it went on it got more and more wearing and more tiring, and we got behind schedule.' Ollie was also drinking heavily, especially at lunch, according to the director. 'He was difficult in the afternoon, a bit brutalized; very unprofessional. Klaus never drank – he was just mad.'

Ollie's drinking was never so bad that Haggard had to send him home. It was just that one knew it was going to get laborious because there would inevitably be a problem or Ollie would get stubborn over something. 'You know how people are a bit pugnacious when they're drunk, but he was still capable of giving a performance. Oliver was one of the finest film actors that we had. When he was right, he was a wonderful, powerful, and authoritative and focused film actor, he really knew how to play the camera. He knew what he had in those wonderful eyes. He gave me a lecture once. "Make sure you shoot these eyes," he said.'

Venom's poor showing at the box office was no great surprise to anyone, but at times the film is quite a suspenseful and exciting drama. Ollie's death is particularly memorable: seized by shock, he's unable to do anything but watch as the mamba crawls up his trouser leg and bites into his knackers. Great stuff.

Josephine

Ollie had stopped off for a quick drink at one of his local pubs, the King's Head in the village of Rudgwick, his custom-built Panther De Ville parked outside and claiming admiring looks from passers-by and people driving through. Coming home on the school bus, sixteen-year-old Josephine Burge caught sight of the car and, curious to see who it belonged to, went inside with a couple of her friends. 'And that's when I first saw him.' It was the beginning of a remarkable love story.

Josephine only vaguely knew who Oliver was, having seen him maybe twice on television. On Friday nights she'd go to friends' houses and often stay up late watching horror movies. 'And I do remember seeing *The Shuttered Room*, which I loved. So I'd seen that. I'd also been sick and off school one day and saw him on this chat show called *Pebble Mill at One*. So I was vaguely aware of him.'

As weeks turned into months Josephine often popped into the King's Head. She lived not far away in a cottage with her mother Anne, a single parent who had done her best to raise her family since their father died when Josephine was eight. From being an irregular customer Ollie had become something of a permanent fixture in the King's Head and always looked forward to seeing Josephine's pleasant, smiling face as she arrived with her friends. 'He used to call us the ducklings baby quack-quacks, and we'd sit in the corner with our soft drinks and crisps and chirp away.' Oliver always made a point of talking to them, engaging them in conversation. 'Then gradually it became apparent that perhaps he and I had more of an interest in each other than just chatting.' The courtship had begun.

There were invitations for her and her friends to come over to Pinkhurst, followed by more intimate dinner dates, always with one of Josephine's brothers or sisters in attendance, chaperones almost. 'An old-fashioned romance,' is how Oliver would later refer to it. Josephine's mother also invited Ollie over to have Sunday lunch with them. 'And he'd arrive bearing a joint of meat and a bunch of flowers,' recalls Josephine. 'And poor Sarah was often dragged along as well. It was a definite courtship. And it was wonderful. Obviously it was fascinating and very flattering for a young girl to have an attractive older man pay so much attention to her. He was very charismatic, and he was very interesting and funny.' Looking back, Josephine recognizes that part of the attraction was that tangible sense of danger Oliver carried around with him, the never knowing what he was going to do next, which countless other women had found impossible to resist ever since the early sixties. 'I suppose being young one always looks for a little bit of danger and one certainly got that with Ollie.' She was smitten, totally, and Oliver too must have surprised even himself that he'd fallen in love with a girl who had yet to take her O levels and was twenty-six years his junior.

Anne Burge took the pursuit of her young daughter by a middle-aged film star surprisingly well, although Josephine admits her family didn't really think it was the greatest thing in the world for her to be doing. 'But I went ahead and did it anyway. My family were actually wonderful and put up with it all. My mother was supportive and mindful and always there for me, and just kept an eye on things.' Anne must have been aware of how innocent Josephine was, a quiet and unassuming girl who had lived all her life in Rudgwick, and one is left to ponder how much of a father figure Oliver represented to her. There had only been the one boyfriend before Oliver and that wasn't at all serious and had fizzled out. Still, this didn't stop Ollie having a 'man to man' chat with him one afternoon in the pub, just to reassure the seventeen-year-old that his intentions were honourable when it came to Josephine. It must have made for a strange scene.

What's perhaps most remarkable about this courtship is that nobody outside of Rudgwick had any inkling of what was going on. 'Nobody leaked it or said anything,' recalls Josephine. 'We quietly got along and got to know each other, and nobody phoned anybody up and said, do you know what's going on?' Even when they went to Dorking for a meal in one of Ollie's favourite restaurants their privacy was respected. 'But again they were all people who Oliver would have known, and just left him alone to get on with things,' says Josephine. Sadly this idyll would not last for long.

First Ollie had a job of work to do. He'd accepted a role in a James Bond-type spoof called *Condorman*, made under the Walt Disney banner. The budget was big, the locations spectacular and the action suitably comic-strip. Best of all, it teamed him up again with Michael Crawford, who since *The Jokers* had attained huge fame as Frank Spencer in the BBC sitcom *Some Mothers Do 'Ave 'Em*. Crawford was playing the dashing hero, a comic-book-illustrator-cum superhero, Ollie the main baddie, a hotshot KGB agent. 'And remembering Ollie's penchant for living roles, I feared for my life,' said Crawford.

The cast all met up for the first time in Monte Carlo, at an exclusive restaurant. Oliver was the last to arrive, with Reg in tow. Barbara Carrera, who was playing a glamorous spy in the film, remembers that Ollie was impeccably dressed in a beautiful suit, Turnbull & Asser shirt, the lot, and he couldn't have been more courteous, walking round the table shaking the hands of the men and kissing the hands of the ladies. 'We had a glass of champagne to welcome everybody and celebrate the beginning of shooting. And it wasn't long after that Oliver stood up. He had this glazed look in his eyes, and ripped open his shirt and jacket, buttons went flying everywhere. Then he went around challenging all the men in the restaurant to arm-wrestling. The next thing, Oliver jumped up and started hanging from the chandelier. That was my first meeting with Oliver.'

What surprised Barbara even more was that the next morning on the set Ollie didn't look hung-over at all, but fresh and alert. 'And totally professional. He was 100 per cent focused. It was when he left the set after we wrapped that Hyde came out. He really was like Jekyll and Hyde. And it was fun working with Jekyll but then frightening spending time with Hyde because when the Hyde came out it was like he almost didn't know what he was doing.'

One afternoon a few of the cast went for lunch in a restaurant on the second floor of a hotel overlooking the harbour. After eating, Barbara took a stroll on to the balcony. 'I was standing there looking out over the Mediterranean when Oliver came up behind me and grabbed me and held me over the balcony. He had this glazed look in his eyes again. It was really scary because he held me completely over the edge. I remember looking at him and I said in the softest voice I could muster, like talking to a little child who was doing something he shouldn't, "Oliver, put me down. Put me down, Oliver." After that I stayed away from Oliver and balconies.'

Certainly Barbara never entertained the thought of socializing with Ollie, but the crew would go out with him and the next day she heard stories about him trying to pick fights with various people. 'One night he was almost killed. He picked a fight with the wrong guys, some Corsicans, and they pulled a knife on him and were really going after him and it

381

was the crew who saved him, who got him out. Although the way they told the story to me, probably by then a little jaded by his behaviour, they said, we thought about it for a second to let the Corsicans have their way with him, then we thought it would only delay the film.'

During the first couple of weeks of production Ollie happily reminisced with Crawford about the good old days when they played brothers in Winner's comedy. But as filming progressed Crawford watched Ollie grow ever deeper into his character, even to the extent of going around speaking with a heavy Russian accent. One evening Crawford was relaxing in the hotel bar when he spied Ollie sitting alone with a drink at a nearby table. Their eyes met. 'Come here and haffff a dreeenk!' shouted Ollie.

'It's OK, Ollie, I'm meeting someone.'

'Come here and haffff a dreeenk!' Ollie growled.

'No, Ollie, really . . .'

Oliver stood up and walked imposingly towards Crawford, who began to sink into his seat. 'Cummmmm here into Russian Embassy and haffff a dreeenk, you little feathered fart!' How could one refuse? And for the rest of filming Crawford was known as Condorman, the Feathered Fart.

Barbara also noticed that Ollie totally immersed himself in his villainous character. So maybe those earlier stunts he'd played on her were his way of implanting fear, an emotion her character had to feel towards him in the film. 'But I wasn't intimidated by Oliver. I wasn't. I was just scared of him. And I think he liked that, I think he liked people to be scared of him. He was always trying to test a person to see how scared they were of him.' Oliver did have a sense of menace about him, a real aura. It was part of his screen image and it was how he was in real life. 'Because his looks were so threatening, if he raised his voice people would start shaking because they thought he was about to punch them out,' remembers Carol Lynley. 'But he had a very sweet smile which, when it broke out in this rather ferocious face, you could almost see a little boy in there.'

Jonathan Vanger, who produced a couple of Oliver's movies in the late eighties, also saw it first-hand, how people were often frightened of him. 'We had difficulty with some of the younger actors. Because Ollie was usually playing a bad guy who would shout or scream, and he did it so credibly, you could actually see them freak out.'

Simon remembers a party held at his home where Oliver was a guest. After he left, one of Simon's television colleagues said, 'There's only two words to describe your brother: fucking terrifying.' And Ollie hadn't done anything. 'It was the first time this friend had met him, but he felt it. Ollie could be scary even when he was behaving himself.'

As had been the case with *The Jokers*, Crawford fell foul of several Ollie pranks. By some margin the weirdest was the time he crept into Crawford's hotel room at the dead of night when the actor was asleep and without a word began slowly and methodically turning over every piece of furniture. Stirred from his slumber, Crawford watched the spectacle and, when Ollie turned to leave whispered, 'Thank you, Oliver,' as he quietly closed the door.

'Michael was a little afraid of Oliver,' *Condorman*'s director, Charles Jarrott, always felt. As for himself, having worked with plenty of tough cookies over the years, from Peter Finch to Richard Burton, Jarrott wasn't going to be intimidated by Oliver Reed and in the end thoroughly enjoyed the experience. 'He was such a character and worked like a real professional. Strange, at work he was fairly quiet. At night, he was always boozed up and boisterous. One tended to steer away from him then. He spent a day and a night on a British cruiser visiting Nice. I hear the rum flowed like water!'

One memorable night shoot took place in the casino at Monte Carlo. Ollie was immaculately dressed in a white tuxedo and his scenes went like clockwork. 'We finished at about 2 a.m. and I went back to my hotel,' Jarrott recalled. 'After changing and enjoying a drink, I sauntered out on to my balcony overlooking the Mediterranean. It was a beautiful moonlit night. I glanced down at the calm sea and noticed a white tuxedo floating away on the waves. Looking back up at the hotel, I saw Ollie, stark naked, climbing from balcony to balcony. An English King Kong was abroad.'

When the film moved to Zermatt in Switzerland, Barbara and Oliver were involved in an episode that very nearly cost them their lives. It was a scene that took place in a helicopter high up the Matterhorn, but confusion reigned when the pilot mistook the signal for Ollie and Barbara to start playing the scene for his signal to take off and swoop down the mountain. 'The shocking thing was, both doors were completely open,' says Barbara. 'And the only thing that kept us in the helicopter was gravity, otherwise we would have fallen out, which is what the director and everyone on the crew thought. They thought that they had lost us, they thought that Oliver and I had fallen out of the helicopter. In the meantime we were so into the scene – our characters are supposed to be fighting – that we ended up really fighting each other. I elbowed Ollie in his stomach. We didn't even realize that we were in danger, not until we came back and landed did we find out. I think the director passed out, he almost had a heart attack. They had to call an ambulance.'

From Barbados to Baghdad

In January 1981 Ollie and Josephine boarded a plane to Barbados, her sixth-form tutor having been told she would be absent from school for several days owing to influenza. Walking on the beach one day, they were spotted and the news was beamed back to Fleet Street. All hell broke loose.

Because he went every year to Barbados, Ollie probably thought nothing of asking Josephine if she cared to accompany him this time; an offer, let's face it, most people would find tough to refuse. 'I looked winningly at my mother, and she let me go.' Then the press descended. 'They were hiding in coconut trees,' recalls Josephine. 'In the gardens where we were staying, in the restaurants where we went for dinner. We'd have great fun trying to avoid them. We'd get a small sail boat to come up to the beach and I'd hop on that and then go off somewhere and Oliver would get into the back of a truck and go off somewhere else and then we'd meet up at some prearranged rendezvous point.'

While all this was going on, back home Ollie was castigated as a 'dirty old man' in the tabloids. But never at any stage in his life did Ollie give a damn about what was said about him in the press. 'People slagging him off as an actor, no, didn't worry him,' says Simon. 'People praising him, whatever, it didn't matter, he didn't care. So his reaction to the press talking about this forty-two-year-old man and this sixteen-year-old girl: they don't understand, fuck 'em. He never did anything to cultivate publicity, and he wouldn't have worried about any adverse publicity either.' The problem was, the spotlight wasn't exclusively shining on him, but on Josephine and her family too, something they'd no experience of and were totally unprepared for. One columnist labelled Anne a poor mother for allowing her daughter to gallivant off halfway around the world with a famous reprobate.

The controversy continued to run for days, reaching a climax when the news hit media outlets that the pair were heading home. 'At the time I had a house close to Pinkhurst,' says David. 'And Fleet Street invaded the village. They had cars outside his main gate, a car down at my gate, they were in all the pubs. They knew they were coming back.' So David rang his brother to warn him. 'We're staked out, Ollie, they're all wanting to get a look at Josephine.' Oliver was at a loss as to what to do. 'Leave it with me,' reassured David, who hadn't the first clue as to how to solve the problem. After much thought he believed he had the answer. 'I'd seen movies where you change your name and come into a country incognito, so I went down to the local Dorking travel agent and I said to this lovely girl behind the desk, how do we do it? Can we get him in under another name? And yes, it was possible.' Obviously the press would have Heathrow and Gatwick covered, so it was arranged for Oliver and Josephine to fly from Barbados out to Mexico, from Mexico to Holland, and from Holland to a little grass airfield in Bournemouth. 'When they landed, Ollie emerged from this tiny plane. I was out on the balcony and when he saw me he stuck his thumb up and then down. I stuck my thumb up, which meant it was all clear, we'd done it.'

Once in the car, David gave them all the tabloid newspapers and the pair just sat and read them with their mouths agape. 'Oh my God.' He followed that with a quick update of what was happening. It wasn't good: the press were swarming all over Rudgwick. 'Listen,' said Ollie. 'Drive into the village and let me out, OK? That will distract them and you whizz up the road to Josephine's house.'

In theory it was a good plan, but the minute Ollie stepped out into the street all these people looking through the pub window suddenly poured out and barged right past him, desperate to get near a cowering Josephine in the car. 'I screamed up the road,' David says, 'with all these guys running after us, slammed on the brakes outside the house, knocked on the door, practically shoved Josephine in, and then drove back.' By the end of the day, once things had calmed down, everyone congregated round the bar of the pub, drinking. 'Come on, Ollie,' the reporters were going. 'How did you do it? How did you get back into the country without us knowing?' Ollie smiled and replied, 'Rubber dinghy. Land's End.'

The press intrusion was far from over, for this was a sensational story and there was no way the tabloids were going to let go of it. 'The press labelled it as this quiet little schoolgirl going out with Britain's biggest hell-raiser,' says Josephine. 'It was fantastic copy, absolute bliss for them all. We couldn't have written it for them better, could we?' It got to the stage where reporters were following her on the school bus. 'I remember my sister and I walking to the bus one morning and spotting this photographer, and I just burst into floods of tears and legged it back to the house, and my sister, who was thirteen at the time, screamed at this guy, "You fucking bastard!" It was pretty awful.'

Another time Josephine got off the bus after school and there was a pack of reporters waiting for her. Running across the road into the pub, she phoned the local policeman to see if there was anything he could do to get rid of them. Nothing, he said. If they were outside on the street it was public property. Josephine had to stay in the pub for hours until they went away.

This kind of thing went on all the time, so it wasn't much fun, especially since the press were also hounding the Burge family, trying to get an interview with Anne. 'I know my mother got so fed up once she actually tipped water out of a window on to them because they were at the front door constantly. Oliver did his best to help me but it was a kind of sink-or-swim situation. Get used to it or don't. I just learned to get used to it.'

Pretty soon the harassment Josephine was facing began to impinge upon her education. Back at school she suffered the usual taunts, and a favourite was to walk behind her singing the chorus of Typically Tropical's 1975 hit 'Whoa, I'm Going to Barbados'. Josephine suffered this in silence, although what she'd done had probably shocked the pants off her classmates too, since she was always considered the quiet shy one, the one least expected to get into any sort of trouble. But when reporters started hanging around outside the school gates, sometimes necessitating Josephine to be smuggled into the building, it couldn't go on. 'It was just quite horrendous. Difficult for everybody. So the headmaster came to see me at my godfather's house and arrived at the decision that it would be best if I left.'

The next decision to make was what to do about her education. Josephine declined to have a private tutor, opting instead to take up a correspondence course since that meant she could travel with Oliver to film sets and locations. 'I wanted to be with him and he wanted me with him when he was working, because it was better for him, more settling, I think. So I'd lug my suitcases around, which my brother William in later years had great fun telling me he packed with the heaviest academic books he could find. And I remember being in Baghdad in this hotel, looking out of the window, and there was Oliver and his mates sunbathing around the pool while I was busy working on my English literature. And I sat there thinking, why am I doing this? So I wrote a very nice letter to my tutor, thanked her very much, but I was quitting. That was my A levels done.'

Baghdad was the first of many locations Josephine remembers going to with Oliver. The film was *A Clash of Loyalties* and was very much a personal project of Iraqi president Saddam Hussein, detailing as it does the end of British colonial influence in the region circa 1920. Ollie stars as a British army major. Ironically there was a real war going on at the time between Iraq and Iran, and, Josephine recalls, you couldn't help but notice. Every night you'd hear the blare of air-raid sirens, or spot a missile go streaking across the cloudless sky. Many of the extras were Iraqi army personnel overjoyed to be away from the front for a few weeks, although filming had to be cancelled once when the soldiers were suddenly ordered to the front to stem an Iranian offensive.

The production itself was totally disorganized, so weeks went by without any filming at all and everyone just sat around getting bored in this beautiful great hotel. 'Luckily Oliver was there and kept us royally entertained,' remembers stuntman Vic Armstrong. 'God, he used to get us into so much trouble. One night we were all drinking in the bar, ending up seeing how many of us could stand on a coffee table. I think we got up to about twelve before it collapsed. It was just killing time.' Then, looking inside the restaurant, Ollie saw a Texas businessman whom he knew. He rushed upstairs to his room, to emerge fifteen minutes later wearing a western shirt and cowboy boots. Strolling into the restaurant John Wayne style, Ollie gave his buddy a Texas handshake, as he called it, which basically meant smashing his cowboy boot down on the table. Cutlery and glass went flying in the air. 'Ollie then stopped and looked at the guy and it wasn't his buddy at all,' recalls Armstrong. 'It was some Arab with his entourage, deeply offended that this Westerner had come stamping on his table and upset everything. The police were called and Ollie was arrested. He didn't go to jail, thank God.'

Ollie very quickly discovered the pool at the hotel and on his days off could be found from fairly early in the morning in a sun chair with a huge bowl of sangria beside him. 'How the hell he ever got sangria made the way he wanted there, I don't know,' remembers Stephan Chase, who had a small part in the film. 'And he'd be there for hours and hours and you can imagine he got very hot, sweaty, and pretty pissed.' This would result in games by the pool, which like everything else with Ollie when he was in this mood, went a bit further than anybody else wanted them to go. 'There was the possibility of being drowned or strangled under the water,' says Chase. 'And Ollie quite liked this, he loved the mischievousness of starting games that would then develop into something potentially really quite dodgy.'

Every night Ollie and Reg would show up in the bar in white suits and there would be the usual jostling and wrestling with each other. After a few days of this the rest of the cast did their best to avoid them whenever possible, even though Chase admits you couldn't help but like Ollie. 'But at arm's length. He was the kind of man who'd walk into a door when it was shut, it might give way and it might not. If it didn't, he'd have a good pummel to try and get through it.'

One night the whole cast had dinner in this vast dining hall in the hotel, along with a number of Arab guests. All of a sudden Ollie leaped to his feet, grabbed the tablecloth and yanked it off. Cups, plates and glasses hit the floor with a loud crash and several of the Arabs jumped to their feet brandishing guns, thinking the hotel was being invaded. Few of Ollie's fellow actors appreciated the prank. 'But Ollie always had that mischief behind the eyes,' admits Chase. 'When he was on form he was amusing, almost scallywaggish, impish. If he was drunk, then you didn't know where it was going to go. Otherwise he was quite sweet, which is a curious word to use about him, but he was. You can almost see him as a little boy with his socks down and a bandage on his knee and a black eye because someone had bashed him.'

To say that Josephine's life had changed out of all recognition since meeting Oliver would be a gross understatement. This was a girl who in just a year had gone from catching a bus to school, and earning spare bits of pocket money babysitting and selling horse manure, to rubbing shoulders with the greats of the film world. Just before they went to Baghdad, Josephine's first taste of Oliver's professional world was a trip to New York for the premiere of *Lion of the Desert*, an experience she's never forgotten. 'That was fantastic. I mean, Anthony Quinn dancing round a handkerchief at dinner. The film was financed by these wonderful people who had far too much money but were very generous and gave us lots of spending money. I remember Oliver saying, "This is ridiculous. What am I going to do with it?" and giving it back. He told them to give it to a charity.' Before the trip both had suits handmade for them at Dougie Hayward the tailor. Josephine's still got hers. 'So all this was happening and then flying out to New York. I remember nearly passing out at one point because I just found the whole thing quite overwhelming.' She was barely seventeen.

Her age certainly wasn't lost on Oliver, for not only did he feel duty bound to protect her from the feeding frenzy of the media but her emotional welfare was also of deep concern. He was fully aware of the fact that for her this whole affair might be nothing more substantial than a schoolgirl crush. These were largely immature and brand-new feelings Josephine was experiencing, emotions that at her tender age she may have had trouble deciphering. It's the reason why he insisted she take her time before committing herself to any serious relationship with him. Yet the subject of her moving into Pinkhurst had already been broached. 'He'd given me the key and said, whenever I felt comfortable and thought it was the right time, I could go and live with him. So I did. I moved in.'

It was a culture shock, no doubt about it, because living with Ollie called for quite a bit of fast growing up on her part.

'Josephine was suddenly thrown into an adult world,' says David. 'She did not experience those teenage things that other girls do, clubbing, dating. She never did any of that, she went from childhood into a drinking, adult life of excess.' And very quickly it began to overwhelm her. 'I was still at school and trying to do some homework and Oliver and one of his friends, Mad Michael, were being utterly annoying, and I thought, what am I doing? So I got on to my moped, with my satchel, and left and went home. It was over half-term and I had a long, hard think about it and realized, no, I miss him, desperately. I wasn't relieved to have got out of it. I thought, I actually really, really do miss him. So I went back and never left again.'

Considering the scandal their love affair caused, Josephine was integrated and accepted surprisingly quickly into Oliver's family and inner circle. Once everyone had got over the initial shock, of course. Simon has still never forgotten the moment Ollie phoned him, not long after he'd first met Josephine, announcing his intention to one day marry her. 'I could not believe it. It was insanity, it seemed to me. Looking back on it, I can absolutely understand it. Yes, it could have been a disaster, but actually it was just what was wanted. But at the time it was just, what on earth are you doing?' And when David and Muriel were first introduced to Josephine they were genuinely shocked, not least because she was only six months younger than their youngest daughter.

That she provoked such reactions from people is something that Josephine can completely understand. It must have been especially difficult for Mark, as here was his father dating a girl who was four years younger than he was, and Josephine admits that it took a little bit longer for them to gel, but eventually a firm friendship developed. 'I've always got on with Josephine,' says Mark. 'I felt that it was brave of her in many ways to get involved with him, because she could have been totally smothered. But then I suppose there was part of him that wanted his own form of normality, for someone to be there. In some ways he had toned himself down a little bit, to become a little bit more acceptable. But it was a challenging time for her. But she stood up to it very well and was a strong enough character to cope with everything.'

As for Sarah, she was relatively unfazed when the news broke. 'I remember everyone else being more affected by it than me. I was eleven. It was like, yeah, OK. I didn't really question it. I remember at school being called into my headmistress's office and her saying, "Listen, Sarah, we need to talk about this, this must be an issue." And I'm going, "It's not an issue. It really isn't." I think I was actually incredibly laid-back in that respect. I'd been used to this madness.'

Ollie's friends were wonderful too, although Johnny Placett used to enjoy endlessly playing Sam Cooke's 'Only Sixteen' on the pub's jukebox until Ollie refused to come in any more and the offending disc was removed. And they were extremely protective of Josephine. 'Bill and Jenny were incredible. There was never a nasty word said to me, no insinuation that I may have been with Oliver for the wrong reasons.' It was said by some, observers looking in from the outside, that Josephine was only with Ollie because he was a rich film star. This couldn't have been further from the truth. Before they went off to Baghdad Ollie took her to Harrods, thrust a wad of cash in her hands, and told her to get whatever she wanted. Josephine came back with a pair of white boots and a skirt. 'Oliver just couldn't believe it, so I was dragged around Harrods by the arm with him going, we'll take that, that and that, and that and that. So the money thing was never an issue for me.'

There was also the suggestion that Oliver chose a young partner so that she would be more compliant and he could carry on misbehaving and indulging his child-like nature. Josephine hopes that it wasn't true, that he was more intelligent than that. Besides, she was no giddy teenager but mature beyond her age.

Because her father died when she was young and her mother spent time in hospital, she'd coped with hardship and helped to manage the family. She was also very countrified and proper. In difficult situations it was very often Josephine who came across as much more of an adult than Ollie.

She was also shy and not particularly talkative, especially in the early years when she was still getting used to her new life and was sometimes overwhelmed by things. Ollie liked to tell the story of when he was in New York for the *Lion of the Desert* premiere and sought advice from the film's Arab director, Moustapha Akkad. 'I'm going crazy, Moustapha. I've got this young girl and she's said absolutely nothing, and it's just driving me potty. I don't know what to do.'

Akkad looked genuinely perplexed. 'Are you mad, Oliver? That sounds like the perfect woman.'

The trials and tribulations Josephine faced in the early months of her liaison with Ollie were to serve her well for the rest of the time she spent with him. But, looking back at that period over thirty years later, she can't quite believe that as a seventeen-year-old she could have behaved in the way she did. She's also equally certain that if her father had still been alive he never would have allowed it.

'Quick poke in the bush, boy?'

As was the pattern for the rest of their lives together, Oliver flew out to his next movie location with Josephine by his side. The destination was Toronto and the film was a hopeless mess called *Spasms*, directed by William Fruet, about a demonic serpent captured from a remote island that goes on the rampage. Oliver, very much on autopilot here, plays a millionaire explorer with some kind of telekinetic connection with the beast. Cast as his daughter was newcomer Kerrie Keane, who, to prepare for her role, read Oliver's then recently published autobiography to get a sense of who he was. 'I learned enough from that book to know that I could never flinch with this man.'

On their first day of shooting, Kerrie was called to the set for her first scene with Oliver, not having met him before. 'There he stood as still as a monument, charismatic and frightening. I was introduced, and he said nothing. He simply stared at me, those eyes boring into mine. I knew that this was some kind of test, so I stared back and didn't blink. Everyone and everything around us stopped in silence. After what felt like for ever, he finally grinned and mumbled something like, you're all right, girl. From then on he seemed to have a respect for me and we worked well together.'

For Kerrie, Ollie was no trouble at all and she remembers his generosity in often inviting her to share lunch with him and

Josephine, though for some reason he took against the way she sipped her wine. 'One day he reached over and tipped the stem of my glass. I managed not to choke as I gulped the wine, at least the wine that didn't spill all over me. "That's the way to drink," he spat. Yes, there was always that potential for violence in him. I guess that's what made him so exciting and exasperating, never knowing what to expect.' Kerrie also observed Ollie and Josephine's fledgling relationship at close quarters. 'He treated her like a doll, always adjusting her hair or clothing.'

There were plenty of night shoots on the film, which had a tendency to drag through inefficiency and delays. One damp, cold night there was a huge lighting set-up. Oliver kept warm drinking Courvoisier, which Kerrie remembers he guzzled like soda pop right out of the bottle. As the night wore on, and the crew were no nearer fixing up the shot, Ollie went for a wander into the neighbouring woods. The crew could hear him in the distance howling like a wolf.

After several hours the director was happy to commence with the scene, only Oliver was still AWOL. A young assistant was sent into the woods to find him. Everyone waited as the clock kept ticking. 'Suddenly, out of the woods came the assistant, his face ashen,' recalls Kerrie. 'He could hardly speak, but he recounted how he had been tracking the wolf sounds when out of a tree dropped Oliver, stark naked, and in a most demonic manner he whispered, "Quick poke in the bush, boy?" I'll never forget the look in that assistant's eyes.'

Oliver did finally show up, back in his costume, and the scene was completed just before dawn. 'I don't think Oliver wanted us to lose the shot that night,' says Kerrie. 'But he needed to protest the lack of professionalism.'

With antics like that, is it any wonder that when Peter Fonda heard Ollie was in the film he accepted the job immediately? 'There was no way I was going to pass up the chance of working with this legendary actor.' Fonda himself liked his booze, and the pair of them were often spotted in Toronto's numerous bars. One evening consisted of drinking Cuba Libres, and when Fonda awoke the next morning, fully clothed on his hotel bed, the several hundred dollars he'd taken with him to pay for his drinks was still in his jacket pocket. Ollie had paid for the whole party.

The drinking, though, did get out of hand. Quinn Donoghue did some publicity for *Spasms*, meeting up with Oliver after a gap of several years, and noticed a significant change in him. 'I went out to interview Ollie and Fonda and I found them both pretty incapacitated. Ollie was drunk and Peter was stoned and they were both enjoying one another's company without any communication whatsoever. This was like at two o'clock in the afternoon, and this was something that surprised me with Ollie because during the *Musketeer* period he didn't drink during the day, maybe a little wine at lunch. It was a night-time problem back then. But on this picture with Fonda they were both heavily indulging and this was the middle of the day.'

While in Toronto, Ollie and Josephine bumped into Yvonne Romain, who automatically assumed this pretty young girl was Oliver's daughter. Yvonne's husband Leslie Bricusse had a musical playing in the city and they invited Ollie and Josephine to dinner. 'I hadn't seen him for years,' says Yvonne. 'And we had a lovely meal. He was so charming, reminiscing about our Hammer films and that he'd wished we'd done more together. And then he ordered a bottle of Armagnac and drank it in twenty minutes and turned into something completely different. It was Jekyll and Hyde. And we thought, what a shame.' It was the last time Yvonne ever saw Ollie. 'I think I respected him more than anyone else I worked with. He was so knowledgeable and had a great instinct as an actor. I think of him now with huge affection. He was so helpful to me as a young actress and we laughed so much together.'

From Toronto Oliver and Josephine flew a short distance to

the US mountain resort of Stowe in Vermont for a short break. In the early morning hours police officer Eben Merrill was at the Stowe Police Department office with Stowe Patrolman Edwin Webster, when they received a call about a disturbance at Ye Old English Inne on Mountain Road. When the two officers arrived they were told by the pub's owner that Oliver Reed was inside causing a disturbance. 'We were asked at that time not to intervene,' Merrill recalls, 'as the owner, his staff, and Mr Reed's friends were trying to get him to leave. The owner and some of his staff had been physically assaulted by Mr Reed, and each time the owner came outside to see us more of his clothing was torn. On his last trip to see us, the owner had had enough and wanted to file charges against Mr Reed.'

By this time Ollie had made his way outside to the parking lot. It was then that he caught sight of the policemen and cried, 'Come on, let's have a go,' while trying to lift up a car by grabbing hold of its fender. 'He then walked over and shook hands with Officer Webster and myself,' continues Merrill, 'and then promptly fell over backwards on to the ground. At this point, Officer Webster and myself placed Mr Reed into handcuffs. Since Mr Reed did not like the idea of being arrested, he was helped to the police car by Officer Webster, myself and State Police Sergeant Loren Croteau, who had just arrived on the scene to lend a hand. The Dispatch Center had been giving area officers up-to-the-minute accounts of Reed tearing apart the pub, and Sergeant Croteau was the first to arrive to assist. Mr Reed was then taken to the Lamoille County Sheriff's Department where he told the alcohol worker to "Bloody well piss off". I returned to the pub to document what had been destroyed and to take statements from those who were assaulted. After his release, Reed sent flowers to the Sheriff's Department Secretary and also made a donation to the Stowe Fire Department.'

Still on the lookout for fun, Ollie decided to see out 1981 in

Los Angeles with Josephine. While she was out shopping one day he hit some bars and in one of them met John Miller, an ex-SAS man who was part of the team who earlier that year snatched Great Train Robber Ronnie Biggs from his bolt hole in Rio and whisked him away to Barbados, in the hope of extraditing him to the UK. Anyway, the two got pally and went from bar to bar and a boozed-up Ollie suddenly decided that he wanted to get a tattoo done. Not on his forearm, or on his knuckles, not even on his backside. No, Ollie wanted a tattoo on his cock.

The pair of them went to the city's Latino quarter but every tattooist they approached was unwilling to perform the task. A cab driver came to the rescue, saying he knew just the place. 'Then take me there, my good fellow,' said Ollie. It was a bit of a slum area and the shop was run by a Chinese man, but even he baulked at Ollie's request. 'I'll do it.' The voice came from the back; it was the man's wife. 'Make bigger, please.'

Two hours later it was finished: an eagle's claws emblazoned on his manhood. He returned to his hotel room with it wrapped in bloodied cotton wool. Josephine remembers being vaguely shocked. 'That possibly wasn't my most favourite thing that he ever did.'

Ollie's tattoo was to become infamous, and indeed world famous. He already had a very small tattoo on his shoulder in the shape of an eagle's head. 'So his party trick in years to come,' says David, 'when the conversation got to him and he couldn't cope, he'd say, "Do you want to see my tattoo?" and show them the eagle's head. Then he'd say, "Do you want to see where it's perched?" And he'd undo his flies and bring out the old sausage.'

Even Carol Lynley got to hear about it, from, of all people, David Niven Junior. 'Have you seen Ol's tattoo?' he said. Of course, Carol hadn't. Niven Junior had run into Ollie and Josephine at Madrid airport and Ollie said, 'Oh, David, I've got to show you my new tattoo,' and dropped his trousers and underpants and said, 'Look, look, David.' And Niven Junior found himself on his knees in a crowded airport lounge staring at Oliver Reed's dick!

In quick succession Ollie made a couple of throwaway American movies. Backed by big studios, the first by Universal and the second by 20th Century Fox, they had a lot of hope riding on them, but both were critically lampooned and tanked at the box office. *The Sting 2* was a belated and lacklustre sequel to the 1973 classic but sadly minus Newman and Redford, their places taken by the less than stellar Jackie Gleason and singer-songwriter turned actor Mac Davis. Strangely, Ollie played Doyle Lonnegan, the role he had turned down in the original movie.

You'd have thought he was on safer ground with *Two of a Kind*, the film that reunited John Travolta with Olivia Newton John, five years after the smash hit *Grease*. In this comedy fantasy Ollie has great fun playing the devil as a poncy Englishman with a walrus moustache, and he also developed a major crush on Olivia Newton John. 'She sent him a Christmas card which he kept for ages,' reveals Josephine. But the film is dreadful rubbish and proved the last he'd make for any of the main Hollywood studios until *Gladiator* over fifteen years later. The problem was, Oliver never came to terms with working in America, never quite felt at home there. 'And he didn't like his American agents, ICM,' confirms David. 'Because they were too po-faced and correct. Ollie was a true Brit.'

So it was back home to the relative tranquillity of Pinkhurst, where he indulged in a sport he'd first taken up during his last years at Broome Hall: lawn-mower racing. This annual event took place in the nearby village of Wisborough Green in West Sussex. 'The first year we entered a standard seated lawn mower from the garden,' says Mark, 'which was, chug-chug-chug-chug, and we were just overtaken by sixty lawn mowers going at great speed.' The following year Ollie was determined to return better equipped and to this end roped in a team of racing car mechanics from a local garage to build a special racing mower made out of aluminium. The sport became something of an obsession that he pursued for years, and at considerable expense, getting these souped-up mowers up to speed, building bigger and better ones. Ollie didn't race them himself, because of his bulk, but instead roped in friends and work pals, including Mark and Bill and Jenny's son Ian. 'Ollie was always pit boss,' says Mark, 'standing in the pit lane with a bottle of beer with his mates, enjoying it, drawing in the atmosphere of it all. It was very serious and very intense for what it was, and in its way very British, the eccentricity of it.' There was even a twelve-hour race, a sort of poor man's Le Mans, in which Ollie entered two machines with three riders for each. The event started on the Saturday night and went through to the Sunday morning, and motor-racing celebrities like Stirling Moss would turn up.

So seriously did Ollie take the sport that he asked David to make a documentary film of one of the twelve-hour races using a video camera. Scenes included footage of the race and Oliver interviewed in the pit lane. The completed film was shown to anyone and everyone, whether they wanted to see it or not. 'That lawn-mower video was one of Ollie's most revered possessions,' says David.

One afternoon producer Harry Alan Towers and director Gerry O'Hara paid Ollie a visit at Pinkhurst. They wanted him to play a small role in their adaptation of John Cleland's eighteenth-century erotic novel *Fanny Hill*. Ollie's involvement in the project was crucial to getting sales interest and a distribution deal. Even though all of his last few films had flopped, Oliver Reed was still a recognizable name. 'We had a drink with Ollie and Josephine, who was a very nice girl,' remembers O'Hara. 'Then Ollie said to me, "Come on, I'll take you round the grounds." So he took me for a walk, we chatted, he was very friendly, very amusing. We went upstairs, he showed me all the bedrooms and everything. We went into the master bedroom and he opened the mullion window and pissed on the flowerbeds outside. I think that was a little demonstration to me about what a wag he was. I didn't comment, we just kept on talking as if he was blowing his nose.'

Harry Alan Towers was an old friend of Ollie's from when they made *And Then There Were None* together, which had also starred Towers's wife, Maria Rohm. Maria remembers being introduced to Josephine for the first time on the set of *Fanny Hill*. 'We both felt that she had "the right stuff" to stay with Ollie and be as much of an anchor as possible. She was very young, yet she seemed to be the mature one.'

Ollie wasn't required on the film very long, in a role that amounted to little more than a cameo. 'But I must say he turned in a very neat performance,' says O'Hara. 'And the one thing I knew about Ollie was, you didn't direct him, that would have been fatal. If you said, wait a minute, Ollie, could you stop doing that silly thing with your eye?, he would have gone mad. You had to go, OK, so he's got a funny eye, very good, Ollie, would you mind doing it just once more, it's so funny?'

Ollie did seem to have a love-hate relationship with many of his directors, commenting once, 'If someone starts dictating to me, I just switch off and think about how much they're paying me. I just phone it in.' Clearly there were directors whom he admired and respected, but there were others who he thought didn't know perhaps as much as he did, and that's when the problems could start and he'd go into misbehave mode. 'If he thought the director was a tosser he'd probably say it,' says Mark.

As a director, John Hough always found Oliver perfectly compliant. If he wanted him to do fifty takes, he'd do it, and he'd do as many or as few as Hough wanted. 'He was great if you had his respect. I'm sure he'd trample all over you if he didn't have respect for the director.' And it was these directors who got into trouble with him or perhaps weren't strong enough to stand up to his bullish nature. 'Some directors never got out of Ollie what I knew was there,' recalls David. 'And a lot of the blame is Ollie's. He was wayward, power corrupts, he began to believe in his own image.' That's why Winner and Russell were so important and why invariably Oliver performed his best for them. 'It wasn't that they were strong,' says David. 'But they knew how to cope with him. Most other directors didn't.'

The Coke-Can Wedding Ring

In spite of their age difference Oliver and Josephine behaved like any normal couple. They dined out quite often, even went to the theatre a couple of times, and were regular moviegoers, despite the fact that Oliver was a nightmare to go to the cinema with. He'd sit there saying, 'The lighting in this film is hopeless.' He'd complain he could see a shadow or the lighting was too harsh, or it was too this, or too that. 'We'd walk out of so many films,' says Josephine. 'He did have his favourites at home that we'd watch again and again on video. He loved Anthony Hopkins. He enjoyed watching his work, he was a big fan. And *The Duellists* he absolutely adored.' Ridley Scott's debut feature as a director was a film Ollie had been obsessed with for years, as Sarah can testify. 'We were all bored to tears by *The Duellists*. That was one of his favourite films. There was a period of about four years where I knew probably every line in that film. He'd say, "Come on, girlie, come and watch this," and it would be something like four o'clock in the morning.'

Mostly, though, Ollie and Josephine were homebodies. A perfect evening for Ollie was snuggling up with Josephine on the sofa watching television or a video after a quiet dinner, which they always ate at six o'clock. Or he might just relax and listen to the radio. 'He loved Radio 4,' says Josephine. 'He was passionate about Radio 4.' For much of his adult life Oliver had terrible trouble sleeping and needed something in the room making a noise, such as the radio, and sometimes very loudly. Jacquie remembers that, rather than walk round and wake him, she would often resort to crawling under the bed to turn down the volume. With Josephine his sleeping disorder persisted. The cause was diagnosed as tinnitus, or ringing in the ear, which Oliver claimed was due to being too close to loud sound-effect bangs on film sets. The radio would be tuned to Radio 4 all night and when they were abroad it was the World Service. If they were filming in a country where the World Service was not available they'd put the television on and cover the screen with a towel. Much later Oliver started taking audiobooks with him to play through the night.

As for television, it was mainly documentaries and sport he watched, primarily rugby, cricket and horse-racing. He loved his gardening programmes, of course. 'Also *One Man and His Dog*,' remembers Josephine. 'He was really into that show. And *Come Dancing*. We used to watch that.' One of the most popular programmes on television in the mid-eighties was *In at the Deep End*. It was a simple format: each week two presenters, Chris Searle and Paul Heiney, undertook various professional jobs as complete beginners, maybe ballroom dancing or becoming a chef at a top London brasserie. The show's producer had come up with a brilliant idea for Heiney's next challenge, playing a movie baddie. 'Our producer was very good at finding people to act as your mentor and adviser,' recalls Heiney. 'And because Ollie was the most famous bad man on the screen at that time they persuaded him to give me a lesson in how to play a screen baddie.' It was an experience Heiney has never forgotten.

Not just Heiney but the whole TV crew were nervous about meeting Oliver. When they arrived at the allotted time outside Pinkhurst and knocked on the front door, there was an ominously long silence. Perhaps he'd forgotten. They knocked again. This time the door opened very, very slowly and an eye appeared, and then the door closed again. It then reopened and Ollie revealed himself. 'He was wearing a heavy army overcoat,' says Heiney. 'Like the ones the Russian army wear, and he said there was nothing underneath. I had no reason to disbelieve him. He was wearing a pair of wire-rimmed spectacles; one of the lenses was cracked. He had a sort of look of death about him, although I'm sure that was put on, and he had in his fist a pint mug with this clear, colourless liquid in it which he said was vodka and tonic, and I've got no reason to doubt that, either. Clearly he'd decided from the outset that he was going to play the bad man every inch of the way. Come in, sit down, shut up, don't sit there, all that kind of stuff, and he was clearly enjoying it. And I wasn't enjoying it.'

The advice Ollie gives in this interview is like a masterclass in how to play a villain on film. His big thing was not to blink: bad men do not blink. 'You don't see a cobra blink, do you?' he says. The next thing was the voice. Villains don't shout, they don't need to. Dangerous men have a great silence and stillness about them. 'Then when he told me to do my villainous foreign accent he took the piss out of me mercilessly.' Tension seemed to be building, until, exasperated at Heiney's feeble line readings, Ollie put down the script, got up and bodily threw the presenter out of the house. 'Piss off!' he yelled as Heiney was unceremoniously deposited on the driveway and the door slammed in his face. 'Now, he clearly planned on doing that. And I remember at the time being really quite scared. Then once the interview was all over he was a completely different man. He was a really nice guy. It was, come on in, have a drink, how are you?'

The team stayed on for maybe an hour or two, during which time Heiney was taken to a room at the back of the house by either a cleaner or the housekeeper. 'This is the games room,' he was told. 'Do you know what that means?' Heiney didn't have the first idea. 'It all happens here,' came the reply. It was now that the presenter noticed a bar in the corner, and was told, 'What happens is that Ollie gets all his mates in here and they drink and they drink and they drink and they drink, and then they smash up all the furniture. Then we come in the next morning and clear it all out and buy some more furniture and then a week later it happens all over again.' That was the games room.

Looking back, the most disturbing aspect of the whole day for Heiney was the sight of Josephine, who sat on the periphery the whole time, observing but not participating in any way in what was going on. 'She looked like a rather nervous creature, like a cat afraid that the dog might go for it. She just sat there all the time at the very back of the room and never moved and never said anything, just sat there completely silently and watched everything. It looked a very strange set-up.'

As a rule Ollie disliked doing publicity. He understood his responsibilities when it came to publicizing a new movie, but premieres and large press junkets left him cold. Some were obviously more bearable than others. Take the occasion in the summer of 1985 when he was asked to take part in a three-day press jamboree on the cruise ship the *Achille Lauro*, a vessel that just a few months later made headlines around the world when she was hijacked by members of the Palestine Liberation Front. The terrorists had obviously waited until Ollie was safely no longer aboard. Scores of journalists and film critics had been invited to watch and then interview members of the cast of a new, Italian-made epic TV mini-series on the life of Christopher Columbus. Gabriel Byrne starred as the famous explorer, while Ollie played Martin Pinzon, who sailed with Columbus on his first voyage to the new world as captain of one of his ships.

Adequately told, the drama featured a top-notch supporting cast of Max Von Sydow, Faye Dunaway and Eli Wallach. In a small role was Murray Melvin, who hadn't seen Ollie since his antics in Budapest on *The Prince and the Pauper*. Everyone was flown to Naples, where the *Achille Lauro* was docked.

Murray remembers Ollie turning up at nine a.m., already on the vodkas. Once aboard they set sail, with the ship merely steaming round in a very large circle for the entire three days. The press were on board all the time and so the actors had breakfast, lunch and dinner at the same table, talking with different media people. And the drink flowed. Like a limpet mine, Ollie attached himself to Murray. 'I used to have to pour my gin and tonics into a plant pot because there was no way I could keep up. Ollie was a big lad, so he absorbed more. I was a matchstick. So after the evening meal it was, "Right, come on, Murray, to the bar." I'd say, "Oh, Ollie, no. Listen, I need an early night." "Don't be ridiculous, come to the bar." So I was in the bar and I'd pour my drinks away when he wasn't looking, but then he'd see my empty glass and go, "Another gin and tonic for Murray." There wasn't a way out. So then I used to try and sip it slowly and of course Ollie would roar, "Drink the bloody thing, Murray!" Two nights I was with him.'

One particular night a group of Italians had gathered round a piano to sing songs, and Murray thought it all rather enchanting. 'Oh, Ollie, let's go over and join them.'

'Italians – don't want to go anywhere near them.'

'Ollie, listen, they're just having a nice time.'

As the clock struck one a.m., Ollie downed another vodka and bang, he was past the point of no return, his face screwed up in pain and confusion. 'Fucking Italians, look at 'em.' He started to make his move.

'Ollie, no, Ollie, you really mustn't, Ollie, no, you cannot,' screeched Murray.

'Why not? They need a jolly good punch.'

'No, Ollie, please don't.' All the time Murray was straining to hold him back.

'Why?' asked Ollie.

'Because you're Brown Owl,' said Murray.

'What do you mean, I'm Brown Owl?'

'You're the head of the English contingent, you're Brown Owl.' Oliver started to laugh and ordered another vodka. 'And that's how I did it,' says Murray proudly. 'All the time I kept saying, "Ollie, you cannot, you're here representing ENGLAND. You're representing the Queen." And of course he was very patriotic, very "raising the flag". And this went on till something like half past two every night, and I'm starting to flag, and you had to be up next morning for interviews, but I had to wait for him to go, "I can't stand this any more, I'm off to bed." And I'd go, "All right, Ollie, I'll see you at breakfast, love. Have a good sleep." I'd get back to my cabin and think, I've got another night of this. But I did it, because it would have caused a diplomatic incident, a scandal beyond belief.'

As for Josephine, who was there for the entire trip, Murray found her no help whatsoever. 'She would sit quietly while he was tipping tables in restaurants. She just sat quietly until he said, "Come on, let's go." It was quite extraordinary, she never said, "Ollie, darling, don't," as most women would have done, but not Josephine, not a word. None of us understood it. I always equated it to, sort of, like the gangster's moll, who just sat there quietly, because sometimes you did think, Josephine, come on, say something.'

To be fair, Josephine was by nature a fairly tolerant, quiet person, and when it just got too rowdy, or Ollie's drinking friends came and things got out of hand, she'd simply take herself out of the situation and go somewhere else. 'I didn't shout, pout, stamp, or berate him. What was the point? This was a man who had been doing this all his life. Who was I to suddenly say, don't? And he did say, right from the outset, that's the way he was. I always said I never wanted to change him. You fall in love with somebody. What's then the point of changing that, because then you end up with someone else.

So I would just sit quietly in the corner if it was just generally exploding.' Ollie also reassured her that if he said something untoward he generally didn't mean it, and if he behaved badly he wanted her to know that wasn't really his true personality and that things generally looked better in the morning, which invariably they did. It was also one of the reasons why he'd put on hold any thoughts of marrying Josephine until they'd been together for five years, 'Because by then I think you'll know me well enough.' Those five years were now up.

Not long after they first met, Oliver put a ring pull from a Coke can on Josephine's finger. It was meant as a joke but she wore it for quite some time, and kept it as a memento for years afterwards. When the couple were having dinner with David and Muriel at Pinkhurst one evening, Muriel suddenly blurted out that really it was about time the two of them tied the knot. Oliver looked over at Josephine and she looked at him. 'Yeah, shall we?' he said. 'All right,' replied Josephine. 'We'll get married this year then.' She was twenty-one.

The wedding took place on Saturday, 7 September 1985 at the register office in Epsom. The couple tried to keep it quiet, with only family members and close friends aware that anything was happening. It was poor Peter, Ollie's dad, who let the cat out of the bag by mistake. Phoned up by a reporter asking if the ceremony was at such and such a venue, he replied, 'Oh no, it's at nine o'clock in Epsom. Oops!' Realizing what he'd done, Peter phoned Ollie to apologize. 'So the press were there,' says Josephine. 'I remember having to drag my brother through the melee to get in.'

They quickly forgave Peter, and Josephine's memories of him are of a 'lovely, sweet, old-fashioned gentleman'. She also met Oliver's mother for the first time at that wedding, one of only two meetings she ever had with her. Just before the ceremony was about to begin, Marcia came over to where Josephine was standing and said, 'So, you're the one marrying Oliver.'

The event passed off without a hitch, much to the disappointment of the press no doubt. As did Oliver's stag party, held at home in a marquee and catered by the local pub. 'I was at the other end of the house watching a film,' Josephine remembers. 'When I went upstairs to bed he was already there, having quietly snuck off and left the others to "party on".' Ollie was appearing at the time in a film called *Captive*, a hostage drama, and was due back on location at London's Albert Docks on the Monday. 'So he was well behaved,' says Josephine. 'He didn't go crazy over the wedding period and we had a lovely day. It was fantastic.' She always loved to lay claim to the fact that she must be one of the only people ever to spend her honeymoon at the Albert Docks.

Oliver's previous important relationships, with Kate and then Jacquie, had produced children, and now he was married he felt a strong desire to begin raising a family with Josephine. 'I remember us arguing about where they'd go to school before we'd even had any,' says Josephine. 'Which we then actually burst out laughing about.' Oliver was full of hope and expectation about having children, talking about it with almost everyone. 'He'd announce it in supermarkets,' says David. 'He'd be stroking babies' heads and saying, "Well, of course we're going to have a baby. We're going to call it Barty." Of course, that was never to happen.'

Perhaps Oliver felt duty bound to give Josephine a child because of her young age, and when it became obvious they couldn't have one (the problem lay with Oliver, not Josephine), the guilt kicked in and it was he who kept insisting they have tests, refused by Josephine, and later that they should think about adoption, again an idea she rejected. 'I had it in the back of my mind that, for us to work and to carry on, I don't think necessarily a child was going to be a good thing. He might have been briefly troubled by this, but then it passed and we were fine. But he loved babies. He spent hours on aeroplanes

411

entertaining babies, especially when he had a big moustache and these little kids would peer back at him and he'd be wiggling his moustache and pulling funny expressions.'

Once when Paul and Nora Friday were visiting Pinkhurst, Oliver turned to their daughter Louise, who was three or four at the time, and said, 'Have you seen the winter dragon?' Louise looked puzzled. 'Dragon?' she replied. 'Yes,' went Ollie. 'A winter dragon. You've not seen the winter dragon?' Louise shook her head. 'Come on then,' said Ollie, grabbing her hand as they all trudged into the woods, 'I'll show you the winter dragon.' Secretly he had got Bill Dobson to hide behind a tree with a large pile of leaves doused in petrol. 'It's over there!' Ollie shrieked. With that, Bill lit a match and, whoosh, a huge flame shot out. Louise looked wide-eyed at her father and mouthed, 'No way,' then turned round, and ran back to the house. 'And Louise believed in dragons till she was fourteen,' says Paul. 'Because she'd seen one! That's the sort of imagination Oliver had.'

Ollie also adored his two nieces, and loved playing with them whenever he visited David and Muriel, which sometimes could be late at night, when he was in a dishevelled state. 'When our girls were very little he used to go up and terrify them and they'd wet their beds for the next three nights,' claims Muriel. But then he'd leave money on the stairs for them to collect in the morning. 'Despite those experiences they all adored him,' says David. 'Oliver loved children. He just didn't know how to cope with them.'

Castaway

Of all the roles he would play in his career, many people have commented upon the fact that Gerald Kingsland in *Castaway* was perhaps the closest to the real Oliver Reed. 'He is a bit of an eccentric and so am I,' revealed Ollie. 'He will do things – not always completely sane – on an impulse and so will I.' The whole ideology of Kingsland's approach to life, going off to a desert island with a very pretty girl who's going to take her clothes off, to live on coconuts and fish, was certainly something Ollie found appealing. And it's no surprise to learn that he was the first and really the only candidate to play Kingsland. The script, too, was almost certainly the best Oliver had read for a very long time. Put simply, *Castaway* was an oasis in the middle of a degenerating run of poor films and poor choices.

Directed by Nicolas Roeg, who'd made such acclaimed films as *Performance* and *Don't Look Now*, *Castaway* was based on true events. Kingsland was a journalist who advertised for a woman to spend a year with him on a deserted tropical island. Lucy Irvine, almost twenty years Kingsland's junior, answered the ad and what should have been an idyll turned into a nightmare.

Ollie took to the role of Gerald wholeheartedly and wore his skin like his own. 'It wasn't often that he'd become a character from one of his films,' reveals Josephine. 'But he was unfortunately a bit of a Gerald for quite a while.' Filming began in London and Oliver had his beard and hair dyed an unflattering ginger, which Josephine found ghastly. The process took place in a make-up van parked in Hanover Square just before his first scene and, according to associate producer Selwyn Roberts, Ollie insisted they also dye his pubic hair. 'The next second Oliver is running around this incredibly exclusive square stark naked, apart from a plastic bag over his cock, shouting, "Look at that!"'

The film's main location was Praslin, the second largest of the Seychelles Islands, and Selwyn Roberts had gone on ahead of the cast and crew to sort out the logistics. He also went to pick up Oliver when he arrived at Seychelles International airport. 'The plane arrived, the door opened, and guess who fell down the stairs first. Yep, Oliver. And of course he also played the game of coming in on the baggage conveyor belt, he did that one as well, and everyone was looking at him and going, "Look, it's Oliver Reed", which he liked.'

Cast as Lucy Irvine was newcomer Amanda Donohoe, who faced not only the daunting task of playing a demanding role in her first film, but having to cope with an often volatile and unpredictable co-star. 'I don't think that anybody understood the state that Oliver was in when he came to do *Castaway*,' she later said. 'Although everybody understood that he drank, nobody knew quite how much. There was this dichotomy. There was this incredibly sweet, charming, sensitive man . . . and the next minute he'd be calling you a bitch.' Strained would be the best way to describe their relationship. As in the past with the likes of Glenda, Redgrave and Rigg, Ollie couldn't get to grips with a strong-willed and independent actress who refused to take any shit from him. Mark was to say, diplomatically, that his father and Amanda 'were not each other's favourite cups of tea'. In playful mood, Oliver summed her up as 'A very pretty girl. Great breasts. But it was definitely a look-don't-touch situation. There was absolutely no way that I would have dared

414

put my mighty mallet anywhere near her bush of content and pumped away. Completely out of the question.'

Nor did the hot and humid conditions help. An amazing experience, to be sure, but *Castaway* was a tough film to make. Ollie was often up early to put on make-up for the shots where his body was covered in scabs, which at the end of the day Josephine spent hours taking off as Ollie fell asleep from sheer exhaustion. At least there was a familiar face among the cast in Georgina Hale, who when she arrived at the island's hotel found a wonderful note welcoming her from Oliver. 'He'd also drawn a duck on it because an old boyfriend of mine used to call me Ducky. I thought that was so sweet of him. I've still got it.'

Georgina had never met Josephine before and came away with the impression that, despite her being very quiet, always reading and keeping herself to herself, it was obvious that she was devoted to Oliver. 'I just think they adored one another. Nobody thought that it would last but it did. And I think it's because even though she was young she was just incredibly mature for her age, and she loved him and he loved her.' As for Ollie, Georgina was more than a little concerned because the drinking had noticeably increased since the last time they'd met. 'He was drunk most of the time on *Castaway*, to my knowledge. But still highly professional.'

It was the sheer volume of Oliver's drinking that drew concern from many on the crew and his unruly behaviour that alienated others. The director of photography, Harvey Harrison, disliked Ollie so intensely that he had it virtually written into his contract that in no way was he ever obliged to socialize with him. And producer Rick McCallum's assistant on the film came to loathe Oliver because of his habit of dropping his trousers in front of her to reveal the old mighty mallet. 'One day she was in the hotel having something to eat,' reveals Selwyn Roberts, 'when Oliver put his cock on her shoulder and without even flinching she stabbed it with her fork. I tell you, he never did it again.'

Ollie seemed to be drinking every day. His routine was to take with him a case of SeyBrew, the local lager, which he would steadily drink through the morning and the afternoon. That was twenty-four bottles and it was quite strong stuff. 'I used to see him sometimes going to the set and he would be as drunk as a skunk,' says Roberts. 'He would then be put into make-up and then when he walked on to the floor he was absolutely bang sober.' Often Amanda Donohoe found it difficult playing scenes opposite Oliver because even though he was delivering the goods there was still a reek of alcohol. She remembers staring at him at times like this and thinking to herself, what could you be if you didn't have this terrible disease? At one point in production Ollie caught a fever from scraping against coral, as did many others. It was easily treated with antibiotics but the doctor who saw him told the producers, 'Oliver's got more alcohol in his blood than blood!'

The drinking, of course, would continue in the evening after work, to the point where the crew couldn't take any more and so used to meet up at a secret rendezvous as far away from Oliver as possible. More often than not he'd find them, barging through the door, usually with Reg, yelling, 'Ya bastards!' He'd always know exactly what everybody drank 'and he'd never buy you a single,' says Roberts. 'It would always be a double. And he wouldn't let any of the crew leave. He used to catch us – gotcha! – if we were heading out of the door.'

This lasted ten weeks and Ollie's behaviour could get so wild it beggared belief, like the time he was so drunk that he attacked an aeroplane. His hotel was close to the island's airport, in reality just a landing strip, and this two-seater job was coming in to land when Ollie charged it and the pilot had to fly over him. Roberts and even Nic Roeg tried to persuade Josephine to talk to Oliver about his drinking, but it was useless. 'You couldn't stop him,' says Roberts. 'And nobody ever made the effort to confront him about it because it was impossible, and what's more he wouldn't listen to you. And yet he delivered a terrific performance. The great shame about the guy was that Oliver Reed having a beer was very nice, charming and rational and funny, but after one drink too many this rather unpleasant snarling beast appeared. He truly was like the wolf man. And it wasn't at that stage violent, it was just, the guy had gone, he was different, and you didn't want to be in his company for that much longer.'

It's no surprise to learn that Roberts was grateful when filming came to an end and he and Rick McCallum deposited Ollie at the airport to fly him home. 'My last ever image of Oliver Reed is going up the steps of the plane, turning to Rick and me and saluting. He got in the plane and away it flew and Rick and I looked at each other and went, thank God for that.'

Towards the end of their time together on Praslin, Ollie and Reg, along with a few friends, were enjoying a meal at a seafront restaurant. As always with these two, there was a lot of banter, copious amounts of drinking, and play-fighting going on. Nobody quite saw what happened next, but Reg ended up falling off a jetty, landing awkwardly fifteen feet below on a coral beach. Was this the result of a disastrous prank that had gone wrong? 'They would have these friendly scuffles where Ollie would think that he was the stronger,' says David Ball. 'But Reg would put him away every time. And I do believe that's what led to Reg's accident.'

Reg's own account of what happened, if true, was shocking. He was leaning against a balustrade outside the restaurant, looking out to sea, when Ollie came up from behind, grabbed his ankles and hurled him over the side. There's no doubt Oliver thought the tide was in, and Reg had lost count of the number of times he'd been thrown into swimming pools. But the tide was out and the result was that he broke his back in two places.

Ollie's account of events, however, differed radically from Reg's. It was, he said, the result of an argument and scuffle that went too far, and when Reg lunged violently towards him he had no option but to dodge out of the way and over he went. It was difficult to know exactly whose story to believe since no eyewitness came forward and both men were so intoxicated that the events of that fateful day were a bit of a muddle. 'I don't think Ollie deliberately went out to hurt Reg,' says Simon. 'But I don't think he was very careful.'

The next thing Oliver heard was that Reg had sold his story to the tabloids, claiming that he was now virtually a cripple, unable to walk without the aid of a walking stick and that his career in movies was over. He also spoke of his intention to sue Oliver for damages. 'My father felt very let down,' admits Sarah. 'He couldn't really understand why Reg went to the press. If he'd wanted money he would have given it to him, he would have helped out.' But Reg was filled with a rage and a bitterness that could not be so easily contained. What else explains his reason for one night arriving at Pinkhurst, armed with a knife, to do who knows what damage to his former employer and best friend? Luckily both Bill and Josephine were in the house and they managed, in Josephine's words, 'to talk him down', even though, at one point, Reg had the knife at Ollie's throat.

Worse was to come. Basing its story largely on an interview with Reg, the *Sun* newspaper made allegations that Oliver had beaten and assaulted Josephine. Usually Ollie never gave a monkey's toss what the press said about him. 'He would just go, "If that's what they want to write, that's what they want to write",' says Josephine. 'It bothered him of course, but he was philosophical enough to know they were always going to print that kind of stuff.' But this was different and he sued. 'That was the one time when he wasn't prepared to let it go because he didn't want my family hurt by the allegations. He stood up and said, "No, this is wrong."' The case was eventually heard in January 1991 and very quickly settled out of court, with the *Sun*'s lawyers agreeing to pay substantial damages and make a full apology, which meant the most to Ollie. It was an episode that deeply upset Josephine, who, despite her husband's propensity to lose his temper and embrace violence, never felt frightened or threatened in his presence. 'I always felt he was extremely protective of me.'

When in December 1993 Reg's case for damages came to court, both men stuck to their original stories and after four days the judge dismissed Reg's claims, believing that, 'through the mists and vapours of drink', neither man knew what the truth was any more. Ollie and Reg never spoke to or saw each other again. 'It was sad that their friendship ended in such an acrimonious way,' says Mark. 'My father wouldn't have dreamt of hurting him. They truly loved each other and it was just an awful shame to watch something that had true value and had been so meaningful for both of them end up so broken.'

While Ollie and Josephine were in the Seychelles for *Castaway* they were also busy buying a new house. David had confronted his brother with the stark truth that since his earning power had decreased since his seventies heyday he needed to downsize yet again. That didn't just mean selling Pinkhurst: he was being advised to leave Britain altogether and reside somewhere more tax-efficient. All through his tough tax years Ollie had defiantly remained a British citizen. As late as 1981 he was telling reporters, 'I just couldn't be a tax exile. I could pay a lot less in taxes if I moved, but I must live in Britain. It's my culture, my home, my heritage.' But the financial reality now facing him was such that he no longer had a choice.

The ideal location was Guernsey, an island Oliver knew well from his stays there for tax purposes and where over the years he'd accumulated a few friendships. So David was instructed to find them a suitable property and Ollie drove away from Pinkhurst to work on *Castaway* knowing he would never see that house again. Every week photographs and property details would arrive in the post for the couple to peruse, but nothing caught their interest. The house they finally decided on was bought unseen. David made all the arrangements. 'It was a very ugly house,' Josephine says of it now. 'I think it was probably one of the only red-brick houses in Guernsey. The rest were all beautiful granite buildings. But it had a lovely garden, and of course David knew that Oliver loved gardens.'

Located ten miles from the island's capital, St Peter Port, the couple moved in after *Castaway* was finished. As a house-warming gift Ollie presented Josephine with a lovely gold chain which, after a few glasses of wine, she draped around her pet terrier. Ollie saw it on the dog and went, right, and buried it in the garden when Josephine was asleep. The next morning she couldn't find her chain anywhere. 'It's all right,' said Ollie. 'I've buried it, because I was very cross.' They never found it. 'We got metal detectors out, you name it,' Josephine recalls. 'I don't know where it went.' Years later when they moved to Ireland Ollie's house-warming gift to Josephine was a hammer.

Along with their furniture good old Hornby was shipped over from England too. At Pinkhurst the rhino was kept in the garden, although for a time he was out on the verge until the council asked them to move him in because it was a dangerous bend and a bit of a shock to drivers. 'He was also kidnapped a few times,' says Josephine. 'We'd get a note – if you want to see Hornby alive again you have to come down to such and such a pub and buy a round of drinks – and so we'd have to go down and get him back. Eventually we put concrete boots on him to stop him being taken.' In Guernsey Keith Moon's mad gift was located in such a way that its horned head protruded from the garden bushes. There was also a new Ollie family heirloom, courtesy of Johnny Placett, a heavy brass knocker cast in the unmistakable shape of a thrusting penis that swivelled on hinges, attached to two equally impressive balls.

While some of the interior of the house was changed and modernized, special attention was paid to the loft above the double garage: Ollie had it totally gutted and rebuilt as a pub christened the Garage Club. It served local draught beer and featured piped music and settees for relaxation. Directly opposite the bar hung a framed blow-up portrait of Ollie as Father Grandier. As well as being a haven for Ollie, the place guaranteed Josephine some peace when her husband's drinking pals came round, whom she didn't especially want in the house: off they'd go to the Garage Club to wreak their havoc. And for her there was no mystery as to what they got up to. 'We'd bought a little camcorder and they used to muck around with it. One day they left it on by mistake and I watched it and I'd never seen such drivel. They were all pretending to be cowboys and sliding drinks down the bar and talking this utter nonsense. I showed it to Ollie and said, "This is what you do." At least they were happy.'

The only thing missing in Guernsey was Bill and Jenny, who had decided to stay put in England, but Oliver made sure they had a house in which to enjoy their retirement.

One of the first guests to visit Ollie and Josephine in Guernsey was Simon. At the airport Ollie was waiting at the Arrivals gate, waving to him. 'We'll go to the bar,' he said. Simon's favourite drink was gin and tonic, and ten gin and tonics were lined up on the bar waiting for him – welcome to Guernsey. 'A thought flashed through my mind,' he recalls. 'Always with Ollie you had to have an escape route, and here I was on a fucking island where you can't get off and I thought, this is dangerous, this could be a problem, especially when I saw ten gin and tonics, but I thought, just go for it.' They went out to eat and had a wonderful evening. Back at Oliver's home, they chatted and talked over old times until 2 a.m. 'And I remember at six in the morning being woken up and Ollie was with Katie, my youngest, and they were out in the garden together and Ollie was taking her round, saying, "I've got a little goblin who lives here." And then we were off at lunchtime for another session. I had a really good time there.'

Sarah also came to visit as often as she could. She was still a shy teenager and her relationship with her father had not much improved. 'As I got older we had fun times, usually when I was old enough to get drunk with him. It sounds terrible, but those were the moments when the awkwardness went and we could actually have a real giggle.'

Josephine had cottoned on quite early to her husband's awkward relationship with his daughter and often told Sarah, 'You do know your dad is really proud of you.' It was just a shame that he was never particularly good at saying it himself. Giving praise wasn't something that came naturally to Oliver, largely because he'd never received it as a child. He never learned how praise was given. 'Occasionally he would come out with, you know, "I love you, girlie, don't ever doubt that," but there was never regular praise or feedback,' Sarah says. 'He would say he was proud but there was a lack of consistency. I figure we just parent differently these days. He did try, though – we both did – but I doubt that either of us was comfortable with these exchanges. I feel there was so much unsaid, unresolved, and very sad that we missed our time.

'I was proud of him, though. Hugely proud. As a child I was accused of boasting about my famous dad but I just wanted to talk about him. Especially when he was absent. And now, despite our sometimes tricky relationship, I am proud of how he embraced life and coloured his surroundings. He touched people from all walks of life. If I could earn half the loyalty that he earned from his friends I would be happy. For those who knew him, the lights were truly dimmed when he went.'

Every morning Ollie's mantra was, go to school and be as

naughty as you can. And that was it. It wasn't, work really hard today, darling. No, it was, be as naughty as you can, and if you get expelled that'll be great. As far as he was concerned, Sarah was a woman, so although her education did matter, it just didn't seem a priority. 'My father was quite sexist, really. He used to tell me this time and time again, that education was important, but perhaps not academia for a woman. I was not academic, so luckily was off the hook in that respect. But he did take great pride in my achievements, especially sporting achievements. "You're just going to get married, have babies, and sit on a cushion and sew a fine seam," was, I suspect, said tongue in cheek, but I believe this is what he expected.'

A few of Ollie's old friends would also pop over the Channel to visit, among them Alex Higgins, who again relied on Oliver to give him safe haven when things weren't going right in his life. 'But Alex was very hyper,' says Josephine. 'Very wound up all the time. So he was quite exhausting. In small doses they got on fine and then they'd get on each other's nerves and he'd be asked to leave.'

During one now legendary drinking session Ollie poured Josephine's Chanel No. 5 into a glass, informing Higgins it was a fine malt whisky. 'I don't drink whisky,' said Alex. 'It sends me crazy.'

'Chicken!' screamed Ollie. 'Chicken boy. Chicken.'

Higgins grabbed the glass and downed it in one. His face twisted up in pain and he spat it out. He was ill for two days. But he had his revenge by treating Oliver to a crème de menthe laced with washing-up liquid. 'Ollie was burping bubbles for weeks,' says Higgins.

Michael Christensen visited a few times and he and Ollie would have lobster-eating contests in one of the island's many seafood restaurants. Christensen was also present when Ollie drank 100 pints from opening time to closing time (which was all day in Guernsey) and finished with a parallel handstand on the bar. It started as a bet. Someone had said, 'Ollie, you really should stop drinking, it's killing you.'

'I only drink beer. That's good for you.'

'Look,' this guy said. 'Any more than three or four pints a day can be harmful.'

'Bollocks. It's only hops and water. I can drink 100 pints and I'll be all right.'

And so a bet was struck that Ollie couldn't do it. The press got involved and people started to come down, and pretty quickly the pub filled up. 'And he bloody did it,' confirms Christensen. 'The only stipulation was, he couldn't be sick. But he did choose a low-alcohol, flat beer, because he couldn't do 100 pints of strong lager. You'd be dead. But he did it. He was out peeing every ten minutes and didn't eat anything. He was doing it quite methodically, timing his intake. It was extraordinary.'

Chat Show Suicide

It's very clear that, after years of appearing in mediocre films in roles that were clearly beneath his talents, *Castaway* represented a real return to form. As Gerald Kingsland Oliver gave one of the best performances of his career, in a film that was both a commercial and critical success. Nicolas Roeg was another of those directors whom he respected, and consequently he'd raised his game. However, according to Selwyn Roberts, Oliver and Roeg seriously fell out one night on location. 'They had a fist fight in the hotel when the pair of them were drunk as skunks. And Nic was a feisty little bugger, and they ended up falling in the water.' But for the vast majority of the time they'd got on well and Ollie's achievement should have put him back on top, with producers queuing up again for his services. So why didn't they? The answer is simple: Ollie hit the self-destruct button. In the lead-up to the UK release of *Castaway* at the beginning of 1987 Ollie seemed to sabotage his own career, either through ego, self-confidence issues, vanity, mischievousness, the bottle, or sheer bloody-mindedness. He was effectively the sniper at his own assassination.

What makes least sense of all is that Oliver knew full well the big chance he was blowing. As he said himself at the time, '*Castaway* has given me the strength to survive and hope that somebody with money in his pocket will see this film and maybe another important film will come out of it.' This was one of the reasons why he'd thrown himself into promotion duties. But things got off on the wrong foot almost immediately. *Castaway* had been chosen to open the London Film Festival the previous November. During the screening Ollie could be heard from the back row giving out piercing whistles and, according to one reporter, 'choice samples from the Oliver lexicon of invective'. Afterwards some of the participants in the film held a Q&A session in front of the audience. Ollie arrived five minutes late on the stage and in a bedraggled state, uttering gibberish before almost falling into the audience. After that he embarked on the chat show circuit and things would never be quite the same again. Following these appearances Oliver Reed the actor no longer existed and the public's perception of him became something very different, a perception that he was never able to shake off and that persists to this day.

Oliver had always been a popular chat show guest during the seventies, though his appearances on them were sporadic. He placed chat shows very much in the same category as premieres: something he felt obliged to do rather than something he enjoyed. 'They weren't really his motivator,' says Mark. 'I never remember him relishing going on a Parkinson or a Russell Harty. It was dread, because of his shyness.' And when in 1986 he was the subject of *This Is Your Life*, well, you can guess his reaction. Halfway up to London he'd worked it out and went, "It's mine, isn't it?" and his whole body language changed. 'Doing that show would have been outrageously painful to him,' says Sarah. 'He hated every minute of it, except probably when Dadi [his driver in Barbados] was the surprise guest at the end. But the rest of it would have been completely grim to him. That was putting him out of his comfort zone.' Probably because he had to be himself.

To combat this insecurity Ollie rarely appeared on chat shows as himself, but instead played some warped version of what he perceived the public thought Oliver Reed behaved like. 'I can never not be a character,' he once admitted to Simon, who says, 'Oliver could be the most charming bloke, a trait that came to a certain extent from his father, but he was just terribly shy. I used to do a lot of TV interviewing and Ollie would watch and say, "I could never ever do that. I can be on TV and I can act and I can be a character or I can go to a press conference and be the movie star, but I could never just be me." That's why he got pissed on chat shows or larked about, because you had to be yourself, and he just couldn't do it, so he'd get slaughtered. He was very shy. I was always terrified whenever he went on a chat show.'

The result could sometimes be fun, like the time Ollie took his trousers off live on *Pebble Mill at One* and performed a Scottish reel up and down the studio floor to the accompaniment of Kenny Ball and his Jazzmen. Or when he turned up in a gorilla suit for *Parkinson*. Or leaped on top of Susan George on Ireland's top chat show with Gay Byrne, pulling the actress off her chair and dragging her behind the set. And there was the occasion Terry Wogan was hosting *Night of a Thousand Stars* on ITV. When introduced, Ollie came striding down a specially built ramp on to the stage but carried on walking straight into the audience. After the show the producer accosted David to complain bitterly. The next day he phoned David, saying it had got a brilliant reaction and could he have him again? 'He had a natural way of creating comedy or creating difference in something that was otherwise going to be rather mundane,' says Mark. 'He would change it and add spice to it. I think he had fun with it. He didn't take it too seriously.'

But sometimes things could get really out of hand. When *Castaway* opened in America, Oliver made an infamous appearance on *The David Letterman Show*. Quite what he hoped to achieve with this performance, for performance it is, and a slightly lubricated one, is difficult to understand. Certainly it didn't do Oliver any favours when it came to offers of work from Tinseltown. Letterman sees through the pretence fairly early on, quipping, 'It's fun to pretend, isn't it?', but is nevertheless unnerved by the strange apparition before him, who right from the off is in turn menacing, incomprehensible and surreal. At one point Ollie starts talking German for no discernible reason. Intriguingly, when Letterman repeatedly asks for anecdotes about drinking Lee Marvin under the table, Ollie seems to lose his cool. 'You'd like to turn my lights out, wouldn't you?' says Letterman. Ollie smiles and his cobra eyes don't blink.

By far the most controversial and celebrated of all Ollie's chat show appearances occurred when he agreed to appear on *Aspel & Company*, which regularly pulled in eight million viewers a week. Graham Stuart, now a top television executive, was then a researcher on the show and a crucial eyewitness to what happened both in front of and off camera. Ollie was booked to promote *Castaway* and it was agreed that a car would be sent to pick him up at his hotel. 'And obviously that car had strict instructions not to stop anywhere. The car was sent but Ollie didn't get in it. Immediately we think we've lost him. Then we hear he's in another car with his brother David, but a car that he's chosen, and that car stops at every pub on the way. So there's mistake number one. The control's lost.'

Anxiety spread around the studio, when was Ollie going to arrive, if at all? The show wasn't going out live, but already the audience had begun to gather for the recording. Finally he showed up, and staff could hear him ranting and raving one floor above. As he appeared to be drunk, discussions took place between the production staff as to whether or not to let him go on. In the end the thought was, well, that's what you expect from Oliver Reed.

Ollie's fellow guests were comedy actress Sue Pollard and TV presenter and writer Clive James. Along with their individual researcher, the guests were led to a little green-room area just behind the set to wait for their cue to go on. 'And that's when it kicked off,' recalls Stuart. 'Ollie goes from being merry drunk to being agitated drunk. He wants a gin and tonic. Now in the backstage area the only instruction that was given to us was, don't give him a drink. So I go off to pretend to get a drink and now it's getting near to show time.' All the while Ollie was getting more and more angry and frustrated. 'Where's my fucking drink? Give me my fucking drink.' Stuart returned empty-handed and tried to avoid Ollie's gaze, but he'd spotted the subterfuge and was furious. 'Where's my fucking drink?' Nearby on a table was a large jug of orange juice. Still shouting and swearing – and by now his shirt had come out of his trousers and his hair was disarranged – Ollie picked up the jug just as he heard his cue to go on. Out he walked and bang, the audience reaction was predictably raucous. Taking in the huge response, Ollie must have thought, right, let's give them a show. Hijacking the band to play the sixties hit 'Wild Thing', Ollie belted out the lyrics like a Neanderthal Elvis and danced like the uncle from hell at a Christmas party. It was a performance that few who watched it have ever forgotten.

Backstage Stuart was watching the horror show unfurl on a TV monitor, and could see that the host, Michael Aspel, was unsettled, that he didn't feel comfortable in the situation. It was left to Clive James to ask the interview's only real probing question, 'Why do you drink?' To which Oliver replied, 'Because the finest people I've ever met in my life are in pubs.' It sounded glib on television, but in reality, from Mick Fryer to Michael Christensen, Ollie's most loyal friendships were indeed hatched over a pint in the bar. As Stuart continued to watch he feared the thing would spiral out of control. He also to this day thinks that Ollie was faking part of it. 'He was not as drunk as that. I think as an actor he'd got to that point and he was going to go with it. And he did.' Afterwards in the hospitality room Oliver was conspicuously sober and behaving in that very English kind of way of pretending nothing had happened. 'Michael Aspel was not happy,' says Stuart. 'He felt the show had been damaged. The producers were also in a bit of a state. And there was Ollie trying to be normal. Afterwards I think there was a feeling of almost regret with him. But, looking back, it was amazing to be part of something like that, to feel the tension and the electricity of something major happening.'

Just how major became clear when ITV aired the show two days later. Switchboards were jammed with angry viewers and the incident made front-page headlines. No one had appeared on television that drunk before. One critic pointed out that it would have been more extraordinary if Oliver had behaved like a bank manager. While Clive James wrote: 'It was one of the most exciting evenings since World War 2, when I was much further from the front line.' But the television authorities took a less flippant view. 'The Independent Broadcasting Authority, who were the regulatory body in the United Kingdom for commercial television, went nuts, as you can probably imagine,' says Greg Dyke, then Director of Programming at ITV. 'Their view was that if he was drunk he shouldn't have been allowed on. I don't think they realized it was recorded, and that we could have edited it out. Now, when you look back, should we have taken it out? No, of course not. You look back now and you say it was a significant moment in the history of British television, not one that you can be proud of, but it was a moment that mattered. It also captured something about Oliver, which is what most of us already knew, that actually a lot of the time he was paralytic.'

Unfortunately it was a view that not only reinforced the public's image of Ollie as a loose cannon but also scared off a lot of potential employers. Producers were just too afraid to work with him and what should have been a revival thanks to *Castaway* ended up another barren wasteland. One wonders if he was aware that he was cutting his own throat with these pantomimic and self-destructive performances. Mark isn't too sure. 'I don't think he was a fool, but he would come away from something where he had behaved badly and think that that was good fun and good television. I'm sure somewhere in the back of his mind he must have thought, hang on, this is all really contributing to my downfall. And yet there was another part of him that didn't care. I don't think he necessarily recognized the full extent of the damage that these little appearances probably did. Great for telly, not great for his film career.'

Nor did Ollie do himself any favours on his next chat show appearance: with Des O'Connor. Again he was clearly not compos mentis here, though Des was his own worst enemy by asking him, 'I understand you have a tattoo in a very unusual place.' Without skipping a beat Oliver replied, 'Yes, on my cock.' The audience burst into hysterical laughter. Again the TV authorities weren't chuffed, for this was live, prime-time television.

It was quite a lively show, that one, because besides Oliver it featured comedian Stan Boardman telling his infamous Focke-Wulf joke, and Freddie Starr. Just before the show Ollie burst into the make-up room brandishing a bottle of whisky and poured some of it into a half-pint tumbler and gave it to Boardman. 'Get that down you.' He then turned to Starr – 'Here you are, Freddie' – but Starr waved the whisky away. 'Oh no,' he said, holding up a large bottle of pills. 'I don't drink, Ollie.'

Not long afterwards Boardman was playing a gig in Guernsey and invited Ollie to come along. On stage Boardman was midway through his act when someone started heckling him. 'I love hecklers, but Ollie didn't understand that comedy and heckling go together. He thought the fella was showing disrespect. So he stretched over the table and grabbed hold of him and gave him a big bear hug, lifted him up on to his feet, dragged him out on to the dance floor, and they collapsed together in front of about three hundred people.'

After the show Ollie invited Boardman and a friend of his, the actor Tony Barton, back to his house. When they arrived, Ollie asked them to join him for a drink in the Garage Club. 'But I've got to initiate you first. You have to wear a tie – and nothing else.' Boardman and Barton stood there thinking, are we going to go along with this? 'Come on, get your clothes off,' Ollie insisted, already stripping. After a couple of minutes all three men stood there completely naked, except for a tie. 'You've never seen anything so ridiculous in your life,' says Boardman. 'We all march up the stairs, and I've got Tony Barton's big fat arse in front of me, and Ollie's behind, probably the worst view in the bloody world. So there I am following these two arseholes. We get into the bar and he'd made a great job of the place: it looked like a small pub. He must have had thirty bottles on the optics.'

Ollie went behind the bar while Boardman and Barton got comfortable on stools. 'For the initiation ceremony you've got to have a drink,' said Ollie and took a half-pint glass and went down every optic, whisky, brandy, vodka, the lot, until it was practically full. He did the same with another one and placed the two glasses in front of his guests. Ollie had one for himself and took a giant gulp. Boardman, a beer man by nature, took a swig. 'It nearly killed me. I managed to get down to about half and he starts filling it up again along the optics. The rest of the night was quite a blur, really.' That's not surprising, but Boardman does remember a bunch of builders arriving, wearing trousers, so they must have already been members, and then the arm-wrestling started, and press-ups. 'All sorts of little games and tests of strength to see if you could beat Ollie.' There was also the singing box, an antique ottoman that you got in, and while Ollie sat on top you weren't allowed out until you'd sung a complete song to his satisfaction.

After the drinking, everybody, now fully clothed again, went into the house, where Boardman noticed in one of the rooms an elaborate chair, almost like a throne, on a raised platform. Ollie sat on it and at once began reciting Shakespeare's *Richard III* but all jumbled up in his own style, ad lib. 'It was absolutely brilliant.' This is something that he often liked to do. He did have his favourite pieces of Shakespeare that he liked to quote or play around with. 'Oliver had a terrific memory,' says Christensen. 'He'd come out with poetry sometimes in the pub, spout something beautiful. Or if you talked about some of the films he'd done, he'd take a speech out of it and deliver it word perfect. Even years later he could do Father Grandier's speeches from *The Devils*. Unbelievable. To have all that rattling round in your head.'

They ate some toast, then Ollie announced that tomorrow he was taking everyone for lunch at a restaurant owned by one of his friends. 'I can't go,' said Barton. 'I'm doing a TV commercial tomorrow in London. I've got to get the first plane out of Guernsey, six-thirty in the morning.' Ollie said, 'No, no, you're not going. You're my guest. Nobody leaves here until I say. We are going to my favourite restaurant.'

As everyone made their way to bed, Barton whispered to Boardman, 'I'll just sneak out at five or something. Ollie will be well out of it.' The following morning Boardman came downstairs and there was Josephine. He asked her, 'Tony Barton, did he manage to go?' Josephine shrugged her shoulders. Boardman guessed he must have gone, as it was past nine o'clock. 'So I go back upstairs and I pass Tony's bedroom and there's Tony on the fucking bed fucking handcuffed. Ollie had gone in during the night and handcuffed him to the rail.'

Bypassing breakfast, everyone headed for the restaurant. When Boardman walked in he couldn't believe it: sitting in the corner was the guy who'd heckled him at the gig the night before. 'Ollie went, "Aarrgghh" and dived over the table and grabbed him, and this guy's fucking terrified, and they rolled around the floor again, the plates and glasses are bouncing off the walls. Ollie then picked him up, straightened the fella's tie and sat him back down and said, "The dinner's on me, but don't ever do that to my friend again."' Ollie returned to his table and sat back down. Clutching a bottle of wine, he continued to watch this guy intently, all the while growling, 'Grrrrr.' The poor guy tried to carry on with his meal but was visibly shaking. 'Suddenly Ollie threw this bottle against the wall behind him,' says Boardman. 'And the fella put his knife and fork down and fucked off out the door. Well, I couldn't stop laughing. And the bloke who owned the restaurant poked his head out. "Ollie, will you stop doing that!" Knowing Ollie, he would have done that as a trick, he liked to shock people. Me, I was doubled up.'

It had certainly been an eventful weekend, and when Boardman left he suggested that since Ollie had looked after him so grandly he'd like to return the favour with an invitation to his home city of Liverpool. Ollie said he'd love to come and after landing at Liverpool airport did his usual trick of falling down the steps of the plane. As a treat Boardman took Ollie to Anfield to watch a match and introduced him to Kenny Dalglish, manager of Liverpool. Ollie was wearing a beautiful red silk jacket from a Who tour, a gift most likely from Moonie. When he saw Kenny, Oliver shook hands and took off his jacket and gave it to Dalglish. 'We had a great time,' says Boardman. 'Ollie met Ian Rush and the team and we watched the match in the directors' box. The Kop were singing, "There's only one Ollie Reed, one Ollie Reed, there's only one Ollie Reed", and he stood up and acknowledged them. He got a standing ovation from the Kop.' In the bar afterwards they were having a drink when Dalglish walked up. 'I've got something for you, Ollie.' One of his assistants ran down to the dugout and came back with a Liverpool tracksuit top. 'You can't give him a crappy Adidas top,' said Stan. 'He's just given you a million-pound fucking Who jacket.' Ollie took it, saying, 'No, I want it,' and insisted on wearing it as they went back to his hotel.

The next day Boardman arrived to pick Ollie up and got landed with a bill by the hotel management for a broken door. In the night Ollie's mate, tired of always being dragged out of bed to go drinking, had gone down to reception and changed rooms. Of course, Ollie had knocked on his door and when he couldn't get a reply smashed the thing off its hinges. Another day of sightseeing and drinking followed. In one restaurant Oliver insisted they swap jackets. 'So I'm now wearing Ollie's coat,' says Boardman. 'And in the top pocket there was a wad of twenties and fifties sticking out. There's £100 in another pocket, £300 in that one. Every fucking pocket I opened, there was cash everywhere. I said, "I want to fucking buy a coat like that. Where do you get them coats, Ollie?"'

Later that day Ollie went off to meet a friend in Halifax to watch a rugby match. Boardman asked the driver who took him if he got there all right. 'It was a nightmare,' was the reply. 'Ollie was wearing that Liverpool tracksuit top and on the dual carriageway he told me to stop the car and he got out and rolled around for ten minutes in the mud to make it look authentic. He said he couldn't go to a rugby match with a new top that wasn't covered in shit.' And when Ollie got there he gave that top to some other guy and took his coat. 'He swapped coats with everybody,' says Boardman. 'When he got on the plane back to Guernsey he had different clothes on to what he started with. I asked him what had happened to the coat with all the money in it. He said, "I don't know."'

Slumming It

In 1987 doctors warned Ollie to ease back considerably on his alcoholic intake or face the consequences of possible kidney damage, coronary disease and ultimately heart failure. But did he care? Not really, brazenly announcing, 'I'd like to think I would be brave enough to drink myself into the grave.'

By now a life on the piss had taken its toll on his appearance. He was pot-bellied, grey-haired, lined and slightly stooping. It was a long way from the brooding sex symbol of the early seventies. His face was now 'a sad reflection of a dissolute life', as one journalist put it, and 'a Hogarthian example of debauchery's perils'.

Of course, growing old is an inevitability, but for someone who set great store by his masculinity it is perhaps surprising to learn that it was something that Ollie had few hang-ups about. 'So long as he had his garden and his Radio 4 and his sport and could walk the dogs, I think he was quite happy and content about getting older,' says Josephine. 'He was perhaps looking forward to the chance of playing different characters. He always laughed that he wanted to be the man who came into the pub and somebody would say, get off that stool, it's his stool, for God's sake, move now. Also that I'd push him everywhere in a wicker Bath chair and he'd have a stick to poke people.'

What did frighten Ollie was the thought of a long, lingering death, of getting some nasty disease and slowly wasting away. 'He didn't want to be in a hospital,' says Josephine. 'He wanted to enjoy his old age disgracefully or however, but he didn't want to be in a hospital or ill.' It was such a morbid fear that Mark was made to swear that he would carry out his father's wish that, 'If I'm there with nurses wiping my nose and my arse, if I'm in that situation, get a shotgun and shoot me. Don't give me one barrel, give me two, make sure you do a proper job.'

Something Ollie did take great pride in was the fact that he was quite indefatigably the last of a dying breed, the last hell-raiser. Burton was dead and Richard Harris and Peter O'Toole had both had to reform to stay alive. Not Ollie, and while most critics in the media looked down on his infantile rabble-rousing, one scribe from the *Mail on Sunday* surely expressed what the majority of the nation thought: 'The world needs Oliver Reed. He's the last great bad boy, a lone, shining beacon in the long dark night of political correctness.'

But after his behaviour on those chat shows producers were by and large afraid to employ him. 'To some degree he chose lifestyle over professional advantage,' says Michael Winner. David, as his manager, did his best to convince people to take him on, telling them, 'You don't have to worry about Oliver. Whatever happens the night before, he'll be there, he'll be on set on time. You've got no fears about losing time or money.' But it had now got to the point where Ollie was accepting almost anything going to pay the bills, even television commercials. In the past David had always advised against doing them, since it smacked of desperation, but now Ollie had no choice. The first had him walking into an off-licence, pointing at the shelves, and saying, 'I'll have one of those, one of those, one of those, and give me half a dozen of those,' and as the camera pulls away he is holding armfuls of potato crisps. 'As a result of that, Ollie got into the idea that maybe commercials were a good idea,' says David.

Next up was an advert for low-alcohol wine with Paula Yates. Of course, the joke is that as Ollie is putting the glass to his lips Paula tells him it's 99.9 per cent alcohol-free and he almost chokes. 'Then I was approached by a very well-known advertising agency who mooted the idea of using Ollie for Bacardi white rum,' David recalls. 'I went in, hard-nosed, and we got the payment up and up and in the end it was going to be the equal of a full-size movie fee. Then, I'm just about to sign the contract and Ollie disgraced himself somewhere, alcoholically, which meant that he wasn't an icon for Bacardi rum, who apparently are rather straight, and they withdrew.' Instead the company sent him a crate of bottles as a goodwill gesture. Paul Friday was visiting one day when Ollie gave him one of them, saying, 'You won't believe how much that bottle of Bacardi cost.'

With no mainstream producer prepared to touch him with a twenty-foot boom mike, Ollie took advantage of a current explosion in the South African film industry, thanks to a government tax shelter scheme that made it cheap to shoot there. Because of apartheid the big Hollywood studios and companies couldn't be seen to be doing business there, but a lot of independent filmmakers took advantage. The same problem arose in relation to actors, so a lot of the high-profile stars didn't come, but people like Ollie, whose careers had stalled but still had name recognition, couldn't afford to be so choosy and saw it as a means to make a fairly quick buck. But the films in question were universally dreadful, starting with *Dragonard* and its sequel, *Master of Dragonard Hill*, shot back to back outside Johannesburg in 1987. Ollie plays the villainous Captain Shanks in this steamy tale of the slave trade in the British colonies of the West Indies in the late 1700s. For young actor Patrick Warburton this was his first job. Now a successful voice-over artist and actor with the US TV series *Rules of Engagement* and *Family Guy*, Warburton doesn't seek to hide both his embarrassment and

438

shame about being roped into playing the story's dashing lead. 'They're horrible films and Oliver was relegated to do these shit movies because I guess he was too much of a liability. But what I always found interesting was that, although he would start drinking in the morning on the set, he's the only watchable thing in them.'

Warburton's first day on the picture was his big sword-fight scene with Oliver. The swords were made of wood and painted to look like steel. 'Oliver must have broken somewhere between seven and nine swords crashing into tables and landing on the extras, and I was doing my best to get out of the way. I was terrified because he was big and scary and if you didn't know him he was very intimidating.' Warburton knew of Ollie's legendary status as a drinker, and as this was the drinking time in his own life, decided to throw it out there on that first day and ask if he'd care to knock a few back. 'And that was the beginning of four months of doing the best I could to keep up with the man. He would offer me a whisky on the set at 10 a.m. and I just let him know that he had to give me till 5 p.m. I've gotta pace myself. But we ended up getting trashed every night.'

One evening after an investors' party Ollie and Warburton were being driven back to their hotel by a local black driver at something like two o'clock in the morning. Ollie suddenly wanted to visit Alexandra, which, along with Soweto, was one of the main townships in Johannesburg, extremely impoverished and entirely black. The driver shook his head violently, but Ollie wouldn't be dissuaded. 'We're going in,' he ordered. 'And when we walked into this shebeen [unlicensed bar] it was like a scene in a movie. There were about fifty townsfolk and everything stopped, their eyes went wide like headlights, and for the very first time ever they saw two white men walk into their shebeen at two o'clock in the morning, this had never happened. Reed says nothing, absolutely nothing. I wanted immediately to put their minds at rest, because there was so much strife and ill will on all sides, so I took Ollie and we walked to the bar and I said, "We're Americans, we're just here to hang out and party." And things were good for about an hour. But then voices started to get raised: the alcohol could only suppress the underlying tension for so long. Some of the men in there were getting very, very angry and looked as though they were going to get violent. We were just drinking and having fun, not exactly understanding what was happening, but then our driver came up to us in a literal panic and said, "You must leave now. You are in danger," so we just got the fuck out. Then we couldn't get out of the township and he hid us in this flat until five in the morning when it was safe to leave. We escaped by the skin of our teeth. We could have been dead and buried and nobody would have known. That driver probably saved our lives and I don't even recall tipping him.'

While stuck in that flat Ollie and Warburton passed the time arm-wrestling. Warburton had been the Southern California arm-wrestling champion in his weight category. He also had youth on his side: he was twenty-two, Oliver forty-nine. 'But he beat me, and that's one department where I still to this day have a pretty good track record. I was amazed the man beat me.'

Another night they were in Ollie's hotel room, living like Romans, eating and drinking, when there was a knock at the door. In walked an elderly gentleman, who, it transpired, was a very well-known South African actor; an executive on the film had brought him up to meet Mr Reed. 'I saw them shake hands,' reports Warburton. 'Then I turned around and within five minutes Reed has this man up against the wall. I have no idea what's going on. Then before you know it he's bundled out of the door and that was it. I was astonished. I don't recall even asking, what the fuck happened? We just carried on our drinking.'

440

These antics were just killing time, since the whole production was a mess, the dialogue, the acting, everything, was tenth-rate, and the director had a background in blue movies. 'This is garbage like you can't fucking believe,' says Warburton. 'And yet Oliver in these films just has a presence.' Worse, it was amateurish. For one scene Warburton was given a flintlock that he had to fire at Ollie. He was told where to stand, but the distance was nowhere near far enough and so when he fired, the gunpowder burned into Ollie's eyes. 'I could tell he was in pain and just raging inside that something as fucked up and stupid like this could happen on a set, but it did. He didn't come after me, he didn't even say anything. I apologized but I don't think he held me responsible. He was so calm in his reaction, I was stunned. And it was then that I realized the guy must have cared for me a little bit.'

Two other films Ollie made in South Africa were produced by Jonathan Vanger, *Rage to Kill* and *The Revenger*, both of them action thrillers that went direct to video and were indicative of the kind of films Ollie now found himself involved in: poor-quality, exploitative fare.

Vanger, of course, knew of Oliver's reputation when he was asked to pick him up at Johannesburg airport. 'The stairs went up to the side of the plane and a couple of people came out and then nothing happened for about ten minutes, no one came out of the aircraft. Suddenly Oliver literally popped out, accompanied by a couple of air hostesses to walk him down the steps. Obviously he'd been having too much of a good time on the aeroplane and getting him off had caused them some problems. They managed to get him through Customs and one of the air hostesses came up to me and said, "You're welcome to him," and pushed him my way.'

The drive to the hotel was strained and uncomfortable. Ollie wasn't belligerent but Vanger guessed that neither was he in the best of moods. The next day the producer was walking through the hotel foyer when Ollie spotted him and invited him to share some lunch. Vanger was nervous, to say the least, about what might happen. 'But he was so polite and charming I was actually taken aback. That was Oliver, he vacillated between this unbelievably charming character whose manners were impeccable and was delightful to talk to, and then once he'd had too much to drink the devil in him came out.'

By and large the devil was on show at night in the hotel, where Ollie got up to all sorts of japes. Vanger remembers him getting into a scuffle with some people who were in the country for a golf tournament. 'I'm not exactly sure what happened but Oliver arrived on set with a black eye. We had to shoot on him from the side so you couldn't see it.'

Josephine was there, as usual, and Vanger recalls that she was for the most part a calming influence. If things got a bit out of control she'd put her hand on Ollie's lap and tell him to calm down, on one occasion stopping him just in time from showing the tattoo on his cock in an exclusive five-star restaurant. 'But sometimes he went so far that there wasn't any way of bringing him back,' says Vanger.

Intimidated at the beginning, Josephine had matured into the marriage, she was now more of a woman than a child and had become a stronger person too, no longer the frightened creature who stayed silent on the fringes. 'As I got older, and perhaps felt a little more secure in how I could behave, I did now and again admonish him. It wouldn't necessarily work but I might have voiced things a little bit more.' But still Josephine didn't feel she could stop Oliver drinking or behaving as he'd always done. 'That was the way he was. This was a man who had lived a lifetime before me, so who was I to come in and say, don't do that? Obviously at times one would wish perhaps not quite so much was taken, but otherwise he was able to control his own drinking, he knew what he was doing. He'd stop and then have several days of quietly being at home, gardening, walking the dogs, listening to the radio, watching sport. Then he'd go, "Right, I'm going off to the pub today."'

As in the past, Oliver's drinking was entirely social. Like Jacquie and members of the Reed family, Josephine never once saw him take a drink on his own. 'He wouldn't come home of an evening and have a glass on his own. He wasn't interested in that. He loved the craic and the laughter, but drink didn't govern his life. He didn't need drink to have a good time. He could equally have a good time without it. But it certainly would create an even wilder time.'

One day director John Hough, who happened to be on business in Johannesburg, bumped into Ollie, and they were having a quiet drink in the hotel bar when the South African rugby team walked in, fifteen really big guys. One of them recognized Oliver and came over and said, 'You're Oliver Reed, aren't you?' 'Yes,' Oliver replied. The guy then sat down next to him and started to have a conversation. In that very quiet and distinguished voice of his Ollie said, 'Sir, did I ask you to sit down?' The guy was perplexed, 'No,' he said. 'Well, fuck off then,' said Ollie. Hough remembers the guy just stood there, with all his mates waiting in the background to see what was going to happen. 'It was just like a western. I thought, oh no, there's going to be chairs flying everywhere. There was a long silence and then the guy sort of shrugged his shoulders and went back to his rugby team. But Oliver was prepared to go the distance. He would never back down, he would have stood there fighting to the very end. He was a genuine tough guy.'

In spite of such escapades Ollie's professionalism remained intact and he was always ready to work and knew his lines. 'And he never seemed to act like he was a movie star,' says Vanger. 'It was never, I want this and that, being a right pain in the neck, not at all. And the crew loved him. Unfortunately you could see that the booze had taken its toll, but what struck me the most about him was the fact that when the director

443

said, "Action", it was almost as if he'd sober up for the take. It was quite extraordinary that he could turn it on and off like that. And the man had the constitution of an ox because I don't know how he drank what he did and managed to carry on, he had many a younger man under the table.'

On *The Revenger*, Oliver's second film with Vanger, the producer had learned his lesson and sent his brother to the airport to fetch him this time. 'I didn't say anything and he came back looking pale, going, oh my God, I couldn't believe it, this happened and that happened, and I'm like, oh really?' Josephine wasn't there this time, either, and so by the time he came to leave, Oliver hadn't spent any of his per diem and there was four thousand dollars' worth of South African money stuffed in his hotel wardrobe. When the director and producers came to see him off, Ollie ordered several bottles of Dom Pérignon and informed them to take the money and distribute it to the entire crew.

With films like this – and also *Gor*, a sword-and-sorcery turkey that co-starred another legendary bad man of cinema, Jack Palance, and *Skeleton Coast*, a mercenary actioner, both of which were again shot in South Africa – Ollie knew that he was making crap, but either didn't have the inclination to try to combat it or had resigned himself to his fate. 'If you look at Oliver's career as the career of an artist,' says Michael Winner, 'it went into the toilet. It basically vanished.'

Many of these films were produced by Harry Alan Towers, 'about the only person who would employ Ollie during this period,' claims David. Unlike others in the film business, Towers had no qualms at all about hiring Ollie. 'We loved and adored him,' says his widow, Maria Rohm. 'He was such an unequalled actor and an amazing person. He never failed us in any way. Ollie could fill a room with his presence – how many people can one say that about these days?' The shame was that Towers was associated with the low end of the market. 'It just seemed to be an awful shame that here was this obviously talented man doing work that was plainly beneath him,' says Vanger. 'OK, he was making money out of them but they couldn't have been terribly satisfying.'

This lack of artistic challenge may well have led to his chronic dependency on alcohol, theorizes John Hough. 'A lot of artists drink because their creativity is not finding an outlet and I think Oliver was a star case for that. He had to do roles he didn't want to do, and he never realized his full potential, he really was a top-line artist. He had the same sort of inner power that people like Kirk Douglas and Bette Davis had, and I don't think he got the chance to really exploit it. And I think he began to see his career slipping away. He needed a part like Richard Burton got with *Who's Afraid of Virginia Wolf*, he needed a part where he could show what he could really do. He just wasn't getting the screenplays that he deserved and the parts he deserved and I think he started to drink more.'

One director who believed it a complete travesty that Oliver's talents were being wasted in low-grade films was Terry Gilliam, who early in 1988 was shooting his lavish comedy fantasy *The Adventures of Baron Munchausen* in Rome. For months he'd been pursuing Marlon Brando to play the god Vulcan in a short sequence. When he finally gave up, a list of replacements was drawn up and Ollie's name leaped out. 'I remembered he'd been so unbelievably funny in *Tommy* and I thought it strange why nobody had really used him in that sort of way since.'

Ollie loved making the movie and working with Gilliam, 'and you can see it,' says Josephine. 'There's a twinkle in his eye.' Ollie would remark that Gilliam was one of the very few directors who allowed him the freedom to take a character to the limit. 'And he's just breathtaking in it,' says Gilliam. 'He and Robin Williams are the funniest things in the film.' And so much of what makes the character work was down to Ollie, who plays Vulcan with a broad Yorkshire accent like some demonic Victorian pit owner. There's one scene where Vulcan throws Munchausen and his gang into a whirlpool and Uma Thurman's goddess Venus tries to soothe his rage. 'Just before the take,' recalls Gilliam, 'he asked me, "Do you mind if I do this?" and he batted his eyelids like a bashful child and it was so funny. He was a great, great comedian. He gave weight to the comedy and his comic timing was just spectacular. I just wish he had a few more films to show how brilliantly comic he was.'

In another scene the Baron and Venus indulge in a romantic waltz and before they shot it Gilliam told Ollie to dance along to the music. 'Just start letting the rhythm get to you.' And as the scene built up Ollie began to bounce slowly up and down and lift his feet in the air. 'I think it's one of the funniest things I've ever seen,' says Gilliam. 'Because you have this dangerous guy suddenly becoming this helpless little dumb creature. And that's the secret to the success of the character, he's so frightening and so funny all at the same time. And Ollie could be absolutely terrifying. On screen he was definitely terrifying and sometimes in life; the first assistant director was scared to death of him. But that's what was so interesting about Ollie, how he could be so utterly dangerous and yet so utterly vulnerable the next moment.'

Uma Thurman was a little over seventeen when she made *Baron Munchausen* and, like the rest of the crew, Ollie vainly lusted after her. One afternoon he took her sightseeing around Rome. 'And there's a story of him taking maybe his frustration out on some Japanese businessman,' says Gilliam. 'I never heard the whole story but I know it got a bit unpleasant and unnecessary, but I think Ollie needed an outlet for his frustration.' Gilliam also remembers how much Oliver enjoyed working with John Neville, the respected stage actor playing Munchausen. 'The two of them got on like a house on fire. There was tremendous mutual respect.'

Ollie was only a couple of weeks in Rome and when he flew back to London he caught the same flight as Gilliam, who remembers him sitting in the back, 'taking advantage of the in-flight drinking'. After they landed, Ollie discovered a bar in the short distance between getting off the plane and getting to Immigration. 'And I have never found that bar again,' claims Gilliam. 'But I swear it was there. The next thing we're walking along, and he's clearly had quite a bit, and he's telling me about this disagreement he had with a director and the story ended with Ollie saying, "And then I headbutted him." By this time he'd swung me round to face him and he then headbutted *me*! But he didn't touch me: he stopped within a millimetre of my skull. And I knew I couldn't move: if I flinched I would have lost and he would have been angry because he wouldn't have been able to prove to me that despite the fact that he was really pissed he was in complete control.'

Return of the Musketeers

In the midst of the heat, dust and mayhem of the original *Musketeer* films, Richard Lester said how much enjoyment he was having and that it would be fun to do another romp in a few years' time when everyone was a little older, and maybe even a bit wiser. 'Then you can see the musketeers having trouble getting on their horse, they've rusted, wouldn't that be fun?' Luckily Dumas had reached that very same conclusion and the result was the novel *Twenty Years After*, a sequel that brought his immortal quartet out of retirement to cross swords once again with the enemies of France. As always in the movie business, Lester and the producers discussed the idea and then it was quietly forgotten.

In 1986 Pierre Spengler was in Los Angeles having dinner with Michael York and mentioned the idea. 'Would you come back and play D'Artagnan?' A smile developed across that still boyish face of York's. 'Sure, I'd love it.' The next call Spengler made was to Oliver in Guernsey. He would be the hardest nut to crack, thought Spengler. If he could persuade Ollie, he could get the rest. Far from reticent, Ollie couldn't wait to get started, his enthusiasm was total. Still, Spengler was concerned enough to contact David to enquire about Ollie's current drinking status. 'He's OK,' was the answer. Later that afternoon Spengler's phone rang: it was David. 'Ollie's told me to tell you that he won't touch a drop.' Nothing was written down, Ollie's contract did not have a specific clause in it, but he'd promised Spengler he wouldn't drink on the picture and he kept his word. 'We didn't know if it was possible,' remembers publicist Quinn Donoghue. 'But he just turned it off. Evidently it was an effortless feat that he could stop drinking. And he was his charming and good self without any bad side to it. A lot of people are charming and fun when they drink but when they stop they become dull and withdrawn. This was not the case with Ollie: during those months shooting *The Return of the Musketeers* he was a pleasure to be with. It was a shame that he ever went back to the drink because, of course, it killed him.'

Things were very different after the film was in the can and due for release. Spengler had arranged a publicity tour in Paris and asked for Ollie's participation. 'I don't like to do promotions,' he told Spengler. 'But I'm doing it because you asked me. But be warned.' That sounded rather ominous. Spengler picked Ollie up at the airport in Paris. 'And when we arrived at the hotel he asked for a quadruple cognac – this was nine o'clock in the morning! I said, "Take it easy, Oliver," and he replied, "During the shooting I didn't, but promotion is different."'

When filming started in the summer of 1988 it was a chance for Ollie to renew former acquaintances. He and Michael York hadn't seen each other since the last *Musketeer* picture and meeting him again, fifteen years on, York identified a stark change in his old colleague. 'He'd actually started to mellow a bit, the wildness had gone slightly. He was getting on a bit now, so I suppose that was bound to happen.' Or was it Josephine's calming influence beginning finally to reap benefits? 'She was fantastic,' says Geraldine Chaplin, back playing the Queen. 'She'd subdued him completely. I suppose she saved his life because if you drink that much and behave that wild it will get to you eventually. I sensed on this picture that he was being a good boy and also I think probably his health was endangered. If you can say "frail" as a term to describe Oliver Reed – you can't really – but he seemed a lot more frail. Of course, we were all getting on a bit, but Ollie was beginning to look his age. He was still handsome, though. He was a beautiful man.'

While it was terrific getting everyone back again – Frank Finlay, Richard Chamberlain, and even Christopher Lee, in spite of the fact he died in the last picture – some began to get the sense that, far from the old magic just not being there, something was seriously wrong. 'It was a very different film and a very different feeling making it,' says York. 'Things were going wrong almost from day one.' There was a general belief that the schedule was too short for what they were trying to accomplish, the same kind of dangerous filming they'd managed on the original *Musketeer* films with actors doing their own stunts. York remembers Christopher Lee saying to him that the film was being made at breakneck speed. 'And he meant it, literally.' On 19 September, shooting in Toledo in Spain, popular British comedy actor Roy Kinnear was thrown from his horse and later died of complications in hospital. Beloved as he was by the cast and crew, Roy's death dampened everybody's spirits, but it was like a knife in the guts for Richard Lester, who as director felt personally responsible for the accident. He would never make another movie.

Back in Guernsey, Ollie and Josephine had settled into life on the island, where the multitude of restaurants and pubs meant that Ollie was never without a place to socialize and have fun in. Sometimes too much fun. One pub banned him and for years after whenever he walked past the place he'd stick his nose in the door and the barman would shout, 'No!' It was a running joke between them. There were less pleasant incidents, like the time he got fined for drink-driving, or the occasion, reeling from the effects of too much rum, when he was arrested in a hotel for trying to smash down the door of one of the chambermaids' quarters in the mistaken belief that Johnny Placett was in there having it away with her. Placett, who was visiting Ollie, remembers the police carting him off on the Saturday night and, because it was a bank holiday, with the magistrate not due to sit until the Tuesday morning, Ollie was moved from the police station cell to the island's prison, where Josephine and Placett were not allowed to see him. In the end Ollie received a heavy fine but reacted to his ordeal with surprising restraint. 'I think he liked the idea of being in prison,' says Placett. 'Because I think if Ollie hadn't been an actor he'd liked to have been a criminal, he'd have liked the excitement. I've always thought that.'

Curiously Ollie and Josephine never entirely warmed to Guernsey: they had a sense of being isolated, cut off. 'Lots of friends did come over and visit us,' says Josephine. 'You could almost say we shipped friends in.' During one stay Christensen couldn't help noticing a change in his friend. 'I saw him looking pensive and sort of wistful on a number of occasions where before I never, ever remember seeing him look like that. Whether he was thinking about things in general or the future, or whether he was looking back on the past, and my being there reminded him of Broome Hall days, I don't know. But things seemed to have changed. Health-wise he still looked pretty good, but he just didn't seem to be that happy. Maybe because all his old mates weren't there.'

At night if Oliver couldn't sleep he'd sometimes call Simon and regale him with some of his poetry. When these recitals, which Simon equated to being like 'someone who had taken LSD every night of their lives', became too much for any human being to bear, Simon took to leaving his answering machine switched on all night. If it wasn't Simon it would be some other luckless friend who'd receive a call, sometimes in the early hours. 'You'd never get a phone call off my father to find out how you were doing,' says Sarah. 'You'd suddenly get this drunken or stoned phone call at four in the morning, and he'd sing you a song and put the phone down, or he'd want to know something or tell you a story. And then that would be it: bored now, gone. Just so childlike, it's like my three-year-old.' Johnny Placett was so pestered by Oliver repeatedly calling him at one or two o'clock in the morning that he ripped out the phone and never replaced it.

One of Ollie's pleasures in Guernsey was walking his dogs along the beach every morning. Whenever she came to visit, Sarah always used to join him, 'and we'd take these long walks together over the golf course and the beaches, a lot of the time in silence, but those were lovely times'.

Oliver had always shown compassion towards animals, dogs in particular. Those who are at odds with the world often prefer the company of animals. 'He found animals easier than people,' says Sarah. David Ball recalls, while on the Mexican set of *The Great Scout & Cathouse Thursday*, taking Ollie and Reg one Sunday afternoon to a bullfight. 'It got started and Ollie couldn't bear it. "Come on, Reg," he said. "Let's fuck off, I can't watch any more of this." He was visibly moved by it. He thought it was cruelty personified and couldn't see any reason for anyone to go to a bullfight. But because it was a tradition he never mentioned it to anybody, he never made a big deal out of it, but he wouldn't go again.'

Ollie was also a sucker for a stray animal, and many a time he'd turn up at Broome Hall with cats, dogs and goodness knows what else, much to the exasperation of Jacquie. While filming in Italy he rescued a street dog that used to hang around the trailers, living on scraps. He paid for it to go through six months of quarantine and the mongrel came to live in Guernsey, going by the name of General. One weekend David and Muriel came to visit. Ollie was out in the garden trying to age some statues he'd bought, white female nudes. He'd heard that if you put yoghurt on them it would turn them green and mouldy.

Someone left the back door open and out ran General, who of course went up and started to lick it all off. 'Ollie laid into it so violently I thought he was going to kill it,' says Muriel. 'I had to pull him off it and scream at him.'

Again the conflicting parts of Ollie's personality were at play even when it came to the treatment of his beloved pets. 'I remember dogs not obeying Ollie, because Ollie liked to be obeyed, and him kicking them,' says David. 'And they used to fawn in front of him. It was if they didn't do his bidding. And that also applied to human beings. He didn't like people contravening him.' And yet there are stories of Ollie spending hours into the night, with a spade and a torch, rescuing one of his terriers that had got stuck below ground in a rabbit warren.

Professionally, film and television work was still coming in but mostly of low artistic quality, like a couple of all-star TV-movie adaptations of Barbara Cartland novels, *The Lady and the Highwayman*, starring a young Hugh Grant, and *A Ghost in Monte Carlo*. 'If there are any decent roles going, they're certainly not coming my way,' Oliver told one reporter. 'People are wary, you see. It's my reputation. Undoubtedly, that's been the ruin of my career.' And it must have been tough to come to terms with because Ollie was a very proud man. Not too proud, though, since Simon remembers him saying more than once that if the career went tits up he could always go back to minicabbing. In fact it had once been his intention to retire at thirty-five and perhaps spend the rest of his life farming or breeding horses. 'That was a dream he had,' confirms David. 'He also firmly believed he was going to be knighted.' But it must have been galling to realize that the booze and the hell-raising that had played such an important part in making him an iconic figure had played an equally important part in his downfall.

The problem was that because everyone thought he was a drunkard, directors didn't particularly want to use him and insurance companies wouldn't underwrite films that he was in, so he was being overlooked for most things that were any good. 'His reputation was worse than what he was,' says Pierre Spengler. 'People would sort of roll their eyes when you'd say Oliver Reed and I would always say, why are you rolling your eyes, the guy's a great actor, and the fact that he drinks is his private business and it doesn't interfere with the work.' The result of all this was that Oliver was left virtually on the sidelines for the next decade, as no one had the balls to give him a chance. 'After Munchausen I would have thought Ollie would have been offered all sorts of work,' says Gilliam. 'That's what I dislike about the film industry, they listen to gossip and they're timid. The man had such extraordinary power on screen.'

David had also noticed a difference in Ollie's work ethic. Where before he had always prided himself on his professionalism and dedication, it now seemed that he didn't give a shit any more. 'I'd take a script to him and he'd say, "How many lines?" and he'd flick through it and see how many times he appeared and say, "No, it's too much." So he got lazy. He wanted an easy life and didn't want to put the effort in.'

It wasn't quite as black and white as that: Ollie had grown disaffected with the movie industry, perhaps because it had largely turned its back on him. On the one hand he needed it to make a living, but on the other hand he didn't miss it when he wasn't working, mainly because he didn't enjoy the process any more. He still loved the crews, but as he'd often complain to Josephine, there was no longer any craft in the business: the whole thing was run by accountants and it was all about the money.

One interesting offer was the chance to play Captain Billy Bones in an American TV movie of *Treasure Island* starring Charlton Heston as Long John Silver and directed by his son Fraser. A long-time fan of Oliver, Fraser was delighted when he accepted the job. 'I had always felt that he was an immensely talented and versatile actor, and he was perfect casting for Billy Bones. He was born to play that kind of period stuff, whether it was Bill Sikes or Athos or Billy Bones: he had that kind of quality. He didn't have to do anything, he just had to look you in the eye and you'd believe that he could skewer you into the wall with his cutlass. He had that kind of truth about him.'

Fraser approached this new adaptation of the classic tale with the idea of making it gritty and realistic; he didn't want to do a jolly Disney pirate film. His first meeting with Oliver took place in the large restaurant at Pinewood, which has a separate little bar, 'and, of course, Oliver knows everybody in the world and people kept dragging him off into the bar, and he'd come back with another gin and tonic under his belt'. Later that day Fraser had arranged for Ollie to have a little time to rehearse his big sword fight in the Admiral Benbow inn. 'But by the time we finished lunch he was about three sheets to the wind, to use a nautical expression. So we arrived at the rehearsal studio and Peter Diamond, our sword master, was standing there with a fistful of rapiers in his hand and went pale as he saw Ollie stagger in. He looked at me and I looked at him and I said, "Ollie, you know, I think you are actually so experienced at sword fights that you can just watch the lads do it today and see how they get on," and he said, "Oh yes, bloody good idea." Fortunately I averted that disaster.'

Then another thought popped into Fraser's head. 'I was completely screwed because, oh my gosh, this poor guy really has a drinking problem and it's too late to replace him: we start shooting in three days.' So he went to his producer, Peter Snell, who listened to his concerns and then replied, 'You know, Fraser, I've been in this business a long time, and I've seen a lot of problems like this come up from time to time, and in this case I would say that you're actually right, you're completely screwed.' As it happened, three days later Oliver showed up on location in Cornwall on time and sober. 'I never had a problem with him,' confirms Fraser. 'He would have one or two beers at lunch and take a little nap and then get on with the day. We learned to really respect Ollie. It was sort of like directing a slightly grumpy and very talented grizzly bear. He was a little prickly at first but I'm kind of a stubborn son of a bitch myself and hung in there with him, and he respected that and we got to have quite a good working relationship, we developed a rapport, and I think he gave us a magnificent performance.'

Ollie dominates the opening of the film, revealing to Jim Hawkins, played by a young Christian Bale, the location of the treasure map before perishing. There's also a wonderfully menacing scene with Christopher Lee as Blind Pew. For one shot Fraser wanted Ollie looking out to sea and found the perfect spot: it was quite safe but near the edge of a crag some one thousand feet above the rocks. It was decided to wire Ollie into a climbing harness, worn under his costume. It was then that Fraser discovered his star's phobia of heights. 'I got Peter Diamond to come and help me rig the harness, and Ollie seemed a little nervous. We were about ten yards from the edge of the cliff and the more we started fiddling with the wire and the shackles the more fidgety he got and pretty soon it turned into a wrestling match, with Peter and I rolling around with him on the ground. And the closer we got to the edge of the cliff the crazier it became until finally I yelled, "Wait a second. We don't have to do this, guys. There's another way." It was clear by then that Ollie was not comfortable, even with a harness.' A double was used instead.

Next came a chance to work with an old friend, Ken Russell, even if the part on offer was again relatively small. Oliver hadn't worked with the director since 1975, although in the early eighties they very nearly made a Beethoven biopic together called *Beethoven's Secret*. Russell had written the script and Ollie would have played Ludwig himself, which would have been glorious to see. All the pre-production arrangements had been made, with Russell earmarking locations in Vienna to shoot, when their backers, a German bank, pulled out just days before filming and the project collapsed.

Now Russell was holding the reins on an American television movie starring Richard Dreyfuss and called *Prisoner of Honor* that told the true story of a French army captain sent to Devil's Island for espionage at the close of the nineteenth century. Ollie was cast as a French general and bestowed upon the role his usual gravitas. Well received upon its broadcast, *Prisoner of Honor* marked the last time Ollie and Ken made a film together. During the shoot Russell couldn't help but notice that the spark in his old sparring partner had burned out. 'There was always an animal lurking under the surface and the animal had either been tamed or driven out of him. It wasn't the same Oliver. He was a different man.'

Ollie was soon up to his old tricks, however, on his next film *Hired to Kill*, yet another low-rent actioner. Director Nico Mastorakis found him a delight to work with when he was sober, 'but when he had downed a couple of bottles of champagne for breakfast he was a nightmare. He never drank on the set but he did come to the set a few times as a raging lunatic after drinking a lot.' As far as co-star Brian Thompson could tell, Ollie was drinking constantly. 'You never saw him with an open bottle on the set, but I do remember smelling alcohol on him.' Thompson, an American actor with a distinctive square-jawed profile and imposing stature, which led to his being cast mostly in action movies, came on to the film a little bit in awe of Ollie and admits, 'He's one of the few actors I've ever performed with that I felt intimidated by because, regardless of his state of inebriation, when those cameras rolled he was a consummate actor, he knew his lines, he hit his marks. It was as if he could sober up and become an artist. It was something to behold.'

He was rather less thrilled with having to kiss Ollie full on the lips in one scene. Although he has long since forgotten the plot relevance behind the kiss, he still shudders at the memory of it. 'I had to kiss Oliver Reed five times, I was counting. After we wrapped I was heading to my car when somebody yelled, "Hair in the gate." In the days of shooting on film you used to get hairs in the gate, but that very seldom ever happened, so I didn't even stop walking because I knew it was a joke, it had to be a joke, this would not be the shot where there would be a hair in the gate and I'd have to go kiss Oliver Reed's wet moustache again. It was not a joke – it was not a friggin' joke! I had to go back and kiss the guy two more times. Actually the fact he drank so much was the reassuring part of kissing him because I'm sure there was no bacteria in his mouth. But it was definitely an act of endurance.'

The film was shot on location in Corfu, with the cast and crew staying at the Hilton, and one afternoon Mastorakis met Ollie in the lobby. He'd obviously been drinking and started complaining that he wasn't being put to work enough. Mastorakis reminded him that they were fully on schedule. Ollie nutted him. 'Fortunately I wasn't seriously injured,' says Mastorakis. 'I went straight to my room but he followed me and started banging on the door.' Unable to get in, Ollie called security and told them that the man inside was a friend who was about to commit suicide. For an inebriated man, that was quite a ruse. In the end Mastorakis talked to security and Oliver was politely removed. 'The very next day he came to the set and was warm, polite and disciplined as if nothing had happened.' Mastorakis empathized with Oliver, as he considered him to be 'a sick man. Even today I don't know if I ever liked or hated him. He was a split personality, really: one personality I hated for the problems and delays he created, another personality (sense of humour, fun) I liked. But I did chew razor blades working with him and never wanted to see him again after he left the movie.'

Oliver saved his best for the very last day of the shoot. He'd met a wealthy couple staying at the hotel and the three of them had indulged in a very late breakfast, consuming nine bottles of champagne by noon. And Oliver's set call was noon. Somehow they managed to get him out of the lobby and into a car and on to the set, which was some kind of old fort. 'They got him into wardrobe,' recalls Thompson. 'But the wardrobe lady had a pretty hard time getting his pants on because he kept pulling out his penis, which he was fond of calling his chopper, and showing her his tattoo.' Finally they managed to get him into costume. Oliver was playing the dictator of a fictitious country. This was the final climactic shot of the movie and all he needed to do was stand in the middle of a courtyard, surrounded by rebel soldiers, and drop his gun. That was all he needed to do. 'So finally he's on the set,' says Thompson. 'Its been quite a delay, the director is furious. All Oliver has to do is drop his gun. We've got two helicopters in the air, we've got fifty rebels surrounding him. So the cameras start rolling and Oliver's kind of staggering in the middle of this courtyard, and he unzips his pants and pulls out his chopper. Niko goes nuts: "Cut! Cut!" And everybody's in shock, including myself. Oliver walks off the set and like an oasis in this moment of confusion he makes eye contact with me and comes charging over and throws his arm around me and says, "Brian, that stupid director wanted me to drop my gun, but you know, the rebels, if I'd dropped my gun they would have killed me. So instead I wanted them to think that I was crazy and that is why I pulled out my chopper." Then somebody escorted him into the back of a car and closed the door, and that was the last we saw of Oliver Reed.'

Obviously in his befuddled mind the film had become very real for Oliver. 'But that is part of what made him such a dynamic actor,' believes Thompson. 'That he could just drop into the reality of the script.'

Next Ollie flew to Italy for a new version of the classic Edgar Allan Poe story *The Pit and the Pendulum*. Director Stuart Gordon, who a few years earlier had achieved notoriety with the gross-out horror film *Re-Animator*, had been a fan of Ollie's ever since *The Curse of the Werewolf* and cast him in the small but crucial role of a cardinal from the Vatican with orders to shut down the bloody Spanish Inquisition. Of course, Gordon had heard stories that Ollie could be difficult, but nothing prepared him for the phone call he now received after the star's arrival at the film's location, a castle in Umbria. 'Oliver had told Tunny, the cook and caretaker of Castello Giove, that he wanted every bottle of wine in the castle to be lined up before him on the enormous banquet table. Tunny thought he was joking, but was soon convinced Reed was not, and so Tunny and his wife Julia had done as they were told. Reed then proceeded to drink bottle after bottle, becoming so inebriated that he began chasing Julia around the table, causing Tunny to lock his wife in their apartment to protect her from being ravaged by this madman who at over 230 pounds was quite a formidable presence.'

When Gordon arrived, Ollie loudly invited him to join the celebration. 'How could I refuse? By this time Oliver was so drunk that he could no longer even get up to pee, so he grabbed an empty bottle and whipped out his dick and pissed into it while still sitting at the table. Before he put it back in his pants he showed us his tattoo.'

The star of the film was Lance Henriksen, who had been employing the Method in playing his role of inquisitor supreme Torquemada. According to historical testimony, this Dominican friar drank only water and ate only stale bread, so this had been Henriksen's diet since the beginning of shooting. 'But the presence of the wild Oliver caused him to join the party and drink for the first time in weeks,' remembers Gordon. 'Oliver took him out on the town and soon Lance was unconscious on the floor. "Can't hold his liquor," Reed said dismissively and again whipped out his dick. I was afraid he was about to piss on his co-star but Josephine handed him another bottle and he quickly filled it.'

The following morning Gordon showed up on the set and nervously asked an assistant if Mr Reed had shown up yet. Indeed he had, Gordon found him in his dressing room already in costume and make-up, totally sober. As for Henriksen, he later stumbled on to the set with a massive hangover. Their scene involved drinking Amontillado wine in a nod to another story by Poe, and Gordon had procured a cask of real Italian white wine, but after a couple of takes Ollie asked for coloured water instead, saying that if he had another glass he wouldn't be able to remember his lines. 'So I discovered that Oliver Reed was a consummate professional,' says Gordon. 'Doing what he wanted – raising hell – on his own time but ready to get the job done, and done magnificently, when on yours.' Gordon was also never to forget another evening, this one much quieter, when he sat with Oliver in front of the castle's enormous fireplace and listened as he recited poetry by Lord Byron. 'It was the most beautiful recitation I have ever heard.'

Ollie was required on the film for only a few days. 'After he had left,' recalls Gordon, 'we discovered the hard way that he had left his urine-filled bottles in the refrigerator. No one drank white wine again.'

'I'll Put My Plonker on the Table If You Don't Give Me My Mushy Peas.'

Early in 1991, at the height of the first Gulf War, Channel 4 decided that it would be a great idea to invite Oliver on to its high-brow and critically lauded live discussion programme *After Dark*, which had been running on and off for several years. The format was simple and effective, assembling a group of experts to debate in depth a particular topic. The 28 January edition was entitled 'Do Men Have To Be Violent?' and questioned militarism, masculine stereotypes and violence to women. For those who stayed up late to watch the ensuing mayhem, it was a spectacle they'd not easily forget.

Over the years many myths have grown up about this programme, principally that Ollie was brought on deliberately to cause chaos and be obnoxious, which of course he ended up doing in grand style. Don Coutts directed just about every episode of *After Dark*, including this one, and remains adamant that Oliver was a legitimate guest. 'I think he was there primarily because he played the stereotype of the male, the drinking and the womanizing male, but underneath all that there was knowledge about his fears about his father, who had been a conscientious objector. I think he had a very vulnerable side and a very soft side.'

Of course, *After Dark* was a highly provocative show that

didn't pull its punches and certainly there was a sense that having Oliver on might be a little bit wild. 'Because you can't control what goes on, you can get that frisson,' says Coutts. 'I mean, inviting the feminist writer Kate Millet on with Oliver Reed was quite a contentious booking. And it worked.'

Then there was the drinks cabinet, fully loaded with bottles of wine and liquor that Ollie made predictable full use of. 'One of the things about *After Dark* was that everybody could drink,' says Coutts. 'It wasn't a case of, let's get Ollie pissed and he'll make a fool of himself. If people wanted to drink or smoke it acted as a great relaxant and worked really well until obviously Ollie couldn't resist drinking more than he should have.'

According to Coutts, Oliver arrived at the studio sober and feeling quite nervous. And you can't blame him: a man who had been self-conscious about his intellectual capabilities his whole adult life was about to go on a live television debate with academics, historians and professors. He was incredibly brave to accept the invitation. Then it began and it didn't take long for the programme makers' hope that Ollie would 'liven things up' to prove horribly accurate. Drinking wine from a pint glass, he became increasingly aggressive and incoherent and lashed out at his fellow guests, who clearly looked intimidated. Sitting next to Kate Millet, who on at least one occasion he called 'Big Tits', Ollie asked the host, 'Is it after midnight yet? It is, good. Well, a woman's role in society depends on whether or not she wants to get shafted.' This didn't go down very well with Ms Millet, nor did Ollie's assertion that 'I've had more punch-ups in pubs than you've had hot dinners, darling.'

If anything, Ollie's behaviour got steadily worse, much to the delight of viewers and the discomfort of his fellow guests, such as when he curtly dismissed an eminent anthropologist by saying, 'What do you know, sitting there covered in dandruff?' In the control room Coutts and his staff watched with a mounting mixture of mirth and incredulity. They could do nothing. One of the show's unwritten rules was never to interfere. It took someone else to take the initiative. The phone suddenly rang in the control room: it was Michael Grade, head of the station, demanding the show be taken off the air immediately. Coutts refused to stop directing. When the commissioning editor repeated Grade's demand to pull the plug, Coutts told him to fuck off.

In the green room nearby, David, who'd driven his brother to the studio, was watching a transmission monitor showing what was going out live to the nation when it suddenly went blank. All the other monitors had the show still running, but David knew the thing had been taken off air. 'What on earth's going on?' he demanded to know. One of the producers reassured him the show was still on. 'No it's not,' said David, pointing to the transmission monitor, which was now running a film about British coal mining in the fifties. Goodness knows what the folk watching at home were thinking.

Back in the control room, Coutts was livid that he had been overruled when somebody mentioned the fact that Michael Grade was currently not in the country. It was a hoax call. 'And no one had taken any kind of proper look into it,' he says. 'So we came back on air and the guests didn't realize that we'd been off them for something like twenty minutes.' In the interim things hadn't changed much, unless it was that Ollie was in an even worse state. After going off to the toilet he came back stumbling through the dark, ran on to the set, and did a leap over the settee into the middle of Kate Millet and kissed her on the cheek, quite aggressively, and you could audibly hear everyone gasp.

Finally stirring his loins, one of the guests suggested to Oliver that he really should go. Then somebody else said it. Ollie took his chastisement like a guilty schoolboy. 'Do you want me to leave?' He asked. 'Yes, yes,' was the chorus from everyone else. Standing up, he apologized gracefully and slouched off. 'The group were terribly proud of themselves that they'd got rid of Ollie,' says Coutts. 'Because Ollie had taken centre stage a lot and they weren't being very assertive and it was amazing watching the group suddenly having the confidence to throw him off. They suddenly felt empowered.'

Ollie didn't leave immediately, but stood beside one of the cameramen for about fifteen minutes watching the debate continue, before bursting into the control room shouting, 'Kissed the bull dyke and they threw me off. Get me a taxi, I'm going clubbing.' Coutts thinks he went off to the Groucho Club in Soho. 'It was just very funny. I laughed for days after. In a funny way he did what they wanted him to do.' And that's exactly the point, but was Ollie deliberately making mischief here or was he just pissed out of his box? It was now difficult to tell: one had become so indistinguishable from the other. Whatever the truth, Channel 4 received a record number of complaints and the tabloids had a field day. Critics were divided. One wrote that it called to mind 'a carriage full of people on a train, reading their papers and chatting amongst themselves, while a drunken loony raves away in the corner . . . superbly entertaining, nail-biting adult television.' Others derided Channel 4 for its mock outrage at the actor's grotesquerie. 'It's just like asking Dennis the Menace to a little girl's birthday party and then throwing up your hands in horror when he jumps on the cake.'

If such a thing were possible, Ollie's appearance on *After Dark* eclipsed even his Stone Age-man rendition of 'Wild Thing' on *Aspel & Company* and sundry other chat show high jinks. Over the years these had been watched, nay endured, by his immediate family. 'And looking back, a few of them do make me cringe,' admits Sarah. 'Because it's, you were better than that.' There was now a very real feeling that Ollie was being exploited, made to dance like a monkey in a cage. 'What do you do if you want to create good telly?' argues Mark. 'You put him in the green room for far too long, you put him up against academics and feminists, and you drop him in there with a trolley full of booze and then ask him a very bright question; he doesn't even know where he is. A lot of the people behind those programmes suddenly go, "oh, isn't that terrible? Look what happened." Well, actually you instigated it, you made it, you put all the components there for the fireworks and when you get the fireworks you go, "oh, we didn't expect that to happen".'

Oliver's nearest and dearest had thus far kept their own counsel, never admonishing their famous relative either publicly or in private. The mood in the family had now changed, for his behaviour had become unacceptable and embarrassing, and it was ruining his career and tarnishing his reputation. Simon remembers watching Ollie's *After Dark* antics literally from behind the sofa. 'Like a kid watching a horror film, I was trying not to look, but not being able to stop myself. Half of me was laughing, half of me dreading what was coming next. Of course, Ollie didn't give a sod.'

After much thought on what to do and how to make their feelings known, his closest relatives wrote a letter to Oliver along the lines of, 'You've got to stop this because it's going to affect your career, and it's affecting the people around you, you're causing a lot of damage. Please understand this is done in love.' Simon, David, Ollie's father Peter and aunt Juliet, for whom he had always had a soft spot, all put their signature to it. 'And it was quite a shock to him,' recalls David. 'Because it came from the closest people to him, within the family. And he didn't like it because we said things like, the reason you're on Guernsey is because you're hardly allowed anywhere in England. We laid it on a bit thick. But it had an element of truth to it because there were so many pubs that had banned him because of his outrageous behaviour. And that's the only time I can remember the family ever getting together and dealing with the situation. Before that he was so successful you couldn't say anything and just had to admire him for what he'd done. And we were very proud.'

Sarah confirms that the letter deeply upset her father. 'He was very hurt by it. He didn't see himself as a bad guy, he just saw himself as wanting to have fun, and he didn't see what was wrong about having fun.'

As Ollie liked to remind people, he discovered very early on that the best way to get flames to rise is by poking the fire. Consequently the room warms up. And Ollie happened to prefer a warm room to a cold room. 'So, if I find the embers dying down, I'll act like a good boy scout and give the fire a good poke. I simply refused to grow up. And it's too fucking late to start now.'

A New Homeland

By the end of 1991 Oliver's career was in a perilous state. Whereas before David had managed to persuade some producers to take a gamble on his client, mostly in inferior product, his hell-raising reputation was now so firmly entrenched in everyone's consciousness that the work had completely dried up. Oliver wouldn't make another feature film for four years. As for David, he was having to sell insurance policies to compensate for the lack of income now that 'Ollie's career had virtually come to an end.' After over twenty years as his brother's manager David was left with no other decision but to quit.

David had done an amazing job with Oliver, but in retrospect there were times when perhaps it would have been more advantageous if he had been managed by a mainstream agent used to dealing with temperamental and challenging artists. Someone who wouldn't have put up with the antics. But then Ollie didn't really want to be managed. And that's the crux of it. David remembers Ollie being particularly rude to a very important agent in America who could have furthered his career. 'And Americans can't put up with bad behaviour for long, they're from puritan stock, and this agent took violent objection to him.' And so it suited Ollie to have David running his affairs, someone he both knew and trusted, someone who understood his foibles and inadequacies, and it worked brilliantly for a very long time.

David wasn't just leaving Oliver, he was quitting the rat race. Yachting had been one of his great passions, ever since Ollie gave him the money to buy his first boat back in the sixties. Now he and Muriel packed everything up and sailed off for almost ten years. 'We didn't have a house, we lived on our boat. We sailed down to the Mediterranean and all the way out to the Greek islands, just very slowly wandering around.'

One of their first ports of call was Guernsey, to see Ollie. Their parting had not been amicable, with Ollie surprised and a little shocked by his brother's departure. The reason for David's visit was to hand over the account books and other business documents to Josephine. 'We arranged to meet at a hotel,' recalls David. 'And so Mickie and I were sitting in this restaurant-cum-bar and Ollie came down the stairs and both of us looked at him and we knew, you could see he'd gone. So we just had a quick drink and then we left, went back to the harbour, jumped on the boat, and off we went to the Mediterranean.' David was never to see his brother alive again.

With his film career in terminal decline, Ollie plumbed new depths by teaming up with Alex Higgins to release an inexcusable version of the Troggs' 'Wild Thing'. To plug the single he appeared on the youth programme *The Word*, another infamous chat show outing in which viewers were left to make up their own minds whether he was pissed out of his skull or play-acting. All Josephine could do, like the rest of his family, was look away. 'God knows why he did *The Word*. If I could stop him doing a chat show I would. I absolutely hated them. Sometimes I did put my foot down. Do you really, really want to do this?'

Like most of the people who cared about Oliver, Josephine knew these types of shows were out to set him up. In the case of *The Word* they put a hidden camera in his dressing room and supplied him with vodka. An obviously intelligent man, why did Ollie keep falling into these traps when he must have known he was being exploited? Perhaps he felt obliged to do them if there was something to promote. It was also a way of keeping his profile alive. Yet it was no longer the profile of an artist but of a public clown, an image that Ollie had cultivated and propagated for so long until it was almost all that was left of him.

One interesting offer did finally come Ollie's way in 1993, a supporting role in the sequel to *Lonesome Dove*, one of the most successful mini-series in American television history and something he himself had watched. 'He fell in love with that first series,' says Sarah. 'He was a big fan of Robert Duvall and would say to me, "Just watch him, he's absolutely magic. He sits on a horse and he'll just flick a fly off him but it's magic." Like Ollie, he had that stillness.' In *Return to Lonesome Dove* Oliver was actually a last-minute replacement for Nicol Williamson, who was forced to pull out of the production. Ollie had been on the original shortlist to play the role of a ruthless cattle baron, but the producers regarded him as too high a risk. Now, with shooting already under way, it was in something of a panic that a call was put through to him and within forty-eight hours he and Josephine were on the set in Montana. 'And from the get-go he was everything we had hoped for in the role,' says director Mike Robe. 'He was glad to be there. He brought with him enormous prestige. He was a commanding personality, even in his silence. And there was not a whiff of attitude and no star treatment.'

In Oliver, Robe sensed a man who was at relative peace with himself. 'For all of his reputation and for all of his purported bad behaviour, I thought he was a man with a really good heart who was, I think, coming to terms with a lot of stuff that had gone on before in his life.' He sensed also someone eager to prove himself and make a good impression. Oliver was smart enough to know that filmmakers talk to other filmmakers. When an actor is considered for a part, the first thing that happens is the last director he or she worked for is contacted to see how things went. Savvy to this, Oliver would, for example, always be the first one back to the set from lunch; he'd be sitting there ready to start before most of the crew even got back. 'I think that showed a great respect for the work,' says Robe. 'I also think it showed a determination that he was going to do well in this role at this particular time in his life and career.' Ollie was also working with a very young actress, playing his wife, by the name of Reese Witherspoon. She'd not done much by that time and he was never less than the perfect gentleman, both patient and giving. 'They worked really well together,' says Robe. 'And Oliver was great in the role. He brought such gravitas to it. When he's on screen he completely commands your attention.'

With David gone, Josephine had taken over all the duties he'd been responsible for, while ICM remained Oliver's agent. After completing work on *Lonesome Dove* Josephine and Oliver were put in contact with an important agent who, it was hoped, might be able to help Ollie. But without David, any momentum that may have been taken by appearing in a high-profile project was lost.

In the summer of 1994 Oliver and Josephine decided to move from Guernsey. Partly it was a financial decision, the need to downsize once again because there wasn't enough work, and partly a realization that they had never been truly happy on the island. 'Guernsey is beautiful and we had lovely friends there,' says Josephine. 'But it was too small and there were too many pubs, and lots of tourists would find him and want to drink with him. I don't think he overly enjoyed his time in Guernsey. It was not the happiest time.'

Briefly they thought about a return to England, but

Josephine's village and those surrounding Pinkhurst had changed almost out of all recognition since they left, with locals priced out of the property market by rich Londoners using the area as a weekend retreat. To a large extent the heart and soul of these places had been ripped out: it was an England Ollie no longer recognized or wanted to be a part of.

'How about Ireland?' he suggested out of the blue one day. For years Ireland had held a special place in Ollie's heart. In the late sixties and early seventies, when life got too much, he'd often flee to his farmhouse in County Clare and as early as 1971 was telling reporters of his dream of one day moving there permanently. 'Ollie loved the Irish,' says David. 'The Irish people are lovely, they're spontaneously social.' But Josephine was unsure: save for a couple of trips to Dublin with Ollie she didn't know the country at all. By chance Josephine's mother Anne was about to embark on a driving holiday there and Josephine was elected to go with her. 'It'll give you a chance to suss the place out,' said Ollie. They went for ten days, driving huge distances, and Josephine fell in love with the idyllic scenery, coming back with handfuls of estate agents' details. Poring over them at home, Ollie and Josephine planned a trip themselves to the south-west to look at houses between the city of Cork and Skibbereen. 'We were trying to find somewhere pretty, and also near to the airport because of work and travelling, but we couldn't see anything we liked.'

It was Anne who found it, an advertisement for a house in *Horse and Hound* magazine. Castle McCarthy was a Georgian house located near Churchtown in north County Cork. It looked so promising that the couple headed over to Ireland to check it out. Having arrived in Churchtown, they popped into a pub called O'Brien's to order two whiskies and seek directions to the house. As they drove up to the place something just clicked. It was perfect and they sealed the deal that very day. While they were back in O'Brien's for more whiskies the bush telegraph was on fire that Oliver Reed was buying Castle McCarthy and the pub soon filled up with inquisitive locals wanting to see the famous film star.

Churchtown is a stone village surrounded by beautiful rolling countryside. Although it has changed a lot in recent years, when Ollie and Josephine moved in nothing much of anything went on. 'There was just one pub and one little shop,' recalls Josephine. 'I wondered at first how we'd manage because we didn't know anybody there. When we moved to Guernsey we already knew lots of people, but we didn't know anybody in Ireland. No one. And I remember thinking, Jesus, what are we doing?' At first the locals were understandably suspicious of their motives for moving there, thinking they'd just be using Castle McCarthy as a holiday home. 'But when they realized we'd sold everything and this was our home, they were lovely,' says Josephine. 'And we very quickly made some lovely friends.'

The house itself wasn't particularly spacious, but what had first caught Ollie's fancy was its eighteen acres of land, another chance to create one of his wild gardens. The first thing he did, aside from finding a space to stand his old faithful Hornby, was to lay a stone path through the grounds. Then up went some fencing and a gazebo and another brick wall that was made to look like it had been there a hundred years. Finally the trees. 'He loved trees,' says Josephine. 'He was always planting trees for the next generation. Always.' And in Ireland Ollie put up something like three hundred hazels and Scots pines, largely to encourage one of his favourite animals, the red squirrel. As with all of his previous homes, he adored creating a space in which nature was left alone to roam. From his bedroom window he often looked through binoculars across the fields, watching a family of hares playing in the field, or a pair of hawks that lived nearby.

In another field Ollie grew vegetables and, in a tradition

that began at Broome Hall, he pitched his gardening prowess against that of other local enthusiasts in an annual vegetable-growing competition. One year it might be beans or marrows and then onions. 'And every year we'd pile down to the local pub for the weighing ceremony,' remembers Josephine. 'And he'd proudly present whatever he'd grown. I don't think he ever won anything, but it never stopped him trying.' One gardening story that still brings a smile to Josephine's face is the time she strapped Ollie into a large grass strimmer and then went off to meet someone for lunch. 'Coming back, he hadn't been able to get out of it, and there he was sitting in a chair in the lounge watching television with it still on.'

For the first time since his Broome Hall days Ollie decided against any major renovations of the house, so about all they did was to knock the kitchen through to the dining room to make it one big room. 'His main thing in Ireland was the garden,' says Josephine. More significantly, whereas Broome Hall had its cellar bar, Pinkhurst its cider shed and Guernsey its bar above the garage, Ollie didn't feel the need in Ireland to build anything at all. Had the great man finally mellowed? Many who knew him from this period suggest that indeed he had – slightly.

Much of that was down to his new life in Ireland. 'He was very content and happy here,' says Josephine. It was a very simple, rural existence. There would be the occasional day trip to Cork or Galway or maybe to the races, but mostly, in Josephine's words, 'We were homebodies.' And visitors were rare, especially those from Ollie's old roaring days. Paul and Nora Friday did pay him a visit, though. 'And he was so sweet,' says Nora. 'He spent days getting the bedrooms ready for you and things like that, just putting nice touches in, especially for our daughter Louise.'

Alex Higgins was another guest. They'd walk the dogs together, drink, and get up to their usual bravado. During one visit Ollie pulled a lance off the wall and chased Higgins round the house with it.

Conspicuous by their absence were David, Simon and Mark. None of them came to see Oliver in Ireland, proof perhaps of a growing remoteness between himself and his immediate family.

Certainly Oliver had chosen to distance himself from his father. When Kay, Simon's mother, died, the Epsom house was sold and Oliver bought Peter a flat in Wimbledon but seldom visited him. 'Ollie was really at a tangent to our lives then,' claims Simon. Josephine simply puts it down to the fact that the Reed siblings were never as needful of one another as perhaps other families were. It was never going to be, let's all get together for Sunday lunch and play happy families. 'They were all very fond of one another but they didn't need each other. So I don't think he was isolated in that sense.'

Sarah, on the other hand, made a number of trips over to Churchtown and was particularly struck by the change in her father. 'I think he felt he'd come home in Ireland. I think he found a great peace there. And he definitely had mellowed: we were getting on far better. He still wasn't always easy, but we were definitely more comfortable in each other's company.'

On one trip Sarah brought her boyfriend Mark to stay. Everything was going well, but it was noticeable that every time Mark went to put his hand on Sarah he'd get a stern look from Ollie. Later that evening, when Sarah wanted to go to bed, poor Mark was on the receiving end of one of Ollie's most menacing glares. 'Er, I'll be up later,' he said. He never was. 'My father couldn't cope with the idea of us being under the same roof in the same bed, he found that quite tricky, even though I was a grown woman,' explains Sarah. 'So he kept him up all night.'

Again one of Ollie's joys was walking the dogs and he'd continued his habit of picking up strays. By the time he died there were six living in the house. 'And all of them used to sleep on the bed,' says Sarah. 'He just loved them. His idea of bliss would be when he was in "clinic", or off the booze. It would be the cricket on the telly and all his dogs with him on the bed.' There's a delightful story of Oliver driving one day near Churchtown and spotting a dog in the middle of the road. He stopped the car at the same time as a woman going the other way. Both of them wound down their windows. 'How many have you got?' she asked. 'Five,' replied Ollie. 'I've got six, you take it,' said the woman.

In Ireland Sarah felt her father could relax more and be himself, without the aggro he could get sometimes in England and in Guernsey when someone wanted to take him on or drink him under the table. Here he could enjoy the craic in O'Brien's bar with his friends, gossip and laugh, or, if he wanted just to sit by himself and mind his own business, he was always given space to do so. 'Ireland made him feel very happy because everyone took him at face value. They didn't give a hoot about who or what he was. He was Ollie and he was a little bit eccentric and because of that he fitted in perfectly.'

Naturally Oliver made many a trip to O'Brien's: it became his second home and the landlord Pat O'Brien a close friend. 'Oliver was a pretty regular customer, but then he'd take a few days off, to give the system a chance to recover. When Oliver was in the pub he liked the place to be lively, he didn't like everybody just looking into their pints and saying nothing. So if that was happening he'd start off with a soliloquy from Shakespeare or one of his movie parts and he was hoping that somebody would tell him to just shut the fuck up. Sometimes it happened and sometimes it didn't.' Anyway it had the desired effect of creating a good atmosphere.

On those nights when the bar was busy the drinks were usually on Ollie. 'Could I have a canter round the paddock?' he'd say when he wanted to buy a round. As in the past, there was a core group of people Ollie drank with but also a bunch of freeloaders whom he tolerated and was never judgemental about. O'Brien remembers one old friend coming down to visit all the way from Northern Ireland. When his taxi arrived the driver presented him with a bill for £450, which Oliver paid without question.

O'Brien recalls few occasions when things got out of control with Oliver. There was one evening, however, when the pub was very quiet, just Ollie and this other fellow who was dressed in what looked like army fatigues. Oliver walked over to him and asked, 'Are you in the IRA?', which was like a red rag to a bull. Straightaway the two men squared up to each other and O'Brien had to jump in and separate them. He manhandled Ollie out of the door and the other guy was allowed to finish his pint in peace. When the man left the bar he drove his car methodically around the roundabout that faced the pub, blazing his headlights straight into Ollie and O'Brien's eyes. He did this six times and each time O'Brien did his best to stop Ollie jumping on the car's bonnet.

As an extra service to his customers O'Brien took horse-racing bets. Sharing his love of horses and racing, Ollie treated him one year to a trip to Epsom for the Derby. They both went over dressed up to the nines in top hat and tails and stayed at the Gatwick Hilton. 'We went out that night and had the usual gargantuan amount of drink,' recalls O'Brien. 'We came back to the hotel and there was this fat, loud American fella with red braces, and Oliver took exception to him straightaway and called the head of security to have him removed from the hotel but to no avail, so he was absolutely in foul humour after that.'

The following morning Johnny Placett hired a stretch limo full of booze to take them to the races. 'And Ollie headed straight into the bar in the Queen's Stand and started ordering champagne,' says O'Brien. 'And he was there for the whole day, he never saw a horse. The Queen, she usually comes out before the Derby to have a look at the horses, and she was coming down the stairs and Oliver was lying down on the floor, with empty champagne bottles all around him, and he was just sober enough to realize who was there and to do the necessary, and he doffed his hat and said, "Ma'am".' When the day finished O'Brien went to collect Ollie and help him back to the car. 'And of course everybody recognized him and they were all shouting, "Good on you, Ollie!"'

The Wound That Never Healed

Oliver had been largely inactive as a film actor for years, though he did have a role in the quirky comedy *Funny Bones*, set in Blackpool, which was so messed about with in the editing that it amounted to little more than a cameo in the finished version. Then, right out of the blue, he received an offer to appear in a Hollywood blockbuster from the director of *Die Hard 2* and *Cliffhanger*. Renny Harlin was planning a 100-million-dollar pirate romp called *Cutthroat Island* starring his wife Geena Davis and wanted Ollie to appear briefly as a scurvy old seadog. In November 1994 Ollie flew to Malta to prepare for what was undoubtedly the biggest production of his career. He lasted twenty-four hours.

At the pre-production party a well-fortified Ollie thought it would be a wheeze to show everyone the tattoo on his cock. Star Geena Davis was not amused, and when he woke up the next morning he was handed a cursory note telling him he'd been fired for 'inappropriate behaviour related to alcohol'. For his friends and supporters it was all too common a tale. 'Oliver lost work through that kind of behaviour, no question,' says Michael Winner.

Vic Armstrong, who'd last seen Oliver over a decade before in Iraq, was stunt coordinator on *Cutthroat Island* and remembers coming down that morning into the hotel breakfast room and seeing Ollie all dressed up and packed. 'Hello, Ollie,' offered Vic. Ollie grimaced. 'Fucking assholes. I'm outta here.' And he was gone. 'And that was the last time I ever saw Ollie, bless him. But it was so typical of him, and perfect.'

It was back to basics again, with Ollie making in quick succession two risible films that blessedly never saw daylight: *Superbrain* was a heist movie and *Russian Roulette – Moscow 95* a hopeless thriller filmed in Minsk. At least he found himself again in the warm company of Barbara Carrera. The two hadn't met since making *Condorman* some fourteen years before and Barbara found Ollie 'a different person, much more sedate. He was such a gentleman, very easy to be around and to talk to, very congenial, very courteous.'

While Barbara was no doubt pleased with this new version of Oliver, there was one incident that reminded her of the old Ollie who'd half-thrown her off a balcony in Monte Carlo. One of the producers on *Russian Roulette* held a birthday celebration at a local castle to which the entire cast and crew were invited. 'We arrived at eleven o'clock in the morning,' remembers Barbara. 'And to meet us was this truck full of vodka. By lunchtime everyone was totally wasted.' After lunch most of the men went outside into the courtyard for bouts of arm-wrestling, with Oliver predictably at the helm. After about an hour he returned to the restaurant and was behaving in a manner Barbara had recognized before, with that glazed look in his eyes, and she knew what was coming. But this time she'd the experience to know how to handle him. 'And I was drunk enough that I didn't care. Ollie grabbed a dining-room chair and held it up as if he was going to smash it over someone's head; it was very menacing. And I said, "Oliver, put that chair down!" He looked at me with this meek expression like a child and he put it down and just left to continue arm-wrestling with the crew. The next day I remember we showed up on the set and everybody had bandages.'

Both *Superbrain* and *Russian Roulette* were directed by Menahem Golan, the former head of Cannon Films, who thoroughly enjoyed working with Oliver and cherished his mischievous sense of humour. On *Russian Roulette* the cast and crew often had dinner together, 'And a couple of times Oliver took out his prick and beat the table with it yelling, "Give me better food, give me meat!" The whole crew screamed, especially the girls. Ollie was really fun and very talented, but he did drink a lot in the evening and had hangovers in the morning, but when we came to shoot he was super-perfect. He was very professional, we didn't argue too much, we had great communication, he let me get on with my directing. I loved him, I simply loved him.'

A little better was a low-budget British film called *The Bruce*, shot in Scotland in the spring of 1995. It told the story of Robert the Bruce and his rebellion against the English and the Bishop, played by Oliver, who recognized the Bruce's claim to be King of Scotland. The bulk of filming took place in Peebles and Ollie was put up at the rather grand Hydro Hotel but, according to Ali Wilson, an extra on the film, he was swiftly kicked out after insulting the guests and rehoused in the Park Hotel. 'I understand that he was kicked out of there too but in the meantime had discovered the Crown Hotel and loved the people and so decided himself he would bloody well move into the Crown.'

While it had only six small rooms, Ollie was perfectly happy at the Crown since it didn't have the aloofness of the Hydro. He soon made friends with the builders and plasterers who drank every night in the public bar, although he only narrowly avoided a few fights. 'Some people tried to have a go at him,' says Wilson. 'A couple of young so-called hard men. I don't think any punches were ever thrown and Ollie gave as good as he got.' Another time Wilson came into the bar and Ollie was drinking with Brian Blessed, cast as Edward I. Both of them were clearly sozzled, and the more they drank, the louder they got. 'It was almost like a rock concert, Brian Blessed's voice was as loud as that, and Ollie wasn't too far behind. They were trying to upstage each other, almost like a shouting competition.'

As much as Ollie loved the Crown he wasn't keen on the public bar's plain wooden benches. Giving one of the staff £400, he ordered, 'Go along to the local furniture shop and get me a bloody chair.' So off this guy went and bought a Parker Knoll armchair and carried it back and stuck it in the corner. For the rest of his time there that was Ollie's place. The chair has remained there ever since.

The Crown was owned by Peter Cassidy, who became a drinking companion during Ollie's stay, and there were tales of all-night drinking sessions and staff arriving the next morning to find them lying unconscious under tables. For the rest of his life Ollie kept in touch with Cassidy, paying him the odd visit and even holding his sixtieth birthday party at the Crown. 'Although he didn't actually make it himself,' says Wilson. 'He was taken to bed before the party really got started. Ollie showed up at quarter past seven for about half an hour and then Josephine ushered him upstairs and that was it. The party continued without him.'

The Bruce was shown barely anywhere, a pity since Oliver's performance proved he could still memorize his lines and hold the attention of an audience with his voice and screen presence. If anything, work became even scarcer afterwards. But he did give a nicely judged performance as General Safan in *Jeremiah*, which was about the prophet, played by Patrick Dempsey, who heard the call to preach against the moral corruption in ancient Jerusalem, and which was shown on US television in 1998.

Then, at home in Ireland, on 9 May 1997 Oliver heard that his father had passed away. Over the past few years their relationship had remained distant and difficult. They'd chat on the phone, which, according to Josephine, 'was probably the best way for them to communicate'. While she believes Oliver was very fond of his father, the psychological wound of his perceived cowardice had still not healed. 'He always used to go on about his father being a conscientious objector. He could never see the strength in that position. And he kept saying how awful it had been as a child to be the son of a conscientious objector.' Johnny Placett recalls times when Ollie would goad his father, 'You bloody conscientious objector.' The words were almost spat into his face.

At the funeral both David and Oliver were unable to read the eulogy, so Simon agreed to take on the duty. 'And I remember thinking, I can't do this, I was flooding up with tears. Then Ollie went up and just danced on the stage, he didn't say anything, he just did a little Irish jig and made people laugh, and it stopped me crying and I went up and I was able to read the eulogy.' It was a touching moment, something singularly lacking when his mother passed away in 1990. Josephine was with Ollie when the news came and she expected to see some emotion from him, but there wasn't any. 'I remember hugging him and him not falling to pieces or anything.'

During the last years of her life Ollie's relationship with Marcia was perhaps even worse than the one he'd had with Peter. It was tenuous at best, as it had been for most of his life. Then when her husband and Oliver's stepfather, Bill Sulis, died, Ollie joked on the phone that if she liked he'd come down and dance round his grave like a Red Indian. Not unnaturally, Marcia refused to have him anywhere near the funeral and, according to David, they never spoke to each other again.

With Peter, it had been his cowardice. With Marcia, she'd been the cause of the marriage breaking up. It's doubtful whether a child ever completely gets over a parent's divorce, and it certainly affected Oliver's relationships with the opposite sex. Just as he had been throughout his time with

Jacquie, Josephine admits that he was extremely possessive of her, especially if she was in a social situation and talking with someone closer to her own age. 'Then he'd panic slightly. I don't know why because I was completely and utterly in love with the man. I guess it was something to do with the age gap between us and also this feeling he had that women always left him. But they didn't, only he felt they did. And I'd say that was probably insecurity from his mother leaving him when he was young, just being very insecure and not trusting women to stay and be a constant.'

With so few opportunities for work, Ollie spent his days peacefully with Josephine at Castle McCarthy or chewing the cud with Pat O'Brien in his pub. They'd watch horse-racing on the telly together, though Ollie rarely if ever bet. He was a fan of the Boat Race, though, because it was a test of strength and endurance, an avid Cambridge man, and followed American football, especially the Pittsburgh Steelers. Sometimes they'd just talk, about subjects ranging from sport to gardening. 'You could have a great conversation with Ollie, especially before he got to the stage where he was over the top. But he never talked about his films or acting or Hollywood, you'd have to drag it out of him. I was very fond of Oliver. He was a great character.'

Whisky was a favourite tipple at O'Brien's, but Oliver was happy to drink whatever the person he was with was drinking, even Guinness, of which he wasn't a great lover. At home Josephine purposely kept Ollie off the whisky, since it had been his downfall for years, and he knew it too. 'Whisky was when Mr Nasty came out to play,' says Mark. 'He used to like single malts, he loved the buzz of it, but you could see the edge that it gave him.' So at home he drank Gordon's gin and Schweppes tonic, with plenty of ice. Or Grolsch. For a special race meeting that happened every year at a nearby course he used to mix a punchbowl and invite all his friends to have a drink before they set off. 'He'd have everything inside, including moonshine,' recalls O'Brien. 'It was absolutely lethal. Everybody would get cock-eyed and fall about the place. And if the punchbowl wasn't finished he'd bring it down to my pub and he'd make everybody there cock-eyed as well.'

Many a time Ollie left O'Brien's in a less than sober condition and more than once he was stopped by the police for drink-driving. 'He didn't have an accident or anything,' says O'Brien. 'And when he used to drive under the influence he'd drive at five miles per hour. There was no danger that he was ever going to do any damage.' After all those Aston Martins, Rollers and Jensens, Oliver's last car was a Suzuki jeep, which he called 'the battle wagon'. Sarah remembers it as an amazing car. 'He could drive it into things, back it into things, and it got him home every time.'

After living in Churchtown for several years Ollie and Josephine felt they had been embraced by the community. And Ollie was always keen to put something back. One morning he read in his local newspaper of a little girl who lived not far away who'd been born with the rare physical condition known as total amelia, that is, with no arms or legs. Her name was Joanne O'Riordan. Immediately, Ollie pledged his support to help fund the medical services she would need. And, as well as contributing handsomely himself, he also fronted the campaign. In 2012 Joanne, then sixteen, addressed the General Assembly of the United Nations. Ollie would have been proud.

Gladiator

Oliver hadn't made a movie now for two years. It was his old friend Michael Winner who brought him back into the limelight with a role in *Parting Shots*, a black comedy about a man, played by rock star Chris Rea, who learns he has only six weeks left to live and so decides to take revenge on the people who screwed him over during his life. The film is poor, but Ollie is effective and beguiling as an ageing hit man. Having promised to behave and not drink, Ollie was true to his word. The problems started after filming, when Winner was plagued by a series of bizarre phone calls, often late at night. The conversation would invariably begin, 'I love you, Michael,' before sliding into a series of slurred messages. 'That's very nice, Oliver,' Winner would say. 'Is Josephine there?' The phone would be handed over and Winner would chat with Josephine while Ollie shouted thoughts and opinions in the background. Suddenly Winner would hear over the line the dull thud of Ollie hitting the floor. 'I've got to go,' Josephine would say. 'Oliver needs me.'

While editing the film Winner requested Oliver's services back in London to dub one particular scene because of an awful sound recording on location. Phoning the Hampstead hotel where Ollie was staying, Winner was told that he had gone out the previous evening, got blind drunk, and been arrested outside the tube station. Winner called Hampstead police station. 'I understand my friend Mr Reed spent the night with you.' The desk sergeant replied, 'We've just released him. He was arrested at ten o'clock for being drunk and disorderly, but we haven't charged him because he was so charming.' Minutes later a taxi drew up outside Winner's house and Ollie clambered out. He was in no fit state to dub his voice and the recording session proved useless. It was a far cry from the days when he was known as the best in the business at 'looping', often able to do it on the first take. Producers would block out an eight-hour day and Ollie would come in and do it in an hour and a half.

As he left Winner's house, Oliver turned to his old friend and said, 'You know, I mustn't travel without Josephine. She looks after me.' The two men embraced. 'He was very humble and ashamed that he'd spent the night in the cells,' says Winner. 'And then he went off, and that was the last time I ever saw Oliver Reed.'

Midway through production of *Parting Shots* Ollie sauntered over to Winner on the set one day to reveal that he'd been approached by Ridley Scott to appear in his forthcoming movie *Gladiator*, but that the director wanted him to do a reading. In essence this was an audition, something he hadn't done since his early acting days. 'I can't believe it! I mean, I'm a star.'

'Oliver, don't fuck with me,' said Winner. 'You're not a fucking star. You're out of work and you're not old enough to retire. You haven't got enough money to retire, so you need a third act to your career. Obviously they think if you're working with me you can't be as drunk as people think you are. So go to Ridley and read. End of story, Oliver. And if he wants you to read twice, read twice.'

Josephine likewise urged her husband to swallow his pride and to go and read for Ridley, a director, after all, whom he hugely respected because of *The Duellists*. 'And I also made him watch *Alien*. Although I don't think Oliver necessarily enjoyed *Alien*.'

In the end Ollie put in a call to Simon. 'This Ridley Scott wants me to audition. Now come on!' Simon was convinced it was a good idea. 'No, no, don't worry, I'm going to do it. But a bit fucking odd.'

It wasn't so much hurt pride that made Ollie reluctant to read for *Gladiator*: it was more fear. 'He was pretty terrified at the prospect,' reveals Simon. 'Having not done it for so long. But I think Ridley had already made up his mind about casting Oliver. I think he was just making sure Ollie was all right, he just wanted a little confirmation.' And so it proved. The deal was done. Ollie had the plum role of Proximo, a world-weary slave merchant and ex-gladiator. Little did anyone know at the time how significant a piece of casting it would turn out to be.

Gladiator had been long in the planning. The script was developed over a two-year period during which Proximo had emerged as one of the most interesting characters, and it was vital that the right actor be found to play him. 'The casting of Proximo was daunting,' recalls producer Douglas Wick. 'Here was this former gladiator, so we had to have someone credible as a fighter, which many of the great English thespians aren't. He had to have that larger-than-life quality, that he could send men to their deaths with a twinkle in his eye and you would forgive him for it. We also knew we had Russell Crowe in the lead, so we had to find someone that would be daunting and intimidating to Russell. He also had to be a great actor.'

A shortlist was drawn up featuring pretty much all the top British actors of that age group, with a few Americans thrown into the mix. As discussions developed and the character evolved, Oliver emerged as not only the obvious choice, but the only choice. He had the charisma, he had the gravitas. 'There were some questions about his viability,' says Wick. 'But Ridley spent some time with him and felt very comfortable with him. We also did our own investigations and people said he was behaving professionally and those representing him were assuring us he was a different guy.'

It was reported that the film's insurers did write to Oliver asking how much he still drank. Ollie returned the form, saying, 'Only at parties.' The insurers wrote back, 'How many parties do you go to?' They were right to be worried: Oliver was still getting into trouble, having recently gone on Sky News live and told presenter Kay Burley to 'Shake your funky stuff to me, hot thing.' She was eight months pregnant at the time and he was clearly drunk. 'He wouldn't leave,' Kay later said. 'So we had to get security to take him out.' In January 1999 he was arrested at Heathrow after throwing beer over shoppers at Terminal 1. He was given a caution and released. It was to be his last reported misdemeanour.

When Ollie and Josephine arrived in Morocco in February 1999 for his first scenes on *Gladiator*, it didn't take them long to grasp the magnitude of the production, the gargantuan sets, the hordes of costumed extras, and the stellar cast of Crowe, Joaquin Phoenix and Richard Harris. This was epic stuff indeed. After languishing in the cinematic wilderness for so long, Ollie was at last back playing with the big boys and, if the film was the hit he was expecting, it was going to completely resurrect his career. So it was no coincidence that Ollie now felt a desire to reach out to his family, to those he had estranged over the years or allowed to drift away, especially his two brothers.

Since quitting as his manager, David hadn't really talked much with Oliver. Nor had their parting been terribly amicable. 'But then he suddenly rang me saying we must meet up. It was only because he was in work again, he was earning, he felt secure. So he rang and said, "David, we're going to be in Malta soon. Why don't you sail down?" I told him, "Do you realize how bloody far it is in a boat that only does five miles an hour?" So in the end we didn't make it, but it was quite revealing that he wanted to touch base again.'

Simon was also invited to visit the *Gladiator* set. His relationship with Oliver had been at best cool these past few years, after he'd had a coffee cup thrown at him in a restaurant. 'I think he meant it as a warning shot. I'd said something flash. It clipped the side of my head and there was a bit of blood, nothing serious, but I said, "That's enough, I'm not driving you home, you can make your own fucking way home. And I'm not talking to you any more," and I left the restaurant. And we didn't speak for quite a while.'

It was an upsetting incident, because Simon had always shared a strong bond with his elder brother, even though there'd always been a little bit of healthy competition between the two of them. 'Ollie wasn't a jealous man, though he was always jealous of my youth, that I was younger than him. And I was quite successful with women, and he was pretty rude to most of the women I was with. But I don't think that was out of jealousy, it was just Ollie being provocative.' But things had never really got out of hand physically before. Well, maybe once or twice: Simon does recall another incident in a restaurant back in the mid-seventies. Joe Frazier was about to fight Muhammad Ali and the brothers got into an argument about who was going to win. Simon contested that Ali would never get caught, while Ollie fancied Frazier. 'He's not that fast,' said Simon. 'It's like you and me, Ollie. You're bigger than me, but you wouldn't be able to catch me.' Fuck, thought Simon, big mistake. 'By this stage we're outside and it got physical. I split his lip, and he punched me in the face, and some people broke it up because it was getting quite heavy. Actually it wasn't too bad. Yes, we had a fight, but I think we were all right after it and got pissed. But when he threw that coffee cup at me we didn't really talk much after that, and then this conversation started happening about how excited he was about *Gladiator* and the future. And I was really thrilled because there had been a sadness in me about the period we didn't see each other. I felt he was easing his way back.'

After three weeks in Morocco, during which time Ollie never touched a drop, cast and crew moved to Malta, where the mighty Colosseum and other ancient structures of Rome had been spectacularly recreated at Fort Ricasoli on the northeast coast. Booked into a palatial five-star hotel in nearby Valletta, the island's capital, Ollie and Josephine settled in for what was going to be a long stay. As they'd done many times before, on days off the pair loved to explore and do the whole tourist bit. And it was on one of these pleasant strolls around the winding and narrow streets of Valletta that they happened upon the Pub in Archbishop Street, a place Ollie immediately gravitated towards and began to use as his local. 'Wherever Dad went he always tried to find somewhere that was like his little community watering hole,' says Sarah. 'He had to find that kind of pub environment wherever he was, just to make him feel at home.' As a bonus there was also a good Chinese restaurant nearby. 'So we would go to the Pub for a drink and then have a Chinese for lunch and then go back to the hotel,' says Josephine. This became a ritual on their days off and at weekends.

Ollie was delighted to learn that David Hemmings had a small role in the film and was staying at the same hotel. They hadn't seen each other for a decade but soon caught up on old times. Hemmings noticed how splendid Oliver appeared. 'With grey flowing hair, a silver beard and a white linen jacket, he looked the quintessential expatriate, swirling an arm at the assembled company, as if he were Her Majesty's representative.' Yet he was distressed to see that the old bad Ollie was still capable of rearing its ugly head. Russell Crowe had organized a cricket match between the cast and crew and a local team. Ollie was supposed to be playing but was instead found by Hemmings at the hotel bar 'well beyond the danger level on his inebriation scale'. With Ollie refusing to leave and feeling the urge to chin someone, the hotel management moved in. Hemmings quickly explained that if they tried to get Ollie out now there'd be real trouble. 'Let me give him a drink, then I'll calm him down and get him upstairs without a scene.' This was accomplished but, according to Hemmings, Oliver was subsequently banned from all public parts of the hotel except the swimming pool.

It was for incidents like this that the British press had encamped in Malta. They seized on one report that while drunk Ollie challenged Crowe to a bout of fisticuffs but the Antipodean star refused to come out of his trailer until the baiting had ceased. Whether this was true or not, Crowe found Oliver difficult to get on with and has spoken about a 'weird energy' that seemed to encircle him. 'I have seen him walk down the street in Malta drunk as a lord and just hit anybody he got near to,' Crowe has said. 'I just found that to be not impressive.' A bit rich, coming from someone who, if as reported, once bit a chunk out of a man's neck and spat it back in his face during a fight in a Sydney bar.

Simon believes Russell's dislike for Oliver probably stemmed from the fact that he saw in him something that was a little too close to home. And Mike Higgins, who was location manager in Malta, says that Ollie was nothing less than totally professional during his time on *Gladiator*. 'I never saw him drunk on the set.'

After five weeks on the island Oliver was looking forward to his final week of filming and going home. On the evening of Saturday, 1 May, Josephine and Ollie invited Hemmings and his wife Lucy out for dinner to a restaurant in Valletta bay. Ollie wasn't drinking heavily, just a couple of glasses of wine. The conversation was merry, with Josephine describing their life together in Ireland in idyllic terms, but Hemmings couldn't help feeling that Ollie was in 'reflective' mood that night. Back at the hotel, they enjoyed coffee in the bar, where the conversation continued but not for long, for Ollie complained of being very tired and he and Josephine went to bed. Hemmings later observed that he'd thought Oliver 'looked worn out in a way I'd never seen him'.

Sunday, 2 May was just like every other Sunday the Reeds had enjoyed during their stay in Malta: a bit of sightseeing, shopping, and a coffee in a charming café in the market. Ready for some lunch, Oliver and Josephine headed towards Archbishop Street but the Chinese restaurant wasn't open yet so instinctively they headed for the Pub. Inside the television was showing the run-up to the Grand Prix from San Marino. A fan of the McLaren team, Ollie got some drinks in and settled down in his favourite chair to watch. He'd never see the end of the race. Even now, when a new Formula One season starts, Josephine gets a sickening, deadening feeling in the pit of her stomach.

As the race got under way the door of the pub crashed open and a gang of Royal Navy ratings from HMS *Cumberland* burst in. Straightaway they recognized Ollie, who, unable to resist anyone in uniform, invited the whole bunch over to watch the race at his table. Out went the order, it was black rums all round, and, as the booze flowed and fuelled his bravado, Ollie challenged the youngsters to an arm-wrestling competition. He was in his element, he was loving every minute.

After about an hour the sailors got up to leave. Ollie happily signed autographs and then, suddenly overcome by exhaustion, fell asleep. 'He was sitting on the floor,' says Josephine. 'So we propped him up on the bench while the rest of us carried on watching the Grand Prix. Then I realized something was wrong. I turned to see if he was all right and he wasn't looking very good. He had gone rigid and he was blue around the lips.' Immediately grasping the seriousness of the situation, Josephine asked for an ambulance to be called. As they waited, Ollie was given mouth-to-mouth resuscitation and heart massages by the staff, but the only sign of any life in him was his fist repeatedly banging on the table. When the ambulance arrived, Ollie was bundled into the back. Josephine jumped in too and it sped off. Inside, as the vehicle made its way through the twisty, bumpy streets, the medics were violently buffeted backwards and forwards, so Josephine grabbed hold of their belts, terrified they might fall over and lose precious seconds in their battle to keep her husband alive.

At the hospital, Ollie was quickly taken into an operating theatre. The wife of the publican had accompanied Josephine and sat with her during the long, unbearable wait until the doctors came out. It was the worst news imaginable. Ollie was gone. He was sixty-one. He'd probably never regained consciousness, and his last words had been spoken in the pub: 'help' and 'hurt'. Josephine can't remember him saying anything after that.

Asked if she wanted to see the body, Josephine said yes, she would, and was led into the room. All was quiet as she stared down at Oliver for what would be the last time. He was at peace now, but his body still showed signs of the frantic efforts the doctors had made to bring him back into the living world. Josephine asked if they could at least remove some of the tubes, but it wasn't allowed. 'So I had to say goodbye to him with them all sticking out of his mouth.'

Back in England, Simon was relaxing at home watching the Grand Prix when the phone rang. It was Josephine. 'Simon he's gone, he's gone.' There was Simon thinking, gone where? Left her? 'He's gone,' the voice said again. 'He's GONE, Simon.' For a few seconds Simon thought this was some sick practical joke and that Ollie would soon come on the line yelling, 'Gotcha!' 'Because Ollie was indestructible. Having lived past forty, which I never thought he would, he was destined to be a ninety-year-old grumpy old man. So it made no sense. I thought Josephine was taking the piss, I thought this was a wind-up, so it took me a little while to take it in. Then I suddenly realized, fuck, he's gone. He's really gone. I couldn't get my head round it, it just seemed so wrong.' In a near daze Simon called Mark and then

David. Walking out into his garden, he picked up a couple of small pebbles and, like a little boy, started throwing them hard against the garden wall.

Mark was walking a dog on Wimbledon Common when Simon called. He'd shared a few drinks with his father just before he went off to make *Gladiator* and there was no sense of the tragedy that was waiting for him. 'I remember him leaving my Wimbledon flat about three in the morning, walking down the stairs, and just catching his eye and saying, "I love you." It's a memory that I hold because it was the last time I saw him.'

David was in Majorca working on his boat when the news reached him. It didn't altogether come as a shock. 'I think deep down we always knew that Ollie would die relatively young. When I ran that office in Piccadilly Circus as his manager there was a newspaper vendor outside and when I arrived some mornings there would be a headline like, Oliver Reed arrested for something or other, and I'd think, oh, for fuck's sake! And I remember thinking that it wouldn't surprise me if I left my office one day and the headline was "Oliver Reed Dead."'

Sarah was at work when it happened. Finishing her shift in a restaurant, she checked her answering machine for any messages and recognized Mark. 'And I could just tell by the tone of his voice that something was wrong. I rang him and he told me and I behaved really awfully: I said, "I don't believe you. I need to speak to somebody else." He said to call Simon. So then I spoke to Simon and he explained what happened and that was that, the world had changed.'

Sarah had rung her father when he'd been in Morocco and he'd asked her to come and see him there, but she couldn't get the time off work. When she rang again he'd already left for Malta. 'That's how rubbish we were as a family: we didn't keep up, we didn't speak weekly.' When she reached him in Malta, Ollie told her, 'It's horrible here, don't come here. I'll be home in a month's time.' Of course he wasn't. 'And I hadn't seen him for a year, because it wasn't always easy to be in his company. It was that whole thing that, as much as you wanted to see someone it wasn't always pleasant, so sometimes you don't put yourself out of your comfort zone. I regretted that for a long time because obviously I thought I would have many more years.'

Sarah remembers the last time her father tried to talk to her on the phone, ringing her at work, but by the time she reached the phone he'd gone, having got bored of waiting, and Sarah never spoke to him again. A week later he was dead. 'When he died I thought, I wish I'd got to that phone quicker.'

Trying as best she could to compose herself, Sarah rang Jacquie. 'Daddy's dead,' she said, her voice trembling. Jacquie was shattered. Like others, she couldn't quite believe it was true. 'He was the sort of person you thought would go on for ever, that he would always be there. I almost felt like saying to Sarah, "Are you sure?" But he died as he would have wanted to die. Josephine was with him and he was doing his usual arm-wrestling with the sailors.'

Back in Valletta, Josephine had called her brother William, who promised to catch the first available flight. Until then she was on her own. It was David Hemmings and Lucy who came to the rescue. 'They were wonderful, both of them sat with me for ages, just keeping me company, looking after me until I said it was all right for them to leave. Then I just curled up into a ball and waited for my brother.'

As Josephine fell into a fretful sleep the news of Ollie's passing was spreading around Malta. By morning, as the cast and crew of *Gladiator* rolled on to the set to begin another day's work, everybody was devastated by what had happened. 'They couldn't believe it,' recalls location manager Mike Higgins. 'There was such a sadness on the set that day because Ollie had really endeared himself to the whole crew and everybody was really, really upset.'

Word of Ollie's death was also filtering out to the world and being taken in by friends and colleagues, most of whom were shocked by the seemingly sudden nature of it. 'I was heartbroken when he died,' remembers Murray Melvin. 'I phoned Georgina Hale. I said, "He's gone. The silly bugger. What did he bloody do that for?" We all loved him. He was a lovely human being. He really was.'

Michael Winner had spoken with Oliver on the phone just two days earlier. A reporter was going over to see him and Winner had urged, 'Do me a favour, dear, don't throw her in the pool, don't take her knickers down and hurl her round the room. Please just be very nice to her.'

'Michael, I promise you,' Ollie told him. 'I've only got a couple more shots in the movie and they've offered me a great role on television.' That role was in *My Uncle Silas*, produced by the team who'd been behind another H. E. Bates adaptation, *The Darling Buds of May*; it was something Ollie was really looking forward to doing. His replacement would be Albert Finney.

Winner could sense in Ollie's voice an optimism about his professional future that he hadn't heard for so long. 'He was just so thrilled because he thought he was washed up and now he was back. Then I got the call, Oliver Reed's dead, and I just burst into tears. Terrible.'

Carol Lynley was at home in California when a friend told her the news. 'And I just started shaking. It was like a chemical reaction, of shock. I hadn't seen him in years, but he was such a huge figure in my life. He was so full of life, and he should have had a longer life, but I don't think he expected to live very long. He went out the way he would have wanted. I could never see Ollie sitting around in an old people's home.'

Michael Christensen had the same feeling. 'I thought, far better that than in a cancer ward. Arm-wrestling with the navy, in a bar, drinking rum, that's the way he'd have wanted to go. But it was much too soon.' And also totally unexpected.

Oliver had undergone a strict medical for *Gladiator*, and passed. But Pat O'Brien recalls Ollie telling him, just before leaving Churchtown for Morocco, that he'd been having niggling pains in his chest and felt that he might have angina. Ollie had also paid a brief visit to Dorking to have some work done on his teeth and met Johnny Placett, who recalls, 'I picked him up from the Hilton at Gatwick, where he was staying. We stopped at a café. He just had an orange juice, and I remember him saying to me, "I haven't been too well. I've had to go off the drink a little bit. And I've been having some pains in my chest, but don't say anything."' Then he went off to make *Gladiator*.

As far as the family was concerned, however, there was no indication of any health issues. Later, though, a photograph turned up that was taken a week before he died, 'And he didn't look like a well man,' says Sarah. 'But I can't imagine my father would have slowed down too much for anything, although he was terrified of death.'

Back at the hotel, Josephine was awoken by her brother William. She was feeling a little stronger now with a familiar face by her side, and when Mark and Sarah arrived her resolve and fortitude were further strengthened. Already the world's press had descended. Josephine remembers not being able to look out of her hotel room, 'because I could see them lined up way down the street, with their huge lenses, so I just kept away from the windows. I suppose they were just doing their job.' Mark and Sarah were less philosophical, having been harassed on their separate flights. And when they both decided to pay a visit to the Pub the next day they had to be smuggled out of the back door of the hotel. They spent a cursory fifteen minutes in the place, a bizarre and chilling episode. 'I don't know why we went there,' admits Sarah. 'It was quite a morbid thing that Mark and I felt we needed to do. I suppose we wanted to know where it had all gone wrong.'

Then there was a trip to the hospital, because the authorities required a second person to identify the body. Brother and sister stood outside the mortuary door debating whether or not they should go inside, then William went in alone. Coming back out, he shook his head and said, 'I wouldn't.' For Sarah, the decision had been made. 'I don't think I wanted to go in anyway. He was so vibrant that to see him like that was not the right way.' Afterwards both made a plea to the hospital authorities to dispense with a post-mortem since it was obvious he'd died of a heart attack. 'We didn't want him interfered with in a foreign land,' says Mark. 'It was a sprawling hospital with people outside smoking fags, it was just really quite horrid.' But for the hospital to have dealt with this request would have caused a further week's delay, so the post-mortem was carried out, since everyone felt the need to get Ollie back home as quickly as possible.

Given this aim, the Reed family will be for ever beholden to the film company, who behaved with remarkable compassion and kindness. 'They were incredible,' says Josephine. 'They looked after everything and told me not to worry about a thing. They were amazing.' In Hollywood, when news broke of Ollie's death, Steven Spielberg, whose DreamWorks was behind *Gladiator*, sent an assistant to Malta to help smooth things over and sort out any problems. Some of the cast also helped, doing simple things like taking the family out to dinner, and Mark found a strange bond developing with Joaquin Phoenix. 'There were a few people on the set that instantly identified with my father, and one of them was Joaquin: he just instantly identified with and related to him. Obviously Joaquin had been through his own challenges with his own family.'

It was people like Joaquin Phoenix who helped Mark get through what he describes as 'a weird, empty, hollow time'. Having to go and see the British consulate and collect his dad's passport and have the corner of it chopped off, picking up his few belongings, and being whisked back to the hotel, driving in through back entrances to avoid the press, using service lifts. 'My memories of it were just remarkably sad and horrid and just wanting to get out of there.'

After a couple of days a flight was arranged for the family to take Ollie back to Ireland. Everyone had just sat down in the plane when they realized they had company: the entire British press contingent had booked the same flight. 'And there we were,' says Josephine, 'laughing hysterically and blubbing the next, emotionally all over the place. But they didn't write a dickie bird, and they didn't print any pictures when we left Malta. So, as grotty as the press boys can be, I think some of them had a soft spot for Ollie.'

From Cork airport the family drove thirty-six miles by hearse to the town of Buttevant, not far from Churchtown, where the funeral home was conveniently located next door to one of Ollie's favourite pubs. 'The Garda had blocked the street so that we could get in with the hearse and unload Oliver,' recalls Josephine. 'And then we went next door to the pub.' By the time they arrived in Churchtown it was late, but still the street was full of people who'd been waiting to welcome them home. O'Brien's pub was crammed with friends and, although exhausted, Josephine found the strength to speak with each and every one.

'People were just absolutely and utterly genuinely touched and lovely,' remembers Mark, for whom one incident in particular stands out. The following morning he was in O'Brien's when he took a call from a friend. The signal was awful, so he stepped outside into the street. 'And there was this young boy with a hurley stick and a ball just knocking it around, and as I was talking to this friend I suddenly started crying. When I finished the call and was walking back inside, this little boy came up to me and said, "Mister, I thought I'd let you know, there's a man over there in a car with a camera." Ireland was amazing in terms of the affinity that people felt for Oliver. They were very protective of who he was to them. So when I go back there each year, it's just the same, it's like walking into a community where I only left yesterday. Amazing people.'

It had been a long day and Josephine was tired as they left O'Brien's well into the evening, but she wasn't looking forward to returning to a home that was going to seem incredibly empty without Oliver's presence. Opening the door, Mark walked in first, and suddenly Ollie's dogs ran into the hall, going crazy. 'They thought it was my dad,' says Sarah. 'Because there was this big tall man who looked like him and sounded like him and then they were all scrambling around looking for Ollie and couldn't understand why he wasn't there. They all ran in going, where's Dad?, waggy tails, and he wasn't there.'

The Mother of All Wakes

Normally in Ireland you're under the sod in two days, but it took Josephine two weeks to make the arrangements for Oliver's funeral, simply because she wanted to give everyone a chance to come over for it. All the while Ollie was being kept in cold storage at Cork University Hospital. Only no one had thought of informing Josephine and she made several trips to the undertakers in Buttevant to talk to Ollie in his coffin not realizing he wasn't there. It was an extraordinary time.

Oliver hadn't really made any arrangements for his funeral. David recalls him once saying, 'If I die I want everyone to come to my funeral and cry. And if they don't cry they're not allowed in.' As for his final resting place, he'd always been rather fond of Bruhenny cemetery in Churchtown, a beautiful quiet spot just across the road from O'Brien's, its ancient gravestones lost for centuries under weeds and brambles. Sometimes at dusk he'd wander out with a drink in his hand to watch hundreds of crows flock into the graveyard to settle on the trees for the night. It was an extraordinary sight that he once shared with Sarah. 'We were sat in the bar and he said, "Come on, girlie, I've got to show you this." And we went out and sat and watched this spectacle and I remember him saying, "Isn't this graveyard amazing?" So it was just so ideal when they allowed us to plant him there.'

As the day of the funeral drew nearer family and friends began arriving. For people like Simon, for whom Ollie's time in Ireland was when he knew him the least, it was to be an enormously moving experience. Seeing where he lived and who his friends were, he sensed a contentedness that must have been Oliver's life in Churchtown. And when Josephine invited him to go through and see the garden, Simon felt a rush of powerful emotions. 'It seemed a tranquil existence. Josephine was telling me that it was his pride and joy and that he used to sit on a seat out there for hours. And I thought, oh my God, that was so far removed from the Ollie that I knew, that I think he had fundamentally changed. I think he'd had enough of the aggression. I think he more or less had come to terms with exactly who he was and why he was like it. Josephine played a big part in all that.'

The funeral service took place at St James's Church in Mallow and was a simple yet memorable affair. From early in the morning people had started to gather outside and by the time the family arrived there was a crowd of several hundred. When Ollie's coffin came out of the hearse spontaneous applause began, along with a few raised voices of, 'Go to it, Ollie', while a lone piper played a melancholy tune as the congregation walked into the church.

Among the first to enter was Michael Winner. Walking down the aisle to where the coffin stood, he touched it gently with his hand and sobbed. 'I didn't cry at my mother's funeral. I didn't cry at my father's funeral. I wept at Oliver's funeral. I was in floods of tears.'

Seated down at the front with the Reed family was a gentleman dressed all in black. Muriel thought he was a priest. It turned out to be Alex Higgins. The snooker ace had insisted on sitting with the family and was his usual twitching, paranoid self, scanning the congregation and nudging David, saying, 'He's IRA. And so's he. He's IRA, too.' Then, with penetrating eyes, he stared at the coffin and yelled, 'Oliver, they're all phonies, get them the fuck out, all these fucking people, they're all fucking phonies.' Mark grabbed hold of him. 'Alex, don't ruin this fucking day. You can fuck around with any other day but you're not fucking around with this day.'

As for the service itself, the family didn't want anything too solemn. 'We wanted to sing "Jerusalem",' says Mark. 'But the vicar thought that might be a little bit hefty in County Cork.' They ended up with 'Abide with Me' and 'All Things Bright and Beautiful', all the verses. 'We tried to keep it light and not too religious, tried to keep it akin with the things that had value to him rather than the godly,' says Mark, whose own contribution was a reading of Robert Frost's poem 'The Road Not Taken'. Sarah also read and Simon did the eulogy, which he'd done just two years before for his father. Afterwards there was a round of applause.

The cortege of at least a hundred cars pulled away from the church to begin Ollie's final journey towards Churchtown, a few miles away, down lanes, roads and streets, every one of them lined with people. 'It was amazing,' remembers Simon. 'There must have been ten thousand people and they all doffed their caps when the cortege went past. Part of it was curiosity, of course, he's a big star, and partly because I think he connected with everyone who lived there. It was an extraordinary day.'

Finally the cortege arrived in the centre of Churchtown, but could barely move for the throng of people. Cheers rang out and there was spontaneous applause. Some onlookers broke out into a verse of 'Consider Yourself' from *Oliver!*. 'I remember getting out of the car and going, wow, this is extraordinary,' says Sarah. 'It was amazing, and lovely as well that he was that loved. He really had come home over there. They understood him.'

The coffin was carried into the cemetery, where the grass had been mowed and the weeds and brambles cut back to clear a space for Ollie. And as the coffin was lowered into the grave, people started throwing in coins.

Of course, the press were much in evidence: TV crews and reporters. Just behind Ollie's grave was a wall and behind that a tree. David has never forgotten it, but suddenly out of the branches fell a cameraman, who landed with a heavy thud. 'So that caused a bit of a distraction.' Afterwards, as is the local custom, Josephine, Sarah and Mark remained at the graveside for something like forty minutes, just shaking hands with people walking past to offer their condolences: 'Sorry for your troubles.'

Oliver had always admired the way the Irish treated their dead, that someone's passing was a cause for celebrating a life that had been well lived. 'I've had some fearsome hangovers burying the dead,' he'd said. So Josephine was determined to throw the mother of all wakes. And it was an open house: Josephine put the word around the village that everyone was most welcome to come. 'And it went on apparently for three days,' reveals Muriel. 'Ollie would have loved it.'

At Castle McCarthy a large marquee was erected in the garden and a microphone set up on a platform so that anyone could go up and tell a story about Ollie or read a poem or sing a song. The place was full of friends, four hundred at the height of the wake, and there was lots of booze and lots of curry and bacon rolls in the morning. There was music, dancing, Irish and rugby songs, a proper celebration. 'And everybody got pretty pissed,' says Simon. 'It was really lovely. Of course, there was a sense of loss, but there was also a sense that we had to get at it because that's what Ollie would have expected.'

Faces from the past mingled with those from the present, and everyone carried with them their own private thoughts and memories of Ollie. Michael Christensen, still in the police, hadn't been able to make the funeral because he was giving evidence at the Old Bailey that day. 'But even if I hadn't I couldn't have gone, to see him in a coffin, he was too larger than life, and to think that he was mortal would just shatter too many of our thoughts and dreams.' However, other old Wimbledon friends were there, like Johnny Placett, Mick Fryer and Mick Monks. Paul and Nora Friday too. And the women in his life: Jacquie came, and so too Kate: 'His harem,' jokes Jacquie. It was the first time the two women had been in the same place since that episode in the pub. It was Jacquie who took the initiative. 'I went up to Kate and told her how sorry I was about what happened with Oliver and she was absolutely gobsmacked. I don't think she liked the fact that I had approached her, so I quietly went away again.'

As the evening wore on people began trickling away, although plenty were still arriving and going strong. For David and Muriel, it was time to leave. Their cab dropped them at their hotel, but before getting out David quietly asked the driver, 'Today was too public for me, would you be very kind and come early tomorrow morning to drive me back out to the cemetery? I'd like to say a private bye-bye.'

Years before, when their friend Pat Clancy died in Ireland, Ollie rang David from some far-flung movie location and told him, 'Go and give him a drink.' David knew what he meant and bought a bottle of hard stuff and poured it over Pat's grave. 'And so I thought, I'll do the same with Ollie. We drove out at the crack of dawn with a bottle of Scotch and I went out to the grave and stood there with my private thoughts, saying bye-bye, Ollie, here's one for the road. It was a bit emotional. I got back in the car and we drove back.'

When David arrived at Cork airport, the Departures lounge was filled with Ollie's friends and family waiting for flights. He decided to buy a paper 'and there on the front page was a photograph taken from the fella who'd fallen out of the tree, and it showed the coffin lying there in the hole and I suddenly realized I'd poured the whisky over Ollie's feet, because I could now see which way up he was. And I can just imagine him saying, you ******!!!'

The Comeback That Never Was

The final shot of *Gladiator* was supposed to have been Proximo, the old entertainer, entering the empty Colosseum and burying in the sandy arena the wooden sword given to him by Marcus Aurelius, the symbol of his freedom. 'That would have been incredibly moving,' says Douglas Wick. 'And what a great final image of Oliver's performance and of his career.' Sadly it was not to be.

Once the shock and tragedy of Oliver's death had passed, the filmmakers were left with what looked like an insurmountable problem. At least 20 per cent of his performance was incomplete, including his most important screen moment, where the cynical Proximo redeems himself. A meeting took place, with the insurance people looking into the option of going back and reshooting all of Proximo's scenes with another actor. 'At that meeting, it was the first time I'd ever seen Ridley Scott really distressed,' recalls Wick. 'Ridley is so impermeable, but he just looked crushed, because aside from the loss of Ollie he knew something extraordinary had happened and he was determined to save that performance. It was irreplaceable.'

Very early on in the production there was a buzz surrounding Oliver's performance. Everyone on the movie was talking about it. And those who knew a little of his history were beginning to speak about a glorious comeback. 'We knew we had lightning in a jar,' says Wick. 'It was a very original performance, just the way his particular qualities, his magnetism, his primitiveness, this strange honesty, intersected with that character. He had found a balance of roughness and cynicism, and you could see just the beginnings of a rumble of a heart. It was a part that he was so wonderfully suited for and it evolved in his hands – Oliver was Proximo.'

The only solution left was to somehow create a new story-line for the character using a combination of body doubles and existing footage. This was done with consummate skill and technical brilliance. What we have in effect is Ollie's ghost saving Crowe's Maximus from imprisonment and meeting his end with nobility at the hands of Roman assassins. It's a fitting denouement to Oliver's cinematic odyssey, and a great rescue job on the filmmaker's part, but one is still left to lament what might have been.

Oliver's death was tragic on so many levels, not least because here was a man thriving and about to have a complete rebirth with the public. The world was going to rediscover Oliver Reed. The enormous success of *Gladiator* would surely have re-energized his career. Producers who had been shit scared of him would have suddenly gone, OK, it's worth taking a little bit of a risk with him, and that would have led to better roles and perhaps some of his best performances because he still had what Ridley Scott termed a 'fantastically powerful screen presence'. As Terry Gilliam notes, 'He's one of the best things in *Gladiator*. If you want to see acting, don't look at Russell Crowe, look at what Ollie's doing, he's magnificent.' When Georgina Hale went to see it at her local cinema she remembers walking out afterwards thinking, 'he was fabulous, drunk or sober, who cares? He was just magic to watch'.

When *Gladiator* was finished, Mike Higgins remembers, there was a private screening in London before the film opened.

'And when the credits came up at the end and it said, "To our friend: Oliver Reed", the entire audience, which was made up of the crew and the actors, burst into applause.'

Ollie

Newspapers everywhere carried the news of Oliver Reed's passing and, as with Richard Burton before him, commentators spoke of a life of waste, a career of great promise thrown away in pubs, chat show embarrassments and gutters of puke. 'When Oliver died a lot of the papers said he had a wasted life,' says Winner. 'It wasn't a wasted life at all: he had a wonderful life. He enjoyed himself. He did a lot of movies, he had a long career considering, he didn't end up broke, he lived in a lovely house in Ireland which he loved, and he had a lovely wife and lovely children. How can that be a wasted life?'

A wasted life perhaps not, then, but a life that ended too soon, unquestionably. 'When he died there was a part of me that felt it was too young,' says Mark. 'But it was a life that he chose to lead. In sixty-one years he packed in a couple of lifetimes. I could never see him lying in a hospital bed with tubes running in and out of him; he couldn't have handled that because to him that would have represented the end of the fun. Lying there suffering, rotting and dying, there was no quality of life in that. But it would have been interesting to have seen him at seventy-one. I really do think he would have been a spectacularly grumpy old fucker. It would have been good to see him live a little longer, for him to have seen the success of *Gladiator*, and to have been recognized: yes, you can still do it, Ollie, you've still got it.'

For Sarah, the passing of her father left a huge gap to fill, for it goes without saying that the bigger the personality the bigger the gap, and Oliver's personality was the size of a small moon. 'Speaking for myself, when he died I was grieving a lot for the man that I didn't have, for what I felt we missed in our relationship rather than what we actually had, because it was so awkward. He wasn't a bad father, he just wasn't always the best father. But you can only do the best you can do with the tools you've been given, that's all you can do. Somebody said to me years ago, you have to let them back in again to be able to let them go, and there was a bit of that for me.'

Perhaps the tragedy of Oliver Reed is that he created a persona for himself that he felt obliged constantly to act out in the public arena. It was part of his creative life. 'He loved acting Oliver Reed, whoever that was,' says actor Stephan Chase. 'He probably didn't know either. All he knew was that he'd cottoned on to something that worked and played it extremely well.' If he'd gone around kissing babies and doing good, the public wouldn't have been at all interested, Oliver often claimed. 'That's not what they expect from Oliver Reed. They want him to fall off the edge of a dustbin, get into fights and get drunk and do all the things you read in the papers.' Mick Monks remembers being in a restaurant with Ollie one night and there was a chap in the corner sitting quietly with a pen and paper. 'See that guy,' said Ollie. 'He's been bloody following me around for weeks, drives me mad.' As they walked out Ollie casually knocked a chair over and said to Monks, 'Wait and see.' The next day a newspaper story was headlined: 'Oliver Reed Wrecks Restaurant'. It was his own fault, of course, all this. 'In a way,' says David. 'Whilst good directors were directing him his career was ascending, but alongside that his notoriety was increasing and one overtook the other. So by the end, far from the press manufacturing events, they were self-generated by Ollie, which led to his downfall because he was always living up to it.'

Oliver had always had a great imagination and a keen sense of the ridiculous, not taking things too seriously, but one wonders whether in later years he did always enjoy playing the fool, or did it become a little stale for him? His antics, which had been so inspired, now seemed all too obvious and staged, like going on a chat show pissed. Spontaneity isn't the same the second time round.

There was a contradiction in his character, no doubt, which can easily be put down to the difference between Oliver Reed sober and Oliver Reed drunk. As many people have observed, he was in important ways two people, 'because sober he was the shyest person that you could ever wish to meet,' says David. 'And that was the real Ollie. The real Ollie was shy.' And vulnerable. It's something Glenda Jackson picked up on during the times they worked together. 'Certainly that was my reading of him, a very vulnerable man. But he would never, ever, ever have shown that. He had great belief in himself when he was in front of a camera which may not have been there in real life.' Perhaps that's why so many people found it easy to forgive his frailties and look upon him with fondness: because they understood this split personality. 'It was something that one couldn't really hold against him,' says Barbara Carrera. 'Because, even though his behaviour was sometimes scary, it was not intentionally malicious. As a person he was so complex, so mercurial.'

For a good few years after Ollie died there was a steady procession of people who came to visit the grave and sup a pint at O'Brien's, but in recent years it has tailed off. Even the family's pilgrimage to Churchtown has somewhat faded, with not everyone able to make it every year. Jacquie has never been back since the funeral and finds it strange that he's lying in the sod in Ireland at all. 'Why did they stick this man in the ground? I'm a great one for cremation and just scatter him and then he can be everywhere, on the wind, in the sea, everywhere. But in that grave in Ireland, what's he doing there? He must be so lonely, so lonely there.'

Josephine visits the grave whenever she's in the area. The last time she went someone had left an empty bottle of vodka next to the headstone. 'People frequently go there to sit and have a drink on the grave; they go to have a drink with Ollie.' Withdrawing to Castle McCarthy after Oliver's death, Josephine continued to live there. After all, it was her home, she had friends locally, and she wasn't ready to leave. Her life was on hold. But Ollie had always been conscious of the fact that in all likelihood he'd die before her. 'So he'd say to me that if he died, to go out and find myself a nice young man and not to sit around and mope.' In 2001 Josephine remarried and moved away from Churchtown, but not too far: she still lives in County Cork and has two lively boys. Ollie would have loved them.

By a coincidence Sarah has two boys and it's perhaps her biggest regret that her father isn't alive to revel in their company and in their innocence, and feed their imagination. 'I always said about my dad, he became a father to become a grandfather. He would have been a sensational grandfather. My children would have had amazing times with him. I can imagine them pottering around the garden, planting things and learning how bees make honey! Buzz, buzz, buzz. Their lives will be paler not knowing him.'

Can one sum up a man like Oliver Reed? Many whose lives he crossed and touched have tried. 'What was so incredible for me was that he was able to have a sense of dignity and fairness and justice, and had an incredible personal human etiquette that I've never experienced in anyone else,' says actor Paul Koslo.

'He was a gentleman's gentleman. They broke the mould when he passed. There'll never be another Ollie.'

'Larger than life' is a phrase often used to describe him; 'an artist' is another, and also 'one of a kind'. 'Ollie was so many things,' says friend Maria Rohm. 'Fiery, yet detached, he exuded a very positive energy and it just felt good to be around him. Of course, these qualities go hand in hand with eccentricity. I don't know that it is possible to have one without the other. Never understood why some people don't seem to understand that.'

Why the public liked and responded to Oliver is easy to grasp: because he was one of them. He appealed as a person, not as a film star. 'He had no airs and graces,' says David. 'And I think his appeal endures because of this, that he was noted more for the pranks he got up to and being a man amongst the people. Whereas film stars tend to live a tinselled lifestyle, above the ordinary man, Ollie drank in his local pub and things like that. He was perceived as very much a down-to-earth sort.'

He also didn't give a fuck, and therein lies much of his appeal. In life it's rare to find a person who has that sense of fun and madness and is also brave enough to go out and just do it and damn the consequences. And yes, get away with it, because he had that presence and personality. 'He was such an extraordinary person,' says Nora Friday. 'He had an enormous zest for life and had such enormous charisma as a person that, even if he had not been a film star, you would have still noticed him when he walked into a pub or a room.'

Some of the stuff Oliver did was hideously unfair, but there was never any malice in his actions. He didn't know venom and spite, he knew how to be a pain in the ass, he knew how to be awkward and horrid, but he didn't know how to be evil: it wasn't in his make-up. He didn't go out to maim and hurt. It was almost ruffian crap, it was gesticulating, it was puffing out his chest. 'Ollie was not a hell-raiser for any vindictive reason,' claims colleague David Ball. 'He didn't have an ounce of hate in his body. He was the eternal naughty boy.'

And a naughty boy capable of almost ridiculous heights of insensitivity. When his old friend Mick Fryer gave up the booze, Ollie did his damnedest to get him started again. 'He came into the Dog and Fox one day,' Fryer relates, 'and stuck a bottle of Rémy Martin and a bottle of champagne on the bar and said, "Right, we're going to stop all this bollocks. Let's get at it." I wouldn't have any of it.' Reckless in the extreme, but done for no other reason than that Ollie wanted the old Mick back, the mad Mick, but he wasn't there any more.

Out of some of this chaos came an almost innocent care and sense of protection for his friends. Johnny Placett was known as a gambler in the seventies. During one visit to a London casino, as Placett was rolling some dice, Ollie picked up this bunny girl who was the croupier and laid her flat across the blackjack table. Of course all the punters leaped out of their seats and their chips went flying. 'Ollie!' Placett yelled. 'You're out of order there.' The girl was trembling with fright and the manager was doing his nut. Ollie just looked at Placett and said, 'I've seen you lose so much money in these casinos, I thought I could get you barred, do you a favour.' It's a story that perhaps sums Oliver Reed up better than most: behind the debris, the screams and the madness was a man whose heart was nearly always in the right place. 'There was always a drama,' says Placett. 'He loved a drama, something always had to happen. He loved excitement in his life.'

It was never easy for anyone living with Ollie, but then the other side of that coin was that it was magical. And that juxtaposition lay at the heart of what it was like to be around Oliver Reed. When he was good he was very, very good, and when he was bad he was horrid. 'Am I proud of him?' says Mark. 'Yes, I am. Am I proud of everything he did? No, of course not. But he was my dad and I loved him. It wasn't always the easiest ride but at the same time it was probably one of the most magical, amazing mystery tours that one could have ever taken. Looking back on it, I wouldn't have missed any of it. But it really was the big dipper, it really was the funfair, and all the lights were flashing. He was well loved and he was lovable. Of course, there were sides to him that were challenging. But he was an amazing person. His like don't come along often.'

Filmography

Hello London (1958)
Director: Sidney Smith
Cast: Sonja Henie, Michael Wilding, Dora Bryan, Roy Castle, Robert Coote, Eunice Gayson, Stanley Holloway, Dennis Price, Oliver Reed (extra).

The Square Peg (1958)
Director: John Paddy Carstairs
Cast: Norman Wisdom, Honor Blackman, Edward Chapman, Campbell Singer, Hattie Jacques, Oliver Reed (extra).

Life is a Circus (1958)
Director: Val Guest
Cast: Bud Flanagan, Teddy Knox, Jimmy Nervo, Charlie Naughton, Jimmy Gold, Eddie Gray, Chesney Allen, Shirley Eaton, Lionel Jeffries, Oliver Reed (extra).

The Captain's Table (1959)
Director: Jack Lee
Cast: John Gregson, Peggy Cummins, Donald Sinden, Maurice Denham, Richard Wattis, Joan Sims, John Le Mesurier, Oliver Reed (extra).

Upstairs and Downstairs (1959)
Director: Ralph Thomas
Cast: Michael Craig, Anne Heywood, Mylene Demongeot,
James Robertson Justice, Claudia Cardinale, Sid James, Joan
Hickson, Joan Sims, Daniel Massey, Oliver Reed (extra).

The League of Gentlemen (1960)
Director: Basil Dearden
Cast: Jack Hawkins, Nigel Patrick, Roger Livesey, Richard
Attenborough, Bryan Forbes, Kieron Moore, Terence
Alexander, Norman Bird, Oliver Reed (young actor).

The Rebel (1960)
Director: Robert Day
Cast: Tony Hancock, George Sanders, Paul Massie, Dennis
Price, Irene Handl, John Le Mesurier, Liz Fraser, Oliver Reed
(artist in cafe).

His and Hers (1960)
Director: Brian Desmond Hurst
Cast: Terry-Thomas, Janette Scott, Wilfrid-Hyde White, Joan
Sims, Kenneth Connor, Kenneth Williams, Oliver Reed (poet).

The Bulldog Breed (1960)
Director: Robert Asher
Cast: Norman Wisdom, Ian Hunter, David Lodge, Robert
Urquhart, Edward Chapman, Eddie Byrne, Michael Caine,
Oliver Reed (Teddy Boy).

The Angry Silence (1960)
Director: Guy Green
Cast: Richard Attenborough, Pier Angeli, Michael Craig,
Bernard Lee, Alfred Burke, Geoffrey Keen, Laurence Naismith,
Brian Bedford, Oliver Reed (Mick).

The Two Faces of Dr Jekyll (1960)
Director: Terence Fisher
Cast: Paul Massie, Dawn Addams, Christopher Lee, David Kossoff, Francis De Wolff, Oliver Reed (uncredited).

Sword of Sherwood Forest (1960)
Director: Terence Fisher
Cast: Richard Greene, Peter Cushing, Richard Pasco, Sarah Branch, Niall MacGinnis, Nigel Green, Derren Nesbitt, Oliver Reed (Lord Melton), Desmond Llewelyn.

Beat Girl (1960)
Director: Edmond T. Greville
Cast: David Farrar, Noelle Adam, Christopher Lee, Adam Faith, Shirley Anne Field, Peter McEnery, Oliver Reed (Plaid Shirt).

The Curse of the Werewolf (1961)
Director: Terence Fisher
Cast: Clifford Evans, Oliver Reed (Leon), Yvonne Romain, Catherine Feller, Anthony Dawson, Richard Wordsworth, Warren Mitchell, Peter Sallis.

The Pirates of Blood River (1961)
Director: John Gilling
Cast: Kerwin Matthews, Christopher Lee, Glenn Corbett, Marla Landi, Oliver Reed (Pirate), Andrew Keir, Peter Arne, Michael Ripper, Marie Devereux, Dennis Waterman.

Captain Clegg (1962)
Director: Peter Graham Scott
Cast: Peter Cushing, Yvonne Romain, Patrick Allen, Oliver Reed (Harry Cobtree), Michael Ripper, Martin Benson, David Lodge, Derek Francis, Milton Reid.

The Damned (1963)
Director: Joseph Losey
Cast: MacDonald Carey, Shirley Anne Field, Viveca Lindfors, Alexander Knox, Oliver Reed (King), Walter Gotel, James Villiers, Kenneth Cope.

Paranoiac (1963)
Director: Freddie Francis
Cast: Janette Scott, Oliver Reed (Simon Ashby), Alexander Davion, Sheila Burrell, Maurice Denham, Liliane Brousse.

The Scarlet Blade (1963)
Director: John Gilling
Cast: Lionel Jeffries, Oliver Reed (Capt. Tom Sylvester), Jack Hedley, June Thorburn, Duncan Lamont, Suzan Farmer.

The System (1964)
Director: Michael Winner
Cast: Oliver Reed (Tinker), Jane Merrow, Barbara Ferris, Julia Foster, Harry Andrews, David Hemmings, John Alderton.

The Brigand of Kandahar (1965)
Director: John Gilling
Cast: Ronald Lewis, Oliver Reed (Eli Khan), Duncan Lamont, Yvonne Romain, Katherine Woodville, Glyn Houston.

The Party's Over (1965)
Director: Guy Hamilton
Cast: Oliver Reed (Moise), Clifford David, Ann Lynn, Katherine Woodville, Louise Sorel, Mike Pratt, Eddie Albert.

The Debussy Film (1965)
Director: Ken Russell
Cast: Oliver Reed (Claude Debussy), Vladek Sheybal, Annette Robertson.

The Trap (1966)
Director: Sidney Hayers
Cast: Rita Tushingham, Oliver Reed (La Bete), Rex Sevenoaks, Barbara Chilcott.

The Jokers (1967)
Director: Michael Winner
Cast: Michael Crawford, Oliver Reed (David Tremayne), Harry Andrews, James Donald, Daniel Massey, Michael Hordern, Gabriella Licudi, Frank Finlay, Warren Mitchell, Edward Fox.

The Shuttered Room (1967)
Director: David Greene
Cast: Gig Young, Carol Lynley, Oliver Reed (Ethan), Flora Robson.

I'll Never Forget What's'isname (1967)
Director: Michael Winner
Cast: Orson Welles, Oliver Reed (Andrew Quint), Carol White, Harry Andrews, Michael Hordern, Wendy Craig, Marianne Faithfull, Frank Finlay, Lyn Ashley, Edward Fox, Mark Eden.

Dante's Inferno (1967)
Director: Ken Russell
Cast: Oliver Reed (Dante Gabriel Rossetti), Judith Paris, Andrew Faulds.

Oliver! (1968)
Director: Carol Reed
Cast: Ron Moody, Shani Wallis, Oliver Reed (Bill Sikes), Mark Lester, Jack Wild, Harry Secombe, Hugh Griffith, Peggy Mount, Leonard Rossiter.

The Assassination Bureau (1969)
Director: Basil Dearden
Cast: Oliver Reed (Ivan Dragomiloff), Diana Rigg, Telly Savalas, Curd Jurgens, Philippe Noiret, Warren Mitchell, Beryl Reid.

Hannibal Brooks (1969)
Director: Michael Winner
Cast: Oliver Reed (Stephen 'Hannibal' Brooks), Michael J. Pollard, Wolfgang Preiss, John Alderton, Karin Baal, Peter Carsten.

Women in Love (1969)
Director: Ken Russell
Cast: Alan Bates, Oliver Reed (Gerald Crich), Glenda Jackson, Jennie Linden, Eleanor Bron, Alan Webb, Vladek Sheybal, Michael Gough.

Take a Girl Like You (1970)
Director: Jonathan Miller
Cast: Hayley Mills, Oliver Reed (Patrick Standish), Noel Harrison, John Bird, Sheila Hancock, Aimi MacDonald, Ronald Lacey, John Fortune, Imogen Hassall, Penelope Keith.

The Lady in the Car with Glasses and a Gun (1970)
Director: Anatole Litvak
Cast: Samantha Eggar, Oliver Reed (Michael Caldwell), John McEnery, Stephane Audran.

The Devils (1971)
Director: Ken Russell
Cast: Vanessa Redgrave, Oliver Reed (Father Urbain Grandier), Dudley Sutton, Max Adrian, Gemma Jones, Murray Melvin, Michael Gothard, Georgina Hale, Brian Murphy.

The Hunting Party (1971)
Director: Don Medford
Cast: Oliver Reed (Frank Calder), Candice Bergen, Gene Hackman, Simon Oakland, L.Q. Jones.

The Triple Echo (1972)
Director: Michael Apted
Cast: Glenda Jackson, Oliver Reed (Sergeant), Brian Deacon, Anthony May, Gavin Richards.

Zero Population Growth (1972)
Director: Michael Campus
Cast: Oliver Reed (Russ McNeil), Geraldine Chaplin, Don Gordon, Diane Cilento.

Sitting Target (1972)
Director: Douglas Hickox
Cast: Oliver Reed (Harry Lomart), Jill St. John, Ian McShane, Edward Woodward, Frank Finlay, Freddie Jones, Jill Townsend.

Fury (aka *Days of Fury*, *One Russian Summer*) (1973)
Director: Antonio Calenda
Cast: Oliver Reed (Palizyn), John McEnery, Carole Andre, Ray Lovelock, Claudia Cardinale.

Dirty Weekend (1973)
Director: Dino Risi
Cast: Marcello Mastroianni, Oliver Reed (Fabrizo), Carole
Andre, Lionel Stander.

Revolver (1973)
Director: Sergio Sollima
Cast: Oliver Reed (Vito Caprini), Fabio Testi, Paola Pitagora,
Agostina Belli.

The Three Musketeers (1973)
Director: Richard Lester
Cast: Oliver Reed (Athos), Raquel Welch, Richard
Chamberlain, Michael York, Frank Finlay, Christopher Lee,
Faye Dunaway, Charlton Heston, Geraldine Chaplin, Jean-
Pierre Cassel, Simon Ward, Spike Milligan, Roy Kinnear.

Blue Blood (1973)
Director: Andrew Sinclair
Cast: Oliver Reed (Tom), Fiona Lewis, Anna Gael, Derek Jacobi.

And Then There Were None (1974)
Director: Peter Collinson
Cast: Oliver Reed (Hugh Lombard), Elke Sommer, Charles
Aznavour, Maria Rohm, Herbert Lom, Richard Attenborough,
Adolfo Celi, Stephane Audran, Alberto de Mendoza, Gert
Frobe, Orson Welles (narrator).

The Four Musketeers (1974)
Director: Richard Lester
Cast: Oliver Reed (Athos), Raquel Welch, Richard
Chamberlain, Michael York, Frank Finlay, Christopher Lee,
Faye Dunaway, Charlton Heston, Geraldine Chaplin, Jean-
Pierre Cassel, Simon Ward, Roy Kinnear, Michael Gothard.

Tommy (1975)
Director: Ken Russell
Cast: Oliver Reed (Frank Hobbs), Ann-Margret, Roger Daltrey, Elton John, Eric Clapton, Keith Moon, Tina Turner, Jack Nicholson, Paul Nicholas, Robert Powell, Pete Townshend, John Entwistle.

Royal Flash (1975)
Director: Richard Lester
Cast: Malcolm McDowell, Alan Bates, Florinda Bolkan, Oliver Reed (Otto von Bismarck), Britt Ekland, Tom Bell, Joss Ackland, Christopher Cazenove, Henry Cooper, Lionel Jeffries, Alastair Sim, Michael Hordern, Bob Hoskins, David Jason.

The Great Scout & Cathouse Thursday (1976)
Director: Don Taylor
Cast: Lee Marvin, Oliver Reed (Joe Knox), Robert Culp, Elizabeth Ashley, Strother Martin, Sylvia Miles.

Burnt Offerings (1976)
Director: Dan Curtis
Cast: Karen Black, Oliver Reed (Ben Rolf), Bette Davis, Burgess Meredith, Lee Montgomery.

The Sell Out (1976)
Director: Peter Collinson
Cast: Oliver Reed (Gabriel Lee), Richard Widmark, Gayle Hunnicutt, Sam Wanamaker.

The Ransom (1977)
Director: Richard Compton
Cast: Oliver Reed (Nick McCormick), Deborah Raffin, James Mitchum, Stuart Whitman, John Ireland, Paul Koslo.

The Prince and the Pauper (1977)
Director: Richard Fleischer
Cast: Oliver Reed (Miles Hendon), Raquel Welch, Mark
Lester, Ernest Borgnine, George C. Scott, David Hemmings,
Rex Harrison, Charlton Heston, Harry Andrews, Murray
Melvin.

Tomorrow Never Comes (1978)
Director: Peter Collinson
Cast: Oliver Reed (Jim Wilson), Susan George, Raymond
Burr, John Ireland, Stephen McHattie, Donald Pleasence,
Paul Koslo.

The Big Sleep (1978)
Director: Michael Winner
Cast: Robert Mitchum, Sarah Miles, Richard Boone, Candy
Clark, Joan Collins, Edward Fox, John Mills, James Stewart,
Oliver Reed (Eddie Mars), Harry Andrews, Richard Todd.

The Class of Miss MacMichael (1979)
Director: Silvio Narizzano
Cast: Glenda Jackson, Oliver Reed (Terence Sutton), Michael
Murphy, Rosalind Cash, John Standing, Phil Daniels.

A Touch of the Sun (1979)
Director: Peter Curran
Cast: Oliver Reed (Capt. Daniel Nelson), Sylvaine Charlet,
Peter Cushing, Keenan Wynn, Wilfrid Hyde-White.

The Brood (1979)
Director: David Cronenberg
Cast: Oliver Reed (Dr Hal Raglan), Samantha Eggar, Art
Hindle, Henry Beckman.

Dr Heckyl and Mr Hype (1980)
Director: Charles B. Griffith
Cast: Oliver Reed (Dr Henry Heckyl/Mr Hype), Sunny Johnson, Maia Danziger, Jackie Coogan.

Lion of the Desert (1981)
Director: Moustapha Akkad
Cast: Anthony Quinn, Oliver Reed (General Rodolfo Granziani), Irene Papas, Raf Vallone, Rod Steiger, John Gielgud, Andrew Keir.

Venom (1981)
Director: Piers Haggard
Cast: Klaus Kinski, Oliver Reed (Dave Averconnelly), Sterling Hayden, Nicol Williamson, Susan George, Sarah Miles, Cornelia Sharpe, Michael Gough.

Condorman (1981)
Director: Charles Jarrott
Cast: Michael Crawford, Oliver Reed (Krokov), Barbara Carrera, James Hampton.

Fanny Hill (1983)
Director: Gerry O'Hara
Cast: Lisa Foster, Oliver Reed (Mr Edward Widdlecome), Wilfrid Hyde-White, Shelley Winters, Alfred Marks.

The Sting II (1983)
Director: Jeremy Kagan
Cast: Jackie Gleason, Mac Davis, Teri Garr, Karl Malden, Oliver Reed (Doyle Lonnegan).

Clash of Loyalties (1983)
Director: Mohamed Shukri Jameel

Cast: Yousef al-Any, Ghari al-Takriti, Bernard Archard, John Barron, James Bolam, Oliver Reed (Colonel Leachman).

Spasms (1983)
Director: William Fruet
Cast: Peter Fonda, Oliver Reed (Jason Kincaid), Kerrie Keane, Al Waxman.

Two of a Kind (1983)
Director: John Herzfeld
Cast: John Travolta, Olivia Newton-John, Charles Durning, Oliver Reed (Beasley), Scatman Crothers.

Black Arrow (1985; TV movie)
Director: John Hough
Cast: Benedict Taylor, Georgia Slowe, Oliver Reed (Sir Daniel), Fernando Rey, Stephan Chase, Donald Pleasence.

Christopher Columbus (1985; TV mini-series)
Director: Alberto Lattuada
Cast: Gabriel Byrne, Rossano Brazzi, Oliver Reed (Martin Pinzon), Raf Vallone, Max Von Sydow, Eli Wallach, Nicol Williamson, Faye Dunaway.

Captive (1986)
Director: Paul Mayersberg
Cast: Irina Brook, Oliver Reed (Gregory Le Vay), Xavier Deluc, Corinne Dacla, Michael Cronin, Hiro Arai.

Castaway (1986)
Director: Nicolas Roeg
Cast: Oliver Reed (Gerald Kingsland), Amanda Donohoe, Georgina Hale, Frances Barber.

Gor (1987)
Director: Fritz Kiersch
Cast: Urbano Barberini, Rebecca Ferratti, Jack Palance, Paul L. Smith, Oliver Reed (Sarm).

Master of Dragonard (1987)
Director: Gerard Kikoine
Cast: Oliver Reed (Captain Shanks), Eartha Kitt, Herbert Lom, Claudia Udy, Patrick Warburton.

The Misfit Brigade (1987)
Director: Gordon Hessler
Cast: Bruce Davison, David Patrick Kelly, D.W. Moffett, Jay O. Sanders, Oliver Reed (The General), David Carradine.

Rage to Kill (1988)
Director: David Winters
Cast: James Ryan, Oliver Reed (Gen. Turner), Cameron Mitchell.

Skeleton Coast (1988)
Director: John Cardos
Cast: Ernest Borgnine, Robert Vaughn, Oliver Reed (Capt. Simpson), Herbert Lom.

The Adventures of Baron Munchausen (1988)
Director: Terry Gilliam
Cast: John Neville, Eric Idle, Sarah Polley, Oliver Reed (Vulcan), Uma Thurman, Charles McKeown, Winston Dennis, Jack Purvis, Jonathan Pryce, Robin Williams, Sting.

Captive Rage (1988)
Director: Cedric Sundstrom
Cast: Oliver Reed (General Belmondo), Robert Vaughn, Claudia Udy, Lisa Rinna.

The Revenger (1989)
Director: Cedric Sundstrom
Cast: Oliver Reed (Jack Fisher), Frank Zagarino, Jeff Celentano, Nancy Mulford.

The Lady and the Highwayman (1989; TV movie)
Director: John Hough
Cast: Emma Samms, Oliver Reed (Sir Phillip Gage), Claire Bloom, Christopher Cazenove, Lysette Anthony, Hugh Grant, Michael York, John Mills, Ian Bannen, Robert Morley, Bernard Miles, Gordon Jackson.

The House of Usher (1989)
Director: Alan Birkinshaw
Cast: Oliver Reed (Roderick Usher), Donald Pleasence, Romy Windsor.

The Return of the Musketeers (1989)
Director: Richard Lester
Cast: Michael York, Oliver Reed (Athos), Frank Finlay, Richard Chamberlain, C. Thomas Howell, Kim Cattrall, Geraldine Chaplin, Roy Kinnear, Christopher Lee, Philippe Noiret, Alan Howard.

Blind Justice (1989)
Director: Terence Ryan
Cast: Christopher Cazenove, Edita Brychta, Oliver Reed (Ballinger).

Treasure Island (1990; TV movie)
Director: Fraser Heston
Cast: Charlton Heston, Christian Bale, Oliver Reed (Billy Bones), Christopher Lee, Richard Johnson, Julian Glover.

A Ghost in Monte Carlo (1990; TV movie)
Director: John Hough
Cast: Sarah Miles, Oliver Reed (The Rajah), Christopher
Plummer, Samantha Eggar, Fiona Fullerton, Lysette
Anthony, Marcus Gilbert, Joanna Lumley, Lewis Collins,
Ron Moody.

Hired to Kill (1990)
Directors: Nico Mastorakis and Peter Rader
Cast: Brian Thompson, Oliver Reed (Michael Bartos), George
Kennedy, Jose Ferrer.

The Pit and the Pendulum (1991)
Director: Stuart Gordon
Cast: Lance Henriksen, Stephen Lee, William J. Norris, Mark
Margolis, Oliver Reed (Cardinal).

Prisoner of Honor (1991; TV movie)
Director: Ken Russell
Cast: Richard Dreyfuss, Oliver Reed (Gen. de Boisdeffre), Peter
Firth, Jeremy Kemp, Brian Blessed, Peter Vaughan, Lindsay
Anderson.

Severed Ties (1992)
Director: Damon Santostefano
Cast: Johnny Legend, Garrett Morris, Billy Morrissette, Oliver
Reed (Dr Hans Vaughan), Elke Sommer.

Return to Lonesome Dove (1993; TV mini-series)
Director: Mike Robe
Cast: Jon Voight, Barbara Hershey, Ricky Schroder,
Louis Gossett Jr, Oliver Reed (Gregor Dunnigan), Reese
Witherspoon, Chris Cooper.

Superbrain (1995)
Director: Menahem Golan
Cast: Torsten Lennie Münchow, Oliver Reed (Superbrain), Hanns Zischler.

Russian Roulette – Moscow 95 (1995)
Director: Menahem Golan
Cast: Barbara Carrera, Karen Moncrieff, Oliver Reed.

Funny Bones (1995)
Director: Peter Chelsom
Cast: Oliver Platt, Jerry Lewis, Lee Evans, Leslie Caron, Richard Griffiths, Oliver Reed (Dolly Hopkins).

The Bruce (1996)
Directors: Bob Carruthers and David McWhinnie
Cast: Brian Blessed, Richard Brimblecombe, Conor Chamberlain, Steven Clark, Oliver Reed (Bishop Wisharton).

Parting Shots (1998)
Director: Michael Winner
Cast: Chris Rea, Felicity Kendal, John Cleese, Bob Hoskins, Diana Rigg, Ben Kingsley, Joanna Lumley, Oliver Reed (Jamie Campbell-Stewart), Gareth Hunt.

The Incredible Adventures of Marco Polo on his Journeys to the Ends of the Earth (1998; TV movie)
Director: George Erschbamer
Cast: Don Diamont, Oliver Reed (Capt. Cornelius Donovan), Jack Palance.

Jeremiah (1998; TV movie)
Director: Harry Winer
Cast: Patrick Dempsey, Oliver Reed (General Safan), Klaus Maria Brandauer.

Gladiator (2000)
Director: Ridley Scott
Cast: Russell Crowe, Joaquin Phoenix, Connie Nielsen, Oliver Reed (Proximo), Richard Harris, Derek Jacobi, Djimon Hounsou, David Hemmings.

Bibliography

Candice Bergen, *Knock Wood* (New York: Simon & Schuster, 1984).

Madeleine Bingham, *The Great Lover: The Life and Art of Herbert Beerbohn Tree* (London: Hamish Hamilton, 1978).

Bill Burrows, *The Hurricane: The Turbulent Life and Times of Alex Higgins* (London: Atlantic Books, 2003).

Michael Crawford, *Parcel Arrived Safely: Tied with String* (London: Random House, 2000).

Tony Fletcher, *Dear Boy: The Life of Keith Moon* (London: Omnibus Press, 1998).

Cliff Goodwin, *Evil Spirits: The Life of Oliver Reed* (London: Virgin Books, 2000).

David Hemmings, *Blow Up… And Other Exaggerations* (London: Robson Books, 2004).

Wayne Kinsey, *Hammer Films: The Bray Studio Years* (London: Reynolds & Hearne, 2002).

Joseph Lanza, *Phallic Frenzy: Ken Russell and his Films* (London: Aurum, 2008).

Christopher Lee, *Tall, Dark and Gruesome* (London: W.H. Allen, 1977)

George MacDonald Fraser, *The Light's On At Signpost* (London: HarperCollins, 2002).

Roger Moore, *Roger Moore: My Word is My Bond* (Michael O'Mara Books, 2008).

Oliver Reed, *Reed All About Me* (London: W.H. Allen, 1979).

Paul Simper, *The Saint: From Big Screen to Small Screen and Back Again* (London: Chameleon Books, 1997).

Carol White with Clifford Thurlow, *Carol Comes Home* (London: New English Library, 1982).

Marco Pierre White, *White Slave* (London: Orion Books, 2006).

Donald Zec, *Marvin: The Story of Lee Marvin* (London: Hodder & Stoughton, 1979).

Index

OR indicates Oliver Reed.

Achille Lauro trip 407–8
Adams, Ritchie 224, 350–1
Adventures of Baron Munchausen
    445–7
advertisements, television 66–7, 169,
    437–8
After Dark 462–6
Akkad, Moustapha 394
All-Star Secrets 298
And Then There Were None 276–9, 402
André, Carole 241–2, 243, 244
Andrews, Lancelot (OR's
    grandfather) 13, 14–15
Angry Silence, The 64
animals, OR and 146–7, 167–8, 452–3,
    473
anniversary of OR's death ix–x,
    513–14
Apted, Michael 92, 225–6, 228–31,
    272
arm-wrestling 33, 87, 131, 201, 381,
    432, 440, 480, 493, 406, 497–8
Armstrong, Vic 389, 479–80
Ashton, Roy 76, 77, 79
Aspel & Company 428–30, 465–6
Assassination Bureau 166
athletics 25–6, 28, 52
Attenborough, Richard 64, 276, 278

auditions 66–7, 68, 69, 91–2, 95, 120,
    487–8

Baird, Roy 180, 198
Baker, Bob 103, 104
Ball, David 112, 113, 302, 304–7, 417,
    452, 516
Bang, Joy 286, 296
Barbados 55, 223–4, 308–10, 385–6
Barton, Tony 399–401
Bates, Alan 172–3, 174–5, 176, 180–1
BBC (British Broadcasting
    Corporation) 109, 126, 268–9, 293
Beat Girl 73–4
Becket, Thomas 281–2
Beerbohm, Max 42
Behan, Brendan 90
Bergen, Candice 206–7
Bernard, Judd 345–6
Beverly Wilshire Hotel, LA, OR at the
    310–14, 322
Big Sleep, The 344–5
Black, Karen 315–16
Bledlow (childhood home) 7–12
Blessed, Brian 481–2
Blue Blood 274–5
Boardman, Stan 431–5
Box, John 148–9, 153
boxing 297–9
Brando, Marlon 91, 110, 445

537

Bray Studios 68, 76, 82, 92–3, 100
Bregman, Martin 376–7
Bricusse, Leslie 314, 397
Brigand of Kandahar 122, 123–4
British Film Institute 99, 176
Bron, Eleanor 172
Brood, The 355–6, 357
Brooke-Little, John 43
Broome Hall (OR's home) 35, 208–13, 215, 219, 224, 227, 232, 233–8, 240, 56, 261, 263, 264, 265, 266, 267, 268, 272–3, 280, 281, 284, 285, 286, 291, 292, 293, 294, 308, 317, 326, 333, 334, 340, 341, 342, 345, 346–7, 348, 349, 350, 353, 362, 363, 364, 365, 367–9, 400, 451, 452, 474
Brown, George H. 124
Bruce, The 481–2
Buck, Jules 301–2, 303–4
Bulldog Breed, The 74
Burge, Anne 378, 379–80, 386, 388, 472
Burge, Josephine *see* Reed, Josephine (OR's second wife)
Burge, William 496, 498, 499
Burgess, Ken 'the Admiral' 87, 101, 162, 291–2
Burke, Jack 56, 59
Burley, Kay 489
Burnt Offerings 315–17
Byrne, Kate (OR's first wife) 66–9, 71–2, 74, 79, 85, 86, 87, 102, 116–17, 128, 132, 133, 134, 143, 156, 162–3, 188, 189, 190, 191, 192, 193, 194–5, 209, 365, 411, 506

Campus, Michael 215
Captain Clegg 82–3
Captain's Table, The 60
Captive 411
car collection 237, 239–40

Carrera, Barbara 380–1, 382, 384, 480, 513
Carreras, Michael 72
Carson, Johnny 316–17
Cassidy, Peter 482
Castaway 413–17, 419–20
Castle McCarthy (Reed Home) 472–4, 484, 505, 514
censors 98, 109, 142, 197, 203–4
Chamberlain, Richard 249, 253–4, 450
Chaplin, Geraldine 151, 214–16, 254, 449–50
Charteris, Leslie 103, 104–5
Chase, Stephan 259, 390, 512
chat shows 203–4, 253, 318, 378–9, 425–31, 437, 465, 469, 511, 513
see also under individual chat show name
chauvinism, OR's 316–20
childhood, OR's 5–6, 7–12 13–30, 39
Christensen, Michael 'Norse' 3, 115, 128–9, 167, 210–11, 232–3, 234, 235, 236, 239, 261–2, 267, 268, 269–70, 279, 287, 291, 292, 308, 309, 310, 341–2, 347–9, 350–1, 362, 370, 421, 423–4, 429, 433, 451, 497, 505–6
Christopher Columbus TV mini-series 407–8
Churchtown cemetery ix–x, 502–3, 505–6
Clancy, Pat 144–6, 147, 506
Clash of Loyalties, A 389–91
Class of Miss MacMichael, The 3, 345, 347–8
Cliffhanger 479
Coleman, Bernie 59, 159, 161, 208
Coleman, Joyce 4, 143, 159–61
Coles, Geoff 25, 26, 28
Collinson, Peter 276–8, 339–40

Compton, Richard 320–1
Condorman 380–4, 480
Cooper, Henry 298–9
Coquillon, John 228–30
Coutts, Don 462–5
Craig, Michael 64
Craig, Wendy 141, 142
Crawford, Michael 92, 134–6, 380, 382, 383
Crazy Elephant nightclub, The, OR attacked in 115–16, 121
Crazy Gang 60
Cricketers Arms, Ockley 235–6, 261, 263, 265, 267, 268, 270, 280, 294, 349, 350, 355
Crist, Judith 203–4
Cronenberg, David 355, 356, 357
Crowe, Russell 488, 489, 491, 492, 509
Crown Hotel, Peebles 481–2
Curse of the Werewolf, The 76–9, 89, 91, 164, 357, 460
Curtis, Dan 315
Cushing, Peter 72–3, 82, 83, 351
Cutthroat Island 479–80

Daily Express 121, 204
Daily Mail 183
Daily Telegraph 163
Dalglish, Kenny 434
Dalton, Timothy 314
Damned, The 80–1, 130
Dante's Inferno 136–7
Dardin, Olivia (OR's grandmother) 13, 34, 35, 37, 55, 56
Daryl, Jacquie (OR's long-term partner) 34, 112–13, 117, 154, 6, 162, 167, 168, 173–4, 188, 189, 190–2, 193, 194–5, 197, 202, 207, 209, 210, 212–13, 219, 220, 223–4, 227, 228, 233, 238, 257, 261, 262, 263–4, 265, 268, 280, 284, 292, 293,

294, 295–6, 317–18, 319, 333–4, 335, 336, 338, 340, 346, 351, 353, 356, 363, 364–5, 366, 372, 373–4, 405, 411, 443, 452, 484, 496, 506, 513–14
David Letterman Show 427–8
David, Pierre 356, 357
Davis, Bette 315, 445
Davis, Geena 479
Day, Robert 75
Days of Fury 240–1
Deacon, Brian 226, 228–30
Dearden, Basil 63, 166
death and burial of OR x–xi, 493–501, 502–7
Debussy, Claude *(The Debussy Film)* 119–20, 121–2, 128, 130, 291
Desert Island Discs 290–1
Devils, The 44, 65, 196–205, 244, 273, 281, 355, 433
Diamond, Peter 455–6
Die Hard 2 479
Ding Hao (OR's Chinese junk) 327
Dirty Weekend 242, 243, 246
divorce from Kate Byrne 190–4
Dobson, Bill and Jenny 87, 212–13, 220, 234, 239, 256, 287–8, 295, 346, 368, 372, 393, 401, 412, 421
Dog and Fox, Wimbledon 1, 4, 59, 88, 100, 127, 129, 143, 159, 194, 208, 232, 516
Donoghue, Quinn 253, 254, 325, 397, 449
Donohoe, Amanda 414, 416
Douglas, Mr (teacher) 26
Dr Heckyl and Mr Hype 357–61
Dragonard 438–9
drink driving 237–8, 450, 485
drinking games 2–4, 55, 227, 233, 235, 239, 245–6, 280, 291–2, 390, 432

Duellists, The (OR's favourite film) 404, 487

Dunaway, Faye 249

Dyke, Greg 430

dyslexia, OR's 21, 198

'Eddie the Arab' 101

Eden, Mark 139–41

education, OR's 14, 16–17, 19, 20–30

Eggar, Samantha 9, 185, 355

18th Field Ambulance – Hong Kong 49–52

elephant in *Hannibal Brooks* 167–8

Elès, Sandor 74, 75

Elstree Studios 74, 266, 374

employment, OR's (non-acting) 35–6, 45–6, 55–6

Entwistle, John 227

Evans, Mike Stanley 95

Evening Standard 134, 204

Ewell Castle school 23–8

extra, OR as film 59–60, 63–4

Faith, Adam 73

Faithfull, Marianne 142

Fanny Hill 401–2

father, OR as a *see under individual child name*

Fearless, HMS 55, 309–10

Feller, Catherine 89

Ferry House, County Clare 146, 147, 472

Field, Shirley Anne 73, 80

Figg, Ray 235

fights and violent outbursts 33–4, 35–6, 45, 64, 82, 91, 92, 98, 104, 107, 108, 115–16, 140, 160, 226, 228, 242–3, 245, 250–1, 253, 276, 277, 282, 301, 314, 325, 329, 364, 375, 381–2, 384, 396, 417, 418, 419, 425, 440, 443, 481–2, 490–1, 512

Films and Filming magazine 80

Finlay, Frank 249, 450

Fisher, Terence 70, 72, 73, 76, 78–9

Fleischer, Richard 326, 332

Flynn, Errol 72, 73, 250, 252, 259, 322–3

Fonda, Peter 396–7

Foster, Julia 107–8, 109–10

Four Musketeers, The 258–60, 448

Francis, Freddie 93

Frankel, Cyril 103, 104

Freeman, Stuart 130–1

Friday, Louise 370–1, 412, 474

Friday, Nora 233, 262, 266–7, 327, 370–1, 474, 506, 515

Friday, Paul 233, 234, 254, 262–3, 266–7, 308, 309–10, 327, 346–7, 369–71, 412, 438, 474, 506

Fruet, William 395

Fryer, Mick 'Mickus' 86–7, 101, 124, 127–8, 129, 162, 335, 429, 506, 516

funeral, OR's *see* death and burial of OR

Funny Bones 479

Galton, Ray 75

Garage Club 421, 432

gardening 212–13, 221, 232–3, 367–8, 473–4

Gate House (Reed home) 157, 158, 159, 183

George, Susan 338, 339, 427

Ghost in Monte Carlo, A 453

Gilbert, Lewis 148

Gilliam, Terry 101, 445–6, 447, 454, 509

Gilling, John 82, 122

Gladiator xi, 117, 361, 400, 486–92, 495, 496, 498, 499, 508–10, 511

Golan, Menahem 481

Golden Spur, The 62, 68
Goodman, Johnny 102–3
Gor 444
Gordon, Stuart 459–60, 461
Grade, Michael 464
Gray, Sheba 137
Great Scout & Cathouse Thursday 301–7, 452
Green, Nigel 73
Greene, David 130–1
Greene, Richard 72
Griffith, Charles B. 357
Guernsey home 419–22, 450–2, 466, 471–2
Guest, Val 60
Guster, Raymond 'Gus' 87, 101, 287, 346

Haggard, Piers 374–7
Hale, Georgina 89–90, 202, 257, 273, 321, 415, 497, 509
Halliwell, Leslie 274
Hamilton, Guy 96, 98
Hamlet cigar advertisements 169
Hammer films 40, 68, 69, 70–84, 89, 92–4, 100, 106, 119, 122–4
Hancock, Tony 74–5, 266
Hand in Hand, Wimbledon 1, 88, 182–3, 238
Hannibal Brooks 166–7
Harlin, Renny 479
Harris, Richard 170, 171, 328, 374, 437, 489
Harrison, Harvey 415
Harrison, Noel 184–5
Harty, Russell 253
Hawkins, Jack 63, 91
Hayers, Sidney 124
health, OR's 450, 451, 498–9
Heiney, Paul 405–7
Hello London 59

Hemmings, David 107–8, 109, 326, 491–3, 496, 459–60
Hendon, Miles 322–3
Henie, Sonja 59
Henriksen, Lance 460–1
Her Majesty's Theatre 39, 295
Heston, Charlton 248–9, 325
Heston, Fraser 454–5
Hickox, Douglas 217
Higgins, Alex 290, 341–3, 423, 469, 474–5, 503–4
Higgins, Mike 153–4, 492, 496, 509–10
Hinds, Anthony 76, 124
Hired to Kill 457–9
Hobbs, William 250
Hoe Place Preparatory School 15–16
Hollywood and OR 261–79, 314–15, 321–2, 400, 479, 499 *see also* LA (Los Angeles), OR in
Holt, Maud 40
Homefield Road (Reed home) 100, 101
Hong Kong 49–52, 55, 61
Hooper, Tobe 374
Hopkins, Anthony 404
horses 207–8, 236–7, 453
Hough, John 110, 163, 402–3, 443, 445
Hunnicutt, Gayle 103–4
Hunt, David 266–7, 342, 373
Hunt, James 328
Hunting Party 206–7, 224

ICM (OR's American agents) 315, 321, 400, 471
I'll Never Forget What's'isname 138–42
In at the Deep End 405–6
interviews 182–3, 252–3, 268–9, 328, 397, 406, 427, 428–31 *see also* press/journalists

Ivan 'Dadi' (taxi driver in Barbados) 223, 308–9, 426

Jackson, Glenda 3, 90, 136–7, 172, 176–80, 202, 224, 225, 226, 228, 229–30, 345, 347–8, 414, 513
James Bond role 164–5
James, Charles 24, 25, 26, 27–8, 33
James, Clive 428, 429, 430
James, Peter 274–5
Jarman, Derek 205
Jarrott, Charles 383, 384
Jaws, OR turns down 273–4
Jeremiah 482
The Jokers 134–6, 380

Keane, Kerrie 395–6
Kidd, Johnny 208, 245
Kidd, Wendy 245
Kings Head, Rudgwick 378
Kingsland, Gerald 413–14, 425
Kinnear, Roy 298, 450
Kinski, Klaus 374–7
Koslo, Paul 320–1, 336–8, 339–41, 514–15

LA, OR in 272–3, 301–5, 310–11, 313–15, 322, 398–9
Lady and the Highwayman 453
Lady in the Car with Glasses and a Gun 185
Langton Green Primary school 17–18, 19
Larthe, Pat 63, 66, 68, 169
lawn mower racing 400–1
Lazenby, George 164, 165
League of Gentlemen 63–4, 166
Lee, Christopher 70, 76, 81, 82, 249–50, 258, 450, 456
'Leith Hill Flying Club' 212, 266
Lester, Mark 149, 152, 153, 323, 324–5

Lester, Richard 134, 248, 249, 250, 258, 298, 448, 450
Letterman, David 427–8
Life is a Circus 60
Lion of the Desert 362, 391
Lisztomania 288
Littlewood, Joan 91–2
Lockwood, Gary 74
Losey, Joseph 80–1
'Lovely Gravy' 11, 15
Lynley, Carol 130, 131–4, 188–9, 192, 216, 217–18, 228, 257–8, 318, 319, 322, 382–3, 399–40, 497
Lyons, Stuart 68, 72
MacDonald Fraser, George 138, 259, 299–300, 323, 325, 332
Mahler 281
Mail on Sunday 437
Malta 479–80, 489, 491, 492, 493, 495–6, 499, 500
Margaret, Princess 256
marijuana 285
marriages *see* Byrne, Kate (OR's first wife); Daryl, Jacquie (OR's long-term partner); Reed, Josephine (OR's second wife)
Martin, Strother 303, 306
Marvin, Lee 113, 301–3, 282–3, 396
Massie, Paul 70, 74
Master of Dragonard Hill 438–9
Mastorakis, Nico 457–9
Mastroianni, Marcello 243
McCallum, Rick 415, 417
McNally, John 349–50
McQueen, Steve 274
Medak, Peter 313–14
Melvin, Murray 197–202, 205, 222, 227, 323–4, 330, 331, 407–9, 497
Merrow, Jane 107–9, 272
Miles, Sarah 344, 373–4
Miller, John 399

Miller, Jonathan 90, 184
Millet, Kate 463, 464
Mills, Hayley 184
Mitchum, Robert 273, 344–5
Monitor 120
Monks, Mick 'Tractors' 1, 88, 100,
    101, 117, 126, 127, 128, 149–50,
    182–3, 235–6, 287, 376, 506, 512
Monthly Film Bulletin 79
Moody, Ron 152
Moon, Keith 280–1, 284–7, 290,
    292–3, 295–6, 299, 310, 311–13,
    322, 342, 353–4
Moore, Roger 102
Morgy (nanny figure) 7, 12
Morris, Oswald 150
Murphy, Brian 198–9

Narizzano, Silvio 345–6
National Service, OR's 46–53, 54,
    240, 266
Neill, Steve 357–61
Neville, John 446
New York magazine 204
News of the World 165–6
newspapers *see* interviews;
    press/journalists; individual
    newspapers by name
Newton John, Olivia 400
Newton, Robert 149
Nielson, Julia 40
Night of a Thousand Stars 427
Niven, David 91, 327
Niven Junior, David 399–400
Norman, Barry 183
nude scene in *Women in Love* 173–7

O'Brien, Pat (and O'Brien's pub)
    472–3, 476–8, 484–5, 498, 500, 501
Observer, The 99
O'Connor, Des 431

Ogilvy, Ian 103–5
O'Hara, Gerry 401–2
Oliver! ix, 148–55, 186
O'Riordan, Joanne 485
Osborne, John 337–8
Owen-Thomas, Dudley 85

Paranoiac 92, 94–5
Parfitt, Rick 346–7
Parkinson 427
Parkinson, Michael 299
Parting Shots 486–7
Party's Over, The 95–9, 112
patriotism, OR's 32–3, 133, 240,
    335–6, 409
Pebble Mill at One 378, 427
Penthouse 68
Perry, Anthony 95, 96–7, 99
Peter the Great, Tsar of Russia 42–3
Phoenix, Joaquin 489, 499–500
Pinewood Studios 60, 63, 81, 148,
    184, 197, 201, 455
Pinkhurst Farm (Reed home) 365–6,
    367–72, 373–4, 379, 386, 391, 400,
    401, 405–6, 410, 412, 418, 419, 420,
    472, 474
Pirates of Blood River 81, 92, 100, 250
Pit and the Pendulum, The 459–60
Placett, Johnny 'the Major' 86, 101,
    132, 256–7, 269, 350, 393, 420–1,
    451, 452, 477, 483, 498, 506, 516
Pleasence, Donald 338
Plomley, Roy 291
police, run-ins with 237–8, 252, 312,
    325, 331, 340–1, 389, 398, 451, 485,
    486–7
Pollard, Michael J. 167
Portley Club, The 161–2, 234–5
press/journalists 170–1, 182–3, 204,
    231, 242, 252, 255, 269, 315, 331,
    332, 407, 385–8, 407, 408, 410, 411,

418–20, 424, 461–2, 492, 498, 500, 505, 513

Prince and the Pauper, The 322–6, 332, 339, 408

Prince, Reggie 112–16, 214, 210, 212–13, 225–6, 228, 229, 242–3, 251, 253, 255, 277, 278, 286, 287, 305, 307, 323, 325, 330, 337, 340, 370, 380, 390, 416, 417–19, 452

Prisoner of Honor 457

Puttnam, David 312–13

Pygmalion (G. B. Shaw) 41

Rage to Kill 441

Raines, Warren 125, 126

Rank Studios 95, 96, 99

Ransom, The 320, 321–2, 336

Rea, Reginald 47

Rebel, The 75

Red Lion, Bedlow, The 8, 9

Redgrave, Vanessa 202–3, 414

Reed, Beatrice 'Granny May' (OR's grandmother) 30, 34, 37, 38, 40–1, 42

Reed, David (OR's brother) 5, 6, 7, 8, 9–11, 13, 15–16, 17–22, 24, 31–2, 34, 35, 37, 38, 39, 42, 44, 46, 48, 49, 55, 56, 57, 58, 61–2, 63–4, 68, 69, 71, 72, 90, 110, 114, 118, 123, 128, 134, 144, 145–7, 151, 157–8, 161, 169–70, 178, 184, 186, 190, 191–2, 194, 209, 210, 215, 218, 219, 220, 222, 223, 236, 237, 238, 239, 240, 243, 255, 257, 262, 266, 269, 272–3, 274, 283, 284–6, 292, 297, 303–4, 310–12, 318–19, 321, 322, 327, 328, 342, 346, 347, 350, 353, 357, 363, 364, 367, 368, 371–2, 386–7, 392, 399, 400, 401, 403, 410, 411, 412, 419–20, 427, 428, 437, 438, 444, 448–9, 452, 453, 454, 464, 466,

468–9, 471, 472, 475, 483, 489, 495, 502, 503, 505, 506–7, 512–13, 516

Reed, Josephine (OR's second wife) ix, x, 20, 33, 54, 107, 122, 227, 293, 294, 378–84, 385, 386, 387, 388, 389, 391, 392 4, 395, 396–8, 399–402, 404 5, 407, 409, 410, 411, 413–14, 415, 416–17, 418–19, 420–1, 422, 423, 433, 436, 437, 442–3, 444, 445, 449, 450–1, 454, 460, 469–70, 471–2, 473, 474, 475, 482–3, 484, 485, 486–7, 489, 491, 492, 493, 494, 496, 498, 499, 500, 501, 502, 503, 505, 514

Reed, Kate (OR's first wife) *see* Byrne, Kate (OR's first wife)

Reed, Kathleen Mary 'Kay' (OR's stepmother) 16, 17, 18, 19–20, 22, 24, 34, 35, 183, 475

Reed, Marcia (later Sulis – OR's mother) 4–5, 6–7, 8, 9, 11–12, 13, 15, 21–2, 31–2, 34, 61, 184, 263, 319, 410, 483

Reed, Mark (OR's son) ix, x, 1, 2, 3, 14, 33, 54, 55, 59, 79, 80, 83, 87, 90–1, 101–2, 117–18, 120, 121, 132, 156, 158–9, 162, 178, 185, 186–9, 191, 192, 193–4, 195, 207, 210, 212, 218, 219–23, 234, 235, 236–7, 246, 263, 264–5, 273, 285, 293–4, 295, 296, 319, 327–8, 334, 335, 336, 338–9, 335–6, 363, 364, 365, 367, 368, 392–3, 400–1, 402, 414, 419, 426, 427, 431, 437, 465–6, 475, 484–5, 494–5, 498, 499–501, 504, 505, 511, 516–17

Reed, Muriel 'Mickie' (OR's sister-in-law) 21–2, 62, 69, 71–2, 123, 157, 161, 190, 220, 222, 237, 238, 266, 346, 347, 371–2, 392, 410, 412, 452, 453, 469, 503, 505, 506

Reed, Peter (OR's father) 4–7, 9–10, 13, 15, 16, 17–21, 22, 23, 25, 27, 28–9, 30, 31, 32, 34, 35, 38, 40, 41–2, 43–4, 46, 57, 169, 183–4, 189, 222–3, 410, 466, 475, 483

Reed, Sarah (OR's daughter) ix, 2, 39, 88, 147, 166, 186, 187, 191–2, 207, 209, 211, 213, 220–1, 223, 226–7, 233–4, 246, 262, 265, 268, 270–1, 285, 286, 294, 295–6, 318, 334, 335, 336, 337, 347, 351, 352, 353, 354, 363, 364, 365, 366, 370, 371, 372–3, 379, 393, 404, 418, 422, 423, 426, 451–2, 465, 467, 470, 475–6, 485, 491, 495, 496, 498, 499, 501, 502, 504, 505, 512, 514

Reed, Simon (OR's brother) 2, 4, 22, 25, 28, 29, 31, 32, 34, 39, 44, 58, 69, 71, 85–6, 88, 128, 140, 149, 152, 161, 162, 164–6, 170–1, 182, 184, 186–7, 190, 192–3, 209, 219, 249, 255–7, 262, 264, 268–9, 271, 272, 277–8, 288, 297, 298, 303, 317, 331–2, 350, 383, 385–6, 392, 418, 421, 427, 451, 453, 466, 475, 483, 488, 490, 492, 494–5, 503, 504, 505

Reed, Sir Carol (OR's uncle) 37, 38, 40, 42, 46, 47, 57–8, 68, 75, 149, 150–2, 155, 184

Return of the Musketeers 449–50

Return of the Saint 103

Return to Lonesome Dove 470–1

Revenger, The 441, 444

Revolver 244–5, 246–7

Richards, Wendy 298–9

Rigg, Diana 166

Ripley, Andrew 163, 261

Robe, Mike 470–1

Roberts, Selwyn 414, 415–17, 425

Robson, Dame Flora 130

Roeg, Nicholas 110–11, 413, 416–17, 425

Rohm, Maria 277, 278, 402, 444, 515

Rokeby School 23

Romain, Yvonne 76, 78, 83, 122–3, 142, 314, 397

Romulus Films 148

Rose and Crown, Wimbledon 1

Rossetti, Dante Gabriel 136, 137

Rosslyn Park rugby club 86, 162–3, 261–2, 291

Rowlatt, Henrietta 42

Rowlatt of Exeter, Canon 42

Royal Army Medical Corps (RAMC) 46–52, 53

Royal Flash 298, 299–300

Royal Oak, Rusper 2–3, 349

Royal Shakespeare Company 89

rugby 162–4, 297

Russell, Ken 44, 80–1, 119–21, 122, 128, 130, 136–7, 171, 172–3, 174, 175–6, 177, 179, 180, 196, 197–9, 200, 201, 202, 203, 204, 205, 264, 280–4, 288–9, 403, 456–7

Russian Roulette – Moscow 95 480–1

Saint, The 102–3, 266

Salkinds, Alexander and Ilya 248, 249, 250, 252, 258, 322

Sangster, Jimmy 92, 93

Scarlet Blade 100

scars, OR's facial 117–8, 120, 130–1, 133

Scott, George C. 325

Scott, Janette 93–5

Scott, Ridley 404, 487, 488, 508, 509

Searle, Chris 405

Second World War 5–13, 14–15, 46

sex, casual 67, 71, 143, 193, 197, 256–7

sex drive, OR's loss of 256–7

Shakespeare, William 89, 433, 476
Shaw, Denis 77, 82
Shaw, George Bernard 39, 41
Shepperton Studios 154, 287
Showtime magazine 164–5
Shuttered Room, The 130–1, 218, 378
shyness, OR's 83, 85, 90, 93, 106, 123, 141, 426, 427, 513
Sikes, Bill ix, 149–54, 164, 165, 259
Simpson, Alan 75
Simpson, O. J. 163
Sitting Target 216–17
Skeleton Coast 444–5
Sky News 489
Smith, Sidney 59
Snell, Peter 455
Snotter Martin (driver) 238–9
Sollima, Sergio 227–8, 229
Sommer, Elke 245, 246–7
Sorel, Louise 97
South Africa, OR in 438–43, 444
South Wimbledon Club 117
Spasms 395–7
Spengler, Pierre 249, 251–2, 254–5, 322, 326, 327, 328–9, 330, 448–9, 454
Spielberg, Steven 499
sports *see* athletics; lawn mower racing; rugby
Square Peg, The 60
St Helier Hospital, Carshalton 45–6
stage acting, rejection of 89–91
Starr, Freddie 431
Starr, Ringo 288, 311
Start the Week 318
Stigwood, Robert 282–3
Sting, The, OR turns down 273–4
Sting 2, The 400–1
strength, OR's tests of physical 33, 114, 252, 432
Stringfellows nightclub 227

Stuart, Graham 428–30
Sulis, Bill 23, 60, 483
Superbrain 480–1
Swan, The, Wimbledon 1, 2, 86–7, 145
sword fighting in *The Three Musketeers* 249–50
Sword of Sherwood Forest 72–3
System, The 106–11, 112–13, 121, 133, 272, 326

Take a Girl Like You 184
Tarantino, Quentin 251
tax issues 335–6, 419–20
Testi, Fabio 245–7
This Is Your Life 426
Thompson, Brian 457, 459–60
Three Musketeers, The xi, 248–55, 257, 258–60, 448
Thurman, Uma 446
Tommy 90, 282–7, 288, 290, 313, 445
Tomorrow Never Comes 336–8, 339
Tonight Show, The 316–17
Touch of the Sun 351–2
Towers, Harry Alan 276, 277, 401, 402, 444–5
Townshend, Pete 282, 283, 284
Trap, The 124–6, 132
Treasure Island 454–5
Tree, Sir Herbert Beerbohm (OR's grandfather) 38–42, 88–9, 184, 209, 295
Trent, John 275–6
Trevelyan, John 98
Triple Echo, The 49, 208–10, 224–5, 228, 230, 231, 348
Turner, Barry 14
Tushingham, Rita 124–5
29 Woodside (Reed home) 74
Two Faces of Dr Jekyll 69, 70
Two of a Kind 400

Universal Studios 134, 400

Valletta, Malta 1–2, 491, 492, 496
Vanger, Jonathan 383, 441–5
Variety magazine 93
Venom 374–8
Villiers, James 101

Walker, Alexander 204
Wallis, Shani 153
Walters, Barbara 269
Warburton, Patrick 438–40, 441
wedding, OR and Josephine Burge
  410–11
wedding, OR and Kate Byrne 68–9
Welch, Raquel 249, 254–5, 325, 326,
  328, 329
Welles, Orson x, 138–9
West Eleven 106
White, Carol 142–3
White Hart, Dorking 219
White Horse Hotel, Dorking 219
White, Oona 154
Who, The *see* Moon, Keith; *Tommy*
Wick, Douglas 488, 508, 509
Wild, Jack 152
'Wild Thing' (by The Troggs) 429,
  465–6
Williams, Billy 174–5, 178, 179
Williams, Kenneth 64

Wilson, Ali 481–2
Wimbledon 1–2, 4–5, 6, 7, 13, 15,
  23, 29, 35, 37, 51, 56, 59, 62, 74,
  86, 87, 88, 112, 117, 126, 127, 128,
  144, 145, 157, 158, 161, 182, 209,
  212, 232, 234, 268, 292, 297, 475,
  495, 506
Wimbledon Common Preparatory
  School 'Squirrels' 14
Winner, Michael 106–7, 110, 122, 123,
  134–8, 139, 140, 141, 142, 166, 167,
  222, 237, 273–4, 344, 345, 382, 403,
  437, 444, 479, 486–7, 497, 503, 511
Winters, Shelley 317
Wisdom, Norman 60, 74
Women in Love 90, 171–7, 179, 182,
  204, 215, 225, 237, 244, 348
Woodland Wines 85–6, 88, 128
Woodville, Katherine 96–7, 99
Woolf, James 148
Woolf, Sir John 148–9
Word, The 469–70

Yates, Paula 438
York, Michael xi, 65, 249, 252, 258,
  259–60, 448, 449, 450

Zanuck, Richard D. 273
Zero Population Growth 215–16
Zuleika Dobson (M. Beerbohm) 42